ROMANTICISM AND COLONIALISM
Writing and Empire, 1780–1830

The relationships between literary discourse and colonial politics have been the subject of much critical investigation since the publication of Edward Said's *Orientalism*. Yet although much has been written about the forms these relationships took in the early modern period and in the nineteenth century, the Romantic period has been comparatively neglected. This volume sets out to redress that imbalance by investigating Romantic writing in its relationship to the people and places with which the British were increasingly coming into contact. Topics examined include slavery, race, climate, tropical disease, religion, and commodity production; a wide range of writers are discussed from Edmund Burke to Hannah More, William Blake to Phillis Wheatley, Olaudah Equiano to Mary Shelley, Thomas Clarkson to Lord Byron. Together the essays constitute a broad assessment of Romanticism's engagement with India, Africa, the West Indies, South America and the Middle East.

Tim Fulford is a Reader in English Literature at Nottingham Trent University. He is the author of *Coleridge's Figurative Language* (1991) and *Landscape, Liberty and Authority* (1996). He edited, with Morton D. Paley, *Coleridge's Visionary Languages* (1993), and has published many articles on Romantic writers. He is currently working on an international study of colonial affairs.

Peter J. Kitson is a Senior Lecturer in the Department of English of the University of Wales, Bangor. He is the editor of *Romantic Criticism, 1800–25* (1989), (with T. N. Corns) *Coleridge and the Armoury of the Human Mind: Essays on His Prose Writings* (1991), and *Coleridge, Keats and Shelley: Contemporary Critical Essays* (1996). He is the current editor of *The Year's Work in English Studies* and has published widely in the field of Coleridge criticism and Romantic studies.

ROMANTICISM AND COLONIALISM

Writing and Empire, 1780–1830

EDITED BY
TIM FULFORD
AND
PETER J. KITSON

CAMBRIDGE
UNIVERSITY PRESS

PUBLISHED BY THE PRESS SYNDICATE OF THE UNIVERSITY OF CAMBRIDGE
The Pitt Building, Trumpington Street, Cambridge CB2 1RP, United Kingdom

CAMBRIDGE UNIVERSITY PRESS
The Edinburgh Building, Cambridge CB2 2RU, United Kingdom
40 West 20th Street, New York, NY 10011–4211, USA
10 Stamford Road, Oakleigh, Melbourne 3166, Australia

First published 1998

Printed in the United Kingdom at the University Press, Cambridge

Typeset in Baskerville 11/12.5pt [CE]

A catalogue record for this book is available from the British Library

Library of Congress cataloguing in publication data
Romanticism and colonialism: writing and empire, 1780–1830 / edited by
Tim Fulford and Peter J. Kitson.
p.   cm.
Includes bibliographical references and index.
ISBN 0 521 59143 0
1. English literature – 19th century – History and criticism.
2. Imperialism in literature.
3. English literature – 18th century – History and criticism.
4. Politics and literature – Great Britain – Colonies.
5. Great Britain – Colonies – History – 19th century.
6. Great Britain – Colonies – History – 18th century.
7. Romanticism – Great Britain.
8. Colonies in literature.
I. Fulford, Tim, 1962– . II. Kitson, Peter.
PR468.I49B66   1998
820.9′358 – dc21   97–44330   CIP

ISBN 0 521 59143 0 hardback

Contents

Notes on contributors

Moira Ferguson holds the James E. Ryan Chair in English and Women's Literature at the University of Nebraska, Lincoln, Nebraska. Recent publications include *Subject to Others: British Women Writers and Colonial Slavery, 1678–1834* (1992); *Colonial and Gender Relations from Mary Wollstonecraft to Jamaica Kincaid* (1994); *Eighteenth-Century Women Poets: Nation, Class, Gender* (1995); *The First Hundred Years: Nine Black Women Writers* (1997).

Caroline Franklin is a lecturer in English at the University of Wales, Swansea. She is author of *Byron's Heroines* (1992), and, among other reprint series, has edited *The Romantics: Women Poets 1770–1835*, 12 vols (1996). At present she is editing a collection of Victorian periodical articles on Romanticism, and is working on a literary life of Byron.

Michael Franklin is Head of English at St. John's School, Aberdare, and has lectured part-time in the Universities of Birmingham and Cardiff. He is the author of *Sir William Jones: A Critical Biography* (1995) and *Sir William Jones: Selected Poetical and Prose Works* (1995), and of articles on medieval love-lyrics and Oriental Gothic. Among other projects, he is working on a biography of Hester Lynch Thrale.

Tim Fulford is a Reader in English Literature at Nottingham Trent University. He is the author of *Coleridge's Figurative Language* (1991) and *Landscape, Liberty and Authority* (1996). He edited, with Morton D. Paley, *Coleridge's Visionary Languages* (1993), and has published many articles on Romantic writers. He is currently working on an international study of colonial affairs.

Lauren Henry is an Assistant Professor of Rhetoric in the College of General Studies at Boston University, Massachusetts. She recently completed her PhD at New York University. Her dissertation, from which this essay is excerpted, examines literary and historical links between the English Romantic movement and the English abolitionist movement, and between black and white writers of the period.

Malcolm Kelsall has been Professor of English at the University of Wales, Cardiff since 1975. His books include *Byron's Politics* (1987) and *The Great Good Place: The Country House and English Literature* (1992). He has also published extensively on British and Irish theatre. He is currently writing on *Jefferson and the Iconography of Romantic Nationalism.*

Peter J. Kitson is a Senior Lecturer in the Department of English of the University of Wales, Bangor. He is the editor of *Romantic Criticism 1800–25* (1989), (with T. N. Corns) *Coleridge and the Armoury of the Human Mind: Essays on His Prose Writings* (1991), and *Coleridge, Keats and Shelley: Contemporary Critical Essays* (1996). He is the current editor of *The Year's Work in English Studies* and has published widely in the field of Coleridge criticism and Romantic studies.

Nigel Leask is a fellow of Queens' College, Cambridge, and a lecturer in the English Faculty. He has published *The Politics of Imagination in Coleridge's Critical Thought* (1988) and *British Romantic Writers and the East: Anxieties of Empire* (1992), as well as numerous articles on Romanticism. He has just completed a new Everyman edition of Coleridge's *Biographia Literaria*, and is currently working on a book about travel-writing and genre in the romantic period.

Joseph W. Lew is Associate Professor of English at the University of Hawaii at Manoa. He has published on a number of eighteenth- and early nineteenth-century writers, and is currently working on a long study of British literature, international trade, and imperial interests.

D. L. Macdonald teaches English at the University of Calgary. He is the author of *Poor Polidori: A Critical Biography of the Author of 'The Vampyre'* (1991). He is currently completing a biography of Matthew Gregory Lewis.

James C. McKusick is Associate Professor of English at the University of Maryland, Baltimore County. He is the author of *Coleridge's Philosophy of Language* (1986) and several articles on Coleridge, Byron and Clare. He is currently completing a book on the emergence of ecological awareness in English Romantic poetry.

Timothy Morton is an Assistant Professor of English at the University of Colorado at Boulder. He has published *Shelley and the Revolution in Taste* (1994), and over fifteen articles, including 'Trade Winds', a study of literary representations of the spice trade from Milton to Shelley (*Essays and Studies*, 1996), and 'Shelley's Green Desert', in the Green issue of *Studies in Romanticism* (Fall, 1996).

Alan Richardson is Professor of English at Boston College, Chestnut Hill, Massachusetts. He is the author of *Literature, Education, and Romanticism: Reading as Social Practice, 1780 1832* (1994) and co-editor of *Romanticism, Race, and Imperial Culture 1780–1834* (1996). He has also published numerous essays on Romantic-era literature and culture, particularly in relation to gender, colonialism, and the social construction of childhood.

John Whale is a Senior Lecturer in the School of English at the University of Leeds. His various publications include *Thomas De Quincey's Reluctant Autobiography* (1984) and, as co-editor with Stephen Copley, *Beyond Romanticism: New Approaches to Texts and Contexts, 1789–1832* (1992). He has just completed a study of aesthetics and politics in the period and is currently editing a volume of *The Works of Thomas De Quincey* to be published by Pickering and Chatto.

Acknowledgements

The editors are most grateful to the following for their help and advice: Linda Jones, Nigel Leask, Debbie Lee, Lucy Newlyn, Morton D. Paley, Alan Richardson, David Simpson.

The illustration *Physical Portrait of the Tropics*, from Alexander von Humboldt and Aimé Bonpland, *Essai sur la géographie des plantes, accompagné d'un tableau des pays équinoxiales* (Paris, 1807) is reproduced by kind permission of the Syndics of Cambridge University Library. Robert Mitchell, *Plans and Views in Perspective of Buildings Erected in England and Scotland*: Plate no. 14, 'A section of the Rotunda in Leicester Square' is reproduced by kind permission of the Yale Center for British Art, Paul Mellon Collection.

CHAPTER I

Romanticism and colonialism: texts, contexts, issues

Tim Fulford and Peter J. Kitson

The publication in 1983 of Jerome J. McGann's *The Romantic Ideology* precipitated a return to historical and political readings of the Romantic period. Critics began to analyse ideas of ideology, class and gender in an attempt to deconstruct previous notions of 'Romanticism' as a mainly aesthetic and literary movement amongst five canonical, male poets. Much effort has been made to return Romantic discourse to the contexts in which it was written and read – the 'actual literary communities as they functioned within their larger communities of time and space'.[1] As a result, it is now accepted that it is impossible to understand writing in the period without examining political responses to the French Revolution and the numerous texts (many of them by women and many far more popular at the time than the work of Wordsworth, Coleridge, Shelley, Blake or Keats) which were excluded from the canon.

Given these critical developments, it is surprizing that, with some recent exceptions,[2] Romanticism's relationship with colonialism has been relatively little studied, although a wealth of critical writing has been devoted to the connection between both early modern and nineteenth-century literature and the histories of colonialism and

[1] Marilyn Butler, 'Repossessing the Past', in Marilyn Butler, Paul Hamilton, Marjorie Levinson, Jerome J. McGann, *Rethinking Historicism* (Oxford, 1989), pp. 64–84 (p. 72).

[2] See, for example, Javed Majeed, *Ungoverned Imaginings: James Mill's 'History of British India' and Orientalism* (Oxford, 1992); John Barrell, *The Infection of Thomas De Quincey: A Psychopathology of Imperialism* (New Haven and London, 1991); Nigel Leask, *British Romantic Writers and the East: Anxieties of Empire* (Cambridge, 1992); H. L. Malchow, *Gothic Images of Race in Nineteenth Century Britain* (Stanford, 1996). The most recent study of the subject, Alan Richardson's and Sonia Hofkosh's, *Romanticism, Race, and Imperial Culture, 1780–1834* (Bloomington and Indianapolis, 1996), comments that 'the considerable effect of these vast social and geo-political developments upon Romantic-era British literature remains largely unanalyzed, despite long-standing associations between Romanticism and literary exoticism, primitivism and Orientalism', p. 4. On race and gender in the eighteenth century see, Laura Brown, *The Ends of Empire: Women and Ideology in Early Eighteenth-Century English Literature* (Ithaca, 1993).

imperialism.[3] Significantly, the most sustained critical attention to
the issues of colonialism and literature in the period has been
afforded to the novels of Jane Austen in Edward Said's noted analysis
of *Mansfield Park* (1814) which considers Sir Thomas Bertram's source
of wealth in his plantations in Antigua in relation to the domestic
values of home and hearth which the novel endorses.[4] Few similar
discussions of the major 'Romantic' writers have yet been forthcoming. In fact the history and politics of the years 1785–1830 were
marked not just by the French Revolution, but by the loss of the
American colonies, the impeachment of Warren Hastings (the
Governor of Bengal), the transportation of convicts to Australia, the
campaign to abolish the slave-trade, the acquisition of new colonies
in the Mediterranean and Africa, the development of Canada and
the administration of older colonies in India, Africa and Ireland.
With Mungo Park's first exploration to the Niger in 1795, the
systematic exploration of the interior of Africa began.[5] That year
Britain also took over the Cape Colony from the Dutch East India
Company for the first time (British rule was confirmed in 1815) and
began to take an interest in Southern Africa. Further afield, Chinese
history became known through De Mailla's translations (1777–85)
and Britain began to countenance the opening up of Chinese
markets through the power of the Royal Navy. By the end of the
nineteenth century, the British Empire was territorially the largest
empire in world history, its population of over 400 million people to

[3] See for instance, ed. Stephen Greenblatt, *New World Encounters* (California, 1993); *Marvellous Possessions* (Chicago and Oxford, 1991); *Learning to Curse* (London and New York, 1990); Hayden White, *Tropics of Discourse* (Baltimore and London, 1978); Peter Hulme, *Colonial Encounters: Europe and the Native Caribbean, 1492–1797* (London and New York, 1986); *Women, 'Race', and Writing in the Early Modern Period*, eds. Margo Hendricks and Patricia Parker (London and New York, 1993); Kim F. Hall, *Things of Darkness: Economies of Race and Gender in Early Modern England* (London and New York, 1995); Edward W. Said, *Culture and Imperialism* (London, 1993); Patrick Brantlinger, *Rule of Darkness: British Literature and Imperialism, 1830–1914* (Ithaca and London, 1988); Dorothy Hammond and Alta Jablow, *The Africa That Never Was: Four Centuries of British Writing About Africa* (New York, 1970); Ashton Nichols, 'Silencing the Other: The Discourse of Domination in Nineteenth-Century Exploration Narratives', *Nineteenth-Century Studies*, 3 (1989), pp. 1–22; Martin Green, *Dreams of Adventure, Deeds of Empire* (London and Henley, 1980); Benita Parry, *Conrad and Imperialism* (London, 1983); Elleke Boehmer, *Colonial and Postcolonial Literature* (Oxford, 1995); Gail Ching-Liang Low, *White Skins Black Masks: Representation and Colonialism* (London and New York, 1996).

[4] For Said, Austen is at 'the centre of an arc of interests and concerns spanning the hemisphere, two major seas, and four continents'. Said, *Culture and Imperialism*, pp. 95–116 (p. 101).

[5] Philip D. Curtin, *The Image of Africa: British Ideas and Actions, 1780–1850* (London and Madison, 1964), pp. 150–51.

be found in all regions of the globe. Colonialism shaped the early nineteenth-century church, with the rise of missionary societies. It affected culture at home, creating new fashions in aesthetics, sport and costume. Indeed, the Romantic period is a watershed in colonial history, witnessing a move from a protectionist colonial system, based upon mercantilist economic principles, to a free-trade empire with a political and moral agenda, proverbially described, after Kipling's poem, as 'the white man's burden'.

Looking at the Romantic-period writing from the perspective of categories of colonialism, imperialism and race is especially challenging because of the very transitional nature of the colonial project in the period. From a Marxist perspective 'colonialism' is 'the conquest and direct control of other people's lands' – a historical phase in the larger process of imperialism, or 'the globalization of the capitalist mode of production'.[6] From a post-Althusserian position it is also possible to discriminate between colonialism, as the material system of conquest and control, and imperialism as a form of colonialism buttressed by hegemonic cultural and ideological imperatives. Although nineteenth-century colonialism is a thing of the past, imperialism is often said to persist in the sense of the continuing global ambitions of Western capitalism. This raises the vexed question of the relationship between culture and imperialism and the complicity of English literature in the imperialist project, and, indeed, the role of a volume such as this in the debate. It is often pointed out that the historical moment which saw the emergence of the academic discipline of English also produced a distinct brand of colonialism.[7] Gauri Viswanathan has argued that 'British colonial administrators, provoked by missionaries on the one hand and fears of native insubordination on the other, discovered an ally in English literature to support them in maintaining control of the natives under the guise of a liberal education'.[8]

Amongst the texts valued by the British in India were those which Romantic critics had helped to establish as embodiments of Englishness and Christianity – Shakespeare and Milton. Indeed,

---

[6] *Colonial Discourse and Post-Colonial Theory: A Reader*, eds. Patrick Williams and Laura Chrisman (New York and London, 1994), pp. 2–3.

[7] *The Empire Writes Back: Theory and Practice in Post-Colonial Literatures*, eds. Bill Ashcroft, Gareth Griffiths and Helen Tiffin (London and New York, 1989), pp. 3–8.

[8] Gauri Viswanathan, 'The beginnings of English literary study in British India', *Oxford Literary Review*, 9 (1987), p. 17. See also her *Masks of Conquest: Literary Study and British Rule in India* (London, 1989).

Wordsworth's own writing anticipates the development of this form of cultural imperialism. In the light of Viswanathan's analysis, the Wanderer's vision of Albion civilizing the rest of the world in *The Excursion* (1814) exhibits a sinister undercurrent:

> So the wide waters, open to the power,
> The will, the instincts, and appointed needs
> Of Britain, do invite her to cast off
> Her swarms, and in succession send them forth;
> Bound to establish new communities
> On every shore whose aspect favours hope
> Of bold adventure . . .
> Earth's universal frame shall feel the effect;
> Even the smallest habitable rock,
> Beaten by lonely billows, hear the songs
> Of humanised society. . .
>   Your Country must complete
> Her glorious destiny. Begin even now.[9]

The Wanderer claims that the world will look to Britain for leadership and that his country's imperial future will be glorious. Coleridge also voiced similar views when, in later life, he commented that 'Colonisation is not only a manifest expedient – but an imperative duty on Great Britain. God seems to hold out his finger to us over the sea'.[10] Noting this connection between Romantic thought and its imperial dimension, Marlon B. Ross comments that:

In a very real sense the Romantics. . . help prepare England for its imperial destiny. They help teach the English to universalize the experience of 'I', a self-conscious task for Wordsworth, whose massive philosophical poem *The Recluse* sets out to organize the universe by celebrating the universal validity of parochial English values.[11]

The Wanderer's hopes for Albion, however, are not unique in this period. Ross's point is actually made in a more emphatic way by an opponent of the conservatism of the later Wordsworth and Southey, Anna Letitia Barbauld. Her remarkable *Eighteen Hundred and Eleven, a Poem* (1812) links colonization, language and culture in a composite imperial endeavour:

[9] *The Poetical Works of William Wordsworth*, vol. v, *The Excursion, The Recluse*, ed. Helen Darbishire (Oxford, 1949; 1972), pp. 295, 299.
[10] *Table Talk*, ed. Carl Woodring, 2 vols. (London and Princeton, 1990), I, p. 369.
[11] Marlon B. Ross, 'Romantic Quest and Conquest', in *Romanticism and Feminism*, ed. Anne K. Mellor (Bloomington, 1988), p. 31.

Wide spreads thy race from Ganges to the pole,
O'er half the Western world thy accents roll:
. . . Thy stores of knowledge the new states shall know,
And think thy thoughts, and with thy fancy glow;
Thy Lockes, thy Paleys shall instruct their youth,
Thy leading star direct their search for truth;
Beneath the spreading Plantain's tent-like shade,
Or by Missouri's rushing waters laid,
'Old father Thames' shall be the Poet's theme,
Of Hagley's woods the enamoured virgin dream,
And Milton's tones the raptured car enthrall,
Mixt with the roar of Niagara's fall.[12]

Barbauld's enthusiastic anticipation of a British cultural imperialism, through which the colonized might be taught to think the thoughts of the poets and philosophers of the mother country, certainly pre-empts the arguments of critics such as Homi K. Bhabha and Viswanathan. And it is certainly true that the Romantic canon did become, as Wordsworth and Barbauld predicted, a part of the later nineteenth-century cultural imperialism of Britain's domination of nearly one quarter of the terrestrial globe. Nevertheless, writing of the Romantic period cannot simply be seen as univocal in its support of that domination: the contributors to this volume investigate some of the ways in which it articulates resistance to, and/or anxiety about, cultural imperialism, even as it also, in other areas, remains complicit with it.

The question of resistance to and complicity with imperialism has been deepened – in discussions which few Romanticists have so far addressed – by Henry Louis Gates Jr, Kwame Anthony Appiah and other writers working on black British and American writers of the period.[13] In the Indian context, the work of Ranajit Guha and the Subaltern Studies group has provided a more nuanced understanding of power within the colonized population.[14] Guha has shown that, beyond the stereotypes constructed by colonizers, colonized peoples are divided in themselves and amongst themselves, so that no one native group, and least of all a nationalist élite educated in the systems of schooling, law, government etc. which are organized

[12] Lines 81–96. *The Poems of Anna Letitia Barbauld*, eds. William McCarthy and Elizabeth Kraft (Athens, Georgia and London, 1994), p. 157.
[13] Henry Louis Gates, Jr., *The Signifying Monkey: A Theory of African-American Criticism* (Oxford and New York, 1988); Kwame Anthony Appiah, *In My Father's House: Africa in the Philosophy of Culture* (New York, 1992).
[14] *Subaltern Studies 1: Writings on South Asian History and Society*, ed. R. Guha (Delhi, 1982).

by the colonizers, can speak for all. Those not educated in the colonizers' discourses often find their voices go unrecorded and unheard in colonial and post-colonial society, although it is often on their labour – and their attitudes to labour – that both the colonial and nationalist élites depend.

The emphasis in the Subaltern Studies group has been on a shift in historiographical method: they have attempted to collect and consider the voices, histories and traditions of those who are often left unrecorded and excluded. In this volume, a similar attempt is made by Lauren Henry, who considers the writings of a number of enslaved and liberated Africans of the period, neither simply as examples of some notional slave or African consciousness, nor purely as responses to the discourses of the colonizers. Instead, she portrays them as artefacts shaped from varied cultural traditions and from differing personal histories, political affiliations and interpretative strategies. Phillis Wheatley, Henry shows, incorporates in her work references to West African forms of worship, references which inflect – and even undercut – the neoclassical style and Christian attitudes of the colonialist society which had enslaved her. Drawing on the work of Gates, Henry argues that by writing and publishing former slaves such as Olaudah Equiano and Ottobah Cugoano asserted the full humanity of blacks, against the arguments of Enlightenment philosophers that their lack of literature demonstrated the inferiority of Africans.

Equiano's history illustrates the difficulties in discussing the issue of 'othering' in the period. Equiano moves from the subject position of marginalized, African slave to speak in the metropolitan and imperial centre. But, to do so, he must take up an assumed, subject position of the converted pagan and present his story in a language not his own, and in the form of the Protestant, spiritual autobiography, uncannily shadowing fictions such as DeFoe's *Crusoe.* The contributors to this volume are well aware of the dangers of 'othering' different nations and cultures, a process in which the writers discussed in this collection are inevitably complicit. The other is always the 'uncanny Other' and othering is a process of alienation and of epistemic violence (often a prelude to material force), whereby an exclusionary distinction is made between the white westerner and the colonized subject. The essays demonstrate how the many and various peoples subject to Western colonial and imperial processes, in the late eighteenth and early nineteenth century, underwent a process of estrangement, frequently being homogenized and often demonized. Imaginary borderlines were constructed on the bases of imputed savagery, cannibalism, and so on. As Homi Bhabha argues, in his critique of Fanon, it is vitally important that:

The Other must not be imaged, as Fanon sometimes suggests, as a fixed phenomenological point, opposed to the self, that represents a culturally alien consciousness. The Other must be seen as the necessary negation of a primordial identity – cultural or psychic – that introduces the system of differentiation which enables the 'cultural' to be signified as a linguistic, symbolic, historic reality. If . . . the subject of desire is never simply a Myself, then the Other is never simply an *It-self*, a font of identity, truth or misrecognition.[15]

Although aware of the economies of desire in producing a colonial Other through identification and alienation, the contributors to this volume focus primarily upon the material, historical conditions and processes of colonialism in the period and their implications for representation itself.

For some British writers, the appearance at the imperial centre of people from the colonies demanded acknowledgement in their depictions of London. Anna Letitia Barbauld describes (in *Eighteen Hundred and Eleven, a Poem*) how, in the streets of London, 'the turban'd Moslem, bearded Jew, / And woolly Afric, met the brown Hindu'[16] and Wordsworth also recalls the national and racial variety of the metropolis: 'The Swede, the Russian; from the genial South, / The Frenchman and the Spaniard; from remote / America, the hunter Indian; Moors, / Malays, Lascars, the Tartar and Chinese, / And Negro ladies in white muslin gowns'.[17] John Whale's contribution to the volume records Hazlitt's troubled response to the performances of a troupe of Indian jugglers playing in popular London theatres. James C. McKusick discusses the celebrated South Sea Island visitors Omai and Lee Boo. It has been estimated that there were probably around 20,000 black people in Britain during the eighteenth century. Of these only a comparative few – Ukawsaw Gronniosaw, Mary Prince and Robert Wedderburn (for example)

---

[15] Homi K. Bhabha, 'Remembering Fanon', in *Colonial Discourse*, eds. Williams and Chrisman, pp. 118–19. See Frantz Fanon, *The Wretched of the Earth* (London, 1965); *Black Skin, White Masks* (London, 1968).

[16] Lines 165–66, *Poems of Anna Letitia Barbauld*, pp. 152–61 (p. 155).

[17] *The Prelude 1799, 1805, 1850*, eds. Jonathan Wordsworth, M. H. Abrams and Stephen Gill (New York and London, 1979), p. 238 (Book VII, lines 239–43).

besides Equiano, Cugoano and Sancho – left records of their experience. Similarly, few black poets of the stature of Phillis Wheatley had yet appeared on the American literary scene.[18] Yet the impact of these black writers in an age which witnessed strenuous intellectual clashes over race and slavery issues, should not be underestimated. Henry's discussion reminds us that several were widely read in the period, in their own right as literary artists. She also shows that they may have been influences on William Blake's poem 'The Little Black Boy'.[19] Iain McCalman's historical research into the activities and writings of black and mixed-race members of the radical underworld of early nineteenth-century Britain, including Robert Wedderburn and William Davidson (both mulatto offspring of slave owners and their black mistresses), has also provided a new ideological context for the writings of Wordsworth, Coleridge, Blake and Shelley.[20] Wedderburn's writings demonstrate how sections of the English Jacobin grouping were alert to colonial issues and their relationship to the political system at home. Indeed, Olaudah Equiano became a member of the London Corresponding Society.

Arranged in a broadly chronological order, the chapters collected here examine representations of individuals and societies in the Western Coast of Africa, the Caribbean, Venice, the South Sea Islands, America, the Ottoman and Hebrew Middle East, as well as India. Representations of India and the West Indies receive most attention because it is our belief that these areas were of most importance to the development of colonialism in the period. The chapters are all informed by a historicist concern with explicating the transformations which were visited on the peoples subject to the colonizing process in this period. And this concern leads them to investigation of the many discourses, economic, ethnographic, aesthetic, religious, colonial, which inform these transformations. This

---

[18] See *Black Writers in Britain, 1760–1890: An Anthology*, eds. Paul Edwards and David Dabydeen (Edinburgh, 1991); *Black Atlantic Writers of the 18th Century: Living the New Exodus in England and the Americas*, eds. Adam Potkay and Sandra Burr (London, 1995); Peter Fryer, *Staying Power: The History of Black People in Britain* (London, 1984); *The Black Presence in English Literature*, ed. David Dabydeen (Manchester, 1985); Keith Sandiford, *Measuring the Moment: Strategies of Protest in Eighteenth-Century Afro-English Writing* (London and Toronto, 1988); Rosalie Murphy Baum, 'Early-American Literature: Reassessing the Black Contribution', *Eighteenth-Century Studies*, 27 (1994), pp. 533–50.

[19] See also Paul Edwards, 'An African Literary Source for Blake's "Little Black Boy"?' *Research in African Literatures*, 21.4 (1990), 179–81.

[20] Robert Wedderburn, *The Horrors of Slavery and Other Writings*, ed. Iain McCalman (Edinburgh, 1992); see also Iain McCalman, *Radical Underworld* (Cambridge, 1988).

is not to say that the critics represented in the volume present a homogenized approach to the texts they discuss, or even agree about the ways such texts are functioning at the level of representation and agency. For instance, Alan Richardson and Timothy Morton read Southey's sonnets on the slave-trade in different ways, Richardson approaching the sonnets from the perspective of altering perceptions of race and Morton from an analysis of the production, commodification and consumption of sugar. Neither do Nigel Leask and Michael Franklin agree over the question of the complicity of William Jones's Indian scholarship in colonial ambitions, Leask being less sanguine than Franklin about its liberationist effects upon the Bengali Renaissance. Rather than presenting a single perspective on Romanticism and colonialism, this volume contains a series of interventions in a number of complex debates, from critics whose work is nuanced in different ways. Nevertheless, all the chapters here are concerned with returning Romantic texts to the context of the material, colonial processes contemporaneous with their imagined versions of colonized people and places. The contributions to this volume also take their bearings both within and outside the Romantic canon. Traditionally, canonical Romantic-period writers, such as Blake, Burke, Coleridge, Percy Shelley, Mary Shelley, Hazlitt and Byron loom large, along with Bowles, Chatterton, Clarkson, Southey, Beckford, Hannah More and Sir William Jones, while Wordsworth and Keats are relegated from their usual starring roles to briefer character appearances in the colonialist drama. These writers have been examined not because they are either canonical or non-canonical *per se*, but because their work has been influential in constructing and propagating different portrayals of cultures, hitherto unfamiliar to an increasingly imperialist Britain. It is not the intention of the contributors to this volume to reinforce traditional notions of canonicity by adding further complexities to the work of canonical writers. Such complexities are not necessarily viewed as unquestioned virtues and, more often, they are seen to reveal the Romantics' material interests, ideological limitations and blind spots. What is presented here is, in Gates's phrase, 'a loose canon' of Romantic-period writers, poets and novelists supplemented by less familiar writers, propagandists, and natural philosophers from the margins of the traditional canon and beyond.

That colonialism shaped literary representation was noted nearly fifty years ago by the French literary historian Raymond Schwab when he defined Romanticism as Europe's response to the over-whelming experience of finding its civilization not unique but merely one of many, those of the East being older and, perhaps, its source.[21] Schwab focused on the Orient, as did Edward Said in *Orientalism* (1978). Said demonstrated that the period saw the consolidation of 'a Western style for dominating, restructuring and having authority over the Orient'.[22] The critics contributing to this volume seek to develop the debates initiated by Schwab, Said and others, by investigating in detail the historical and aesthetic relations of writing of the period, not only to the Orient, but also to the other geo-political zones primarily colonized by Britain, and also by other European powers. Said's work has stimulated a dramatic growth in theoretical analysis of colonialism. Later theorists, most notably Aijaz Ahmad, Abdul R. JanMohamed, Kwame Anthony Appiah, Homi K. Bhabha, Benita Parry, and Gayatri Chakravorty Spivak, reviving the insights of earlier writers, – Frantz Fanon, Freud, Bahktin – have revealed the limitations of Said's model of colonial discourse.[23] Rather than working at the purely theoretical level the contributors to this volume are more interested in developing applications of some of the perspectives opened by these writers, mixing historicist and new historicist approaches. Implicit in many of the contributions is the recent questioning of the overly rigid, binary distinctions implicit in the notion of the Other that is such an important element in the work of Said and JanMohamed. Several of the chapters move in the area opened by the work of Homi K. Bhabha who showed how Said underestimated the ambivalence and indeterminacy which appeared within colonialist discourse when it

[21] Raymond Schwab, *The Oriental Renaissance: Europe's Rediscovery of India and the East, 1680–1880*, tr. Gene Patterson Black and Victor Reinking (New York, 1984).

[22] Edward W. Said, *Orientalism* (London, 1978); see also, John M. MacKenzie, *Orientalism: History, theory and the arts* (Manchester and New York, 1995); Rana Kabbani, *Imperial Fictions: Europe's Myths of Orient* (London, 1986); Mohammed Sharafuddin, *Islam and Romantic Orientalism: Literary Encounters with the Orient* (London, 1995); Gail Ching-Liang Low, *White Skins Black Masks*.

[23] Homi K. Bhabha, 'Signs Taken for Wonders', in *Europe and its Others*, ed. Francis Barker et al., 2 vols. (Colchester, 1985), I, pp. 89–106; 'The Other Question . . . the Stereotype and Colonial Discourse', *Screen*, 24.6 (Nov/Dec. 1983), pp. 18–36; Gayatri Chakravorty Spivak, *In Other Worlds: Essays in Cultural Politics* (New York and London, 1987); Abdul R. JanMohamed, 'The Economy of Manichean Allegory: The Function of Racial Difference in Colonialist Literature', in *'Race,' Writing, and Difference*, ed. Henry Louis Gates, Jr. (Chicago and London, 1985), pp. 78–106; Marilyn Butler, 'Orientalism', in *The Penguin History of Literature*. Vol. V: *The Romantic Period*, ed. David B. Pirie (Harmondsworth, 1994), pp. 395–447. See also Benita Parry, 'Problems in Current Theories of Colonial Discourse', *Oxford Literary Review*, 9 (1987), pp. 26–58.

was decentred from its imperial origin and mimicked by the colonized subject. Bhabha's notion of hybridity is also important here, in postulating that colonial subjects inevitably include the trace of the repressed.[24]

The works collected here are all, in some sense or other, after Said. While, however, it is Said's work that has made the most impact in the field of historicist Romantic studies, several of the contributions are informed by other post-colonial theories and modifications of Said's model, including John Barrell's *The Infection of Thomas De Quincey: A Psychopathology of Imperialism* (1991) and Nigel Leask's *British Romantic Writers and the East: Anxieties of Empire* (1992). Leask and Barrell, working more closely on Romantic texts than Said, have highlighted anxiety and unease as elements which disturb from within writers' attempts to delineate and so imaginatively control the people of Britain's colonies, who were unfamiliar to them. Like Leask's study these works share a common concern to articulate in detail the instabilities, ambiguities and contradictions which Romantic-period texts reveal at the heart of colonialism's discourses. Morton, for instance, argues that slaves, as conceived in the writings of Southey and Coleridge, exist between the categories of subject and object, in the hybrid condition that Bhabha hypothesizes. Many of the British Romantics saw themselves as being in opposition to aspects of colonialism – Coleridge and Southey actively campaigned against slavery and Blake wrote against it. Discussions of their work are placed next to analyses of Evangelical women abolitionists, Hannah More and Mary Butt Sherwood – writers opposed to their politics and aesthetics. What is revealed in this contextualization is that, on neither side of the gender and ideological divisions, was a self-consistent discourse on colonialism possible: men and women, Romantic and Evangelical opposed slavery in different ways, but both reinstated some of its informing assumptions within their opposition.

At best, as Malcolm Kelsall argues, the instability of the writings highlighted in this collection deconstructs the binary oppositions and

---

[24] Aijaz Ahmad, 'Jameson's Rhetoric of Otherness and the "National Allegory"', *Social Text*, 17 (Fall), 1987, pp. 3–25; Appiah, *In My Father's House*; see also Robert Young, *White Mythologies: Writing History and the West* (London, 1990) and *Colonial Desire: Hybridity in Theory, Culture and Race* (London and New York, 1995); Homi K. Bhabha, 'Of Mimicry and Man: The Ambivalence of Colonial Discourse', in *Modern Literary Theory*, eds. Philip Rice and Patricia Waugh (London, 1989), pp. 234–41 and 'Signs Taken for Wonders'.

apparent truths by which imperialist ideology becomes hegemonic, establishing itself as an apparently natural and inevitable authority. Often, this deconstructive element resulted from Romantic writers' juxtaposition of different forms of theoretical and aesthetic discourse in their work, a juxtaposition paralleled by their reading of different geo-political spaces in each other's terms. It is appropriate, then, that this collection both focuses on a variety of colonial areas and utilizes a range of contemporary theorists. The ethnography of James Clifford, the race debate of Appiah, Gates and Jon Michael Spencer, the historiography of Stephen Bann, variously inform the contributions which, taken together, demonstrate that Romanticism cannot be properly questioned without an investigation of its complicity with, and its resistance to, the colonialist discourses of a Britain becoming steadily more imperialist as the nineteenth century progressed.

CHAPTER 2

Romanticism and colonialism: races, places, peoples, 1785–1800

Peter J. Kitson

In the Romantic period, the processes of colonialism underwent significant transformation, both at the material and ideological level. The rather rigid Marxist distinction between colonialism and imperialism is complicated by the late eighteenth and early nineteenth centuries. The traditional, historical periodization of the Romantic Age as one which coincided with the rise and fall of the old colonial system prior to its supersession by the 'New Imperialism' from around 1870 onwards, has been problematized by recent writing. In fact, a new system of British imperialism appears to have been emerging at roughly the same time as what we know as Romanticism began to appear.[1] Gananath Obeyesekere has recently argued that it was in the late eighteenth century that the concept of the 'colonialist' changed. Obeyesekere regards the three voyages of Captain James Cook as crucial to this transformation: 'the voyages that he led heralded a shift in the goals of discovery from conquest, plunder, and imperial appropriation to scientific exploration devoid of any explicit agenda for conquest of and for the exploitation and terrorization of native peoples'.[2] Similarly, Mary Louise Pratt noticed that, around this time, there occurred the end of the 'last great navigational phase' of discovery and its replacement by a growing concern with the exploration of the interiors of the continents. This was fuelled by the concomitant emergence of a new 'planetary consciousness', altering the ways in which Europeans perceived themselves and understood their place on the planet. Pratt argues that this led to a kind of 'anti-colonialist' literature which conceals an

---

[1] For a summary of the historical debate about colonialism and imperialism in the period, see Frank McDonough, *The British Empire* (London, 1994), pp. 1–25.

[2] Gananath Obeyesekere, *The Apotheosis of Captain Cook: European Mythmaking in the Pacific* (Oxford and Princeton, 1992), p. 5.

underlying colonial purpose.[3] Pratt's point about the movement to
interior exploration still needs qualifying. The sublime polar landscapes, the last remote areas of the globe, remained unexplored. On
his second voyage Cook explored the Antarctic regions and his third
and final voyage began, in 1776, as an attempt to discover the North
West Passage, a navigable waterway, which, it was believed, crossed
North America from East to West.[4] In 1818, the British government
organized the first of several Arctic explorations, and in 1845 the ill-
fated Franklin expedition left in search of the elusive passage. The
sublime polar sea-scapes which haunt the Romantic imagination
are, in part, a response to this scientific endeavour. It was to seek the
North West Passage, as well as to discover the secrets of the magnet,
that Captain Robert Walton, one of the 'sons' of Captain Cook, left
for the Arctic Circle in Mary Shelley's *Frankenstein* (1818), where he
encountered the dying creator and his unnatural progeny in extremes of cold and ice. Coleridge's 'The Rime of the Ancient
Mariner' (1798) similarly uses the Antarctic as a means to explore the
metaphor of mental and maritime exploration, describing a voyage
bearing remarkable similarities with Cook's second expedition
(1772–1775).[5] Several commentators have pointed out that the guilt
felt by the mariner after shooting the albatross might be a displacement of a more general guilt experienced by the Western maritime
nations for their treatment of other cultures.[6]

The treatment of other cultures became a central issue in British
Romanticism and in the new variety of British imperialism after 16

[3] Mary Louise Pratt, *Imperial Eyes: Travel Writing and Transculturation* (New York and London, 1992), pp. 15–37. Pratt argues that the 'eighteenth-century systematizing of nature as a European knowledge-building project . . . created a new kind of Eurocentred planetary consciousness' (p. 39). See also David Killingray, *A Plague of Europeans: Westerners in Africa since the fifteenth century* (Harmondsworth, 1973).

[4] Obeyesekere, *Apotheosis of Captain Cook*, pp. 40–43.

[5] For the Romantic obsession with polar landscapes see Francis Spurford, *I May Be Some Time: Ice and the English Imagination* (London, 1996), pp. 1–53. For Cook's voyages, see J. C. Beaglehole, *The Exploration of the Pacific*, 2nd edn (London, 1947); Alan Frost, 'New Geographical Perspectives and the Emergence of the Romantic Imagination', in *Captain James Cook and His Times*, eds. Robin Fisher and Hugh Johnston (Vancouver and London, 1979), pp. 5–20. William Wales, who was an astronomer on Cook's second voyage, was also Coleridge's and Lamb's mathematics tutor at Christ's Hospital, known for entertaining his pupils with stories of his travels. See also Bernard Smith, 'Coleridge's Ancient Mariner and Cook's Second Voyage', *Journal of the Warburg and Courtauld Institutes*, 19 (1956), pp. 117–54.

[6] William Empson, 'The Ancient Mariner', *Critical Quarterly*, 6 (1964), pp. 298–319; J. R. Ebbatson, 'Coleridge's Mariner and the Rights of Man', *Studies in Romanticism*, 11 (1972), pp. 171–206; Patrick J. Keane, *Coleridge's Submerged Politics: The Ancient Mariner and Robinson Crusoe* (Columbia and London, 1994).

February 1788. On that day, Edmund Burke rose to his feet in
Westminster Hall and began the impeachment of the Governor of
Bengal, Warren Hastings. Burke's speeches, and the impeachment
which they launched, were the first powerful manifestations of
colonial guilt at the centre of British political life. An audience of
MPs and members of the public were confronted with a narrative
determined to expose the brutal and violent acts done in the interest
of the Company's profits. Burke's sensational narrative was not anti-
colonialist. Rather, it contained a reading of Indian society from
which Burke argued for a different, and, he believed, more effective
colonialist policy than that executed by Hastings. As Michael
Franklin points out in his chapter in this volume, Burke 'saw the
politics of the subcontinent as the imperial and ethical challenge of
his time'. He represented Indian society, for the benefit of his
Westminster audience, as a complex civilization bound by traditional
institutions, social distinctions and laws. Hastings had violated this
traditional structure, humiliating Indians of power and wealth,
reducing all to the level of subjects equally vulnerable to the
Company's arbitrary power. In a critique that he was to develop in
the 1790s in his attacks on the French Revolution, Burke showed
Hastings' colonialism to depend upon the destruction of pre-colonial
society and upon the construction in its place of an inherently
tyrannical (and unstable) despotism. The Company monopolized
power: Indian society was levelled, Indians of different ranks, castes,
wealth all now equally subject to its authority. Hastings, Burke
claimed, was playing God: in claiming 'arbitrary power' he was
forgetting that he was 'bound by the external laws of Him, that gave
it, with which no human authority can dispense'.[7] But playing God
in the colonial space of India was a Satanic temptation prompted by
the culture's unending and complex difference, by the very variety
that enabled it so effectively to elude the colonialist's desire for
control. The colonialist seeking such control was led into an expan-
sionary, but unavailing, logic of terror, becoming bloodier and
bloodier in his efforts to make India assume a pattern over which he
could have knowledge and authority.[8]

---

[7] *The Writings and Speeches of Edmund Burke*, gen. ed. Paul Langford, 17 vols (Oxford, 1981–), VI,
pp. 350.
[8] Sara Suleri, in *The Rhetoric of English India* (Chicago and London, 1992), p. 65, shows the same
logic to have structured Burke's rhetoric as he strove to encompass India's cultural and
geographical vastness.

Burke's case against Hastings was implicitly also a case for a colonialism based on rule through the adaptation and manipulation, rather than the destruction, of the existing Indian power-structures. As such it mirrored, as Michael Franklin's chapter shows, the kind of colonial administration practised by Burke's friend Sir William Jones (although Jones's detailed knowledge of Indian culture eventually led him to perspectives rather different from Burke's). But Burke's impeachment speeches were also important in other, related, ways. They brought debate about Britain's colonial role in the East to the heart of public life. Their rhetoric of horror vividly animated some of the oppositions produced by colonialism – showing the subjection of those who were colonized to be a process inherent in the attempt by the colonizing power to construct itself in a position of exclusive authority. And they suggested that this attempt was the more dangerous, for colonizer and colonized, the greater the exclusivity claimed.

Both Jones and Burke shaped the discourse of Romanticism. 'All-accomplished Jones', as Anna Letitia Barbauld described him, showed that Oriental culture could be translated into terms familiar to Europeans without the figurative excess of Burke. India became more easily read, more easily grafted on to existing aesthetic modes, because his translations represented it as different but not alien. Franklin shows too that Jones did not simply, as Aijaz Ahmad and others have implied, conservatively identify Hindu culture with the work of the Brahman élite at the expense of popular movements.[9] Although concerned to remove aspects of popular Hinduism likely to confirm European readers in their prejudices about Indian savagery, Jones was appreciative, to a degree most Orientalists were not, of the continuity between ancient Sanskrit devotional texts and contemporary popular cults. And Franklin also shows, contra Said, that Jones's Orientalism did not *simply* impose a colonialist discourse upon India, facilitating British administration. It also partially fostered Indian nationalism by helping in the process of liberating its writings from Brahman control.

Jones's neoplatonic translations made Hinduism available to the Romantic poets – as the work of Southey, Shelley and Coleridge reveals. But Burke's anti-Hastings language also left an enduring rhetorical legacy. Its figurative power, its enthralling excess, its

---

[9] Aijaz Ahmad, *In Theory: Classes, Nations, Literatures* (London and New York, 1992), pp. 257–65. See also George D. Bearce, *British Attitudes Towards India 1784–1858* (Oxford, 1961) and S. N. Mukherjee, *Sir William Jones: a Study in Eighteenth-Century Attitudes to India* (Cambridge, 1968).

violent attack upon colonial violence fascinated Cowper, Wordsworth, Coleridge and their radical mentors. All admired Burke's
rhetoric and echoed it in their own attacks upon the slave-trade,
even as they bemoaned Burke's later use of similar rhetoric to attack
enthusiasts for the French Revolution. Historians of Romanticism
have too often read Wordsworth's and Coleridge's 1790s use of
Burke as evidence of a 'reactionary' abandonment of pro-French
radicalism. If, however, we trace their Burkean rhetoric to their
participation in the anti-slavery campaign, it can be seen to derive
from Burke's attack on the current forms of British colonialism.
Coleridge paid tribute to Burke as 'the bold Encomiast of the
American Rebellion' against Britain.[10] And in his lecture against the
slave-trade, he developed Burke's own rhetoric in a racist portrait of
American Indians as 'human Tygers' that was intended to make
readers guilty about the imperialism of the British government who
employed them to attack white settlers.[11] Guilt about British
imperialism did not necessarily entail opposition to all forms of
colonialism: like other opponents of the slave-trade Coleridge came
to favour colonial expansion. Burke himself argued for more prin-
cipled, colonial government whilst opposing the trade:[12] in 1789 and
1791, he supported Wilberforce's motions for total abolition, and in
1792, he sent Henry Dundas his *Sketch of a Negro Code* which
characteristically proposed the expedient of regularization and
humanization of the trade and of the institution of slavery to
accompany its gradual abolition.[13]

Burke's version of British India was one of several colonialist
discourses which shaped Romanticism. The campaign against the
slave-trade was also vital in shaping the radical politics and the
characteristic forms of expression adopted by the young poets
Southey, Coleridge and Wordsworth. Thomas Clarkson was already
resident in the Lake District when Coleridge and Wordsworth met
him there, in November 1799. The two poets had known his *Essay on*

[10] S. T. Coleridge, *Lectures 1795 On Politics and Religion*, eds. Lewis Patton and Peter Mann
(London and Princeton, 1971), p. 325.

[11] Ibid., pp. 56–58.

[12] Eric Williams argued in *Capitalism and Slavery* (London, 1944) that the industrial revolution
in Britain was financed by the profits of slavery and that an increasingly unviable system of
slavery was merely replaced by other forms of bonded labour and the exploitation of
African and Asian workers. For an overview of the debate, see Robin Blackburn, *The
Overthrow of Colonial Slavery 1776–1848* (London and New York, 1988), pp. 24–28.

[13] Quoted in *Slavery: Abolition and Emancipation*, eds. Michael Craton, James Walvin and David
Wright (London and New York, 1976), p. 222.

the Impolicy of the African Slave Trade for several years.[14] Clarkson's detailed evidence, along with further information found in the work of the Quaker Anthony Benezet[15] had provided an essential component of Coleridge's and Southey's political radicalism. The influence of writers such as Clarkson and Benezet and the impact of the whole race/slavery debate on the first generation of Romantic writers has never been fully acknowledged. Indeed, the debate about the slave-trade was conducted within the parameters of a larger discourse about race. The prevailing view of race in the eighteenth century is summarized by Robert Young: 'The dominant view at that time was that the idea of humans being of different species, and therefore of different origins, conflicted with the Biblical account; moreover, the pressure of the Anti-Slavery campaign meant that the emphasis was very much on all humans belonging to a single family'.[16] What Wylie Sypher calls the 'egalitarian dogma of the eighteenth century,' with its acceptance of the hypothesis of one species of humanity, remained the consensus throughout the nineteenth-century.[17] However, the idea that there was a hierarchy of 'races' within the family of humanity and that the Negro was at, or near, the foot became generally accepted as a result of 'the rise of a new science of human taxonomy' and 'the homogenizing pressure of imperialism and the slave-trade'.[18] It

[14] Coleridge borrowed the second edition of Clarkson's *Essay* (London, 1788) from the Bristol Library in June 1795. For Clarkson, see E. L. Griggs, *Thomas Clarkson: The Friend of Slaves* (London, 1936); Ellen Gibson Wilson, *Thomas Clarkson: A Biography* (London and New York, 1990).

[15] Anthony Benezet, *Some Historical Account of Guinea . . . with an Inquiry into the Rise and Progress of the Slave-Trade . . . also a Republication of the Sentiments of Several Authors of Note, on This Interesting Subject. Particularly an Extract of a Treatise, by Granville Sharp*, 2 vols. (Philadelphia, 1781).

[16] Robert Young, *Colonial Desire: Hybridity in Theory, Culture and Race* (London and New York, 1995), p. 7.

[17] Wylie Sypher, *Guinea's Captive Kings: British Anti-Slavery Literature of the XVIII Century* (New York, 1969), p. 55.

[18] See Nicholas Hudson, 'From "Nation" to "Race": The Origins of Racial Classification in Eighteenth-Century Thought', *Eighteenth-Century Studies*, 29 (1996), pp. 247–64 (p. 258). See also, Eric Voeglin, 'The Growth of the Race Idea', *Review of Politics*, 2 (1940), pp. 283–317; Richard H. Popkin, 'The Philosophical Basis of Eighteenth-Century Racism', in *Racism in the Eighteenth Century. Studies in Eighteenth-Century Culture*, vol. 2, ed. Harold E. Pagliaro (Cleveland and London, 1973), pp. 245–62 (pp. 246–47); Stephen Jay Gould, *The Mismeasure of Man* (Harmondsworth, 1981); Nancy L. Stepan, *The Idea of Race in Science: Great Britain* (London, 1982), pp. 1–82; Michael Banton, *Racial Theories* (Cambridge, 1987); Robert Miles, *Racism* (London and New York, 1989); David Lloyd, 'Race Under Representation', *Oxford Literary Review*, 13 (1991), pp. 62–94; Anne McClintock, *Imperial Leather: Race, Gender and Sexuality in the Colonial Contest* (New York and London, 1995), pp. 33–56; Londa Schiebinger, 'The Anatomy of Difference: Race and Sex in Eighteenth-Century Science', *Eighteenth-Century Studies*, 23 (1990), pp. 387–405.

appears that the discourse on race underwent a shift in the late eighteenth century from being a system of arbitrary marks to 'an ascription of natural signs'.[19] This new conception of race derived, perhaps unfairly, its most influential and scientific justification from the work of J. F. Blumenbach.[20] Blumenbach followed the biblical account of race, arguing that the different varieties of humanity could be accounted for by the idea of 'degeneration'. The pure origin of humanity was the white male, all other forms were descended from this race according to gender or geography or a combination of the two. The European race (Caucasian) was the most beautiful and least degenerate and, therefore, constituted the historic race. For Blumenbach white was 'the primitive colour of mankind' since it 'was very easy for that to degenerate into brown, but much more difficult for dark to become white'.[21] He enumerated four other races (Malayan, American, Mongolian, and Ethiopian) which deviated from the norm, with the Mongolian and Ethiopian being the two extremes.[22] Coleridge had attended Blumenbach's lectures while at Göttingen in 1798–99 and he annotated his work.[23] His later speculations on race are deeply indebted to Blumenbach's pioneering anthropology.[24] Blumenbach, following Montesquieu, argued that climate accounted for change and denied that mental ability was a key determinant of race. He has been described by one recent writer as 'the champion of the Africans' and had a noted collection of literature by black writers, which Coleridge may well have seen.[25] Yet it is not difficult to see how his ideas about racial degeneration could be adapted to justify

---

[19] Lloyd, 'Race Under Representation', p. 69.
[20] For the contributions of Carl Linnaeus and G. L. Buffon, see Hudson, 'From "Nation" to "Race"', pp. 252–53; Banton, *Racial Theories*, pp. 3–5; Pratt, *Imperial Eyes*, pp. 24–37; James L. Larson, *Interpreting Nature: The Science of Living Form from Linnaeus to Kant* (Baltimore and London, 1994).
[21] *The Anthropological Treatises of Johann Friedrich Blumenbach*, tr. and ed. Thomas Bendyshe (London, 1865), p. 269.
[22] Ibid., pp. 264–76, 302–4; Banton, *Racial Theories*, pp. 5–6; Young, *Colonial Desire*, pp. 64–65. For the gender implications of Blumenbach's racial theories, see Schiebinger, 'The Anatomy of Difference: Race and Sex in Eighteenth-Century Science'.
[23] See S. T. Coleridge, *Marginalia*, ed. George Whalley, 5 vols (Princeton and London, 1980), I, pp. 535–41.
[24] J. Haeger, 'Coleridge's Speculations on Race', *Studies in Romanticism*, 13 (1974), pp. 333–57; Patrick J. Keane, *Coleridge's Submerged Politics*. See also Trevor H. Levere, *Poetry Realized in Nature: Samuel Taylor Coleridge and Early Nineteenth-Century Science* (Cambridge, 1981), pp. 114–15.
[25] *Anthropological Treatises of Blumenbach*, pp. 310–12.

later nineteenth-century theories of imperialism and, later, of racial supremacy.[26] The Romantic period thus witnessed the beginnings of a paradigm shift in race theory and in the ways 'race' was related to nationality and culture. By discussing various representations or constructions of the African in a number of writers of the time, we can see how this paradigm shift was manifesting itself, and how, in speaking for and/or giving voice to an estranged and silenced 'Other', the literature of the period was complicit with, and/or resistant to, such trends.[27]

The idea that the human race was essentially one species, although generally accepted, did not go unchallenged. The Jamaican slave owner, Edward Long, argued, in his influential *History of Jamaica* (1774), that the white and the black were two distinct species and that the African is closer to the ape or ourang outang than to mankind. Long's refusal of the status of humanity to the African slave suited his defence of slavery. Following Hume, Long found that Western descriptions of Africans as bestial reflected an absence of moral, intellectual and artistic capacity. The Africans 'have no moral sensations' and they are the 'vilest of the human kind'.[28] In 1799, the Manchester surgeon, Charles White, published his *Account of the Regular Gradation of Man*, allowing 'Long's expedient prejudices [to] move into the realm of scientific theory'.[29]

It was the pseudo-scientific view of the African that the opponents of the slave-trade were trying to excise. Two writers who were important for Coleridge's and Southey's early views of race were Anthony Benezet and Thomas Clarkson. Benezet, America's most prominent opponent of the slave-trade, published his *Some Historical Account of Guinea . . . with an Inquiry into the Rise and Progress of the Slave-Trade* (1771) to persuade his readers to end the trade and to swiftly emancipate the slaves.[30] His work was hugely influential in England

---

[26] See Patrick Brantlinger, *Rule of Darkness: British Literature and Imperialism* (Ithaca and London, 1988), pp. 184–88.

[27] For an overview of the debate about the nature of the 'Negro' see, Sypher, *Guinea's Captive Kings*, pp. 50–55.

[28] Edward Long, *History of Jamaica*, 3 vols (London 1774), II, pp. 51–83. On Long see Peter Fryer, *Staying Power: The History of Black People in Britain* (London, 1940), pp. 157–60.

[29] Young, *Colonial Desire*, pp. 7–8; Banton, *Racial Theories*, pp. 13–15.

[30] Anthony Benezet, *Some Historical Account of Guinea its situation, produce, and the general disposition of its inhabitants with an Inquiry into the Rise and Progress of the Slave Trade its Nature and Lamentable Effects* (London, 1771; 2nd edn, 1788; rpt 1968), p. 56. Further references to this edition are cited in the text by title *Account* and page number.

and France.[31] He represented the inhabitants of Guinea as noble savages living a happy and pastoral life until interrupted by Europeans. In fact, it was probably Benezet who was instrumental in fashioning the eighteenth-century abolitionist myth of the noble Negro. For Wylie Sypher, Benezet's work is important, in that it 'marks the point at which religious, primitivistic, humanitarian, "philosophic", and practical objections against slavery fuse'.[32]

Benezet stated that the Africans had a developed, if not sophisticated, civilization involving agricultural cultivation, and several trades (smiths, potters, saddlers, and weavers), as well as established systems of law and justice. He paid tribute to the quality of the work of the goldsmith and silversmith and the fine cloths of the weavers. He employed a range of sources to authenticate the quality of the Africans' work and their industry in trade, fishing and agriculture. Guinea appeared a fertile and Edenic place where the inhabitants had a sense of a one true God and a future state, but they were also 'superstitiously and idolatrously inclined' (*Account*, p. 32). Yet ultimately, for Benezet, the Africans were barbarous and savage and he exhorted Europeans to use 'their endeavours to make the nations of Africa acquainted with the nature of the Christian religion' (*Account*, pp. 58, 82). He questioned the moral superiority of the Europeans who had behaved so cruelly and immorally to the Africans, but he never accepted that the Africans had achieved parity with the European. He did not mention any linguistic or artistic excellence that they possessed. He could not imagine African cultures on their own terms, but only as primitive states of European culture. Throughout he spoke for, or allowed others to speak for, the silenced African and he accepted the oppositions of enlightenment and barbarity, and the equivalence of darkness, ignorance and savagery, the terms which drive JanMohamed's 'manichean allegory'.

If both Long and Benezet, despite both their differing views of race and their conflicting aims, can be seen to accept the inferiority of the black races, Thomas Clarkson, who paid generous tribute to the effects of Benezet's work, went further than most in stressing the equality of the African.[33] Underlying Clarkson's arguments against

[31] David Brion Davis, *The Problem of Slavery in the Age of Revolution* (Cornell and London, 1975), p. 214.
[32] Sypher, *Guinea's Captive Kings*, pp. 69, 92–93.
[33] For Clarkson, see Griggs, *Thomas Clarkson: The Friend of Slaves*; Wilson, *Thomas Clarkson: A Biography*.

the slave-trade was his Christian universalist view of race. He believed that all mankind sprang from the 'same original' and that the notion of separate species contradicted scripture and science.[34] His first work on the subject, the prize-winning Cambridge dissertation, *An Essay on the Slavery and Commerce of the Human Species* (1788), makes the case for the humanity of the African race in a rigorous and compelling way. The premise behind Clarkson's writing, which becomes one of the central creeds of Coleridge's later political philosophy, is that a man is not a thing and thus cannot be traded as a commodity. Clarkson's essay argues for the original equality of all men and the contractual state of government. Slavery must always be illegal unless the person consents to being placed in that position. Clarkson informed his audience of the horrors of the slave-trade in a way that no other writer had so far done. He also attempted to demolish the main arguments concerning black inferiority. Clarkson's more-than-apologia for African industry and culture marks him out as someone whose writings push the parameters of Eurocentric views of Africa to their limits, making his readers rethink their assumptions about European superiority.

Clarkson argues that the Africans in their own country 'exercise the same arts, as the ancestors of those very Europeans, who boast their great superiority, are described to have done in the same uncultivated state'. Although he sees African societies as at an earlier state of development than those of European nations, he is keen to stress the African's linguistic abilities, arguing that their songs 'afford us a high proof of their poetical powers, as the works of the most acknowledged poets' (*Essay*, pp. 118, 120). As evidence of this Clarkson cites the work of Phillis Wheatley. He is able to make the important statement that, if Wheatley 'was designed for slavery, (as the argument must confess) the greater part of the inhabitants of Britain must lose their claim to freedom' (*Essay*, p. 122). Furthermore Clarkson regards certain aspects of the African manufacturing arts as surpassing those currently practised in Europe. African skill in ironwork goes beyond 'the workmen in our towns' and African cotton cloths are 'not to be exceeded by the finest artists in Europe' (*Essay*, p. 124).

Clarkson's second major argument concerning race relates to

[34] Thomas Clarkson, *An Essay on the Slavery and Commerce of the Human Species, particularly the African; translated from a Latin Dissertation*, 2nd edn (London, 1788), p. 131. Further references to this essay are cited in the text by title, *Essay*, and page number.

colour. He attacks at some length the argument that the Africans suffer the curse of Ham and Canaan by showing that the descendants of Ham were not known by their colour and that this colour could not be used to distinguish them. The descendants of Cush, however, were 'of the colour' yet no such curse was placed upon them.[35] Clarkson's explanation of difference accepts the current synthesis of Christian and Enlightenment reasonings. Either the Deity interposed and created such variation or it springs from climatic causes. In both cases differences in colour must exist for human convenience and not as a sign of moral difference. Adopting contemporary notions of race, Clarkson argues against the polygenist hypothesis of those, such as Long, who posit the existence of separate species by pointing to the fertility of the offspring of black and white (Long claimed, against overwhelming evidence, that such offspring were sterile). This fertility test was, as Robert Young has pointed out, the key eighteenth-century argument for the existence of one species of humanity as 'if two animals of a different species propagate, their offspring is unable to continue its own species' (*Essay*, p. 132).

Clarkson's speculations about secondary characteristics are quite fascinating in their mixture of Christian essentialism and contemporary scientific awareness. He postulates that the colour of 'dark olive; a beautiful colour, and a just medium between black and white' was probably the complexion of Noah and that of all our ancestors. He does not see white as the primary colour, and he accepts its equivalence with black; 'there is great reason to presume, that the purest white is as far removed from the primitive colour as the deepest black' (*Essay*, p. 134). Clarkson's insistence on the relativity of our perceptions of the primacy or beauty of skin colour is not exactly unprecedented: Sir Thomas Browne, Joshua Reynolds and others had made the same point. What is new is Clarkson's attempt to confute pseudo-scientific racialists such as Long by giving his arguments a scientific underpinning. His speculations into the origin of colour led him to minimize the key difference as simply resulting from the 'mucosum corpus' which lies under the skin. The actual

---

[35] The demolition of this biblical justification for black slavery was a necessary task for the Christian Clarkson as it was for his contemporary, the black writer and convert, Quobna Ottobah Cugoano in his *Thoughts and Sentiments on the Evil and Wicked Traffic of the Slavery and Commerce of the Human Species* (London, 1787). See *Black Atlantic Writers of the 18th Century*, eds. Adam Potkay and Sandra Burr (London, 1995), pp. 139–43.

skin of the 'blackest negroe' is of the same transparency as 'that of
the purest white'. Not having an awareness of modern-day genetic
theory, Clarkson cannot account for the gradations of colour or its
inheritance but he assumes 'the epidemic complexion' in all its many
and various gradations to result from climate. He even goes so far as
to conceive of 'a black skin' as like a 'universal freckle' (*Essay*, pp.
134–38, 144–45). It is clear that Clarkson is attempting to efface the
sign of difference between white and black, unsettling such binary
oppositions by positing a dark olive as the primary colour, so
removing the grounds for the workings of any manichean allegory
based on such an opposition. Although he does not explicitly state
them, Clarkson must have realized the implications of his discussion
in decentring Western assumptions of white as privileged and
primary. Yet ultimately the African is positioned as a being at a more
primitive level of development than that of the European and in his
Essay on the Impolicy of the Slave Trade (1788) Clarkson does look
forward, like most of the abolitionist writers (John Thelwall being an
exception), to his Christianization.[36]

Clarkson's writings and activities helped to provide the dynamism
for Coleridge's and Southey's radical campaigning in the 1790s. In
this period, Coleridge preached and lectured against the slave-trade,
finding his first audience amongst Bristol and West-Country dissenters. He attacked slavery in his 'Ode to the Departing Year' and
'Fears in Solitude', thereby incorporating political comment in what
scholars of Romanticism have sometimes been content to read as
uncontroversial nature poetry. Yet colonial debate was at the centre
of Coleridge's 1790s activities. Anti-slavery discourse acted as one of
the few forms of opposition to Pitt's government possible after the
passing of the Two Acts gagging the press in December 1795. It
acted too as a form of imaginative displacement – Thelwall's novel
The Daughter of Adoption contained discussions of the slave rebellion in
French St Domingue (present-day Haiti) which served as an analogue for the author's own experience of persecution and marginalization as a radical subjected to the repressive power of established
Church and State. Here (as was later the case with Byron for
different reasons) the writer's experience of physical displacement
and intellectual alienation led him to identify with rebels against and

---

[36] Thomas Clarkson, *An Essay on the Impolicy of the African Slave Trade* (London, 1788),
pp. 98–107.

victims of colonization and to generate through his portrayal of them a critique which showed that repression at home and abroad was central to the imperialist nation (a critique later made from the position of colonized subjects in C. L. R. James's treatment of the same rebellion).[37]

Abolitionism often acted in the Romantic period as a coded language of opposition to the dominant culture within Britain as well as a direct campaign against the cruelties of empire. For dissenters the campaign for the recognition of black Africans' human equality was fuelled by, and in turn refuelled, their campaign to remove the Test and Corporation Acts which prevented them from holding public office. For Evangelicals within the Church of England such as Wilberforce, anti slave-trade agitation was part of a larger attempt to effect a moral reform of the governing classes. In this attempt campaigners spoke on behalf of those who had been colonized, using 'their' words to prick consciences at home about exploitation abroad but also to serve domestic agendas. Even the most assiduous abolitionists rarely let those who had been subjected to colonization speak: instead they appropriated the words of the colonized from mixed motives of their own.[38] Nevertheless, their imagined versions of the speech of colonized people had powerful results, being astutely organized to move the sensibilities of middle-class English readers. Timothy Morton, in his essay, shows how Southey and Coleridge radicalized a topos already made familiar by the anti-slavery writing of Cowper, William Fox and Thomas Cooper,[39] in which the sugar sweetening the tea of polite Englishmen and women was figuratively turned to the blood shed by the slaves who produced it. In the hands of the young Southey and Coleridge, Morton argues, this topos became ambivalent: intended to arouse a shared guilt and compassion in its audiences it also hinted that the poets vicariously enjoyed the prospect of revolutionary violence. The blood of the sugar-producing slaves would be

[37] C. L. R. James, *The Black Jacobins: Toussaint L'Ouverture and the San Domingo Revolution* (London, 1938).

[38] For a theoretical discussion of the appropriation of the speech of the colonized see Gayatri Chakravorty Spivak, 'Can the Subaltern Speak?' in *Marxism and the Interpretation of Culture*, eds. Cary Nelson and Lawrence Grossberg (London, 1988), pp. 271–313.

[39] Fox's *An Address to the People of Great Britain, on the Propriety of Abstaining from West India Sugar and Rum*, went through twenty-six editions by 1793. Thomas Cooper, *Considerations on the Slave Trade; and the Consumption of West Indian Produce* (London, 1791).

mingled with the blood of sugar-consuming ladies and gentlemen if the writers' warnings were not heeded and slave revolt followed.

The first-generation Romantics developed an existing topos in a way that manifests great tension with regard to a polite audience and its likely social position. They also developed an existing poetic genre in a similar way. Coleridge's and Wordsworth's *Lyrical Ballads* have often been put in the context of domestic radicalism. Wordsworth's claim to be speaking the real language of rural labourers made poetic style an issue in the politics of culture. The poems challenged, in form and diction as well as subject-matter, the values by which the governing classes legitimized their power. Yet whilst this challenge has been clearly understood, it is still too often assumed that Wordsworth and Coleridge derived their lyrical ballads from the folk ballad, which Percy's *Reliques* had revived.[40] It is arguable, however, that Cowper's popular 'The Negro's Complaint' (1788) was just as relevant an influence, as well as a more recent one. In this poem, written in response to the request of John Newton for popular verse in support of abolition, Cowper presented the voice of a slave in deliberately simple form and diction. He thereby rendered his enslaved African a victim whose brutal exploitation had not destroyed his innocence. That innocence both demands compassion from the reader and assures him/her that the slave is not a violent – or savage – threat. It allows the slave to question the colonialist's hypocrisy without alienating the reader in the colonizing nation:

> Is there, as ye sometimes tell us,
>   Is there one who reigns on high?
> Has he bid you buy and sell us,
>   Speaking from his throne the sky?
> Ask him, if your knotted scourges,
>   Matches, blood-extorting screws,
>
> Are the means which duty urges
>   Agents of his will to use?

Having gained the readers' compassion and appealed to their religious conscience, Cowper's Negro is able to overturn their racist assumption of moral superiority:

> Deem our nation brutes no longer
>   Till some reason ye shall find
> Worthier of regard and stronger

---

[40] Thomas Percy, *Reliques of Ancient English Poetry*, 3 vols (London, 1765).

Than the colour of our kind.
Slaves of gold, whose sordid dealings
Tarnish all your boasted pow'rs,
Prove that you have human feelings,
Ere you proudly question ours![41]

Here, as in Blake's *Songs of Innocence* and in *Lyrical Ballads*, the innocence of the voice and simplicity of the style lull the readers, allowing a challenge to their prejudices to succeed because it is unexpected. The Negro's complaint becomes an inquisition, the slave, first victim, and then, interrogator. In an age when Reason, as Cora Kaplan has argued, was 'marked from the beginning by exclusions of gender, race, and class',[42] Cowper's attribution of powers of rational enquiry to the Negro is exceptional. Of course, Cowper's Negro is characterized in terms of the debate of the time. 'Fleecy locks and black complexion / Cannot forfeit nature's claim' defensively concedes the point made by racists such as Edward Long that the African's physical features should be read as animalistic.[43]

As Blake's 'The Little Black Boy' and many of the poems in Wordsworth's and Coleridge's *Lyrical Ballads* indicate, the forms of expression developed in abolitionist discourse were vital to the discourses we have come to term 'Romantic'.[44] As Cowper and Burke also reveal, opposition to current forms of colonialism within a colonizing culture does not make a writer immune from colonialist stereotyping: Cowper makes no concessions to the African's own idiom of speech.[45] Yet at its best, as in 'The Negro's Complaint', abolitionist discourse transforms the stereotype with which it operates, so that it destabilizes rather than reinforces the assumptions of the imperialist culture.

William Blake's awareness of the slavery issue and his verbal and visual representations of it have been well discussed by David

[41] *The Poems of William Cowper*, ed. John D. Baird and Charles Ryskamp, 3 vols (Oxford, 1980–95), III, pp. 13–14.
[42] Cora Kaplan, 'Pandora's Box: Subjectivity, Class and Sexuality in Socialist Feminist Criticism', in *Making a Difference: Feminist Literary Criticism*, eds. G. Greene and C. Kahn (London and New York, 1985), pp. 146–76 (p. 150). For the exclusions of race from Reason see, Popkin, 'Racism', pp. 245–62 (pp. 246–47).
[43] Long, *History of Jamaica*.
[44] See Alan Richardson, 'Colonialism, Race, and Lyric Irony in Blake's "The Little Black Boy"', *Papers on Language and Literature*, 26 (1990), pp. 64–90 and *Literature, Education, and Romanticism* (Cambridge, 1994), pp. 153–66.
[45] See D. L. Macdonald, 'Pre-Romantic and Romantic Abolitionism: Cowper and Blake', *European Romantic Review*, 4 (1994), pp. 163–82.

Erdman.[46] As well as 'The Little Black Boy', Blake also produced his illuminated poem *Visions of the Daughters of Albion* in 1793, making explicit the connection between racial and gender oppressions. It has been argued that Blake elaborated Mary Wollstonecraft's questioning conflation of the issues of race and slavery in her *A Vindication of the Rights of Woman* (1792). Wollstonecraft, commenting on the racial and gender exclusions of 'Reason' had asked:

Is sugar always to be produced by vital blood? Is one half of the human species, like the poor African slaves, to be subjected to prejudices that brutalize them, when principles would be a surer guard, only to sweeten the cup of man? Is not this indirectly to deny woman reason?[47]

Blake elaborates on the psychology of the colonialist Theotormon's own mental oppression and on his oppression of both woman and African in the person of Oothoon who is the victim of colonial and sexual violence. Erdman argued that Blake's Theotormon functioned as a critique of John Gabriel Stedman who, in 1796, published his *A Narrative, of a Five Years' Expedition, against the Revolted Negroes of Surinam, in Guiana, on the Wild Coast of South America; from the year 1772 to 1777*. Blake produced, at Joseph Johnson's behest, around fourteen plates for Stedman's *Narrative* between 1792 and 1793, the time of his etching of *Visions of the Daughters of Albion*.[48] Erdman claimed that the momentum of the poem is

. . . supplied by the oratory of Oothoon, a female slave, free in spirit but physically bound; Bromion, the slave-driver who owns her and has raped her to increase her market value; and Theotormon, her jealous but inhibited lover who fails to recognize her divine humanity. . . the frustrated lover . . . being analogous to the wavering abolitionist who cannot bring himself openly to condemn slavery although he deplores the trade.[49]

Erdman's historicization of *Visions* is convincing in locating the poem as a response to the debate about the slave revolt in St Domingue (Blake's 'vales of Leutha'). Blake's slaver certainly repeats Said's later explication of the clichés of Africanist discourse in his proprietorial claim:

---

[46] David V. Erdman, *Blake: Prophet Against Empire*, 3rd edn (Princeton, 1977), pp. 226–42; 'Blake's Vision of Slavery', in *Blake: A Collection of Critical Essays*, ed. Northrop Frye (Englewood Cliffs, 1966), pp. 88–103.

[47] Mary Wollstonecraft, *A Vindication of the Rights of Woman*, ed. Miriam Brody (Harmondsworth, 1985), p. 257.

[48] Martin Esslin, *Blake's Commercial Engravings* (Oxford, 1993). For Stedman, see Pratt, *Imperial Eyes*, pp. 90–102.

[49] Erdman, *Blake: Prophet Against Empire*, p. 228.

> Stamped with my signet are the swarthy children of the sun;
> They are obedient, they resist not, they obey the scourge;
> Their daughters worship terrors and obey the violent.[50]

Erdman's historical insights into the revolutionary potential of *Visions* have, however, been problematized in Steven Vine's recent account of the occlusions made by the poem, an account which 'maps the struggle of the poem to expose structures of sexual and colonial enslavement in the name of visionary Enlightenment' yet also shows how, 'while affirming its radical potential', Blake's language 'dramatizes the historical and ideological uncertainty of its own limitations'.[51] Certainly Blake had a tendency to subordinate issues of race and gender to the dictates of his own highly-developed symbolic structures, so much so that in *The Song of Los* (c. 1795) skin colour is a sign of the fall into materialism and rationalism:

> Adam shuddered; Noah faded. Black grew the sunny African,
> When Rintrah gave abstract philosophy to Brahma in the East.[52]

Responses to discovery of the island of Tahiti (or Otaheite as Europe knew it in the period) and its inhabitants were very different but equally complex. The natives of Tahiti were made an indicator for European attitudes to the peoples with whose culture Europeans were unfamiliar. At first the natives were regarded as conforming to Rousseau's notions of the 'noble savage'. The French navigator Louis Antoine de Bougainville visited Tahiti in 1768 after its discovery by Samuel Wallis. Bougainville believed he had been transported to the Garden of Eden and he named the island 'La Nouvelle Cythère', from the island in Greece where Venus first emerged from the sea.[53] Tahiti was an island of peace and plenty

---

[50] *Blake: The Complete Poems*, ed. W. H. Stevenson, 2nd edn (London and New York, 1989), p. 174. For Said, Africanist discourse stereotypes the African mind in an analogous way to Orientalist discourse: it contains 'the notion of bringing civilization to primitive or barbaric peoples, the disturbingly familiar ideas about flogging to death or extended punishment being required when "they" misbehaved or became rebellious because "they" understood force or violence best; "they" were not like "us" and for that reason deserved to be ruled'. *Culture and Imperialism* (London, 1993), pp. xi-xii.

[51] Stephen Vine, '"That Mild Beam": Enlightenment and enslavement in William Blake's *Visions of the Daughters of Albion*', in *The Discourse of Slavery: Aphra Behn to Toni Morrison*, eds. Carl Plasa and Betty J. Ring (London and New York, 1994), pp. 40–63 (p. 41).

[52] *Blake: The Complete Poems*, p. 242.

[53] Alan Moorehead, *The Fatal Impact: The Invasion of the South Pacific 1767–1840* (New York and Cambridge, 1966), p. 51. See Beaglehole, *The Exploration of the Pacific*, pp. 198–381. For a discussion of the various accounts of the voyages to the South Seas in the period see Philip Edwards, *The Story of the Voyage: Sea-Narratives in Eighteenth-Century England* (Cambridge, 1994)

where nature supplied all the wants of mankind. Bougainville stressed that the islanders had no personal property and that they were free of the stringent sexual taboos of Christian Europe. Diderot penned a *Supplement* (1772) to Bougainville's account of his voyage. The mental voyage to Tahiti made by the philosophe described a land free from the Enlightenment bêtes noires of orthodox Christianity and despotic government. Tahiti became as Philip Edwards puts it 'a showpiece for the advantages of the natural or pre-civilized state', a place from which to criticize the warped values of civilized Christian Europe.[54] Cook arrived in Tahiti in 1769, returning in 1773, 1774 and finally in 1777. Cook, a practical man formed from the traditions of Enlightenment Christianity, regarded the myth-making of Diderot and Bougainville with scepticism. He viewed Tahitian society with a degree of tolerance and practised a kind of cultural relativism with regard to its sexual mores.

It was also in Tahiti that William Bligh landed in 1788 on a mission to secure the bread-fruit plant which was intended for transplantation in the West Indies to be used as a food source for the slaves. The mutiny on board *The Bounty* on Bligh's leaving the island for the West Indies helped crystallize notions of Northern duty and Southern pleasure for the British reading public. By the time of Bligh's visit the Tahitian way of life was suffering from its contact with the West. Many of the natives became addicted to drink and were infected with venereal disease. In the new Evangelical climate that began to dominate British opinion in the early nineteenth century, the Tahitians were no longer seen as noble savages but as unfortunate pagans. An expedition sent by the London Missionary Society arrived on the island in 1797. These missionaries were not the enlightened natural philosophers like those who sailed with Cook, but instead determined servants of their Lord who had little ethnological respect for the cultures of others evident in late eighteenth-century exploration. Subsequently in this new climate the Tahitians were viewed as a primitive, or degraded, crude and super-stitious people in need of revelation.[55]

Tahiti, more than New Holland or New Zealand where the

---

and Neil Rennie, *Far Fetched Facts: The Literature of Travel and The Idea of the South Seas* (Oxford, 1992).

[54] Edwards, *Story of the Voyage*, pp. 110–11.

[55] Moorehead, *The Fatal Impact*, pp. 69–104 (p. 104); Bernard Smith, *European Vision and the South Pacific, 1768–1850* (Oxford, 1960), pp. 24–25.

natives were either considered as primitive or vicious, occasioned modifications in aesthetic theories and practices at home. Bernard Smith has shown how the artists who voyaged with Cook, such as William Hodges, altered picturesque and Claudian assumptions about landscape art in their representations of the Pacific Islands. Tahiti figured in British poetry as an ideal paradise, although sometimes this was used ironically. The figure of the noble savage received added credence when the Tahitian native Omai returned to Britain and created a sensation. He was introduced to George III and dined with Dr Johnson (not himself an adherent to the noble savage creed). Eight years after Omai returned to Tahiti, a popular pantomime by John O'Keefe, *Omai: or a Trip Round the World* was performed in 1785 at the Theatre Royal, Covent Garden. Omai, transformed into a Tahitian prince, woos and marries Londina before returning home.[56] Not everyone, however, accepted the noble savage idea. The first book of Cowper's *The Task* argued that humanity perfects itself in civil society, even in 'the favour'd isles' of the South Pacific. Omai is imagined returning to Tahiti with his former joys ruined by comparison with those he had enjoyed in Britain, forlornly surveying the seas for sight of British vessels. Omai and Tahiti are abandoned because

> Doing good,
> Disinterested good is not our trade.
> We travel far 'tis true, but not for nought.
> (Book I, lines 673–75)[57]

The contrasting views towards the South Sea islanders put forward by Diderot and Cowper informed writing about this geo-political area in the Romantic period. The relationship of Coleridge's 'The Rime of the Ancient Mariner' to numerous accounts of South Sea travel has been well-documented.[58] Additionally Wordsworth, Coleridge, Southey and Byron were fascinated by the story of the Bounty mutiny. Wordsworth drew upon it for his drama *The Borderers* in 1797, Coleridge planned to write a narrative work on the 'Adventures of Christian, the mutineer' and Byron published his version of the

---

[56] Smith, *European Vision*, pp. 80–81.
[57] *The Poems of William Cowper*, II, pp. 133–34.
[58] John Livingston Lowes, *The Road to Xanadu* (London, 1927); Smith, 'Coleridge's Ancient Mariner and Cook's Second Voyage'; James C. McKusick, '"That Silent Sea": Coleridge, Lee Boo, and the Exploration of the South Pacific', *The Wordsworth Circle*, 24 (1993), pp. 102–6.

event as *The Island* in 1823.[59] Southey, in a letter to John Rickman of
1803, alludes to 'Coleridge's scheme to mend' the Tahitians by
'extirpating the bread-fruit from their island, and making them live
by the sweat of their brows'.[60] The bread-fruit which Bligh had
come to gather was increasingly seen as the source of the indolence
which made the island a 'paradise of sin' in which promiscuity and
infanticide flourished.

In this volume James C. McKusick explores the hitherto neglected
context of accounts of the South Pacific in Coleridge and Southey's
Pantisocratic project. An essential part of Romanticism's destabiliza-
tion of the values of imperialist Britain was its capacity to imagine
radical grounds on which social and political ideologies could be
overturned. Pantisocracy, Coleridge's and Southey's scheme to
establish a settlement in America, was an attempt to realize radical
social equality in a country which had successfully rebelled against
Britain's colonial power. McKusick argues that Pantisocracy arose
from 'an imaginary representation of America that assimilates it to
the South Sea Islands'. Coleridge and Southey, bidding to escape the
boundaries of imperialist Britain, are seen to have constructed an
idealizing colonialism of their own, one which collapsed the historical and geographical differences of remote societies so as better to
be able to write inland America in the image of an exotic and fertile
paradise. As was the case in Burke's representation of India, an
attack on Britain's imperialist policy still retains a colonialist understanding: 'what it seeks to escape', McKusick concludes, 'it instead
reinscribes within the text of its own geo-political unconscious'.

The sense of 'place' is a key issue in most works in this collection.
Remote locations are often dislocated in terms of time and space by
Romantic writing and the various discourses which inform it. This
can be seen in those essays dealing with the West Indies. D. L.
Macdonald, utilizing James Clifford's notions of the allegorical basis
of ethnography, shows how Matthew Lewis views Jamaica through a
Gothic lens, whilst Timothy Morton argues that the economic tracts
turn the colony into 'a supplementary island growing an imported,
supplementary crop'. Although accepting the idea that Romantic

---

[59] *The Notebooks of Samuel Taylor Coleridge*, ed. Kathleen Coburn, 5 vols (London and Princeton,
1957–), I, 179; Geoffrey Sanbourn, 'The Madness of Mutiny: Wordsworth, the *Bounty* and
The Borderers', *The Wordsworth Circle*, 23 (1992), pp. 35–42.

[60] *The Life and Correspondence of Robert Southey*, ed. Rev. Charles Cuthbert Southey, 6 vols
(London, 1849–50), II, pp. 243.

writing dissolves the referents of place, the contributors to this volume also consider the ways in which such geo-political re-imaginings show resistance to and complicity with the material progress of colonialism and imperialism. One should not forget, as Marilyn Butler has pointed out with regard to the East, that these re-imagined places were the sites of a 'pragmatic contest among the nations for world power' in the period.[61]

Alan Richardson broadens the focus in his chapter by placing Southey's and Coleridge's writing in the context of other Bristol abolitionist poetry by Thomas Chatterton, Hannah More and Anne Yearsley. Richardson questions whether Romanticism is complicit – even in its early abolitionist form – with the naturalization of racial categories that characterized nineteenth-century racism. He finds not a series of consistent – or even fully formed – attitudes towards race but internally unstable schemes from which 'race' is only beginning to emerge in a modern sense. And he notes how the class and gender of the writer shaped the portrayal of black slaves.[62]

This whole question of race, class and gender, commented on by Wollstonecraft, represented in Blake's *Visions of the Daughters of Albion*, has become a subject for a wide-ranging and hotly-contested debate in criticism informed by post-colonial writing. It had been argued that in many different societies patriarchal authority has relegated women to subjugated status and, furthermore, that the congruence of the position of women with those subjected to colonization indicates a shared experience and understanding of oppression. Sander L. Gilman has argued that in the nineteenth century black females and white prostitutes were labelled as both primitive and sexualized subjects, this labelling shown in the iconography of medical and artistic discourse.[63] Nancy Stepan has demonstrated

---

[61] 'The Orientalism of Byron's Giaour', in *Byron: the Limits of Fiction*, ed. Bernard Beatty (Totowa, New Jersey, 1988), p. 78.

[62] For a judicious discussion of the effect of women's subordinate gender position on their representations of the colonized see Laura E. Donaldson, *Decolonizing Feminisms: Race, Gender and Empire-Building* (London, 1993). See also, Moira Ferguson, *Subject to Others: British Women Writers and Colonial Slavery, 1760–1834* (London and New York, 1992); Anne McClintock, *Imperial Leather: Race, Gender, and Sexuality in the Colonial Contest* (New York, 1995); Moira Ferguson, *Colonialism and Gender Relations from Mary Wollstonecraft to Jamaica Kincaid: East Caribbean Connections* (New York, 1993); Susan Meyer, *Imperialism at Home: Race and Victorian Women's Fiction* (Ithaca and London, 1996).

[63] Sander L. Gilman, 'Black Bodies, White Bodies: Toward an Iconography of Female Sexuality in Late Nineteenth-Century Art, Medicine, and Literature', in *'Race,' Writing, and Difference*, ed. Henry Louis Gates, Jr. (Chicago and London, 1985), pp. 223–61. For discussion of the representation of women and the historical phase of eighteenth-century

the fundamental nature of 'the analogy between race and gender' in
the nineteenth century where 'the major modes of interpretation of
racial traits were inevitably evoked to explain sexual traits'.[64]
Deirdre Coleman, in a recent essay, has employed such insights in
discussing women's abolitionist writing in the 1790s, arguing that 'in
seeking to capitalize upon fashionable anti-slavery rhetoric for their
own political objectives, women only increased the general murki-
ness of abolitionist rhetoric, an effect most evident in their employment of the emotive but clichéd analogy between their own
disenfranchised lot and the plight of enslaved Africans'.[65] Anne
McClintock, writing about the later period of European imperialism,
similarly criticized the tendency in some post-colonial thinking to
produce ahistorical and monolithic terms, such as 'Third World
Woman' and 'Post-Colonial Condition' which flatten distinct realms
of experience.[66] Such complicated debates about the triangulated
conflicts of race, gender and class, informing the essays in this
volume by Richardson and Ferguson, show the need for awareness
of the interplay of these three key terms in Romantic-period writing
about colonialism.

colonialism see Laura Brown, 'Reading Race and Gender', *Eighteenth-Century Studies*, 23
(1990), pp. 425–43.

[64] Nancy L. Stepan, 'Race and Gender: The Role of Analogy in Science', *Isis*, 77 (1986),
pp. 261–77 (p. 263).

[65] Deirdre Coleman, 'Conspicuous Consumption: White Abolitionism and English Women's
Protest Writing in the 1790s', *ELH*, 61 (1994), pp. 341–62 (p. 341).

[66] McClintock, *Imperial Leather*, pp. 5, 12–13. For recent discussions of these areas see Lisa
Lowe, *Critical Terrains: French and British Orientalisms* (Ithaca, 1991); Suvendrini Perera, *Reaches
of Empire: The English Novel from Edgeworth to Dickens* (Chicago, 1992); Jenny Sharpe, *Allegories of
Empire: The Figure of the Woman in the Colonial Text* (Minneapolis, 1993); Chandra Talpade
Mohanty, 'Under Western Eyes: Feminist Scholarship and Colonial Discourses', in *Third
World Women and the Politics of Feminism*, eds. Chandra Talpade Mohanty, Ann Russo, and
Lourdes Torres (Bloomington, 1991), pp. 51–80.

CHAPTER 3

Romanticism and colonialism: races, places, peoples, 1800–30

Tim Fulford

These years saw the emergence of several writers for whom race and gender were related concerns: Mary Shelley, Mary Butt Sherwood and Matthew Lewis are discussed here by Joseph W. Lew, Moira Ferguson, and D. L. Macdonald. The period brought the formal abolition of the slave-trade (1807) and a subsequent rise in illegal slave smuggling. It saw the development of missionary societies and the increasing influence of colonial government by Evangelical precepts. After 1815 successive governors-general vastly expanded British rule in India and in 1828 the then Governor-General, Lord William Bentinck, introduced a comprehensive policy of 'Westernization', instituting English as the official language of law, administration, and education, and outlawing Indian customs such as sati.

Britain became the colonial power in Malta and the Mediterranean, giving Coleridge first-hand experience of colonial administration. Colonialist interest also expanded to the West: the discovery and subsequent conquest and government of the South American tribes was a popular subject for poetry in the period. Helen Maria Williams's long poem *Peru* (1786) had told the story of Pizarro's conquest of the Incas; Joel Barlow glorified the Inca state in *The Vision of Columbus* (1787) and R. B. Sheridan adapted Koetzebue's *Pizarro* (1799) for the London stage. Advised by Samuel Rogers and Robert Southey, William Lisle Bowles described Spanish rapacity in Chile in *The Missionary* (1811–13). This poem developed the sentimental topoi of Williams's *Peru*. It indicted Spanish colonialism and advocated instead a 'benevolent' paternalism by idealizing the Christian missionary Anselmo, himself a victim of torture at the Spanish Inquisition's hands. It enlisted male readers' chivalric feelings against the Spanish by portraying their cruelty to helpless Indian maidens. The heroine Olola is abandoned by her Spanish lover and is forced to watch her father being tortured; doubly betrayed, she drowns herself, singing of her love in a scene intended to be reminiscent of Ophelia. Thomas Campbell, likewise, used the death of an innocent maiden, lamented by a faithful Indian, to oppose the military conquest of America in *Gertrude of Wyoming* (1809). Byron, who admired both Campbell and Bowles, adopted a similar method of structuring his analyses of colonial relations through stories of cross-cultural love in which the woman suffers. His Eastern Tales, the age's most popular imperial fictions, were founded on the sentimental depiction of the conquest of the West.

In 1805, Southey published his romance *Madoc* (begun in 1789 but heavily revised in 1804). Southey's poem imagines an encounter between his twelfth-century, Welsh, Christian hero and New World Amerindians, repeating the stereotypes of the good and bad Indians (pacifist Hoamen and the barbaric, devil-worshipping Aztecs) found in the literature of colonial encounter from Columbus onward.[1] Madoc's militant religion and his wish to suppress the native customs of human sacrifice and flesh eating made him resemble Thalaba, Muslim hero of Southey's 1801 Orientalist epic. And his later poem, *The Curse of Kehama* (1810), also began with a condemnation of the superstitious customs of native peoples. Southey's poetic narratives, however, displayed enough disturbing similarity between Britain and the peoples of its empire to invalidate their ideological aims. In using poetic licence to explore foreign cultures, he seemed to be asking British readers to believe in the mythology of heathens. *The Curse of Kehama* was condemned by reviewers for this reason. And his portrait of Madoc was termed a 'deification of a marauder, possibly as savage as the Indians themselves'.[2] His counter-productive poetry had collapsed the distinctions it had been attempting to make, infecting the colonizer with the barbarity he found in the natives. Thus, his colonialist poetry made renewed attempts to construct an ideology of imperialism all the more necessary as it reminded Britons of similarities they would rather forget between their own culture and those of the countries they ruled.

Southey made renewed attempts to do so, turning to the medium of prose, and becoming one of the age's most influential commenta-

---

[1] Benjamin Keen, *The Aztec Image in Western Thought* (New Brunswick, New Jersey, 1971), pp. 271–72; T. Todorov, *The Conquest of the Americas: The Question of the Other* (New York, 1987).

[2] *The Eclectic Review*, quoted in *Robert Southey: The Critical Heritage*, ed. Lionel Madden (London and Boston, 1972), pp. 106–7.

tors on the politics of empire. In discussions of Ireland, India, Polynesia and South America he strove to eradicate the similarity of homeland to colony, precisely because that similarity was partly produced by the export to the colonies of the repressed fear that the 'infections' of commercialism, Jacobinism, sensuality and superstition were endemic to the British character and not just diseases that threatened the nation from without. Locating (and exterminating) the sources of infection in the colonies, then became a mission by which Britons assured themselves of their own purity, whilst subordinating the colonized to their 'righteous' authority.

For the nineteenth-century public, Southey's most influential, imperialist work was his *Life of Horatio, Lord Nelson* (1813): thirteen editions were published before 1853. This biography was presented as a training in imperial duty: Southey's preface hoped the book would be carried by the young sailor 'till he has treasured up the example in his memory and his heart'.[3] In 1828, Grosvenor Charles Bedford told the author that the biography 'ought to be in the chest of every seaman, from the admiral to the cabin boy'.[4] In the later Victorian period, it was included in the 'Every Boy's Library' series and was made a school-book (in an edition which included examination questions).[5] The *Life* sought to define British imperialism by embodying it in a paternalist, dutiful and Protestant hero. Instrumental in forming the values of generations of Victorian schoolboys, many of whom went on to become soldiers, sailors and colonial officials, Southey's *Life* was one of the texts by which Romanticism educated the British in an ideology of empire.

Other texts had a similar educative role, not least Romantic discussions of Ireland. Closer to home than the new colonies in India, Africa and the West Indies, the anxiety Ireland caused in Britain was more familiar, the authoritarian response longer tried. The leader of the 1803 Irish rebellion, Robert Emmet, was executed in 1803, arousing Coleridge's regret at Britain's harsh treatment of its oldest colony.[6] But after the Act of Union (1800), which gave the Irish seats at Westminster, regret turned to fear of Catholic influence

---

[3] Quoted in David Eastwood, 'Patriotism Personified: Robert Southey's *Life of Nelson* Reconsidered', *The Mariner's Mirror*, 77 (1991), pp. 143–49 (p. 145).

[4] Quoted in Eastwood, 'Patriotism Personified', p. 149.

[5] In the Intermediate Education Series, ed. G. A. Green (London, 1879).

[6] See Tom Paulin, 'English Political Writers on Ireland: Robert Southey to Douglas Hurd', in *Critical Approaches to Anglo-Irish Literature*, eds. Michael Allen and Angela Wilcox (Gerrards Cross, 1989), pp. 132–45.

on the state. In essays of 1809, 1812 and 1828 Southey played on the traditional British distrust of Irish Catholicism as he argued against Catholic emancipation. 'Religious madness is infectious', he wrote, and the revival of monasteries allowed the Catholic clergy to 'communicate the contagion'. This contagion would be made political, as well as religious, by emancipation, and would 'introduce Irish priests into our army and navy; men acting under orders from a church which Buonaparte has ostentatiously restored'.[7] Equating religious enthusiasm with Jacobinism, Southey demonized the latter as a disease to which the uneducated were prone, just as credulous, Irish peasants were prone to the superstitions peddled by Catholic priests. This demonization was ultimately reassuring, however, since it allowed him to suggest that the removal of the priesthood's influence (by the refusal of emancipation, by the Protestant education of the populace, by the suppression of popular ceremonies and by the prevention of travel to Britain) would stop the spread of revolutionary politics, just as it would that of Catholicism – as if that politics was a foreign infection rather than a product of domestic radicalism. The familiar authoritarianism used to suppress insurrection in Ireland since Spenser's time was, thus, in Southey's colonized version of domestic politics, a prophylactic against the political infection of Britain itself. And, lest his readers quail at his draconian proposals, Southey compared the Irish to African kings notorious for their savagery and likened Catholic processions to the Hindu custom of sati. Ireland became Africanized and Indianized in his account, as he sought to portray the military government he thought necessary to prevent Irish infections as a civilizing paternalism that, as in the newer colonies, would save heathens from themselves. In this racist solution, those Irish too intransigent to accept military rule became 'refractory savages' to be shipped off to the colonies. Having proved themselves 'savages' by resisting British authority, any difference between them and the Africans, Indians and aborigines who inhabited the newer colonies (also 'savage climes'[8]) could be disregarded. In the East Indies, Africa and Australia, the Irish, now identified with the dangerous natives of Britain's remoter territories, would, at least, be at a safe distance. Here Southey's writing exhibits a process of import/export in which

[7] See Robert Southey, *Essays Moral and Political*, 2 vols. (London, 1832), II, p. 280.
[8] From the 'Botany Bay Eclogues', in *The Poetical Works of Robert Southey Collected By Himself*, 10 vols. (London, 1853), II, p. 72.

one imagined colony is shaped by (and in turn reshapes) the writer's interpretation (from reading and direct contact) of others. In this process, it is not simply the imagined colony's otherness, but its uncanny combination of similarity and difference from its fellows and from the home culture, that is most notable.

Coleridge also referred to India, and to *The Curse of Kehama*, when writing of Ireland. In 1814, he published in *The Courier* a series of open letters to Mr Justice Fletcher. These alarmist letters feared a Catholic rebellion and defended 'the name of Orange dear and religious in the heart of every patriotic and loyal Irish Protestant'.[9] The causes for alarm included the persistence of Jacobinism which 'still *walks* in Great Britain and Ireland . . . like the Kehama of our laurel-honouring laureat, one and the same, yet many and multiform and dividuous, assaulting with combined attack all the gates and portals of law and usage'.[10] It was a 'contagion most widely dispersed' by 'Priests and Prophets' exploiting 'Irish superstition, and the barbarism and virulence of Irish clanship'.[11]

At the root of Coleridge's alarm was an interpretation of Catholicism and Hinduism as forms of idolatry. Reverence for 'supernatural power transferred to objects of the senses' encouraged 'blind submission to remorseless leaders'.[12] Ireland merged into India in Coleridge's account, because its Catholicism made it fanatical. Or rather, it merged with the Orientalist and Protestant suspicion of Hinduism that Coleridge had adopted from Southey's poem. In the Romantic conservatism of the Lake Poets, then, Ireland was the victim of religious and political prejudice which Britain's exposure to Eastern beliefs only deepened. The more favourable (yet still ambivalent) portraits presented by Thomas Moore's *Irish Melodies* (1808–13) and the Edgeworths' *Essay on Irish Bulls* (1802) were exceptions to Romanticism's reinforcement of English stereotypes about the Irish.

Southey's idea of shipping Irish Catholics to the colonies became reality as the politics of landownership forced the poor to emigrate. But it depended on the rapid growth of new colonies in the period. In 1815, Cape Colony was confirmed under British rule after being twice taken from the Dutch in 1795 and 1806. Despite the fact that ninety per cent of the colony was Dutch, it became the focus for British territorial expansion. In 1809, the legal status of the indi-

---

[9] S. T. Coleridge, *Essays on his Times*, ed. David V. Erdman, 3 vols. (London and Princeton, 1978), II, p. 409.
[10] Ibid., pp. 384–85.   [11] Ibid., pp. 387, 405.   [12] Ibid., p. 411.

genous population was defined in such a way as to oblige them to
work for the Europeans, and in 1812 they were virtually enslaved by
the Boers. In 1820, British settlement of the Cape began in earnest
when 5,000 emigrants arrived, bringing with them the London
Missionary Society.[13] British law was imposed in their wake and
English became the colony's official language in 1822. The native
Khoikhoi ('Hottentot') were given legal protection and slavery was
abolished in 1833, leading to the Great Trek of the Boers, in which
thousands moved Northward, establishing the Orange Free State
and the Transvaal republics. Although the Cape did not catch the
attention of Romantic writers to the extent of other geo-political
regions, it was a source for the popular tale by Mary Butt Sherwood
which Moira Ferguson analyses in this volume. It was the subject for
the work of the Scottish poet, Thomas Pringle. Pringle emigrated
there in 1820 as part of the British drive to colonize the Cape. His
collections of verse and prose, *Ephemerides* (1828) and *African Sketches*
(1834), applied the rhetoric of the picturesque to the South African
landscape. J. M. Coetzee argues that the intractability of the South
African landscape to European notions of the sublime may have
been linked to the absence of an aggressive politics of expansion in
the area, which lacked the great American frontiers.[14] Pringle also
adapts the typical Romantic ballad to subjects native to South Africa
in poems such as 'The Bechuana Boy', 'Song of the Wild Bushman',
and his sonnets on the three tribal groups of the Cape, 'The
Hottentot', 'The Caffer' and 'The Bushmen'.[15]

A further colony of settlement was added to the British Empire
when James Cook charted the coast of Australia in 1770, on his first
voyage of exploration. In 1788, a colony was established in what Cook
had named New South Wales when a fleet of eleven vessels containing
736 convicted criminals, a Governor and some officials arrived there.
Transportation was an important part of the British penal system and,
after the revolution of 1776 prevented any further convict settlements
in North America, an alternative destination needed to be found. By

---

[13] Mary Louise Pratt, *Imperial Eyes: Travel Writing and Transculturation* (New York and London,
1992), pp. 67–68.
[14] J. M. Coetzee, *White Writing: On the Culture of Letters in South Africa* (New Haven and London,
1988), pp. 35–62.
[15] *The African Poems of Thomas Pringle*, eds. Ernest Pereira and Michael Chapman (Durban,
1989); John Robert Doyle, *Thomas Pringle* (New York, 1972). See also David Bunn, ' "Our
Wattled Cot": Mercantile and Domestic Spaces in Thomas Pringle's African Landscapes',
in *Landscape and Power*, ed. W. J. T. Mitchell (Chicago and London, 1994).

1852, some 160,000 convicts were transported to the new colony which became a major supplier of wool for the British textile industry.[16] Not surprisingly, it is the penal aspect of the colony's character which features in writing of the period. Up until 1820, views of Australian nature were largely created by the experience of the colonists who settled around Sydney Harbour and Cumberland Plain. For the colonists, Australian scenery appeared visually mono-tonous and led to feelings of melancholy in those who surveyed it.[17] Southey's 'Botany Bay Eclogues' (1794) use 'this savage shore' at the 'farthest limits of the world' as a background for an indictment of social injustice and penal severity, yet also depict a land of potential opportunity, uncorrupted by European civilization. Southey's 'Eclo-gues' gloss over the real hardship endured by the colony:

> Welcome, ye wild plains
> Unbroken by the plough, undelved by hand
> Of patient rustic; where for lowing herds,
> And for the music of the bleating flocks,
> Alone is heard the kangaroo's sad note
> Deepening in distance. Welcome, wilderness,
> Nature's domain! for here, as yet unknown
> The comforts and the crimes of polish'd life,
> Nature benignly gives to all enough,
> Denies to all superfluity.[18]

Ironically, it was to a 'moral' Botany Bay that Byron, perhaps with the 'Eclogues' in mind, was to sentence Southey, Wordsworth and Coleridge for their 'apostacy' in *Don Juan* (Canto III, stanza xciv).[19] Byron may have been alluding to the Crown's 1790s practice of transporting reformers to Botany Bay under legislation against sedition. Transportation was one of the fates that Coleridge's radical friend, John Thelwall, would have had in mind as an alternative destiny to being hanged for treason when he penned his sonnet 'On the Report of the Death of Thomas Muir, on Board the Surprise, in his Passage to Botany Bay'.[20] But, by and large, the colony is simply represented as a land unwounded by plough or spade and suitable

---

[16] *The Cambridge Illustrated History of the British Empire*, ed. Peter J. Marshall (Cambridge, 1996), pp. 36–39.

[17] Bernard Smith, *European Vision and the South Pacific, 1768–1850* (Oxford, 1960), p. 184.

[18] *The Poetical Works of Robert Southey*, II, p. 73.

[19] *Lord Byron: The Complete Poetical Works*, ed. Jerome J. McGann, 7 vols. (Oxford, 1980–91), v.

[20] John Thelwall, *Poems Written in Close Confinement in the Tower and Newgate Under a Charge of High Treason* (London, 1795), p. 8.

for the erasure of either the individual's guilt or society's iniquities. From the start, Australian nature was, as Bernard Smith puts it, seen as 'something to be worked upon and made congenial for human occupation'.[21] This was the tenor of the medallion Josiah Wedgwood fashioned out of clay which had been sent from New South Wales. On it was stamped the legend, 'Hope encouraging Art and Labour, under the Influence of Peace, to pursue the employment necessary to give security and happiness to an infant settlement.' The medallion was accompanied with a dedicatory poem by Erasmus Darwin, *The Visit of Hope to Botany Bay*, which envisaged a municipal and agricultural future for the colony. Australia provided a congenial space for Darwin's 'progressive and evolutionary speculations in natural philosophy'.[22] The aborigines, although a frequent subject in the colony's visual art, scarcely feature in the poetry of the time. Despite an initial attempt to idealize the inhabitants of New Holland as noble savages, it was the aborigines who were to rival the 'Hottentot' for the distinction of being, in European eyes, the lowest link in nature's chain between man and animal.[23]

Higher up the chain were the inhabitants of the ancient civilizations of the East, high enough for Orientalism to become an established fashion in architecture, decoration, costume and poetry, as Byron's 'Eastern Tales' and his *Don Juan* indicate. Caroline Franklin's contribution to this volume situates Byron's *The Siege of Corinth* (1816) and *Hebrew Melodies* (1815) in the context of their author's sceptical critique of Orientalism and his discourse of sentimental nationalism. Franklin considers the poems as symbolic meditations on the poetry of imperialism as well as discourses oppositional to the Evangelical movement at home. In Byron's work, colonialism was interrogated through a survey of the Europe of Napoleonic conquest and Bourbon reaction, and through an examination of the historical space in which Western and Eastern empires met, fought and melded – the unstable space of Venice, considered here by Malcolm Kelsall. Kelsall seeks to undermine the assumptions on which Said's *Orientalism* was founded, by returning Byron's and Wordsworth's geo-political imaginations to the liminal space of a republic, in which the construction of the West as its opposite by an imperialist East (and South) was as legible as the West's colonialism

---

[21] Smith, *European Vision*, pp. 132, 117–57.   [22] Ibid., pp. 132–33.
[23] Ibid., pp. 125–32.

of the 'Orient'. Byron, Kelsall shows, destabilizes the ideologies of empire by reversing the gender and sexual hierarchies implicit in the cultural representations, by which Venetians had imaged their colonial dominance, celebrating a feminized and Orientalized culture of sexual fecundity and social melding, rather than one of masculine authority.[24] Pointing to the persistence of Sir William Jones's translations of sexually explicit Hindu poetry, in Shelley as well as Byron, Kelsall develops in the context of 1820s Europe the arguments of Michael Franklin's essay later in this volume.

Shelley also exploited the East in a series of visionary poems and dramas, including *The Revolt of Islam* (1818), 'The Witch of Atlas' (1824), and *Prometheus Unbound* (composed 1818–19; published 1820), which stressed the redemptive aspects of Prometheus' soul mate Asia. Like Sir William Jones, Shelley in such poems genders the East as female and represents it as a source of renewal, if not redemption. Significantly, it is towards the East that Mary Shelley's Henry Clerval directed his talents in *Frankenstein* (1818). Like Sir William Jones, Clerval wished to master the languages of India with the aim of materially assisting in the progress of colonization and trade.[25]

The East is not always so redemptive a force. Shelley's 'Ozymandias' may follow Volney's *Ruins* in deriving comfort from the end of empires, but, for others in the period, the East was the source of anxiety and infection. With extraordinary prescience, Thomas Paine had pre-empted this fear back in 1775 in his remarkable tract 'Reflections on the Life and Death of Lord Clive' where he imagined a guilt-ridden and tormented Clive' haunted by memories of his colonial rapacity in India.[26] The topos of the confident imperialist, stricken with colonial guilt and subject to a mysterious, even occult, punishment in later life is analysed in D. L. Macdonald's discussion in this volume of Matthew Lewis's Gothic depictions of his slave plantations in Jamaica.[27] The topos was to reappear later in the

---

[24] For a persuasive reading of Byron's manipulation of the categories of gender and Orient see, Susan J. Wolfson, '"A Problem Few Dare Imitate": Byron's Sardanapalus and the "Effeminate Character"', *ELH*, 58 (1991), pp. 867–902. See Marilyn Butler's argument that Byron's Nineveh 'as a realized imagined Otherworld, is the familiar world – London – at once turned upside down, and satirically reproduced'. See her 'John Bull's Other Kingdom', *Studies in Romanticism*, 31 (1991), pp. 281–94.

[25] See also Elizabeth A. Bohls, 'Standards of Taste, Discourses of Race, and the Aesthetic Education of a Monster', *Eighteenth-Century Life*, 18 (1994), pp. 23–36 (p. 27).

[26] Thomas Paine, 'Reflections on the Life and Death of Lord Clive' (1775), *The Thomas Paine Reader*, eds. Michael Foot and Isaac Kramnick (Harmondsworth, 1987), pp. 57–62.

[27] On colonialism and the Gothic, see H. W. Malchow, *Gothic Images of Race in Nineteenth Century*

nineteenth century, finding its most popular manifestations in the
thrillers of Wilkie Collins and Arthur Conan Doyle and in J. Milton
Hayes's melodramatic, music-hall monologue, 'The Green Eye of
the Yellow God'. But in the Romantic period, the Bedouin Arab,
who features in Wordsworth's account of Coleridge's dream in Book
Five of *The Prelude*, fleeing from 'the fleet of waters of the drowning
world' is a prophet of apocalypse. For Anna Letitia Barbauld back in
1791, the East was the source of divine punishment for Britain's
involvement in the slave-trade. In her verse *Epistle to William
Wilberforce, Esq.*, she combines themes from the discourses of colonialism, fashion and medicine with politics, by representing the
modish Orientalism of the time, and the mercantile and commercial
success which underlaid it, as an infectious and sybaritic luxury
which corrupted and feminized civilization and encouraged despotism.

> Nor less from the gay East, on essenc'd wings,
> Breathing unnam'd perfumes, Contagion springs;
> The soft luxurious plague alike pervades
> The marble palaces and rural shades;
> Hence, throng'd Augusta builds her rosy bowers,
> And decks in summer wreaths her smoky towers;
> And hence, in summer bow'rs, Arts costly hand
> Pours courtly splendours o'er the dazzled land:
> The manners melt – One undistinguish'd blaze
> O'erwhelms the sober pomp of elder days;
> Corruption follows with gigantic stride,
> And scarce vouchsafes his shameless front to hide:
> The spreading leprosy taints ev'ry part,
> Infects each limb, and sickens at the heart.
> Simplicity! most dear of rural maids,
> Weeping resigns her violated shades:
> Stern Independence from his glebe retires,
> And anxious Freedom eyes her drooping fires;
> By foreign wealth are British morals chang'd,
> And Afric's sons, and India's, smile aveng'd.[28]

Britain (Stanford, 1996), pp. 9–40. Bohls, 'Standards of Taste', p. 27; Joseph W. Lew, 'The
Deceptive Other: Mary Shelley's Critique of Orientalism in Frankenstein', *Studies in
Romanticism*, 30 (1991), pp. 255–83. Kari J. Winter, *Subjects of Slavery, Agents of Change: Women
and Power in Gothic Novels and Slave Narratives, 1790–1865* (Athens, Georgia and London, 1992),
pp. 49–52.
[28] Lines 86–105, *The Poems of Anna Letitia Barbauld*, eds. William McCarthy and Elizabeth
Kraft (Athens, Georgia and London, 1994), pp. 117–18.

Similarly, De Quincey's *Confessions of an English Opium Eater* (1821) presents the alternative, negative aspect of Eastern influence, one which threatens and infects, albeit this time through the psychic agency of dreams. The East as a nexus of fears of despotism, corruption, effeminacy and infection is discussed by Joseph W. Lew in his analysis of Mary Shelley's apocalyptic novel *The Last Man* (1826). The novel deals with the total annihilation of the human race resulting from a plague emanating from the East. Such subject matter brings the theories of Montesquieu's *L'Esprit de Lois* (1748) into the context of the imperial doubt, the inevitable result of colonial encounters. Arguably Shelley's novel prefigures, in a more sophisticated way, the mode of imperial Gothic, practised by writers such as H. Rider Haggard and Bram Stoker in the fin de siècle years of the nineteenth century.[29] Shelley's Eastern plague and De Quincey's opium nightmares oddly pre-empt the threats of invasion posed by Stoker's Dracula and Haggard's Ayesha, with their ambitions to colonize the West in an unholy parody of contemporary Western imperialism.

In the more classically Hellenistic poetry of John Keats, whose work is the least marked by Orientalist and colonialist influences, we can, perhaps, see how the anxieties occasioned by the contemplation of other worlds may have influenced his representation of the fall of empires in the Hyperion poems.[30] Generally for Keats the East is emptied of meaning, its place names exploited for their exotic and euphonic qualities, as in the sumptuous feast Porphyro sets before Madelaine in 'The Eve of St Agnes' (1819) with its

> Manna and dates, in argosy transferred
> From Fez; and spiced dainties, every one,
> From silken Samarcand to cedared Lebanon.[31]

Nevertheless, in Keats's 'Isabella; or, The Pot of Basil' (1818), we can see a condemnation of the mercantile mentality and its propagation of the trade in slaves. In up-dating Boccaccio's tale, Keats made Isabella's capitalist brothers into speculators in colonial ventures:

---

[29] See Patrick Brantlinger, *Rule of Darkness: British Literature and Imperialism* (Ithaca, 1988), pp. 227–53; Nicholas Daly, 'That Obscure Object of Desire: Victorian Commodity Culture and the Fictions of the Mummy', *Novel*, 28 (1994), pp. 42–70; Laura Chrisman, 'The Imperial Unconscious', *Critical Quarterly*, 32 (1990), pp. 38–58.

[30] Marilyn Butler, 'Orientalism', in *The Penguin History of Literature*. Vol. 5: *The Romantic Period*, ed. David B. Pirie (Harmondsworth, 1994), p. 438.

[31] *The Poems of John Keats*, ed. Miriam Allott. Longman Annotated Poets (Harlow and New York, 1970), p. 471.

For them the Ceylon diver held his breath,
   And went all naked to the hungry shark;
For them his ears gushed blood; for them in death
   The seal on the cold ice with piteous bark
Lay full of darts; for them alone did seethe
   A thousand men in troubles wide and dark
Half-ignorant, they turned an easy wheel
That set sharp racks at work to pinch and peel.[32]

Joan Baum comments that Ceylon was 'very much a public issue in 1818, a prime example of the East India Company's widespread corruption and repressive rule'.[33] 'Isabella' is unusually explicit for a Keats poem in its criticism of colonial and commercial endeavour. Far more typical of this work is the sense of cultural unease and anxiety occasioned by Classical Greek art. Recently, John Whale has shown how Keats's response to the Elgin Marbles is analogous to the various responses of De Quincey, Hazlitt, Shelley and of the pioneering showman and Egyptologist, the 'Great Belzoni', when confronted with the sacred objects of Eastern art:

The various representations ... are subject not to a monolithic and synchronic authority, but to a binary play which is just as coercive and dangerous, especially when it enacts the fiction of its own collapse. The appropriating power of the Romantic ideology takes place side by side with claims of its own incapacity: sublime abstraction continues with bodily disgust; critiques of power alongside worship of power.[34]

The imagined exotic places of 'Kubla Khan' and *Don Juan*, like that of 'Ozymandias', exhibit the binary play to which Whale refers. What Nigel Leask has termed the multiple 'anxieties of empire'[35] became manifest as instability, ambivalence – as a cross-hatching of narratives which disturbs the apparent logic of each. This is the case in the texts which Leask examines in this volume, including Southey's Orientalist epics, Byron's tales, travel narratives and the new and highly popular visual forms – large-scale topographical painting and panoramic displays. Without ignoring the ideological suppression of alterity present in those texts, Leask seeks to retrieve from them evidence of

---

[32] Ibid., p. 334.

[33] Joan Baum, *Mind-Forg'd Manacles: Slavery and the English Romantic Poets* (North Haven, 1994), pp. 117–18.

[34] John Whale, 'Sacred Objects and the Sublime Ruins of Art', in *Beyond Romanticism: New Approaches to Texts and Contexts, 1780–1832*, eds. Stephen Copley and John Whale (London and New York, 1992), pp. 218–36 (p. 236).

[35] Nigel Leask, *British Romantic Writers and the East: Anxieties of Empire* (Cambridge, 1992), pp. 6–12.

the disturbance which contact with another culture caused to traditional European modes of seeing and describing. He constructs a methodology which enables him to find within Romantic Orientalism an aesthetics by which the viewer/reader is dislocated from his/her cultural vantage-point and temporarily absorbed into the scene being represented – collapsing subject/object distinctions. Leask's discussion continues the critical inquiry into the cultural politics of the aesthetic sphere which has been foregrounded in recent works by John Barrell, Terry Eagleton and others.[36]

The essays in this volume reveal the heterogeneous nature of British colonialism in the period and demonstrate how the material basis of conquest and direct rule is configured in a large variety of Romantic-period writers, both within and outside the traditional canon. They reveal that challenges to and re-inscriptions of colonialist ideology often co-existed in the same text, that apologies for imperialism often contained a radical element potentially subversive of that imperialism – and vice versa. They show that, rather than a simple opposition between colonizing Britain and its Oriental empire, a more complex geo-political imaginary was crucial to the formation of Romanticism. This imaginary, shaped and reshaped in the varied texts of the Romantic period, influenced, and continues to influence, the cultural imperialism and nationalism of Britain and America, movements in which Romantic literature and aesthetics were awarded key places. Given that this Romantic imaginary had, and has, influence of this kind, it is essential that we continue with the project of making ourselves conscious of its complex origins in the social, political and psychological questions posed by the development of colonialism. In showing Romanticism to have been dependent on writers' historical understandings of the British empire and other empires, to have been shaped by their views on race, slavery and gender, to have been influenced by their domestic politics, to have been motivated by their desire to imagine – and rule – the exotic, this volume attempts to provide a beginning to that project.

[36] John Barrell, *The Political Theory of Painting from Reynolds to Hazlitt: 'The Body of the Public'* (New Haven and London, 1986); Terry Eagleton, *The Ideology of the Aesthetic* (Oxford, 1990). Elizabeth A. Bohls has recently argued that, from the latter half of the eighteenth century, certain writings 'draw on the cultural power of the aesthetic to legitimize the region's colonial plantation culture'. See, 'The Aesthetics of Colonialism: Janet Schaw in the West Indies, 1774–1775', *Eighteenth-Century Studies*, 27 (1994), pp. 363–90 (p. 365). See David Lloyd, 'Race Under Representation', *Oxford Literary Review*, 13 (1991), 62–94 on the racist implications of Kantian aesthetics.

CHAPTER 4

Accessing India: Orientalism, anti-'Indianism' and the rhetoric of Jones and Burke

Michael J. Franklin

The extent to which Edward Said found himself 'enslaved to an ideological construct of his own design',[1] utilizing an all-encompassing 'Occidentalism' to essentialize and indict the West where 'every European, in what he could say about the Orient, was consequently a racist, an imperialist, and almost totally ethnocentric'[2] has reinforced the need to produce discriminating and nuanced readings of Orientalism and the production of Orientalist knowledge. Said adopts the very discursive structures which he anathematizes; he decries rigidity and the imposition of generalization,[3] only to produce a concept of Orientalism as a sinister, singular, and transhistorical 'discourse', accommodating in one totalizing sweep Aeschylus, Victor Hugo, Dante and Karl Marx.

By contrast with such a unitary construction, this chapter seeks to demonstrate the complex, diverse, and changing specificities of Orientalism by investigating the techniques of representing India employed by two friends and fellow members of Johnson's Turk's Head Club, Edmund Burke and Sir William Jones, from the discrete perspectives of metropolitan Westminster and colonial Calcutta in the mid 1780s. Their friendship was to be broken by their divergent estimates of the career and character of Warren Hastings, the Governor-General of Bengal, whom Jones was to invite to be President of his newly-formed Asiatick Society and Burke was to impeach.

In the years before Sir William Jones's 1783 departure for the Supreme Court bench of Calcutta, Burke had consulted him

---

[1] Elinor Shaffer, 'Editor's Note', *Comparative Criticism*, 3 (1981), p. xxi. See also the critique of Said in Aijaz Ahmad, *In Theory: Classes, Nations, Literatures* (London and New York, 1992), pp. 159–219.

[2] Edward W. Said, *Orientalism* (London, 1978), p. 204.

[3] Ibid., pp. 149, 155.

repeatedly on various East India Bills. Burke, requesting his friend to join him for a working breakfast to elicit advice on the conduct of the Bengal Judiciary Bill, complimented Jones on his support for Asian cultures, both as poet and jurist: 'The natives of the East, to whose literature you have done so much justice, are particularly under your protection for their rights.'[4] It was just such a role of protector and paternalistic guardian for which Burke was grooming himself by means of his increasing interest in Indian affairs. In a letter of 29 June 1781 to his former pupil and lifelong correspondent, Viscount Althorp, Jones characterizes Burke's politics:

We are very good friends; but, in serious truth, he is too *aristocratical* (as most of his countrymen are) for me. His system about America is to me incomprehensible; and his system of national Liberty still more sublime, that is, obscure. He froze and blighted the great business of the petitions for reducing the influence of the Crown, which, I believe, he does not think too great.[5]

It was the 'great melody' of the Burkean, aristocratical sublime which was not to the Welshman's taste. They had already clashed over a separate issue, Burke's cost-cutting proposal to abolish the circuits of the Welsh judicature. Jones was totally committed to the principle of economical reform, but not at the expense of his already underprivileged, fellow countrymen. With his considerable experience as a barrister on the Welsh circuits, he could see the measure might augment the despotic power of landlords, as he wrote on 26 March 1780 from Haverfordwest:

Ought a few thousand to be saved to the revenue by a plan, which will either distress the yeomanry and peasantry of Wales or deter them from applying at all for justice? How many industrious tenants will then be even greater *slaves* than they are even now to the *tyrannical* agents and stewards of indolent gentlemen. (Emphasis mine) (*Letters*, I, p. 354)

The natives of the West, it would seem, were also under Jones's protection for their rights, and his references to slavery and tyranny are reminiscent of one of the most remarkable causes he had argued that spring at Haverfordwest. Jones's client was a certain Isaac Phillips, a yeoman of St Martin, indicted for 'alarming a village on the coast of Pembrokeshire with a report that a hostile ship of war

[4] *The Works of Sir William Jones*, ed. Anna Maria Jones, 13 vols. (London, 1807), I, p. 360.
[5] *The Letters of Sir William Jones*, ed. Garland Cannon, 2 vols. (Oxford, 1970), II, p. 479. Henceforth cited in the text as *Letters*.

was approaching' by two local magistrates, one of whom was John Zephaniah Holwell, the former Governor of Bengal.[6] Holwell, a survivor of the notorious Black Hole of Calcutta, had been one of Voltaire's chief informants on India, and was the author of *Interesting Historical Events, Relative to the Province of Bengal* (1766–67), an account of which Burke was to make substantial use in the Hastings impeachment. It is a piquant coincidence that Jones was to face a Governor of Bengal in legal combat some eight years before Burke was to open the lengthy impeachment of Governor-General Hastings.[7] Holwell, of course, was not on trial, nor do we have any transcript of the Haverfordwest proceedings as the serried ranks of the press and the beau monde were absent on this occasion, but we do have the sardonic account Jones gave to Althorp:

The prosecutors were two magistrates, one of them *governor Holwell*, who were angry at *having been made fools of*; a point, however, which they could not easily prove, inasmuch as they were fools *ready made*. I defended the prosecuted man with success, and mingled in my speech many bitter reflections on the state of the country at the time of the alarm, and on the attempt, because the English laws were not relished in India, to import the Indian laws into England, by imprisoning and indicting an honest man, who had done no more than his duty, and, whose only fault was fear, of which both his prosecutors were equally guilty. (*Letters*, 1, 430–31)

It is perhaps significant, especially when this case is compared with the Hastings impeachment, that Jones's forensic harangue, like much in that of Burke, relates to public prejudice and centres on the nature of Indian law. Burke at the outset of the impeachment appeared to tower above contemporary prejudice by constructing an elaborate antithesis between the supremely just and equitable nature of Islamic law and the arbitrary despotism of Warren Hastings and his minions. Jones, on the other hand, panders to the popular prejudice that Oriental law equated despotic tyranny, in order to direct a particularly barbed and appropriate invective at the 'returned nabob' Holwell. The Member for Malton, in attempting to demolish Hastings' defence (or rather the caricature of Hastings' position which Burke himself had constructed) that local circumstances necessitated the exercise of arbitrary power, vehemently argues that the very concept is alien to the East: 'I do challenge the whole race of man to show me any of the Oriental Governors

---

[6] National Library of Wales, MS 4 Wales 821/5.
[7] See pp. 14–17 above.

claiming to themselves a right to act by arbitrary will.'[8] The Welsh lawyer deprecates autocratic, discretionary power as an 'Oriental' importation, foreign to the constitution, an insidious symptom of arbitrary and decadent court government.

There are manifold ironies here, especially as Burke's newly attained expertise in Indian law was largely acquired through his conversations with Jones who was busily translating the Moslem law of inheritance.[9] For the purposes of sharpening his courtroom rhetoric, Jones was prepared to reverse his scholarly and sympathetic championing of Oriental law and culture by impugning Indian law and implying that mere contact with India was corrupting. Jones was clearly appalled at what he saw as Holwell's high-handedness, and the operation of what amounted to caprice and discretionary power in the judicial system; a British magistrate ought not to behave like the popular perception of an Eastern potentate. Burke was later to refer to this Orientally nurtured compound of tyranny and wilfulness as 'Indianism', horrified by its virulent potential to infect public life.[10]

The depth of Burke's knowledge of Indian affairs was, perhaps, unrivalled by that of any other contemporary British politician. From 1778 when his close friend and distant relative, William Burke, returned from Tanjore, his interest was centred in Madras; his attentions moved northwards in 1781 when he was appointed to a Select Committee on the administration of justice in Bengal, and were intensified the following year when Philip Francis returned from six years of opposing Hastings on the Bengal Supreme Council. Without prejudice to the question of whether his advocacy of the interests of the Raja of Tanjore was motivated by self-interest, one is bound to question the wisdom of his reliance upon the jaundiced perspectives of disgruntled officials such as William Burke and Philip Francis.[11] The idealized picture of traditional Indian life which

---

[8] Speech on the Opening of Impeachment, 16 February 1788, *The Writings and Speeches of Edmund Burke*, vol. VI *India: The Launching of the Hastings Impeachment, 1786–88*, ed. P. J. Marshall (Oxford, 1991), p. 353. Seven years earlier in 1781 'Burke was reported to have said that he was willing to see "arbitrary power" given to "the Governor and Council"', P. J. Marshall, *The Impeachment of Warren Hastings* (Oxford, 1965), p.13.

[9] *The Mahomedan Law of Succession to the Property of Intestates* (1782), *The Works of Sir William Jones*, XI, pp. 166–98.

[10] Burke viewed 'Indianism and Jacobinism' as 'the two great Evils of our time', see *The Correspondence of Edmund Burke*, ed. Thomas W. Copeland, 10 vols. (Cambridge and Chicago, 1965), VII, p. 553.

[11] See P. J. Marshall's detailed and scrupulously objective account in *The Writings and Speeches of Edmund Burke*, vol. V *India: Madras and Bengal, 1774–85* (Oxford, 1981), pp. 3–27.

Burke painted bore as little relation to reality as did Holwell's panegyric of Bishnapor which had allowed Voltaire to rhapsodize on natural savages in the subcontinent. Burke himself quoted this description from Holwell's *Interesting Historical Events* on the first day of the impeachment proceedings:

'In truth', says this author, 'it would be almost cruelty to molest this happy people; for in this district are the only vestiges of the beauty, purity, piety, regularity, equity, and strictness, of the ancient Hindostan Government. Here the property as well as the liberty of the people are inviolate. Here no robberies are heard of, either public or private.'[12]

It matters little that Burke incorrectly cites this as a description of the province of Burdwan rather than Bishnapor; it is the myth of an innocent, pre-lapsarian India 'before it was disturbed by the barbarism of foreign conquests' that he wishes to convey. Indeed, Burke's critique of Company affairs, though apparently guided by high-minded principles, was in many respects shaped by biased information and a distinct vein of credulousness.

In his 'Essay on the Poetry of the Eastern Nations' (1772) William Jones in an investigation of 'the scene of pastoral poetry' turns briefly from Arabia Felix to the Indian subcontinent:

There is a valley, indeed, to the North of *Indostan*, called *Cashmere*, which, according to an account written by a native of it, is a perfect garden, exceedingly fruitful, and watered by a thousand rivulets: but when its inhabitants were subdued by the stratagem of a *Mogul* prince, they lost their happiness with their liberty.[13]

Burke's rhetoric, in laying the grounds of impeachment, created similarly paradisical havens of abundance and liberty, pastoral idylls to be cruelly subdued by 'Mogul' Hastings:

Was not this country, prior to the dirty and miserable interference of English politics, so plentiful, so well cultivated and so rich, as to deserve the name of the Eden of the East. . . . But where was now this beautiful paradise? This delightful spot, the joint effect of nature and art, the united work of God and man, was no more. The country was extirpated. *Haman Dowlah*, ['the security of the state'] the well-known appellation of Mr. Hastings in India, had reduced the whole to a waste, howling desert, where no creature could exist.[14]

---

[12] *Writings and Speeches of Edmund Burke*, VI, p. 306.
[13] See my *Selected Poetical and Prose Writings of Sir William Jones* (Cardiff, 1995), p. 321.
[14] *Writings and Speeches of Edmund Burke*, V, p. 466.

In the Rohilla War Speech of 1 June 1786 the tone becomes decidedly biblical, and Burke seems to owe as much to Milton as to his Indian informants; Hastings, overlooking the paradise of Rohilkhand, assumes the character of envious Satan:

... the devil hovered for a while in the Garden of Eden. It was such a paradise as he had not seen before, and he regarded its populous and splendid town, its beautiful villas, and its rich vineyards, with envy. This was the origin of all the mischief which befel that innocent and industrious people.[15]

The rhetoric encourages the Members to contemplate this diabolical overview of an Asian paradise and the howling waste of its loss in order to implicate them in colonial guilt, to acknowledge as English politicians their participation in this 'dirty and miserable interference'. The colonial gaze, for Burke, was essentially a Satanic and intrusive way of looking, characterized by a powerful but unhealthy mixture of envy, greed, desire and guilt.

In offering the House and the country an affective narrative Burke had recourse to the imaginative sensationalist discourses of the Gothic and the sublime.[16] Battening on tendentious and unsubstantiated reports from Rangpur concerning horrific brutality and the sexual humiliation and torture of women, allegedly committed by Devi Singh, a revenue farmer chosen by Hastings, he wrote to Philip Francis:

Oh! what an affair – I am clear that I must dilate upon that; for it has stuff in it, that will, if anything, work upon the popular Sense. But how to do this without making a monstrous and disproportioned member; I know not.[17]

Unconcerned by either the accuracy or the relevance of these reports to the charges against Hastings, Burke's dilation upon these alleged atrocities on the third day of the opening of impeachment reveals his confidence that Hastings would ultimately be tried not by the Lords, but by the press and the public, whom Burke acknowledged as 'the ultimate judges under God of all our actions'.[18]

There was a consummate artistry in the way he manipulated his material, modulating from the perfumed Oriental tale evocation of

---

[15] Ibid., VI, p. 110.
[16] See Frans De Bruyn, 'Edmund Burke's Gothic Romance: The Portrayal of Warren Hastings in Burke's Writing and Speeches on India', *Criticism*, 29:4 (1987), pp. 415–38.
[17] *The Correspondence of Edmund Burke*, V, p. 372.
[18] Minutes, 20 May 1789, Add. MS 24230, f.147, quoted in Marshall, *The Impeachment of Warren Hastings*, p. 84.

Devi Singh's 'Seraglio' to the detailed description of crushed fingers and virgins raped in front of their fathers, sounding new depths of Oriental Gothic as he hinted at unspeakable vaginal violation:

Grown from ferocity to ferocity, from cruelty to cruelty, they applied burning torches and cruel slow fires (My Lords, I am ashamed to go further); those infernal fiends, in defiance of every thing divine and human, planted death in the source of life, and where that modesty which more distinguishes man even than his rational nature from the base creation, turns from the view and dare not meet the expression, dared those infernal fiends execute their cruel and nefarious tortures where the modesty of nature and the sanctity of justice dare not follow them or even describe their practices. These, my Lords, were the horrors that arose from bribery, the cruelties that arose from giving power into the hands of such persons as Debi Singh and such infernal villains as Gunga Govin Sing.[19]

Burke's determination to arouse public indignation against Hastings militates against his frequently expressed desire to create sympathy for the plight of the Hindus. The rehearsal of atrocities only serves to reinforce stereotypes of the Oriental capacity for capricious and diabolically inventive cruelty.

Burke enlists his newly acquired knowledge of Indian botany to illustrate the exquisite refinements which these Hindus had introduced to the art of torture:

But refining in their cruelty, searching every thing through the devious paths of nature, where she seems to have forgotten her usual plan and produces things unfavourable to the life of man, they found a poisonous plant called the Bechettea plant, a plant, which is deadly caustic, which inflames the parts that are cut, and leaves the body a crust of leprous sores. . .[20]

The Indian rapists and torturers, both mirroring and accentuating the hostile and deviant aspects of Oriental nature, human and environmental, perform their masterpiece of misapplication as 'they put the nipples of the women into the sharp edges of split bamboos and tore them from their bodies'. Even divorced from the theatricality of their original Westminster Hall presentation, these passages still have the power to disturb and dismay; after the unspeakable horror of 'they planted death in the source of life', we have the appalling precision of this sexual torture. India is characterized as an abused woman; the sources of her fecundity cruelly mutilated or

[19] *Writings and Speeches of Edmund Burke*, VI, p. 421.
[20] Ibid., VI, p. 420.

cauterized, simultaneously spoiled and despoiled. This is compatible with the conquest of India figured in terms of predatory sexuality, the brutal and brutalizing effects of empire. But rather than serving as a repulsive variation on the recurring theme of Burke's indictment of the East India Company for its lack of 'reverence paid to the female sex in general, and particularly to women of rank and condition',[21] the images force the audience to contemplate the atrocities at the hands of Devi Singh, Gunga Govind Singh and their native minions. From the narrative Burke has constructed, it appears that Hastings has empowered dark and sinister elements in the Oriental psyche which delight in mutilation and inventive torture, a stereotype radically opposed to that of the innocent, passive, feminized Indian which Burke is normally anxious to portray. In opening the impeachment he had successfully 'work[ed] upon the popular Sense', India had become X-rated entertainment, Mrs Sheridan had fainted, and tickets for admission to the proceedings were soon to be exchanged for fifty guineas, but this had been achieved only at the expense of 'making', in Burke's ominously ithyphallic phrase, 'a monstrous and disproportioned member'.

Frans De Bruyn has argued that: 'Burke's flights into the gothic are intended to clarify the fundamental moral issues obscured by the welter of facts, details, motives, and opinions put forward in the course of Hastings's trial.'[22] If this were his intention it would seem that his handling of the Rangpur atrocities constitutes a signal failure. Indeed Burke's fundamental approach to laying the charges of impeachment lacked clarity or legal precision. The obscuring 'welter of facts, details' and so on, proceeded from Burke himself, from his capacious mind, his ingestion of bales of India knowledge, and ultimately testified to his superiority as an orator rather than as an advocate. In his speech on Fox's East India Bill, Burke had attempted to make the manifest difficulties of the Indian situation intelligible to his fellow members, but the massive density of his geographical inventory, the cataloguing of tens and hundreds of thousands of square miles of territory, communicates only an obscure sublimity and a failure of classification. As Sara Suleri has convincingly demonstrated: 'With his characteristic reliance upon the locutions of astonishment and horror, Burke's speech insists on

---

[21] Ibid., v, p. 417.
[22] De Bruyn, 'Edmund Burke's Gothic Romance', pp. 435–36.

the futility of approaching India as though it could be catalogued or would ever be categorizable.'[23]

Jones had arrived in Calcutta on 25 September 1783 as a Judge of the Bengal Supreme Court, immediately embarking upon a rigorous programme of Indian studies in the Hastings tradition, founding the ground-breaking Asiatick Society in 1784. One of the first Europeans to learn Sanskrit, he co-operated closely with native informants in the Orientalist project to compile a Digest of Indian Law; translated Hindu literature; composed his Hymns to Hindu Deities; and in 1786 disturbed the West with his thesis of an Indo-European family of languages.

Burke was a colonial spectator gazing with astonishment and terror at the ungraspable sublimity of India: Jones, a participator in the processes of empire, was astonished only at the grandeur of the classical texts which Sanskrit placed within his grasp. India holds no terrors for Jones; what for Burke was an unreadable subcontinental palimpsest obscured by the scrawlings of foreign conquests and depredations is for Jones a revelation, but one that needs to be communicated. Both men were equally involved in creating narrative representations of India, but while Burke in London was constructing, in Suleri's phrase, 'a discourse of difficulty', in Calcutta Jones was responding in a radically different way to the sublimity of India and the problems of making its difficulties accessible.

A particularly apposite example comes to hand in Jones's 'Hymn to Durgá' (1788), composed during the opening months of the Hastings impeachment. Significantly the name of this Vedic goddess and consort of Śiva means, as Jones explains in his prefatory Argument, 'of difficult access'; she represents the power of cognition and transcendent knowledge, she is the destroyer of the world of illusion. Jones's poetic treatment of Durgā perfectly exemplifies the subtle cultural tact with which he made Indian civilization accessible to the West. She is represented in the Purāṇas as a formidable female warrior, astride a lion, destroying giant demons whose blood she drinks. Her principal temple was in Calcutta where she received during her autumn festival of Durgā Pūjā the heads of some seven or eight hundred goats. Both blood sacrifice and communal copulation in the surrounding fields were most acceptable to this immensely popular mother goddess, but likely to be rather less so to the

---

[23] Sara Suleri *The Rhetoric of English India* (Chicago and London, 1992), p. 26.

sensibilities of a metropolitan audience. Jones, therefore, avoids representing Durgā in her Kālī aspect – black, naked, four-armed, standing on a corpse, holding a severed head, and wearing only a necklace of skulls – such traditional iconography might create reader resistance. He portrays her instead as the gentle and devout Pārvatī, the Lady of the Mountain, and daughter of Himalaya, and in this Jones was inspired by his reading of the *Kumārasambhava* of Kālidāsa, the flower of Gupta high culture. Aware of the awesome responsibility of his role as a cultural mediator he uses the balanced symmetry of the Pindaric ode and the grandeur of the Himalayan setting to lend dignity to what is essentially an erotic encounter between the austere Śiva and his impassioned neophyte Pārvatī. Her virginal calm is reflected in the placid lakes and like the lake-born lotos her transcendent beauty silently unfurls:

> On a morn, when edg'd with light,
> The lake-born flowers their sapphire cups expanded
> Laughing at the scatter'd night,
> A vale remote and silent pool she sought,
> Smooth-footed, lotos-handed,
>
> ('Hymn to Durgá', ii, 1, lines 5–9)[24]

But neither her loveliness nor her garlands of sacred blossoms seem immediately effective in gaining the love of the ascetic 'who, fix'd in thought, / Sat in a crystal cave new worlds designing'. The flower-tipped arrow of Cáma, the god of love, awakens Śiva from his yogic meditation, but in his fiery wrath he reduces Cáma to ashes, and retreats to the mountain fastnesses. In a physical and spiritual ascent which stresses her liminal nature, the distraught Pārvatī seeks 'the mountain drear', and against a backdrop which reflects in its terrifying and vertiginous sublimity the nature of the storm god, she practises powerful austerities:

> There on a crag, whose icy rift
> Hurl'd night and horror o'er the pool profound,
> That with madding eddy swift
> Revengeful bark'd his rugged base around,
> The beauteous hermit sat; . . .
>
> ('Hymn to Durgá', iv, 3, lines 1–5)

In such a landscape and such a metre a British audience might expect to find Gray's Bard; Pārvatī perceives 'A *Bráhmen* old before her stand' and the syncretic point is made. The testing Brahman (the disguised Śiva) suggests she direct her devotion towards more appealingly conducive divinities, the festive Indra, or the handsome Cuvera:

> 'But spurn that sullen wayward God,
> That three-eye'd monster, hideous, fierce, untam'd,
> Unattir'd, ill-girt, unshod – '
>
> ('Hymn to Durgá', v, 3, lines 1–3)

The Brahman's representation of Śiva anticipates and in a sense forestalls the conventional Eurocentric rejection of monstrous Indian deities, and the reader is encouraged to empathize with Pārvatī's horrified reaction to the appalling blasphemy:

> 'Such fell impiety, the nymph exclaim'd,
> 'Who speaks, must agonize, who hears, must die;'
>
> ('Hymn to Durgá', v, 3, lines 4–5)

The unspeakable is also the unhearable; in a self-sacrificial attempt to atone for the blasphemy, Pārvatī hurls herself from the crag:

> But beneath her floating locks
> And waving robes a thousand breezes flew,
> Knitting close their silky plumes,
> And in mid-air a downy pillow spreading;
> Till, in clouds of rich perfumes
> Embalm'd, they bore her to a mystick wood;
> Where streams of glory shedding,
> The well-feign'd *Bráhmen*, śiva stood.
>
> ('Hymn to Durgá', vi, 1, lines 3–10)

The last two words of the strophe emphasize Pārvatī's successful arousal of Śiva and the perfumed pillowing foreshadows their marital intimacy. The final canto of Kālidāsa's poem contains explicit scenes of passionate love-making but Jones, ever aware of Occidental sensibilities, merely hints at the power of cosmic coitus:

> The rest, my song conceal:
> Unhallow'd ears the sacrilege might rue.
> Gods alone to Gods reveal
> In what stupendous notes th'immortals woo.
>
> ('Hymn to Durgá', vi, 2, lines 1–4)

In contrast to Burke's sentimental idealization of women which results in his obsessive emphasis on the Company's victimization of Indian women of 'quality', Jones reveals in this poem an enlightened

understanding of traditional constructions of womanhood in India.[25]
This proceeds from his interest in the concepts of *prakriti* (created
nature seen as the female principle) and *śakti* wherein, as he explains
in the Argument, 'The *female* divinity. . . represents the active power
of the *male*' in a union of immanent goddess and transcendent god.
The manner in which Jones keeps the god Śiva in passive contemplation, together with his foregrounding of the active role of Pārvatī,
underscores the fundamental importance of *śakti* in Hindu culture.
Pārvatī abandoned the protection of her parents against the advice
of her mother, determined in heroic mood to win Śiva through her
dedicated austerities and calm self-control, thus accomplishing single
handed what the gods had failed to achieve. Although this hymn
relegates Durgā as battle queen and demonslayer to the final stanza,
it portrays Pārvatī's fierce independence, allowing her to represent
something of a challenge to the submissive stereotype of Hindu
woman which emerges from the law-code of Manu.[26] Pārvatī is the
vulva which must hold, stabilize, and actualize the *Śiva-linga*, the
phallus of concentrated enlightenment. She tames and domesticates
the wild and dangerously anti-social ascetic, providing a role-model
for Indian womanhood and arguably for Jones himself in his attempt
to offer a more classically acceptable Hinduism to a classically
educated domestic audience. The success of Jones's contribution to
the shaping of Romantic sensibilities lay in the cultural tact with
which he augmented aesthetic possibilities, adjusting and extending
contemporary taste by introducing the Other as unfamiliar but not
alien.

Avoiding the predatory sexuality or the 'robust hypermasculinity'
of the colonizer, Jones reacted to differing constructions of gender
and the primacy of female divinity with remarkable cultural
empathy.[27] He demonstrates precisely the kind of sensitivity required
when missionaries and Evangelicals were anxious to locate Hindu
culture and religion in a morass of satī, thuggee, and infanticide.
Writing in February 1790 to his friend Jonathan Duncan, Resident at
Benares, who by appealing to the dictates of the Hindu *śastras* and

---

[25] Ashis Nandy, considering Gandhi's privileging of *nāritva* or femininity, maintains that the
culture has always underwritten 'a closer conjunction between power, activism and
femininity than between power, activism and masculinity', *The Intimate Enemy: Loss and
Recovery of Self under Colonialism* (Delhi, 1983), p. 53.

[26] See *The Works of Sir William Jones*, VII, pp. 245–73.

[27] Nandy, *Intimate Enemy*, p. 32.

offering government compensation had effectively ended the practice of infanticide among the Rajputs, Jones differentiated between
the clear spring of Hinduism and what he saw as some of its murkier
rivulets:

With all my admiration of the truly learned Brahmens, I abhor the sordid
priestcraft of Durgā's ministers, but such fraud no more affects the sound
religion of the Hindus, than the lady of Loretto and the Romish impositions
affect our own rational faith. (*Letters*, II, p. 856)

For all this Jones did not simply reinforce the distinction favoured by
contemporary scholars between a rational, ethical Brahman élite
and the repulsive superstitions of the masses. Jones was not at all
unsympathetic to the devoted fervour of popular cults, and found no
difficulty in accepting the apparent eroticism of temple imagery,
writing in his path-breaking 'On the Gods of Greece, Italy and
India' (1784):

it never seems to have entered the heads of the legislators or people that
anything natural could be offensively obscene; a singularity, which pervades
all their writing and conversation, but is no proof of the depravity of their
morals.[28]

Jones was faithful to the spirit of contemporary Bengali Hinduism
both in his attention to the cult of *śakti* and in his representation of
the cult of Vaishnavism (devotion to Vishnu, especially in his
important eighth *avatār*, or incarnation, as Krishna). Even before he
had mastered Sanskrit, Jones enthusiastically devoured his friend
Charles Wilkins's translation of the *Bhăgvăt-Gēēta* (1785) in which
Krishna advocates the spiritual path of *bhakti* or loving devotion.
Indeed it is in the impassioned tones of a *bhakta* that Jones writes of
the Hindu gods and heroes to his friend Richard Johnson:

I am in love with the *Gopia*, charmed with *Crishen*, an enthusiastick admirer
of *Rām* and a devout adorer of *Brihma-bishen-mehais* not to mention that,
Jūdishteīr, Arjen, Corno, and the other warriours of the *M'hab'harat* appear
greater in my eyes than Agamemnon, Ajax, and Achilles appeared, when I
first read the Iliad. (*Letters*, II, p. 652)

Jones was well aware of the huge popular following of the Gaudīya
Vaishnava sect, especially among the lower castes of Bengal.[29] The
founder of this sect had been the sixteenth-century Caitanya, a

[28] *The Works of Sir William Jones*, III, p. 367.
[29] W. Ward, *An Account of the Writings, Religion and Manners of the Hindoos*, 4 vols (Serampore, 1811), III, p. 241.

sainted and ecstatic disciple of Krishna as Jagannātha, but understandably Jones does not foreground the hysteria of the great Ratha-
yātra festival in which suicidal devotees threw themselves under the
wheels of the huge processional image of 'Juggernaut'. Again Jones's
problem, to use Burke's terms, was how 'to work upon the Popular
sense' without creating monstrosity or disproportion.

In his effort to represent the popular tradition in a more acceptable guise Jones turns to that other central focus of the Bengali
Gaudīya sect, the love of Krishna and Rādhā. Jones had touched
upon the cowherd-god Krishna and his relationship with the
beautiful *gopī* or milkmaid Rādhā in 'A Hymn to Lacshmí' (lines
82–108), but aware of the immense influence the *Gītagovinda* exerted
upon popular Bengal Krishna devotion, he decided to translate this
central poem of the twelfth-century Jayadeva. Jones appreciated that
it was in Rādhā that the cults of Vaishnavism and *śakti* coalesced for
whereas Pārvatī as the meditative but impassioned *yoginī* represents a
paradigm for devotees of Śiva, the disciples of Krishna identify with
Rādhā, his *hlādinī-śakti* ('infinite energy of bliss') in a contemplation
at once divine and erotic.[30] Not content with the traditional contrast
between ancestral purity and contemporary degeneration, Jones
viewed Bengal as a crucial site in the evolution of Hinduism
exhibiting a vigorous continuity between this classical, devotional
Sanskrit text and contemporary Bengali devotees. Appending the
poem to his paper 'On the Mystical Poetry of the Persians and
Hindus' given before the Asiatick Society on 8 December 1791, Jones
commented:

Let us return to the *Hindus*, among whom we now find the same
emblematical theology, which Pythagoras admired and adopted. The loves
of CRISHNA and RADHA, or the reciprocal attraction between the divine
goodness and the human soul . . . it consists almost wholly of a mystical
religious allegory, though it seems on a transient view to contain only the
sentiments of a wild and voluptuous libertinism.[31]

In preparing his translation for a Western audience he was, as ever,
concerned that scholarly accuracy should be compromised only by
the abiding necessity of avoiding any offence to metropolitan tastes,
as he knew well that nothing could be more certain to create rather

[30] See *The Divine Consort: Rādhā and the Goddesses of India*, ed. John Stratton Hawley and Donna
Marie Wulff (Boston, 1986).
[31] *Selected Writings*, p. 299.

than dispel prejudice. Consequently he omitted 'only those passages, which are too luxuriant and too bold for an *European* taste'.[32]

His appreciation that the Rādhā-Krishna cult linked Hindu high tradition and contemporary Bengali worship provides further evidence that Jones was no ivory-towered intellectual lingering in a remote, passive and textualized India. The members of the Asiatick Society which Jones had founded in 1784 were profoundly practical men for whom India was very much a dynamic reality, and their 'amateur' enthusiasm was infectious:

It is not here, as in Europe, where there are many scholars and Philosophers professedly, without any other business: here every member of our Society is a man of business, occupied in his respective line of revenue, commerce, law, medicine, military affairs, and so forth: his leisure must be allotted, in great part, to the care of his health, even if pleasure engage no share in it. What part remains then for literature? Instead, therefore, of being surprised, that we have done so little, the world, if they are candid, will wonder, that we have done so much. *Sanscrit* literature is, indeed, a new world:. . . In Sanscrit are written half a million of Stanzas on Sacred history – literature, Epick and Lyrick poems innumerable, and (what is wonderful) Tragedies & Comedies not to be counted, above 2000 years old, besides works on Law (my great object), on Medicine, on Theology, on Arithmetick, on Ethicks, and so on to infinity. (*Letters*, II, p. 747)

Where Burke seems obsessed with loss,[33] Jones is obsessed with what he has discovered, anxious only that Europe should share his excitement. If the former's astonished and horrified response to the vastness of India constitutes the characteristic Burkean sublime, Jones can be seen to anticipate the Romantic sublime, enabling, revelatory, communicating power to the researcher. It was the dynamism and diversity of Indian culture that Jones wished to communicate not merely at the level of international scholarship through the pages of *Asiatick Researches*, given the tendencies and capabilities of his mindset that was comparatively easy, but also at a more popular level in terms of a metropolitan audience.

With respect to political representation, Indian experience confirmed the need for relativism and gradualism, and the first observation of the twenty-three point document entitled 'The Best Practicable System of Judicature' which he sent to Burke from

---

[32] For Jones's treatment of such topoi as cross-dressing, inverse sexual positions, love-bites and nail-wounds in the *Gītagovinda*, see my *Sir William Jones* (Cardiff, 1995), pp. 106–10.

[33] Suleri, *The Rhetoric of English India*, p. 26.

Calcutta in the spring of 1784 underlined the point: 'A system of *liberty*, forced upon a people invincibly attached to opposite *habits*, would in truth be a system of cruel *tyranny* (*Letters*, II, p. 643). Two years later, in correspondence with the Virginia diplomat, Arthur Lee, Jones rehearsed the same arguments:

I shall never cease thinking, that rational liberty makes men virtuous; and virtue, happy: wishing therefore ardently for universal liberty. But your observation on the Hindus is too just: they are incapable of civil liberty; few of them have any idea of it; and those, who have, do not wish it. They must (I deplore the evil, but know the necessity of it) they must be ruled by an absolute power; and I feel my pain much alleviated by knowing the natives themselves as well as from observation, that they are happier under us than they were or could have been under the Sultans of Delhi or petty Rājās. (*Letters*, II, pp. 712–13)

It would be valuable to place in juxtaposition to this magisterial if regretful rhetoric the authentic Indian voice of the colonized. Such responses have unfortunately not been recorded, but the writings of Bhudev Mukhopadhay (1827–94) have been seen as representing orthodox Bengali Brahman scholarship. In his polemical collection of essays *The Nineteenth Purana* he argues against the view, still very much in vogue, that imposed and authoritarian British rule was a necessary evil.[34] Respect for traditional customs, a legal system based on indigenous codes of law, undisturbed inheritance, freedom from invasion, security, a disciplined and impartial administration: these were some of the benefits Bhudev associated with the Orientalist policies of the East India Company. Neither were commercial profit-driven motives necessarily counter-productive to Indian integration as 'only a prosperous India would be of benefit to England.'[35]

So Sir William Jones, despite his membership of the Society for Constitutional Information, or the fact that his *Principles of Government* was the subject of a seditious libel case even as he sailed for India, was not to be found distributing either pamphlets or muskets to the

---

[34] See Tapan Raychaudhuri, *Europe Reconsidered: Perceptions of the West in Nineteenth Century Bengal* (Delhi, 1988), pp. 64–67.

[35] Bhudev claims that even in its dissimulation the Company produced positive effects for Indian political development: 'So long as India was under the East India Company, the English used to say, "We are here to prepare the people of India for self-government" . . . The statement was entirely false, but it had one great merit. It expressed beautifully the [belief] that the governance of India must be informed by a very high ideal', *Different Types of English Officials*, quoted in Raychaudhuri, *Europe Reconsidered*, pp. 65–66.

Bengal peasantry.[36] It is dangerous to impose a twentieth-century post-colonial sensitivity upon an earlier age; a species of historicism and relativism had and has to operate. P. J. Marshall's reminder is timely and deserves to be quoted in full:

> Virtually no one believed that the absolutes on which a purely British empire had been based, Protestant truth, free government or the common law, had any application to India for the foreseeable future. The British must operate a despotism, preserving laws and customs which had become adapted to the needs of Indians over centuries of slow evolution. Undue change would disorientate a people who were entirely unready for it.[37]

Jones had no intention of disorientating the Orient. The whole burden of the rhetoric of his Hymns to Hindu Deities emphasized a vision of benign imperialism in an eighteenth-century Whig version of Pax Britannica. He was, in fact, acknowledging a nexus of responsibilities not wholly dissimilar from what a century later became known as 'the white man's burden'. Motivated by a desire to legitimize British rule in India, in the hymns Jones frequently poses as a Hindu poet. 'A Hymn to Gangá', as he explains in its prefacing Argument, 'is feigned to be the work of a Brahmen, in an early age of Hindu antiquity, who, by a prophetical spirit, discerns the toleration and equality of the BRITISH government, and concludes with a prayer *for its peaceful duration under good laws well administered*'. The italicization and the use of capitals remind us of the intended metropolitan destination and the propagandist purposes of these odes; Jones had a clear conception of a benign and responsible imperialism. This brief extract seems totally characteristic of Jones's thinking about India: the philosophical emphasis upon Hindu antiquity and a practical concern for India's future, past and future bridged and balanced by equality and good law; the easy empathy with the Brahman and the powerful goddess to whom he prays for an enduring imperium. It might be argued that the transient tyrant is apt to favour illusions of permanence, but Jones, like Hastings, could clearly conceive of a time when British empire was forgotten and Indian literature celebrated.[38]

---

[36] See *Selected Writings*, p. 383.

[37] In P. J. Marshall, 'Empire and Authority in the Eighteenth Century', *Journal of Imperial and Commonwealth History*, 15 (1987), pp. 105–22 (p. 118).

[38] '(Indian writings) will survive when the British dominion in India shall have long ceased to exist, and when the sources which it once yielded of wealth and power are lost to remembrance.' 'Letter to Nathaniel Smith' prefacing Charles Wilkins, *The Bhágvát Gēēta* (London, 1785), p. 13.

Both Jones and Burke were concerned to make India comprehensible to metropolitan audiences, earnestly combatting provincialism, prejudice and complacency. Burke, it has been argued, 'envisaged an empire not of administration but of justice'[39] but these were never alternatives for Jones who respected Hastings's deliberate policy decision to adopt Orientalism in the firm belief that efficient administration relies upon understanding of indigenous cultures and responsiveness to Indian languages and traditions.

Burke, the barrister *manqué*, with a disconcertingly sublime mix of misinformation and high principle, utter credulity and accurate analysis, constructed an anthropomorphic model of the Indian problem, characterized by a failure of empathy not for the Indians but for Orientalist policy, evading rather than engaging with the central problems. While the competing monstrosities of Hastings's criminality and Burke's rage were commanding attention, it is difficult to judge whether the British public were being introduced to colonial guilt or imperial theatre, with the accompanying danger that progressive boredom with the proceedings might prove destructive of the very sympathies he had laboured to arouse. He appreciated his engagement with India was at once too close and too distant as sublimity and clarity are binary opposites:

India might be approximated to our understandings, and if possible to our feelings; in order to awaken something of sympathy for the unfortunate natives, of which I am afraid we are not perfectly susceptible, whilst we look at this very remote object through a false and cloudy medium.[40]

In Calcutta face to face with the realities of empire Jones described European misconceptions in imagery which links the biblical and the technological:

In Europe you see India through a glass darkly: here, we are in a strong light; and a thousand little *nuances* are perceptible to us, which are not visible through your best telescopes, and which could not be explained without writing volumes. (*Letters*, II, p. 749)

Burke had seen the politics of the subcontinent as the imperial and ethical challenge of his time, but he failed to produce any kind of nuanced reading of India despite, or perhaps on account of, his attempt 'to wind himself into the inmost recesses and labyrinths of

[39] *Writings and Speeches of Edmund Burke*, VI, p. 35.
[40] Ibid., V, p. 390.

the Indian detail'.[41] Burke's rhetoric hermetically immures himself
in the sublime vacuity and incomprehensible darkness of Marabar-
like caves and sealed chambers. Jones, however, depicts himself in
his 'A Hymn to Súrya' (significantly, the Vedic Sun-god) as moving
into the light, revealing and retrieving, liberating knowledge from
the abysm of the past:

> Draws orient knowledge from its fountains pure,
> Through caves obstructed long, and paths too long obscure.
> (lines 186–87)[42]

[41] Ibid., v, p. 382.
[42] *Selected Writings*, p. 152.

CHAPTER 5

'Sunshine and Shady Groves': what Blake's 'Little Black Boy' learned from African writers[1]

Lauren Henry

At first glance, the poetic diction, heroic verse, and classical allusions characterizing Phillis Wheatley's 1773 *Poems on Various Subjects, Religious and Moral* would seem to suggest that her poetry has everything to do with neo-classicism and nothing at all to do with Romanticism. Yet a closer examination of Wheatley's collection reveals its significance, not just to the neoclassical tradition from which it derives, nor even to the African–American literary tradition which it initiates,[2] but also, and quite surprisingly, to a particularly problematic poem of the English Romantic tradition. The problematic poem is William Blake's 'The Little Black Boy,' and I will argue that reading this Song of Innocence alongside Wheatley's 'An Hymn to the Morning,' one of the poems in her 1773 volume, leads to a better understanding of Blake's child speaker and of the intense irony used to portray his situation.[3] Also arising from the juxtaposition of these two poems is the interesting possibility that Blake had some familiarity with Wheatley's work in particular, and with eighteenth-century England's small but notable African literary community in general.[4]

[1] I am grateful to Morris Eaves and Morton D. Paley for giving me permission to reprint material used in a shorter version of this chapter published in *Blake: An Illustrated Quarterly*.

[2] Henry Louis Gates, Jr. credits Wheatley with launching both 'the black American literary tradition *and* the black woman's literary tradition'. See his Foreword to *Six Women's Slave Narratives* (New York, 1988), p. x.

[3] Harold Bloom calls 'The Little Black Boy' 'one of the most deliberately misleading and ironic of all Blake's lyrics'. *Blake's Apocalypse* (Ithaca, 1963), p. 48. For other readings of the poem which suggest that irony is its central element, see Howard Hinkel, 'From Pivotal Idea to Poetic Ideal: Blake's Theory of Contraries and "The Little Black Boy"', *Papers on Language and Literature*, 11 (1975), pp. 39–45; C.N. Manlove, 'Engineered Innocence: Blake's "The Little Black Boy" and "The Fly"', *Essays in Criticism*, 27 (1977), pp. 112–21; or, more recently, Alan Richardson, 'Colonialism, Race, and Lyric Irony in Blake's "The Little Black Boy"', *Papers on Language and Literature*, 26 (1990), pp. 233–48.

[4] For an introduction to African English literature of the eighteenth century, see Keith Sandiford, *Measuring the Moment: Strategies of Protest in Eighteenth-Century Afro-English Writing* (London and Toronto, 1988). For an anthology of extracts, see *Black Writers in Britain, 1760–1890: An Anthology*, eds. Paul Edwards and David Dabydeen (Edinburgh, 1991).

In the eighteenth century, as Henry Louis Gates, Jr. tells us, a tradition of African writing in England was born in 'response to allegations of its absence', allegations which had been made by European writers such as Hume, Kant, and Hegel (among others), and which had led to 'metaphors of the childlike nature of the slaves', and 'of the masked, puppetlike personality of the black'.[5] Eighteenth-century Africans wrote, Gates explains, to deny 'these profoundly serious allegations about their "nature" as directly as they could'[6] and to affirm their humanity, since it was only through literary accomplishments that the African had any hope of communicating with a society which saw writing 'as the most salient repository of "genius," the visible sign of reason itself'.[7]

The individual eighteenth-century Africans who took on the challenge of confronting English society's denial of their intellectual and literary abilities included, along with Phillis Wheatley, James Albert Ukawsaw Gronniosaw, an African prince who ended up an impoverished English peasant; Ignatius Sancho, a poor but popular London grocer, who also happened to be a favourite correspondent of a number of bluestocking socialites; John Marrant, a free black born in America, who became an ordained minister in the Countess of Huntingdon's Calvinistic Methodist 'Connection'; Ottobah Cugoano, a slave who became a London servant and well-known anti-slavery activist; and Olaudah Equiano, a friend of Cugoano and a slave who bought his own freedom, embarked on a career as an English sailor, and eventually became known as Britain's most important and most influential black abolitionist. In their poetry, narratives, letters, and essays, these individuals asked that the English reading public recognize them as living, thinking, and writing human beings. In the process, they attracted a great deal of attention.

Phillis Wheatley, for example, although the slave of a Boston family, was given celebrity status by élite London society when, in 1773, she accompanied her master to England in order to oversee the publication of her collection of poetry. She was called on by members of some of the 'best' bluestocking circles,[8] and years after

[5] 'Race,' Writing, and Difference, ed. Henry Louis Gates, Jr. (Chicago and London, 1986), p. 11.
[6] Ibid., p. 11.   [7] Ibid., p. 9.
[8] See Critical Essays on Phillis Wheatley, ed. William H. Robinson (Boston, 1982), pp. 26, 33; see also Wylie Sypher, Guinea's Captive Kings: British Anti-Slavery Literature of the XVIII Century (New York, 1969), p. 4.

her visit, she was still being remembered in celebratory poems by prominent female writers.[9] Upon its publication in London, Wheatley's volume of poetry was widely and enthusiastically reviewed in British periodicals, and her literary abilities were to be held up as evidence of African intelligence in abolitionist documents for many years to come.[10]

James Gronniosaw was not as well known to the upper ranks of English society, but his autobiography, *A Narrative of the Most Remarkable Particulars in the Life of James Albert Ukawsaw Gronniosaw, an African Prince*, first published in Bath around 1770, was immensely popular, for the work was reissued in numerous editions and under various titles throughout Great Britain and America for at least the next seventy years.[11] *The Letters of the Late Ignatius Sancho*, however, had an even bigger impact on the English public, for upon its initial publication, in 1782,[12] the two volume collection was accompanied by a subscription list 'said to have been of a length unknown since the first issue of *The Spectator*, with well over six hundred people subscribing.'[13] The list reads like a 'who's who' of eighteenth-century English society, with numerous nobles, parliamentarians, and well-known bluestockings comprising a large portion of it. And just in case the status of the subscribers was not enough of an endorsement of Sancho's collection, the *European Magazine* also gave it a very favourable review.[14] John Marrant also appears to have received a very favourable response from the English people. Like Phillis Wheatley, Marrant was a visitor to England from America and was first published in London. As was true of his fellow Africans

---

[9] Moira Ferguson points out that Phillis Wheatley's work was celebrated in poems by Mary Scott and Mary Deverell. *Subject to Others: British Women Writers and Colonial Slavery, 1760–1834* (London and New York, 1992), pp. 127, 129.

[10] For excerpts from the reviews, see Mukhtar Ali Isani, 'The British Reception of Wheatley's *Poems on Various Subjects*', *Journal of Negro History*, 66 (1981), pp. 144–49. References to Wheatley's work in Thomas Clarkson's *An Essay on the Slavery and Commerce of the Human Species, Particularly the African* (Philadelphia, 1786; Miami, 1969), and in numerous issues of the American anti-slavery weekly, *The Liberator*, attest to the poet's considerable impact on both English and American abolitionist writing.

[11] Henry Louis Gates, Jr. writes that the narrative 'had by 1811 been published in seven editions, including American editions in 1774 and 1810, and a Dublin edition in 1790,' adding that '[i]n 1840, another edition was published simultaneously in London, Manchester, and Glasgow'. See 'James Gronniosaw and the Trope of the Talking Book' in *Studies in Autobiography*, ed. James Olney (Oxford, 1988), p. 57.

[12] At least two later editions were published. See *Black Writers in Britain, 1760–1890*, eds. Edwards and Dabydeen, p. 26.

[13] Folarin O. Shyllon, *Black People in Britain, 1555–1833* (London, 1977), p. 191.

[14] See Sandiford, *Measuring the Moment*, p. 74.

residing in England, Marrant impressed the English people not just with his 1785 autobiography, *A Narrative of the Lord's Wonderful Dealings with John Marrant, a Black . . . Born in New York, in North-America*, but also with his personality and with what they saw as his intellectual and spiritual 'potential'. One member of the Countess of Huntingdon's 'Connection' present in the congregation on the day of Marrant's ordination was so inspired by the African's speech and demeanour that he published a poem describing the experience,[15] and thus gave English society one more introduction to an African intellectual in its midst.

Ottobah Cugoano and Olaudah Equiano were perhaps the most visible of eighteenth-century African writers in England. Cugoano's abolitionist treatise, *Thoughts and Sentiments on the Evil and Wicked Traffic of the Slavery and Commerce of the Human Species*, first published in London in 1787, appears to have reached a fairly large number of readers, for the work was popular enough to have been translated into French,[16] and its later (1791) edition includes a list of approximately 170 subscribers.[17] And there is certainly no question about the positive response to Equiano's autobiographical work, *The Interesting Narrative of the Life of Olaudah Equiano, or Gustavus Vassa the African*, the first edition of which was published in 1789, for as Paul Edwards and David Dabydeen point out, the work 'was a best seller in its day, being published in eight English editions and one American in [Equiano's] own lifetime as well as translations into Dutch (1790), German (1792), and Russian (1794)'.[18] In addition, the narrative was reviewed in a number of periodicals, including the *Monthly Review*, the *General Magazine*, and the *Gentleman's Magazine*.[19]

Cugoano and Equiano were known for more than their literary accomplishments, however. Both were key players in the abolitionist campaign and spokesmen for the black community. In these capacities, they became well acquainted with some of the prominent

[15] S. Whitchurch, *The Negro Convert, A Poem; Being the Substance of the Experience of Mr. John Marrant, A Negro, As Related by Himself, Previous to his Ordination, at the Countess of Huntingdon's Chapel, in Bath, on Sunday the 15th of May, 1785, Together with a Concise Account of the Most Remarkable Events in His Very Singular Life* (Bath, 1785?).

[16] Eva Beatrice Dykes, *The Negro in English Romantic Thought; or, A Study in Sympathy for the Oppressed* (Washington, D.C., 1942), p. 61.

[17] Shyllon, *Black People in Britain, 1555–1833*, p. 174.

[18] *Black Writers in Britain, 1760–1890*, eds. Edwards and Dabydeen, p. 54.

[19] Sandiford, *Measuring the Moment*, p. 147.

white abolitionists of the period.[20] Equiano, in particular, was 'on friendly terms' with Thomas Clarkson, Granville Sharp, James Ramsay, and a number of other Englishmen critical to the anti-slavery cause.[21] He was quite clearly an important public figure, for his marriage and death were both reported in the *Gentleman's Magazine*,[22] and in 1797 the *Anti-Jacobin; or, Weekly Examiner* printed a satire on the radicals in which 'Olaudah Equiano, the African' appears in the company of Charles James Fox.[23]

This African literary community was much better known to the eighteenth-century English reading public than we might have expected, especially given our own relative unawareness of it today. William Blake would not have to have done much more than pick up the latest literary review or pay some small amount of attention to the progress of the abolitionist campaign to have heard something about one or more of these writers. As we know, however, Blake was, in fact, doing much more than this.

Blake's interest in issues of race and slavery was not just a passing fancy which began and ended with his composition of 'The Little Black Boy'. As David Erdman's crucial study of 'Blake's Vision of Slavery' has shown, the poet continued to explore these issues in later works, most notably *The Visions of the Daughters of Albion*.[24] Here, Erdman tells us, Blake expressed his anger towards those who passively supported the institution of slavery while professing their distaste for it. He had in mind, Erdman claims, those individuals who, like John Gabriel Stedman, considered themselves humanitarians but still saw Africans as chattels to be bought and sold, or those who called themselves abolitionists but did nothing to support the cause of African emancipation.[25]

In *Visions*, Blake blames Oothoon's state of enslavement not just on Bromion, the rapist and slave owner, but also on Theotormon and his oppressive religious beliefs.[26] In this sense, Blake seems to pick up in *Visions* right where he left off in 'The Little Black Boy', for

[20] See Sandiford's chapters on each in *Measuring the Moment*.

[21] Shyllon, *Black People in Britain, 1555–1833*, p. 443.

[22] O. R. Dathorne, 'African Writers of the Eighteenth Century', *The London Magazine* (September, 1965), pp. 51–58 (p. 57).

[23] See 'Meeting of the Friends of Freedom' in *The Anti-Jacobin; or Weekly Examiner*, 4 (4 December 1797), p. 29. I am grateful to Paul Magnuson for bringing this reference to my attention.

[24] See David V. Erdman, *Blake: Prophet Against Empire*, 3rd edn (Princeton, 1977), pp. 226–42.

[25] Ibid., pp. 232–34.   [26] Ibid., p. 234.

both Oothoon and the child speaker of the song of innocence suffer most of all from the spiritual slavery to which they have been subjected. Oothoon manages to break free and leave behind the 'religious caves'[27] she has been bound in, but 'the little black boy' sees no such escape in his future.

He remains, instead, perpetually chained by the Christianity of his oppressors. The only sign we have that 'the little black boy' may be yearning for something more than the religion which has cast him in an inferior role, destined to serve forever those with lighter skin than he, is the irony with which his story is told. This irony becomes much more visible, though, when we recognize this poem's affinities with Phillis Wheatley's 'An Hymn to the Morning'.

Blake could have been exposed to Wheatley's poem in any number of ways. Perhaps he read one of the many reviews of Wheatley's collection when it came out in 1773, or perhaps he learned about the African poet as he composed his *Songs of Innocence* at the height of the English abolitionist movement in the late 1780s. This is the more plausible possibility, for one critic has suggested the likelihood that 'Blake drew on' Thomas Clarkson's celebrated 1786 *Essay on the Slavery and Commerce of the Human Species* as he wrote 'The Little Black Boy'[28] and, as it happens, Clarkson discusses Wheatley and her poetry in the third part of this essay.

Here, in a chapter pointing out the faulty reasoning in the pro-slavery argument 'that the Africans are an inferiour link of the chain of nature, and are made for slavery', Clarkson cites Wheatley as an example of African intellectual potential.[29] He suggests that Wheatley's situation illustrates that with the proper education and appropriate training in the language of composition, Africans can produce poetry which is, at least, 'less objectionable' than the 'incoherent and nonsensical' songs heard on the plantations.[30] He tells Wheatley's story, explaining that after being kidnapped at the age of eight and sold as a slave in America, the young girl learned to read and write, displayed an interest in Latin, and eventually, with the permission of her master, published a collection of poetical works which 'con-

---

[27] William Blake, *The Complete Poetry and Prose of William Blake*, ed. David V. Erdman (Garden City, New York, 1982), p. 46.

[28] D.L. Macdonald, 'Pre-Romantic and Romantic Abolitionism: Cowper and Blake', *European Romantic Review*, 4 (1994), pp. 163–82 (p. 178).

[29] Thomas Clarkson, *An Essay on the Slavery and Commerce of the Human Species* (Philadelphia, 1786; Miami, 1969), p. 110.

[30] Ibid., pp. 110, 109.

tain[ed] thirty-eight pieces on different subjects'.[31] As he goes on to provide the reader with extracts from three of these poems, Clarkson includes the opening of 'An Hymn to the Morning' among them.[32]

Clarkson clearly asks that we view these extracts as proof of his belief that blacks could be educated to sound and write like whites. He wants us to see, in other words, that Africans were not simply 'inferiour', but only lacking in opportunity. What Clarkson himself fails to see about Wheatley, however, is just what Blake may have understood: that Wheatley's poetry does more than illustrate the African writer's ability to imitate her oppressors, since it also reveals that such acts of imitation were painful as well as representative of all the other sacrifices blacks had to make, particularly in the realm of religion. This, in fact, seems to be the issue which Wheatley subtly invites the reader to consider in her 'An Hymn to the Morning'.

Any examination of 'An Hymn to the Morning' must be preceded by an understanding of Wheatley's complex situation as a woman who was an African, an American, a slave, a Christian and a poet. Wheatley's poetry has for many years been criticized by readers who see her verse as imitative (as Clarkson did) and who see her reluctance clearly to condemn the institution of slavery as reprehensible.[33] More recent critics, however, point out African elements in Wheatley's form and comment on her use of irony and subtle manipulations of language to condemn the society that has enslaved her.[34] They suggest that Wheatley's poetry must be read with the knowledge that she has been forced to speak 'with a double tongue'.[35]

Approaching 'An Hymn to the Morning' with this knowledge, we find that the speaker communicates complex feelings about Nature, religion, and her role as a poet in imagery that brings 'The Little

---

[31] Ibid., p. 110.   [32] Ibid., p. 111.

[33] As Sondra O'Neale puts it, Wheatley has been 'castigated' by 'many modern critics of Black American literature' as 'an unfeeling woman foolishly immersed in colonial refinements, oblivious to her own status and to that of her African peers'. 'A Slave's Subtle War: Phillis Wheatley's Use of Biblical Myth and Symbol', *Early American Literature*, 21 (1986), pp. 144–65 (p. 144).

[34] Lucy Hayden suggests that Wheatley may have been 'drawing subliminally on the storytelling tradition of her African past' in her poem 'Goliath at Gath'. 'Classical Tidings from the Afric Muse: Phillis Wheatley's Use of Greek and Roman Mythology', *CLA Journal*, 35 (1992), pp. 432–47 (p. 435). See also John Shields, 'Phillis Wheatley', *African American Writers: Profiles of their Lives and Works from the 1700s to the Present*, eds. Valerie Smith, Lea Beachler, and A. Walton Litz (New York, 1993), p. 357.

[35] Betsy Erkkila, 'Revolutionary Women', *Tulsa Studies in Women's Literature*, 6 (1987), pp. 189–221 (p. 205).

Black Boy' to mind. '[W]ritten in heroic verse, [though] embody[-ing] the spirit of the hymn', the poem begins as the speaker proclaims her intention to celebrate the dawn through her song.[36]

> Attend my lays, ye ever honour'd nine,
> Assist my labours, and my strains refine;
> In smoothest numbers pour the notes along,
> For bright Aurora now demands my song.
>
> Aurora hail, and all the thousand dies,
> Which deck thy progress through the vaulted skies:
> The morn awakes, and wide extends her rays,
> On ev'ry leaf the gentle zephyr plays;
> Harmonious lays the feather'd race resume,
> Dart the bright eye, and shake the painted plume.
>
> Ye shady groves, your verdant gloom display
> To shield your poet from the burning day:
> Calliope awake the sacred lyre,
> While thy fair sisters fan the pleasing fire:
> The bow'rs, the gales, the variegated skies
> In all their pleasures in my bosom rise.
>
> See in the East th'illustrious king of day!
> His rising radiance drives the shades away—
> But Oh! I feel his fervid beams too strong,
> And scarce begun, concludes th'abortive song.[37]

In the first stanza, Wheatley calls upon the muses for assistance as she composes her pæn to the rising sun, confidently situating this poem within the classical, poetic tradition of the society which has enslaved her. Her description of the beauty and brilliance of the awakening morning progresses uneventfully throughout the second stanza, but, by the third stanza, a discordant note becomes apparent, as the speaker makes a curious request: 'Ye shady groves, your verdant gloom display / To shield your poet from the burning day'. At this point, the poet seems to feel a need for protection from the very object of her praise. And, in the final stanza, it becomes evident that her apprehension was not unwarranted, for here the sun, or 'th'illustrious king of day' has, with his 'rising radiance', driven 'the shades away'. Thus, the now unprotected poet finds that she 'feel[s]

---

[36] John Shields, 'Phillis Wheatley and Mather Byles', *CLA Journal*, 23 (1980), pp. 377–90 (p. 380).

[37] Phillis Wheatley, *The Poems of Phillis Wheatley*, ed. Julian D. Mason, Jr. (Chapel Hill, 1989), p. 74.

his fervid beams too strong' and must abruptly end her composition: 'And scarce begun, concludes th'abortive song'.

Clearly, the poet has mixed feelings about her purpose and her potential to accomplish it in this poem. We can only begin to understand the nature of those feelings if we are aware of the traditions which collide in these verses. The poem was certainly meant to be read by its original white English and American audiences as a melding of Classicism and Christianity, in which the Greek gods of the sun and the dawn are celebrated at the same time that Christianity's God and His Son are praised and glorified. Subsequent readers have continued to emphasize these elements of Wheatley's work, as is evident in Julian Mason's remark that Wheatley's 'mixing of Christian and classical in the many invocations in her poems (as well as in other parts of the poems) reflects the two greatest influences on her work, religion and neoclassicism'.[38]

Yet, an integrated reading of Wheatley's work (and of 'An Hymn to the Morning' and its sun imagery in particular) requires recognition of cultural influences with non-Western roots. The reader needs to consider, for example, the strong possibility that Wheatley came from an African community in which sun worship was a religious practice, for Wheatley's first biographer claimed that the poet could remember only one thing about her life in Africa, and that was that every day her mother 'poured out water before the sun at his rising'.[39] Because Wheatley was kidnapped and brought to America when she was only seven or eight years old, there is no way to be certain of either her place of birth or her native religious traditions, although it has been suggested that 'she was very likely of the Fulani people in the Gambia region of West Africa', and that the ritual she remembered may have been a 'complex, syncretized version of Islam and solar worship', as 'Islam had long before penetrated into the Gambia region'.[40] In any case, Wheatley's intense preoccupation with the sun in this poem and others,[41] certainly can be traced to African origins, since, for many African cultures, God is ' "the Sun"

[38] Julian D. Mason, Introduction, *The Poems of Phillis Wheatley*, p. 38.

[39] Margaretta M. Odell, *Memoirs and Poems of Phillis Wheatley, A Native African and a Slave*, 2nd edn. (Boston, 1835), pp. 10–11.

[40] John Shields, 'Phillis Wheatley', *African American Writers: Profiles in their Lives and Works*, eds. Smith, Baechler, and Litz, p. 356.

[41] John Shields writes that 'solar imagery constitutes the dominant image pattern in [Wheatley's] poetry'. Ibid., p. 356.

which beams its light everywhere'.[42] Both James Gronniosaw and Olaudah Equiano also mention sun worship rituals in their narratives (discussed below); for them and for Wheatley, incorporating images of such rituals into their literature may have been a way of quietly confirming that they each had had another life and another religion before both were lost to the slave system.

Because it is so fraught with contradictions, the sun imagery of 'An Hymn to the Morning' calls attention to itself and to the various cultural and religious roles that it is asked to play. Perhaps while Wheatley encourages the reader to consider the cultural convergence in her depiction of this Christian/classical/African sun, she concurrently questions the role that the sun in its Christian manifestation has played in her own life. We would certainly expect a slave carried to America and converted to the religion of her captors to have doubts about that religion, and, of course, the only way for her to communicate those doubts would be to cloak them in conventionality. Thus, the tension that exists between the poet's glorification of the sun and her discomfort when exposed to its 'fervid beams' may be the result of Wheatley's ironic attitude towards her subject: while ostensibly praising her Christian God, she also implies that His presence in her life has made it impossible for her to fully express her beliefs and emotions, and therefore, to write the kind of poem she envisions.

The speaker's attempt to seek refuge in a 'shady grove' and its 'verdant gloom' may also be seen as evidence of Wheatley's conflicting feelings about Christianity and her abiding interest in the religious traditions she left behind in Africa. For just as the sun in this poem suggests an aspect of the poet's African past, so too does the shade. As Wheatley was composing her *Poems on Various Subjects* in colonial America, both England and America were amassing voluminous accounts of the life and land of Africa.[43] These geographic/ethnographic reports were sometimes written (or compiled) by those interested in abolitionism, but most often by 'slave-traders or naval officers involved in protecting the trade'; yet, in spite of

---

[42] John S. Mbiti, *African Religions and Philosophy* (Oxford, 1989), p. 31.

[43] Many of these works are discussed in Chapter Eight of P. J. Marshall's and Glyndwr Williams's *The Great Map of Mankind: British Perceptions of the World in the Age of Enlightenment* (London, 1982). Philip Curtin also refers to the genre throughout *The Image of Africa: British Ideas and Action, 1780–1850*, vol. 1 (London and Madison, 1964), as does William Lloyd James in his dissertation, 'The Black Man in English Romantic Literature, 1772–1833' (UCLA, 1977).

their glaring flaws and prejudices, they were invaluable to those who wanted at least a glimpse of the continent they were colonizing.[44] It seems likely that Wheatley's lack of information about her homeland and 'easy access' to 'the three largest libraries in the colonies'[45] would have led her to peruse some of these widely published accounts, and a reference to one of them in a 1774 letter suggests that she was, in fact, familiar with the genre.[46] Examination of some of these works reinforces this suggestion, for one of the African traditions repeatedly remarked upon concerns the practice of meeting and worshipping in a 'shady grove'.

One work typical of this genre is William Smith's *A New Voyage to Guinea*, first published in 1744. In his depiction of what was then known to the English as the country of Whydah (also referred to as Fida by the Dutch, and Juda by the French), on the Slave Coast of Africa, Smith writes that '[a]ll who have ever been here, allow this to be one of the most delightful Countries in the World', in part because of '[t]he great Number and Variety of tall, beautiful and shady Trees, which seem as if planted in fine Groves for orna-ment'.[47] He later recognizes, however, that the groves serve a more than ornamental purpose, when he notes that '[a]lmost every Village has a Grove or publick Place of Worship, to which the principal Inhabitants on a set Day resort to make their Offerings, &c.'[48]

Thomas Salmon devotes the twenty-seventh volume of his ency-clopaedic *Modern History; or the Present State of All Nations* (1735) to an examination of Africa, and in so doing, also notes the importance of public, shady groves in various African societies. In a discussion of the Congo, for example, he writes

[as] to the Towns belonging to the Negroes, most of them consist of a few Huts, built with Clay and Reeds, in an irregular manner; and as every Tribe or Clan has its particular King or Soveraign, his Palace is usually distinguished by a spreading Tree before his Door, under which he sits and converses, or administers Justice to his Subjects. But I perceive most of their Towns are in or near a Grove of Trees; for our Sailors always

[44] Marshall and Williams, *The Great Map of Mankind: British Perceptions of the World in the Age of Enlightenment*, p. 228.

[45] Shields, 'Phillis Wheatley and Mather Byles,' p. 380.

[46] In a letter to the 'Rev'd Mr. Saml. Hopkins of New Port, Rhode Island', Wheatley writes that she 'observe[s] [his] reference to the Maps of Guinea & Salmon's Gazetteer, and shall consult them'. Thus it appears that Reverend Hopkins has directed her to some information on Africa in one of Thomas Salmon's popular accounts. See *The Poems of Phillis Wheatley*, ed. Mason, p. 208.

[47] William Smith, *A New Voyage to Guinea* (London, 1744), p. 194.   [48] Ibid., p. 214.

conclude, there is a Negroe Town, wherever they observe a Tuft of Trees upon the Coast.[49]

As Salmon goes on to discuss other areas of Africa, he, like Smith, pays particular attention to Whydah in a description he appropriates from Willem Bosman's firsthand account of the region in *A New and Accurate Description of the Coast of Guinea* (translated from Dutch into English in 1705). He writes that Bosman's inquiry into the religion of this society revealed that, along with serpents and the sea, the natives of this land show reverence for trees and groves:

The next Things the Fidaians pay Divine Honours to, are fine lofty Trees and Groves. To these they apply in their Sickness, or on any private Misfortune; and I ought to have taken Notice, that all the Serpents Temples are in some Grove, or under some spreading Tree.[50]

Salmon's appropriation of Bosman's text is not unusual in this genre, for many writing these early accounts of Africa incorporate entire paragraphs and even pages from the works of their predecessors. This is especially true in the case of Anthony Benezet's *Some Historical Account of Guinea . . .* , an abolitionist text first published in 1771. For Benezet's attempt to establish the spiritual potential of Africans is partially based on passages taken directly from both William Smith and Bosman, and these happen to be the passages portraying the religious practices of the Whydah blacks, which, of course, include worshipping in a shady grove.[51]

Although we must read eighteenth-century travel accounts of Africa with caution, remembering that 'travellers with closed minds can tell us little except about themselves',[52] the likelihood that Wheatley consulted one or more of the works in this genre nonetheless sheds new light on the 'shady grove' of 'An Hymn to the Morning'. The image now seems to say less about the burning sun and desire for relief from it and more about Christianity and possible alternatives to it. Unearthing African roots in Wheatley's 'shady grove'[53] thus relocates the reader somewhere beyond the poem's

---

[49] Thomas Salmon, *Modern History; or the Present State of All Nations. . .* (London, 1735), p. 160.

[50] Ibid., p. 228.

[51] Anthony Benezet, *Some Historical Account of Guinea . . . with an Inquiry into the Rise and Progress of the Slave-Trade . . . also a Republication of the Sentiments of Several Authors of Note, on This Interesting Subject Particularly an Extract of a Treatise, by Granville Sharp* (Philadelphia, 1781, 1788, Rpt. 1968), pp. 23–28.

[52] Chinua Achebe, quoted in Patrick Brantlinger, 'Victorians and Africans: The Genealogy of the Myth of the Dark Continent', in *'Race,' Writing, and Difference*, ed. Gates, p. 95.

[53] Modern studies of African religions attest to the continuing significance of 'shady groves' in

pious, conventional, Christian surface. From this new vantage point, we see Wheatley giving credence to a religious ritual that might have been her own had she not been enslaved, and we recognize the note of bitterness in the poem's abrupt conclusion where a potentially African shade is driven away by a Christian incarnation of the sun.

Turning to 'The Little Black Boy', we find that Blake's poem brings Wheatley's to mind, as it, too, makes the reader aware of irony and bitterness through tensions and contradictions in its depiction of the sun and a 'shady grove'. As the child of Blake's poem relates his story, he brings the reader to 'the Southern wild' where he was born and tells us of his mother's religious lessons.[54] We find that she, like Wheatley and her own mother, worships a God which she associates with the sun. Yet it is difficult to discern the true nature of the mother's relationship to this sun/God because, like Wheatley, she presents Him both as an object of devotion and as an entity from which she and her child need protection. She instructs her little boy to celebrate this God who lives in 'the rising sun', yet at the same time explains that they have been 'put on earth a little space / That [they] may learn to bear the beams of love', suggesting that these are in fact harsh beams to bear and that the lesson she most wants her son to learn is one of Christian patience and fortitude (p. 9).

In this sense, she sounds very much like some of the other mother figures in *Innocence* and *Experience* who ask that the children in their care adhere to repressive ideologies. In the two 'Nurse's Song[s]', for example, the freedom of children to continue laughing and playing is either threatened (*Innocence*) or taken away (*Experience*) by a nurse supposedly responsible for protecting and nurturing them. While the nurse of *Innocence* gives in to the children's pleas and is much kinder and gentler than her counterpart in *Experience* (who tells her charges that they are wasting their lives in play and fun), both maternal figures make attempts to restrict the children's worlds. Similarly, in

---

many African societies. For example, in a chapter on places and objects of worship, Dominique Zahan writes that 'the tree acquires an even greater value when it forms a part of the thickets and groves in which man holds religious meetings', and claims that '[i]n fact, groves are the most preferred places of worship in African religion'. *The Religion, Spirituality, and Thought of Traditional Africa*, tr. Kate Ezra and Lawrence M. Martin (Chicago, 1979), p. 28. Similarly, John S. Mbiti writes of the importance of trees and groves in the worship practices of many African cultures. *African Religions and Philosophy*, p. 73.

[54] *The Complete Poetry and Prose of William Blake*, ed. Erdman, p. 9. Subsequent page references appear parenthetically in the text.

'A Cradle Song' of *Innocence*, the mother, says Norma Greco, 'subsumes [her] child's identity', and in deluding herself with conventional Christian doctrine is also 'sublimating and thwarting' not only 'her own energies but those of her child as well'.[55] The mother of 'the little black boy' probably has much better reasons for her repressive lessons than these other maternal figures; i.e. she may realize that her son will soon find himself in a situation where acceptance of his lot in life could keep him alive and rebellion against it almost ensure his demise. Yet, like these other mothers of *Innocence* and *Experience*, the African mother still takes something away from her child by teaching him that he must quietly shoulder his burden, follow the rules, and learn to bear the 'harsh beams' of so-called Christian love. As in the other Songs concerning maternal repression, then, Blake probably means for us to recognize irony in his portrayal of the African mother and of the religious principles she passes on to her little boy.

We should also recognize, however, that this mother, presenting her child with an image of the sun, evocative of both Christian and African religiosity, and espousing beliefs about God and His association with the sun which clearly contradict each other, sounds remarkably like the speaker of Wheatley's 'An Hymn to the Morning'. The parallel between the two poems becomes even more evident as the child quotes his mother as saying that 'these black bodies and this sunburnt face / Is but a cloud, and like a shady grove' (p. 9). The mother also proclaims that some day, when their 'souls have learn'd the heat to bear', she and her son will be called 'out from the grove' by the loving voice of God (p. 9). The relationship Blake is establishing here between the image of a 'shady grove' and an African sense of self and blackness clearly duplicates the one developed in 'An Hymn to the Morning'. In both poems the 'shady grove' is associated with an African speaker's struggle to construct an identity (either poetic or personal), and, in both poems, the image of the protective grove is set up in opposition to the sun and to Christianity.

The complexity of the images of sun and shade in these two poems continually conducts the reader back to critical questions about Christianity, and more specifically, about the role that Chris-

---

[55] Norma A. Greco, 'Mother Figures in Blake's *Songs of Innocence* and the Female Will', *Romanticism Past and Present*, 10 (1986), pp. 1–15 (pp. 3, 4).

tianity plays in the life of an enslaved African. Christian doctrine was being deployed during this period by pro-slavery apologists who argued that African servitude was ordained by God. There were of course the pseudo-biblical theories concerning the Hamitic curse and the mark of Cain that were routinely advanced by early defenders of the slave-trade.[56] There was also a more general notion among whites that Christianity somehow sanctioned slavery, the pervasiveness of which is illustrated in a 1786 letter from Daniel Burton, secretary of London's Society for the Propagation of the Gospel, to the Quaker abolitionist Anthony Benezet. In this letter, Burton explains that the Society is unwilling to support Benezet's anti-slavery efforts because it

cannot condemn the Practice of keeping Slaves as unlawful, finding the contrary very plainly implied in the precepts given by the Apostles, both to Masters and Servants, which last were for the most part Slaves . . .[57]

At the same time, abolitionists were asserting that the institution of slavery was completely incompatible with Christian teachings and the Christian way of life.[58] Considering, then, this vexed relationship between Christianity and slavery, the relevance and significance of the questions that arise when examining the symbolic import of sun and shade in Wheatley's and Blake's poems become incontrovertible. Blake's reformulation of some of the ideas and images of 'An Hymn to the Morning' in 'The Little Black Boy' can thus be seen as indicative of his struggle to provide his own representation of some of the bleak but unavoidable answers to these questions.

Blake's struggle to come to terms with these questions and answers is reflected in his depiction of the child speaker of his poem. The 'little black boy' is clearly confused by the complexity of the religious and social lessons he has been taught, and in his confusion, seems very much like another oppressed child of *Innocence*, the chimney sweeper. Both of these little boys do their best to make sense of a senseless society, in which children are not only sold and enslaved, but also taught to believe that it is their duty to serve and

---

[56] For commentary on some of these pseudo-biblical theories, see Charles Lyons' *To Wash an Aethiop White: British Ideas About Black African Educability, 1530–1960* (New York, 1975), p. 12 or Sandiford's *Measuring the Moment*, p. 100.

[57] Quoted in Winthrop D. Jordan's *White Over Black: American Attitudes Toward the Negro, 1550–1812* (New York, 1975), p. 197.

[58] For one discussion of the argument that slaveholding was in violation of the Christian condition, see Jordan's chapter, 'Quaker Conscience and Consciousness' in ibid., pp. 271–76.

to suffer. Both also find themselves caught in a web of contradictions. In the case of 'the little black boy', it is his dual role as a child of Africa and a child of God that makes it most difficult for him to come to any satisfactory conclusions about his life. All he is able to do, then, is collect attitudes and ideas which clearly conflict with each other. He looks to God for love and protection and, yet, needs protection from Him; he sees his blackness as a sign that he is 'bereav'd of light' (p. 9) and as a gift from God; and he believes that when he goes to Heaven, he and the white English boy will both shed their cloud-bodies, and thus achieve some kind of equality, and yet still envisions himself serving the white child, 'shad[ing] him from the heat', and 'stand[ing] and strok[ing] his silver hair' (p. 9).

Some readers of the poem see the child's 'fractured theology'[59] as evidence that he has mingled the religion his mother taught him with the Christianity he was exposed to through missionaries or English Sunday schools in order to 'produc[e] a self affirming discourse of his own.'[60] While it is difficult to extricate the separate strands of religion and culture here, I think that it is safe to say that there is little of a self-affirming nature in the tensions and contradictions that comprise the resulting religious views of 'the little black boy'. Like Wheatley, he has clearly learned that the spiritual teachings of his homeland are considered at best insufficient, and at worst, mere superstition by the society he now lives in. And, like Wheatley, he has learned that in order to be tolerated by this society, he is expected to embrace Christianity, but not to expect too much out of Christianity in return. Thus, as the little boy of this poem grapples with the religions of his past and his present, Blake suggests that confusion, contradictions, and irony are the necessary results of Christianity's involvement in Africa and the slave-trade, and, perhaps also of Evangelical involvement in the anti-slavery movement, since most Evangelicals had more of an interest in converting Africans than in freeing them, as Moira Ferguson shows later in this volume.[61]

In any case, Blake, nonetheless, provides the reader of 'The Little Black Boy' with more than a bleak example of Christianity's impact on Africa and Africans. In the language and images that his poem

---

[59] D.L. Macdonald, 'Pre-Romantic and Romantic Abolitionism: Cowper and Blake', p. 168.

[60] Alan Richardson, 'Colonialism, Race, and Lyric Irony in Blake's "The Little Black Boy"', p. 243.

[61] See Ford K. Brown, *Fathers of the Victorians: The Age of Wilberforce* (Cambridge, 1961), p. 383.

shares with Wheatley's, Blake attests to the significance of beliefs and rituals with African origins and thus offers a revised reading of religion to eighteenth-century England and a new perspective on his poetry to readers today. While the sun and groves are, of course, elements of both Christian and classical tradition, they are also symbols belonging to African culture, and once the 'The Little Black Boy' is set alongside Wheatley's poem, we can no longer ignore this fact. Instead, we must consider 'The Little Black Boy' from a new point of view. When we do so, we can see that, although Blake's *Song of Innocence* is obviously limited by its historical situation, it still presents a picture of traditional African belief systems that is both accepting and appreciative of their differences from British Christian creeds. But this accepting and appreciative attitude is evident, not only in the sun worship and the retreat to a 'shady grove' central to Blake's and Wheatley's poems, but also in 'The Little Black Boy's' affinities with the writings of other eighteenth-century Africans.

Blake's portrait of childhood in Africa, for example, reminds Paul Edwards of James Albert Gronniosaw's slave narrative, published in at least four editions in England and America from the 1770s to the 1790s. Edwards suggests an admittedly shaky, circumstantial link between Blake and Gronniosaw's narrative, as he explains that Blake was good friends with the painter Richard Cosway, whose house servant was Ottobah Cugoano, one of the leaders of Britain's black abolitionists. Because Cugoano's anti-slavery document, first published in 1787, mentions Gronniosaw's work, Edwards proposes that Blake may have been introduced to Gronniosaw's narrative on a visit to the Cosways.[62]

In any case, the story told by 'the little black boy' of Blake's poem bears an uncanny resemblance to the story Gronniosaw tells of his own childhood. Gronniosaw writes of a conversation he once had with his mother in Africa about the author of creation, and reports that when he 'raised [his] hands toward heaven', and asked 'who lived there', he was 'much dissatisfied when she told [him] sun, moon, and stars, being persuaded in [his] own mind that there must be some superior Power'.[63] Gronniosaw then remarks that the

---

[62] See Paul Edwards, 'An African Literary Source for Blake's "Little Black Boy"?', *Research in African Literatures*, 21 (1990), pp. 179–81 (p. 181).

[63] James Albert Ukawsaw Gronniosaw, *A Narrative of the Most Remarkable Particulars in the Life of James Albert Ukawsaw Gronniosaw, an African Prince, as Related by Himself* (Bath, c. 1770 and many later editions), p. 3.

members of his village often congregated under a number of 'large palm tree[s]' for their early morning worship.[64] Edwards notes the resemblance of these lines to the second and third stanzas of 'The Little Black Boy', and sums up the relationship by saying that 'the two passages share a conversation between mother and child, a sheltering tree, and an identification of the Heavenly Power with the sun, [though] in Gronniosaw it is the child who appears more aware of the Heavenly Power than the mother'.[65]

Once again encountering the tradition of worshipping the sun from the protective covering of a 'shady grove', we find that Blake's poem and Gronniosaw's narrative share more than the specifics of plot outlined by Edwards.[66] Gronniosaw unmistakably establishes the tree and the shade it provides as emblems of African religion, for his initial image of the tree is extended later in the narrative when he explains that even after he had been enslaved and converted to Christianity, he continued to pray under a tree, although he had to replace the palm trees of Africa with a 'large, remarkably fine' American oak, 'about a quarter of a mile from [his first] master's house'.[67] Reading Blake's poem in the light of Gronniosaw's *Narrative*, thus, reinforces the suggestion that the specific setting of the religious lesson in 'The Little Black Boy', 'underneath a tree', 'before the heat of day', is intended as acknowledgement of the little that Blake could have known of African religious practices. And because a thorough reading of Gronniosaw's *Narrative* confirms that tension and irony inevitably accompany the Christian conversion of an enslaved African, we can recognize in this writer one more likely model for Blake's child speaker.

If Blake was indeed familiar with Gronniosaw's *Narrative*, it is almost certain that he would also have been aware of the work of Olaudah Equiano, since Equiano, as was mentioned earlier, was a close friend of Cosway's servant Cugoano, and probably the most

---

[64] Ibid., p. 8.

[65] Paul Edwards, 'An African Literary Source for Blake's "Little Black Boy"?', p. 180.

[66] Michael Echeruo recently suggested that Paul Edwards's article on the possible link between 'The Little Black Boy' and Gronniosaw's *Narrative* is in need of 'some expansion and revision' and stated that such a project might begin with research into various 'instances of the habit of "theologizing under a tree" in written and oral African literature'. 'Theologizing "Underneath the Tree": An African Topos in Ukawsaw Gronniosaw, William Blake, and William Cole', *Research in African Literatures*, 23 (1992), pp. 51–58 (pp. 51, 56).

[67] James Albert Ukawsaw Gronniosaw, *A Narrative of . . . the Life of James Albert Ukawsaw Gronniosaw*, p. 24.

famous of Britain's black abolitionists. Along with exposing some of the horrors of slavery, Equiano's autobiography depicts the same kind of spiritual struggle as is seen in Wheatley's poem and Gronniosaw's *Narrative*. Equiano appears in one part of the narrative to have completely supplanted his African religious training with Christianity and in another to be revolting against such a distasteful idea. We find him at his most direct when he compares English society to cultures with non-Christian belief systems, and when he presents the reader with an account of his 'early life in Eboe'.[68] In this account, he describes many of the traditional practices and beliefs with which he was raised, and after considering subjects such as the homes, the food, and the daily occupations of the Eboes, he states that 'as to Religion, the natives believe that there is one Creator of all things and that he lives in the sun',[69] thus presenting us with another possible source for the mother's message to her child in 'The Little Black Boy'.

As Blake's poem concludes, the 'little black boy' offers the reader a vision of his hopes for the future. He sees himself and the little English boy, free from their respective clouds, together in a Heaven in which Christ is depicted as the good shepherd[70] and where 'round the tent of God like lambs [they] joy' (p. 9). This conclusion has been condemned for its evasion of historical realities and its imperialist implications,[71] and the black child's contented, unquestioning acceptance of this Christian afterlife in which he is the playmate and yet still the servant of the white child may seem on the surface to substantiate such criticism.

Yet the ending of this poem is clearly an ironic one, much like the ending of the 'Holy Thursday' of *Innocence*. 'Holy Thursday's' concluding irony becomes apparent when we pay attention to relationships within the poem, for as Robert Gleckner has pointed out, in the last stanza of this *Song*, the innocent, charity children seem almost literally to rise above their hypocritical patrons.[72] 'The

---

[68] Olaudah Equiano, *The Interesting Narrative of the Life of Olaudah Equiano, or Gustavus Vassa, the African, Written by Himself*, 2 vols. (London, 1789; London, 1969), p. 1.

[69] Ibid., p. 10.

[70] See William Blake, *Songs of Innocence and of Experience*, ed. Sir Geoffrey Keynes (Oxford, 1967), Plate 10.

[71] For these assertions, see D.L. Macdonald, 'Pre-Romantic and Romantic Abolitionism', p. 168; and Ngugi wa Thiongo, *Writers in Politics: Essays* (London, 1981), p. 20.

[72] Robert F. Gleckner, 'Irony in Blake's "Holy Thursday"', *Modern Language Notes*, 71 (1956), pp. 412–15.

Little Black Boy's' closing irony, however, becomes most evident
when we look instead at relationships outside of the poem; namely
the relationship between Blake's final vision for his anti-slavery
statement, and that of one of his African contemporaries, Ottobah
Cugoano.

Cugoano's condemnation of the slave-trade, *Thoughts and Sentiments
on the Evil and Wicked Traffic of the Slavery and Commerce of the Human
Species* . . . , closes with three proposals for the people of England.
First, Cugoano recommends that the English pray for forgiveness for
'making merchandize' of human beings; then, he suggests that they
completely abolish slavery; and finally, he says that after doing so,
they should convert all of the forts and factories used for the slave-
trade in West Africa into Christian missions or 'shepherd's tents',
where 'good shepherds' sent from England will 'call the flocks to
feed beside them'.[73] In this third proposal we find a parallel to the
ending of Blake's poem and are left with this question: if Ottobah
Cugoano was unable to represent anything other than an English/
Christian vision of the future, then why should we be surprised that
Blake's 'little black boy' finds himself in the same situation? Essentially, he has learned the lessons of Phillis Wheatley and his other
real life counterparts only too well.

[73] Ottobah Cugoano, *Thoughts and Sentiments on the Evil and Wicked Traffic of the Slavery and
Commerce of the Human Species: Humbly Submitted to the Inhabitants of Great Britain by Ottobah
Cugoano, a Native of Africa* (London, 1787; Rpt. London, 1969), pp. 129, 133.

CHAPTER 6

Blood Sugar

Timothy Morton

Transmitted miseries, and successive chains.
Hannah More, *Slavery* (1788), line 103

INTRODUCTION

How did the representation of sugar interact with discourses on trade and slavery? As a supplement produced by slaves, consumed and discussed by the British, sugar is ideal for testing connections between colonialism, materialism and representation.[1] The rhetoric of abstinence from West Indian sugar and rum, where East Indian sugar or honey was substituted for the former, operated in the discourse of the Anti-Slavery Society, reaching its peak in the late 1780s and early 1790s. The texts discussed here are belated in relation both to this tradition of abstinence, and to the slave uprisings with which they are preoccupied. During the period, anti-slavery came to be used by different factions.

The rhetoric of abstinence involved an aversive topos, often directed towards the female consumer, here called the 'blood sugar' topos.[2] Sweetened drinks of tea, coffee and chocolate were rendered suddenly nauseating by the notion that they contained the blood of

---

[1] Sidney Mintz's *Sweetness and Power: the Place of Sugar in Modern History* (New York, 1985) is a resonant Marxist analysis of the sugar industry in advancing capitalism, and is strong on Caribbean history. See also Sidney Mintz, 'Tropical Production and Mass Consumption: a Historical Comment', *Bulletin of the Institute of Ethnology*, Academica Sinica, 70 (Autumn, 1990), pp. 1–12, and Clare Midgley, *Women Against Slavery: the British Campaigns, 1780–1870* (London and New York, 1992). In addition, I have drawn on historical and anthropological work on the fetish, the gift and money (Braudel, Taussig, Pietz, Buck-Morss and Harvey), and work on notions of supplementarity in representation, crossing over into studies of the subaltern subject (Derrida, Spivak). I am grateful to Peter Kitson and Tim Fulford and to Margaret Ferguson, Barbara Foley, Kay Fowler, Strother Purdy, David Simpson, Charlotte Sussman and those who commented on a version of this article at the 1994 GEMCS conference.

[2] See Charlotte Sussman, 'Women and the Politics of Sugar, 1792', *Representations*, 48 (1994), pp. 1–22.

87

slaves. As a poem in the *Scots Magazine* for 1788 put it, 'Are drops of blood the horrible manure / That fills with luscious juice the teeming cane?' Cowper's 'Epigram' contains the lines, 'No nostrum, planters say, is half so good / To make fine sugar, as a Negro's blood.'[3] Cowper employed the topos in 'Sweet Meat has Sour Sauce, or, the Slave Trader in the Dumps' (1788, a potent year for anti-slavery poetry).

This essay explores the function of the 'blood sugar' topos in Coleridge's 1795 lecture on the slave-trade and Southey's sonnets on the slave-trade (1797). Southey is read with close attention to figurative language and questions of materiality. The metonymic chains which relate the colony to colonial power (the 'successive chains' quoted in the epigraph) are condensed into a powerful and ambiguous metaphor, in which sugar stands for the blood of the slaves. The sonnets treat the commodity as metonymized body in a remarkably sophisticated, ambiguous way.

THE GUILT TROPE

Paul Gilroy has written: 'A sense of the body's place in the natural world can provide . . . a social ecology and an alternative rationality that articulate a cultural and moral challenge to the exploitation and domination of "the nature within us and without us" '.[4] Within anti-slavery literature, Coleridge's 1795 address is a striking example of the discourse of 'natural' and 'unnatural'; the latter implies notions of luxury, barbarity and social injustice.[5]

Coleridge used the 'blood sugar' topos to highlight the unnaturalness and artificiality of certain desires, and ways in which acts of consumption comply with forces of colonialism and exploitation. Coleridge was probably not trying to induce guilt in the specific audience which the speech addresses, made up of middle-class Bristol Dissenters and reformers, perhaps including his Dissenting friends and associates such as the Unitarian minister, John Prior Estlin, the publisher, Joseph Cottle (1770–1853), and his brothers,

---

[3] Ibid., p. 7.

[4] Paul Gilroy, 'Urban Social Movements, "Race" and Community', in *Colonial Discourse and Post-Colonial Theory: a Reader*, eds. Patrick Williams and Laura Chrisman (New York and London, 1994), p. 407.

[5] For a recent discussion of the lecture, see Joan Baum, *Mind-Forg'd Manacles: Slavery and the English Romantic Poets* (North Haven, 1994), chapter 1.

Robert and Amos. Coleridge may have been preaching to the converted, in which case the blood sugar topos was designed to invoke self-righteousness, or even complacency: most of the audience may be assumed to have been abstainers.

Coleridge spoke on the slave-trade on 16 June 1795 at Bristol, before his quarrel with Southey and abandonment of Pantisocracy. The lecture, part of a series intended to raise money for the project, was later printed 'in condensed and revised form' in the fourth number of *The Watchman*.[6] Bristol had long been a centre for the slave-trade. During Chatterton's time, slaves were kept in the crypt of St Mary Redcliffe. Bristol was part of the triangle that included Jamaica and Africa, balancing the trade in timber, tobacco, spices, cocoa and other goods against the trade in human beings.

The lecture addresses the consumer and the abstainer. The first paragraph resonates directly with other discourses on luxury and artificiality in the period, for example Shelley's 1813 pamphlet on vegetarianism: 'Miseries' and 'Vices' arise 'From Artificial Wants'; in contrast, 'What Nature demands Nature everywhere supplies.' The purpose of humans is 'To develope the powers of the Creator', to finish the job that He started: to supplement nature safely.[7] The rhetoric distinguishes this 'good' mode of supplementarity from the 'bad' one of artificial wants in excess of a naturalized norm. Coleridge then focuses on his subject:

> We receive from the West Indies Sugar, Rum, Cotton, log-wood, cocoa, coffee, pimento [allspice], ginger, indigo, mahogany, and conserves – not one of these are necessary – indeed with the exception of cotton and mahogany we cannot with truth call them even useful, and not one is at present attainable by the poor and labouring part of Society . . . If the Trade had never existed, no one human being would have been less comfortably cloathed, housed, or nourished – Such is its value.[8]

Many products in this list could be considered luxuries: spices, coffee and to a certain extent, sugar. The eighteenth-century debate on luxury concentrated on oppositions between mercantilism and the development of wide-ranging protectionist trading policies on the one hand, and attempts to fuse aristocratic modes of consumption with emergent capitalism on the other. The protectionism of

---

[6] *The Collected Works of Samuel Taylor Coleridge*, vol. 1 (*Lectures 1795 on Politics and Religion*), eds. L. Patton and P. Mann (London and Princeton, 1971), p. xxxviii.

[7] Ibid., p. 235.

[8] Ibid., pp. 236–37.

English-based companies often countered the protectionism of
colonial ones. Early mercantilist debates about consumption delineated the problem of 'necessary' luxuries.[9] 'Luxury' was condemned and feminized by writers like Addison and Steele, and
praised only half-comically in Mandeville. Adam Smith later developed ways of thinking about modes of individual overconsumption
that became providential for society at large, deploying the rhetoric
of the invisible hand. During the American and French Revolutions,
anti-luxury discourses also appeared in the Evangelical opposition of
writers like Cowper and Hannah More. It is fair to say, however, that
Coleridge's remark is aimed towards a middle-class and largely
Dissenting audience.[10]

A contribution by Southey contrasts the Europeans, who dabble
with dangerous supplements, with the holistic culture of the Africans: 'The Africans, who are situated beyond the contagion of
European vice – are innocent and happy – the peaceful inhabitants
of a fertile soil, they cultivate their fields in common and reap the
crop as the common property of all.'[11] This image of primitive
communism, close to the ideal of Pantisocracy, was designed explicitly to counteract the effect of works categorizing Africans as savage
and, hence, in need of Christian improvement, a rationalization for
slavery. It conflicts with the more realistic account of African
involvement in the slave-trade, later in the essay.

Coleridge starts using the blood sugar topos by criticizing consumers for what is primarily the fault of capitalists and speculators,
castigating the politics of abstinence:

Had all the people who petitioned for the abolition of this execrable
Commerce instead of bustling about and shewing off with all the vanity of
pretended Sensibility, simply left off the use of Sugar and Rum, it is
demonstrable that the Slave-merchants and Planters must either have
applied to Parliament for the abolition of the Slave Trade or have suffered
the West India Trade altogether to perish – a consummation most devoutly
to be wished – .[12]

Quoting *Hamlet*, III, i, 63–64, Coleridge tightens the rhetorical screw.
Twenty six editions of William Fox's *An Address to the People of Great*

---

[9] For further discussion, see Joyce Oldham Appleby, *Economic Thought and Ideology in Seventeenth-Century England* (Princeton, 1978).

[10] In particular, it was Unitarian and also probably Quaker.

[11] Coleridge, *Lectures 1795*, p. 240.

[12] Ibid., p. 246.

Britain, on the Propriety of Abstaining from West India Sugar and Rum had been published by 1793; the discourse of radical abstinence was already in place. 'Blood sugar' was even somewhat outmoded: *A Second Address* had expressed a more anti-sentimental, literalist form of paranoia about the actual contamination of sugar by the sweat of slaves.[13] Coleridge taps this vein by citing the 'cause' of the slave-trade as the 'consumption of its Products! and does not then Guilt rest on the Consumers? and is it not an allowed axiom in Morality That Wickedness may be multiplied but cannot be divided and that the Guilt of all attaches to each one who is knowingly an accomplice?'[14] The language of complicity registers the faults of the capitalists on the blushing cheeks of the consumer.[15] Coleridge speaks through the already fetishized language of the commodity form, as if all that was required was to resist by refraining from consumption. On the other hand, in that civil society is shown to be playing a part in mercantile life, he is empowering the consumer's aggravated sense of choice. Like any other discourse of the fetish, his rhetoric works in multiple directions simultaneously, establishing a bizarre, contradictory reciprocity between the consumed and the consumer.

Coleridge's address to the Christians in the audience, rhetorically coded through the special and radical meanings of an appellation connoting Unitarianism, portrays Jesus as a figure who brushes history against the grain. If he were alive today, Jesus would not turn water into wine but sugar back into blood, luxury back into barbarism:

Surely if the inspired Philanthropist of Galilee were to revisit earth and be among the feasters as at Cana he would not change Water into Wine but haply convert the produce into the things producing, the occasioned into the things occasioning! Then with our fleshly eye should we behold what even now truth-painting Imagination should exhibit to us – instead of sweetmeats Tears and Blood, and Anguish – and instead of music groaning and the loud Peals of the Lash.[16]

Coleridge exploits the long-held, Christian fascination and anxiety over what was called *metabole* in the Middle Ages,[17] and from which

---

[13] Sussman, 'Women and the Politics of Sugar, 1792', p. 8.

[14] Coleridge, *Lectures 1795*, p. 247.

[15] The student 'Boycott Barclays' campaign in 1980s Britain (against its complicity with South African apartheid) was similar.

[16] Coleridge, *Lectures 1795*, p. 247.

[17] See Marc Shell, *Money, Language, and Thought: Literary and Philosophical Economies from the*

we obtain the notion of 'metabolism': the transubstantial changes involved in the sacrament of the Eucharist (or thanksgiving: 'Bless the Food'), predicated on ways in which potentially cannibalistic food is transmuted into the food of grace. The rhetoric of metabolism raises the question of metaphorical language itself. Coleridge's effort to find a suitable, linguistic philosophy for his radical politics is an attempt to construct a notion of 'natural signification'.[18] Could a metaphor be read in reverse, as it were 'back into' literality? Jesus acts as the good, inspired man of Unitarian belief: rather than miraculously transforming substances into emblems of divine power, he radically defetishizes the object, turning the product into the process of production. Needless to say, it is the metaphorical power of language which enables the retroactive construction of 'literality', separating Coleridge's richly ambivalent engagements with language in his early writing from other modes of Unitarian discourse.

The blood sugar topos reverses consumption into production, figurality into literality and supplementarity into essence. But the topos is remarkable in its underlying assumptions about figurative language, and complex in its ideological effects. The topos does not simply reveal a 'Real' of slavery underlying the figure of sugar; the materiality of the figure itself is at stake. It is an apocalyptic rhetoric that decodes the slave-trade, but its unveiling process draws attention to the materiality of the very veil which has been torn away. Abstinence in itself appears not to be an adequate means of resistance. It is not disillusioning enough; it becomes questionable whether abandoning 'false consciousness' is a way of subverting ideology.

Disgust is evoked as the sweet supplement turns clotted and sour in the mouth. Thomas Somerville's *A Discourse on Our Obligation to Thanksgiving, for the Prospect of the Abolition of the African Slave-Trade* (1792) similarly exploited the potential for Christian shock: 'Were men, whose hands were *full of blood*, the fit instruments to promulgate the gospel of peace?'[19] In *The French Constitution* Benjamin Flower

---

Medieval to the Modern Era (Berkeley, Los Angeles and London, 1982), pp. 41–43; a discussion of the Holy Grail, another kind of blood container.

[18] James C. McKusick, *Coleridge's Philosophy of Language* (New Haven and London, 1986), p. 26; pp. 18–26 discuss the lectures.

[19] Thomas Somerville, *A Discourse on Our Obligation to Thanksgiving, for the Prospect of the Abolition of the African Slave-Trade. With a Prayer* (Kelso, 1792), p. 17; see pp. 48–49.

wrote: 'let [the Ladies], if they can . . . continue morning and evening, to sweeten their tea, and the tea of their families and visitors, with the blood of their fellow creatures'.[20] Coleridge relates oppression in the colonies to the oppression of the peasantry at home:

But I have heard another argument in favour of the Slave Trade, namely, that the slaves are as well off as the Peasantry in England! . . . I appeal to common sense whether to affirm [this] . . . be not the same as to assert that our Peasantry are as bad off as Negro Slaves – and whether if the Peasantry believed it there is a man amongst them who [would] not rebel? and be justified in Rebellion?[21]

Marx would concur that capitalism imposes forms of slavery, if not economically in the form of wage-slavery in the metropolis, then actually in the colony. Just as he wants to strip trade to its bare essentials (an impossibility?), discarding the intensive labour of slaves in plantations, so Coleridge wishes to reverse language's tropology towards some essential, necessary, causally logical encapsulation of the Real. The lecture is a pattern of supplements and reversals between luxury and necessity, sugar and blood, Jamaica and England, slave and peasant. Coleridge searches for a radical, miraculous language that might reverse a metonymic chain of commodity flow by undoing a metaphorical substitution of blood for sugar, power for sweetness. For the virtuous, temperate radical, sweetness is a mode of enjoyment predicated on the repression of production, whose unrepression tips the sweet into the sour.

TROPICS AND TOPICS

In exploring a topos, the notion of 'place' becomes important, especially considering the topical and tropical qualities of the colonies. Capitalism tends to liquidate the local meanings and values that make a certain territory into a 'place'; it functions better between more abstractly conceived 'spaces', what Castells might call the 'space of flows'.[22] This is why the colonial project was often extraordinarily problematic. The West Indies needed the support of

---

[20] Coleridge, *Lectures 1795*, p. 248.
[21] Ibid., pp. 250–51.
[22] Manuel Castells, *The Informational City: Information Technology, Economic Restructuring, and the Urban-Regional Process* (Oxford, 1989), pp. 169–71; this discussion of the consequences for spatial organization of electronic information networks may be applied in a broader sense.

England: for example, in 1783, 16,576 tons of salted meat had to be imported. Planters were 'not usually' rich, and Jamaica performed the function of 'a wealth-creating machine' for England, whose net benefit in 1773 was about one and a half million pounds.[23] It is, thus, no surprise to find literature on the sugar plantations oscillating between a sense of place and a sense of space. Jamaica is never quite as solidly 'there' as the Hellenic or English pastoral *loci amoeni* with which the literature strives to bestow the local colour of 'place'. Jamaica threatens to dissolve and decode all 'placedness' into the pure space of sugar monoculture: a supplementary island growing an imported, supplementary crop.

This need not necessarily have disappointed radical writers. Jamaica's instability could threaten to destabilize the metropolitan culture which it so dangerously supplemented. Reactionaries tried to 'reterritorialize' Jamaica, presenting it as another Europe, another belated subject for Shakespeare or Milton. But the need to rely on figures such as *occupatio* ('would that those writers were present to describe the island . . .'),[24] threatened their project, let alone the newer, more capital-happy modes of representation, celebrating the instability of 'space' through the language of the fetish. Like it or not, sugar became the hero of the story, and all other voices (Shakespeare *and* the Africans) competed with it.

Relationships between indigenous cultures in Jamaica often contradicted ways in which non-indigenous writers and artists conceived of them.[25] Jamaica's culinary culture was rich and diverse. From the Arawaks, Jamaicans inherited cassava, corn, sweet potatoes, yampie, beans, callaloo, hot peppers, pimento, fish, conies, iguanas, crabs, guavas, pineapples, prickly pears, paw-paw and cocoa. The Spanish brought bananas, plantains, sugar-cane, lemons, limes, oranges, coconuts, tamarind, ginger, date palms, pomegranates, grapes and figs, while the guinep and naseberry were introduced from other New World tropics. Along with beef, cakes and tarts, the English

---

[23] Fernand Braudel, *Civilization and Capitalism, 15th-18th Century*, tr. S. Reynolds, 3 vols (Berkeley and Los Angeles, 1992), 1,158, II, pp. 275, 279.

[24] For example, see William Beckford, *A Descriptive Account of the Island of Jamaica: with Remarks upon the Cultivation of the Sugar-Cane, throughout the Different Seasons of the Year, and Chiefly Considered in a Picturesque Point of View; also Observations and Reflections upon what would probably be the Consequences of an Abolition of the Slave-Trade, and of the Emancipation of the Slaves*, 2 vols. (London, 1790), I, p. 44.

[25] A recent conference highlighted problems of unity and diversity in Caribbean literary culture: 'Sisyphus and Eldorado: Literary Culture in Two Caribbeans?', 31st Annual Eastern Comparative Literature Conference, 7 May 1994, New York University. •

introduced bread-fruit (via Captain Bligh and the Oceanic islands), the otaheite apple, ackee, mango, rose apple, mandarin orange, cheirmoyer, turmeric, black pepper and coffee. Jewish settlers brought egg-plant and sesame. African Jamaicans used a wide variety of foods including yam, pigeon-peas, okra, callaloo, corn, cocoa, coffee, oranges, shaddock, hot peppers, pimento, pumpkin and ackee.[26]

The culinary folk culture of the Jamaican slaves differed, not surprisingly, from cultural work on Jamaica for outside audiences. It drew upon utopian registers such as the idea of soul food, the notion that 'slave food . . . nourished the individual's very essence since it provided a kind of freedom in which he could express himself'.[27] The *Columbian Magazine* for May 1797 reported a slave work song about food, home and longing:

> Guinea corn, I long to see you
> Guinea corn, I long to plant you
> Guinea corn, I long to mould you
> Guinea corn, I long to weed you
> Guinea corn, I long to hoe you
> Guinea corn, I long to top you
> Guinea corn, I long to cut you
> Guinea corn, I long to dry you
> Guinea corn, I long to beat you
> Guinea corn, I long to thrash you
> Guinea corn, I long to parch you
> Guinea corn, I long to grind you
> Guinea corn, I long to turn you
> Guinea corn, I long to eat you.[28]

'Monk' Lewis, who had an estate on the island, wrote in his *Journal* (1834) about overhearing a song thanking Wilberforce but also encouraging its listeners to '*Take force by force! Take force by force!*'[29] Those traditions which represented Jamaica for an outside audience, however, tended merely to concentrate on the fact of slavery and the sugar monoculture.

Benjamin Moseley (1742–1819) settled in Jamaica in 1768, and

[26] On Jamaican produce see Norma Benghiat, *Traditional Jamaican Cookery* (London, 1985), pp. 17–20.

[27] Sidney Mintz, 'Tasting Food, Tasting Freedom', in *Slavery in the Americas*, ed. Wolfgang Binder (Würzburg, 1993), pp. 257–75; the citation is from p. 269.

[28] *Columbian Magazine* (May 1797), II, p. 766; see Edward Kamau Brathwaite, *The Folk Culture of the Slaves in Jamaica* (London and Port of Spain, 1971; revised, 1981), p. 18.

[29] Quoted in Brathwaite, *Folk Culture*, p. 19.

became surgeon-general. *A Treatise on Sugar* (1800), scorning the
fetishism of African religion or 'Obi', worships its own kinds of
fetish.[30] Moseley describes the history of the commodity as 'a subject
of the first importance in commerce', extolling the spurious idea that
sugar-cane grew spontaneously in the West Indies and Southern
America. He explores sugar's Indo-European past through philology
and depicts its medicinal use in India and Arabia.[31] Unlike Coleridge and Southey, Moseley does not employ the language of
supplementarity in his discussion of sugar's virtues. He emphasizes
what he calls the saccharine element in vegetables: the use of sugar
as a restorative, a 'salubrious luxury' for African children in the West
Indies; and the increase in 'vigour' and sustenance of 'nature' that it
imparts in 'tea, milk, and beer'. Europeans were healthier through
the supply of sugar from the East and West Indies.[32]

Moseley employs vegetarian language, demonstrating an interest
in modernizing diet. Animal food is not necessary for 'mental
pleasure and health' – it could even be deleterious; nevertheless in
London 'Blood flows in almost every gutter.' His picture of foul
Smithfield slaughterhouses exemplifies the vegetarian rhetoric of
butchery or *macellogia*, with its vision of 'poor trembling victims . . .
gazing on'.[33] Moseley links this rhetoric with sugar in ways which
more radical writers, matching it with the barbarity of treating
humans like cattle, would have found bizarre: 'In the time of
PYTHAGORAS, sugar was unknown . . . Otherwise his philosophy
would have had more converts.'[34] The odd link is confirmed by
Moseley's negative judgement of the rebellion in French St Domingue (Haiti) as threatening to sugar: 'Of such importance has the
agriculture of half a million of Africans, become to the Europeans.'[35]

William Beckford's *A Descriptive Account of the Island of Jamaica* (1790)

---

[30] See Alan Richardson, 'Romantic Voodoo: Obeah and British Culture, 1797–1807', *Studies in Romanticism*, 32 (1993), pp. 3–28; the citation is from p. 9.

[31] Benjamin Moseley, *A Treatise on Sugar. With Miscellaneous Medical Observations* (London, 1800), pp. 5–74, 53.

[32] Ibid., pp. 139, 144, 157, 168–69. Moseley also discusses the importance of spices in the Old Testament (pp. 128–33).

[33] Ibid., pp. 159–60; see Timothy Morton, *Shelley and the Revolution in Taste: the Body and the Natural World* (Cambridge, 1994), chapter 1.

[34] Moseley, *Treatise*, p. 160; the vegetarian passage extends to p. 161. Beckford also makes a vegetarian reference about killing turtles: 'What would the simple and unlettered Bramin [sic], or what would the Pythagorean philosophy say to this cruel instance of refinement and gluttony?' (*Jamaica*, I, pp. 374–75).

[35] Ibid., p. 164.

is less optimistic about the suitability of the West Indies for sugar, but having been transplanted he hopes that it will stay, along with slavery. Beckford (1744–99), the cousin of the author of *Vathek*, was a historian who had lived in Jamaica for thirteen years. Gothic and picturesque language permeates the text. There is the 'saffron glow' of the sunset (a luxury marker, typical of imperial and colonial travel writing), and the 'many very pleasing and romantic situations' on the island, like the Gothic caverns worthy of quotations by poets who had never visited, reputedly containing the remains of Arawaks exterminated by the Spanish.[36] Production is prettified: 'There is something particularly picturesque and striking in a gang of negroes, when employed in cutting canes upon the swelling projections of a hill.'[37] The picturesque, distancing the aesthetic from the practical, often appropriated scenes where labouring figures seemed ornamental. But it also served to aestheticize surplus value. Janet Schaw's journal of her visit to the West Indies (1774–75) aestheticizes the sugar-cane fields in this fashion.[38]

The politics of slavery is threateningly absent in Beckford, but in a monoculture, not even climatology is politically irrelevant, given sugar's precocious and unstable qualities: 'A sugar plantation is like a little town . . . I have often been surprised . . . how intimately connected is every thing that grows, and every thing that labours, with this very singular, and at one time luxurious, but now very necessary, as it is deemed to be a highly useful and wholesome, plant.'[39] Each word gravitates towards 'plant', in the sentence, as in life. Beckford animates the cane like a fetish: '[It] is perhaps, through all its different stages, the most uncertain production upon the face of the earth; and has . . . the greatest number of foreign and local enemies . . . of any plant that either contributes to the wants, or that administers to the comforts and luxuries of man.'[40] He feels sorrier for it than for the slaves, with whose suffering he only sympathizes minimally: 'Happy are those, in some instances, who are without property, and are consequently ignorant of law! Such are the *peasantry* in most countries, and such are the *slaves* in all.'[41] This is

---

[36] Beckford, *Jamaica*, I, pp. 84, 233–48.
[37] Ibid., I, p. 48.
[38] See Elizabeth A. Bohls, 'The Aesthetics of Colonialism: Janet Schaw in the West Indies, 1774–75', *Eighteenth-Century Studies*, 27 (1994), pp. 363–90 (pp. 370, 374–75).
[39] Beckford, *Jamaica*, I, p. 141.
[40] Ibid., II, p. 11.
[41] Ibid., II, p. 132.

especially true in Jamaica for 'The negroes are slaves by nature.'[42]
Beckford hopes that an integrated, 'consistent' picture of Jamaica
might contribute to an aesthetic ideology to preserve the colonies –
precisely what Coleridge and Southey were opposing.[43]

SWEET REVENGE

Raimond argues that 'By the end of the eighteenth century, Southey,
not Coleridge or Wordsworth, was regarded as the leading champion
of a new spirit in English poetry.'[44] Even if it were not the case that
Southey is neglected in relation to his contemporaries, assessing the
ideological range of his sonnets on the slave-trade in *Poems* (1797)
would still be hard. Several contradictory modes and objects of
address are involved. Is Southey supporting a slave rebellion or
reform by planters and consumers? Are the Africans victims or
agents? As in Coleridge's lecture, the possibility of rebellion haunts a
reformist text. Is this a threat and goad to reform, or a more
complex celebration of revolutionary struggle?

It should be remembered that the slaves themselves were *commodities* as well as *subjects*. Some poets had articulated the slave as
subject. In Hugh Mulligan's *The Slave, an American Eclogue* (1788) the
protagonist, Adala, does all the talking, though supplemented with
copious notes.[45] Blake's *Visions of the Daughters of Albion* (1793) had
discussed slavery through three allegorical characters. Other work,
such as Hannah More's *Slavery* (1788), emphasized the slaves as
commodities: 'MAN the traffic, SOULS the merchandize!' (line 145).[46]
Southey's sonnets are haunting because they figuratively demonstrate the revolutionary potential of people existing *between* the
categories of subject and object: as Bhabha might remark, a state of
hybridity.

The Preface to the *Poems on the Slave Trade* summarizes the history
of abolitionism. The Government intended to destroy the trade or to
stop using

[42] Ibid., II, p. 382.
[43] Ibid., II, p. 399.
[44] Jean Raimond, 'Southey's Early Writings and the Revolution', *Yearbook of English Studies*, 19
(1989), pp. 181–96.
[45] Hugh Mulligan, *Poems Chiefly on Slavery and Oppression, with Notes and Illustrations* (London,
1788).
[46] Hannah More, *Slavery, a Poem* (London, 1788).

West-Indian productions: a slow but certain method. For a while Government held the language of justice, and individuals with enthusiasm banished sugar from their tables. This enthusiasm soon cooled; the majority of those who had made this *sacrifice*, (I prostitute the word, but they thought it a *sacrifice*) persuaded themselves that Parliament would do all, and that individual efforts were no longer necessary.[47]

Southey criticizes the tenacity of the so-called enthusiasts, a loaded term in the context of contemporary, radical, religious movements. Wilberforce is attacked for his 'duplicity'.[48] Southey is concerned that 'humanity', invoked early on, should not be *supplemented* by revenge. He presents the alternatives:

There are yet two other methods remaining, by which this traffic will be abolished. By the introduction of East-Indian or Maple Sugar, or by the just and general rebellion of the Negroes: by the vindictive justice of the Africans, or by the civilized Christians finding it their interest to be humane.[49]

The chiastic slip between 'just and general rebellion' and 'vindictive justice' is repeated in the sonnet sequence itself. Unsure of how to address his audience, or even of who precisely his audience is, Southey slides between supporting revolution and advocating reform.

The first sonnet pictures the violence of capitalism:

> the pale fiend, cold-hearted Commerce there
> Breathes his gold-gendered pestilence afar,
> And calls to share the prey his kindred Daemon War.
>
> (lines 12–14)

This kind of invective was employed by Percy Shelley, one of the early Southey's admirers, in *Queen Mab* v (1813).[50] The anti-slavery passage in the millennial, eighth section of *Queen Mab* incorporates the 'mangling scourge' found in Southey's third Sonnet (VIII, line 179); the later passage on vegetarianism in the same section (VIII, line 211ff) also represents mangling. The rhetoric of mangling flesh or *macellogia* was a feature of anti-slavery and animal rights rhetoric, often found together as Pratt's *Humanity* (1788) demonstrates.[51]

---

[47] Robert Southey, *Poems* (Bristol and London, 1797), p. 31.
[48] Ibid., p. 31.
[49] Ibid., p. 32.
[50] Shelley's debts in *Queen Mab* to Southey's *Joan of Arc* have already been noted: see Raimond, 'Southey's Early Writings', p. 194.
[51] See Morton, *Shelley and the Revolution in Taste*, pp. 94–96.

Southey describes capitalism as a devourer. Commerce as a cannibal appears again in the sixth sonnet, in which a slave is hung like Prometheus and consumed by vultures, 'their living food' (line 2). In *To the Genius of Africa*, 'The Daemon COMMERCE on your shore / Pours all the horrors of his train' (lines 20–21), and surveys 'Europe's blood-fed plains' (line 49). The language of consumption is politicized.

The sun's heat, for Southey, as for Thomson and Shelley, becomes an emblem of tyranny

> The scorching Sun,
> As pityless as proud prosperity,
> Darts on him his full beams; gasping he lies
> Arraigning with his looks the patient skies,
> While that inhuman trader lifts on high
> The mangling scourge. Oh ye who at your ease
> Sip the blood-sweeten'd beverage! thoughts like these
> Haply ye scorn: I thank thee Gracious God!
> That I do feel upon my cheek the glow
> Of indignation, when beneath the rod
> A sable brother writhes in silent woe.
>
> (Sonnet III, lines 4–14)

The blood-sugar topos is spliced between two acts of physical marking: the mangling scourge in the colony, and the blush of indignation in the colonizing country. Whereas in the New World those marks are represented in blood on the surface of the body, in the Old World they appear in the internalized mode of the blush. 'Sip', 'ease' and 'Haply ye scorn' are juxtaposed with language that registers literality, truth: the truth of colonial power and the truth of sympathetic passion. The language of marks relegates the sweetness of the beverage to the status of something useless, a supplement to be discarded.

The blood sugar passage is echoed uncannily in the fifth sonnet: 'No more on Heaven he [the slave] calls with fruitless breath, / But sweetens with revenge, the draught of death' (lines 13–14). Death is figured as a beverage that must be sweetened, and justice is imagined as a kind of wild revenge. 'Wild justice' was a theme in the discourses of anxiety about the justness of the French and American Revolutions and the threat of insurrection in England, where revenge was considered supplementary to law.[52] The figure uses the same image

---

[52] See Paul Magnuson, 'Wild Justice', *The Wordsworth Circle*, 19 (1988), pp. 88–91.

of oppression as the 'blood-sweeten'd beverage', but turns it into an image of revolution.

In Southey's sonnets, sugar is figured both as specious pretence and as deep substance. It is a superficial luxury, but also has a bloody history, a viscerality that belies its sweetness. Sugar is an emblem for toil, pain, death and slavery: 'Oh ye who at your ease / Sip the blood-sweetn'd beverage! thoughts like these / Haply ye scorn' (Sonnet III, lines 9–11). Southey forces the sippers to read the barbarism stirred into their luxuries, enacting this in the conventional enjambment between the sonnet's ninth and tenth lines. Sipping is a refined gesture; 'ease' and 'sweetn'd' chime. The luxurious culture of the eighteenth century *was* the culture of 'ease'.

Can the flow of blood into sugar be counteracted? Three options are presented: a slave uprising; abstaining from the condiment; and redirecting its flow (looking to the East). The last two options are reformist. Abstinence as a means of psychic and social control is itself an affordable luxury: there needs to be enough money in one's pocket to be able to *refuse* food. Redirecting the flow is a legal move within existing trade structures. Sugar appears supplementary in both cases. It is an unnecessary luxury, not befitting a moral, social and psychic restricted economy. And the West Indies are an unnecessarily barbaric supplement of the East Indies.

The image of revenge as a blood-sweetened beverage is extraordinary. Where is the critical tone located? Southey is either trying impossibly to overhear the voice of the Other (the object of colonialism), or mimicking a universal voice that castigates from afar. The revision of Old Testament, prophetic registers adds complexity. Unlike the Oriental voices in *Thalaba* or *The Curse of Kehama*, the voices of the slaves are tantalizingly out of reach. This non-placedness may be positive. The Orientalist works locate Oriental despotism; a sense of non-location may subvert the fixities of power.[53] Alternatively, non-location may be a way of beating capitalist ideology at its own game. Then are the sonnets' addressees guilty or converted? Moreover, radical understanding may emerge, reasons why the slaves might have to revolt, not just rationalizations of reform. A varied series of identifications and divergences, within which various forms of ideological fantasy play, is structured around

---

[53] See Marilyn Butler, 'Plotting the Revolution: the Political Narratives of Romantic Poetry and Criticism', in *Romantic Revolutions: Criticism and Theory*, eds. K. R. Johnston, K. H. Chaitin and H. Marks (Bloomington and Indianapolis, 1990), pp. 144–49.

the hard kernel of the viscerally real cup of blood. The beverage is a fantasy object that shows colonial enjoyment to be predicated on cannibalistic consumption.[54]

What stands in a *metonymic* relation to others along a chain of commodities becomes *metaphorically* present in the sugar. Several mediating links of time and space are removed, collapsing the colonial body from East and West into the tea-cup. The flows of blood, rum and tea are all pooled in the same space, generating revulsion (and revolution). Beauty, the sweet, mutates into sublimity, the bloody. The image is catastrophic for moral rectitude. It resembles Kant's articulation of absolute evil as the form of good: the shocking secret is that sugar and rebellion only *appear* as supplementary to a justice that is *already* wild, precisely in the fact of the ownership of slaves. The bloody cup highlights the non-identity of the law and capitalism, and implicates certain forms of religion and spirituality as modes of oppression. Southey was also horrified about the Trinity and the transubstantiation of blood into wine. He was satirizing the religiosity of consumption, the way in which the consumer fetishizes commodities, treating them as 'The Real Thing' (as sugary Coke has been advertised).

Which subject position is supplementing the other? 'I', 'you' and 'them' shift between rectitude and rebelliousness, bigotry and sympathy, objects of colonial reform and subjects of revolution. Southey's sonnets are didactic texts that become radically unstable. The status of the object, the fetishized sugar and the fetishized cup, becomes significant as an index of capital. Southey's storm in a tea-cup resembles Marx's two mutually exclusive positions on capital. Capital is either an alienated substance (the labour of the worker transformed under capitalism), in which case revolution is a mode of disalienation, of getting back/going forward to some essential, non-alienated state; or it is a substantive subject, in which case revolution is to be achieved *through* alienation.[55] It is precisely this image of sugar-as-revolution, of rebellion as sweet, which holds these two meanings in (dis)solution together.

There are thus two main ways of reading Southey's sonnets, either from the 'inside out' or from the 'outside in'. From the 'inside out', they are about interpreting the behaviour of the English consumer,

[54] See Slavoj Žižek, *Tarrying with the Negative: Kant, Hegel, and the Critique of Ideology* (Durham, 1993), pp. 116–17.
[55] See ibid., p. 27.

speaking for the Other, goading and advocating reform. But, from the 'outside in', the poem is inwardly fractured by the possibility of revolution. Moreover, this is not only a possibility but a historical event in relation to which the sonnets can only be belated. The Maroon revolt was fresh in the memory, as was the revolution in French St Domingue (1791). Indeed, 'London merchant firms held investments in Santo Domingo in the then large sum of £300,000', which explains 'why the British government in [1793–98] sacrificed more than £4,000,000 in an effort to conquer the French colony and maintain or restore Negro slavery'.[56] This chance of revolution operates as what Fredric Jameson calls a 'vanishing mediator', indicating the 'open' situation of the emergence of a new kind of political state, before it has been 'closed'. The logic of the supplement is overturned and surpassed: the 'threat' function of the bloody cup fails to exhaust its power. The bloody cup is a stain on the whitewashed walls of the reformist project, in non-relation to which Southey, the liberal, articulates nothing less than the positive chance of revolution. The Enlightenment reformism implicit in Wedgwood's medallions 'Am I Not a Man and a Brother?' and 'Am I Not a Woman and a Sister?', influenced by the reasoned sentimentalism of Cowper's 'The Negro's Complaint' (1781), is unavailable here.

The reality of Caribbean revolution gives the poems their bite. They exemplify anti-colonial infiltration of the 'centre' culture by the culture of the 'periphery'.[57] The supplement emerges as their *most* material (though hardly the most 'natural') element. Reformism has been surpassed by history, bestowing upon the blood sugar image its awkward ambiguities. Southey was caricatured by Hazlitt for moving from 'Ultra-jacobin' and 'fantastic demagogue' to 'Ultra-royalist' and 'senile court-tool'. The former 'maintained second-hand paradoxes' while the latter 'repeats second-hand commonplaces'.[58] In his anti-slavery poetry, he was less in control of his meanings than Hazlitt asserts. His use of the blood sugar topos not only evokes the politics of sympathy, but also suggests revolution. The slave-trade sonnets materialize the supplement, making it rich and sticky, heavy with history and suffering, while simultaneously construing it as arbitrary and artificial, capable of being cast aside. They offer the possibility of scratching the grooves

56 David V. Erdman, *Blake: Prophet Against Empire* (Princeton, 1977), p. 237.
57 See *Colonial Discourse*, eds. Williams and Chrisman, pp. 16–17.
58 William Hazlitt, *Selected Writings*, ed. R. Blythe (London, 1970; rpt. 1982), pp. 245–46.

of the commodity fetish to create unexpected, revolutionary meanings. Whether these meanings are achieved *against* the commodity fetish (boycotting sugar, transcending capitalism), or *through* it, in the revenge of the commodities themselves (an uprising of slaves), is left in the balance.

The eighteenth-century politics of boycotting and abstinence were ambiguous. In the 1760s, the abolitionist Quaker essayist John Woolman (1720–72) advocated not dyeing clothes; but the clothes remained. In the 1780s and 1790s, sugar symbolized unnecessary luxury, but what about the luxury drinks into which it was poured? The trade in coffee and tea had eclipsed the spice trade as the main motor of long-distance capitalism. Sugar, as the supplement of a luxury, is overdetermined in this respect, but consent was involved in boycotting some but not all articles of colonial and imperial trade. Moreover, among Southey's remedial options, why is there no mention of sugar beet, grown successfully in Germany since the 1740s, whose farming was being attempted in England? One answer might be that he is being triumphalist, celebrating the possibility of a revolutionary outcome in the war against the slave-trade, while not assuming much responsibility for that war himself.

The study of literary and cultural representations of consumption and the commodity provides fresh ways of considering Orientalism and colonialism, which are often construed through a psychoanalytic discourse of 'Self' and 'Other'. This history of the subject can be expanded with histories of the *object*. The study of the object often aims at a naively empirical collection of detail. But the study of consumption raises the question of enjoyment and suffering: colonial discourses included *fantasies* about the commodity.

Cultural analysis may appeal to a metaphysical Real beyond the text, but in the ones explored here, the Real appears much as it does in Žižek's reading of Lacan, as a hard kernel of desire which aggravates the reformist. The desire for and possibility of (and historical actuality of) revolution in the West Indies forms a visceral excrescence on the sickly sweet rhetoric of humanitarianism. The production of surplus leads to a contradictory set of discourses on supplements, broaching the question of radical social transformation. From the boycotters' point of view, the question is: what do you want after you have what you need? One answer concerns the reality of desire.

Alan Liu has investigated the fetishistic coexistence of transcendence and detail in Romanticist historical work, criticizing the prose of writers in which culture *is*, not *means*, 'with all the ontological zing of the Real'.[59] 'Zing' is poised between the fetishism of detail and a totalizing effect, as of a sudden illumination: 'the ontological zing of the Real' sounds like 'the ring of truth'. 'Zing' chimes punningly with Kant's *das Ding*, but also embodies the *jouissance* of a glow of detail on a fetishized object: a glint on the surface of a brand new car, the sparkle of some advertised clean teeth, or the 'zing' imparted by The Real Thing. 'Zing' indicates the enjoyment of hallucinatory detail. For this queasy, Kantian blend of detail and transcendence, Liu substitutes a Barthesian notion of culture as reality-effect. But this only pushes the problem back a stage further. What is interesting about 'the Real' is not merely its reality but its 'zing'. 'Zing' is about enjoyment, not just realism.

The fascination for 'zing' in historicizing prose is illusory given what Sloterdijk calls cynical reason, the fact that one never actually quite believes in 'reality-effects' anyway. 'None of us would actually believe' an advertisement, however much 'zing' it had. This is bad news for Moseley's marketing of sugar. Nevertheless, it need not disqualify advertisements from working. Ideology, never more potent than when one believes one has seen through it (the vision of the blood-swilling, tea drinkers), does not necessarily operate through convincing reality-effects. It would be fairer to say, with Žižek, that cynicism may be ideologically effective: 'They know that, in their activity, they are following an illusion, but still, they are doing it.' In this sense, 'falsity lies on the side of what we do', not say.[60]

The blood sugar topos is naively economistic, placing us in an imaginary relation to a sentimentalized, pain-drenched mode of production, developed in Marx's notion of the commodity as *alienated substance*. Southey, the reformist, wishes us to lift the veil of this trite, easily-reversible topos. Seeing that slaves produce sugar is not a disillusionment; it is crassly obvious. But a hole in Southey's symbolic structure, the implications of the sweetness of revenge, outlines the Real of revolutionary desire elaborated in Marx's concept of the commodity as *substantive subject*. This hole is more real than the sentimental scene onto which the curtain of the topos rises,

[59] Alan Liu, 'Local Transcendence: Cultural Criticism, Postmodernism, and the Romanticism of Detail', *Representations*, 32 (1990), p. 86.
[60] Terry Eagleton, *Ideology: an Introduction* (London and New York, 1991), p. 40. Eagleton is quoting from Slavoj Žižek, *The Sublime Object of Ideology* (London and New York, 1989, 1991).

since it appears through the historical chance of revolution in the West Indies. In which case, Southey's accidental poetics of revolution paradoxically resembles Beckford's fetishistic aesthetics of capital more than the humanitarian poetics of sympathy.

CHAPTER 7

'Wisely forgetful': Coleridge and the politics of Pantisocracy

James C. McKusick

During the summer of 1794, Robert Southey and Samuel Taylor Coleridge planned to establish an egalitarian community on the banks of the Susquehanna River in Pennsylvania. It was Coleridge who invented the name for this ideal community, 'Pantisocracy', meaning 'government by all'. The historical origins of Pantisocracy have been thoroughly scrutinized by Coleridge scholars; an especially insightful, biographical overview is provided by Richard Holmes, who gives a sympathetic account of the project as a major intellectual enterprise that left Coleridge with an enduring sense of his political and poetic vocation.[1] A more detailed historical perspective is afforded by Nicholas Roe, who elucidates the role of Pantisocracy within the intricate discourse of contemporary, radical politics.[2] However, the intellectual significance of Pantisocracy within the larger context of British maritime exploration and the colonization of the New World has not been adequately examined.

This essay will discuss two previously unrecognized narrative sources for the Pantisocracy scheme: Edward Christian's pamphlet concerning the mutiny on the *Bounty* (1794) and George Keate's *Account of the Pelew Islands* (1788). Pantisocracy arises from an imaginary representation of America that assimilates it to the South Sea Islands, with their fabled luxuriance and remoteness from European politics. Coleridge was especially intrigued by the figure of Fletcher Christian, whose imaginary adventures he intended to write. Christian was regarded by many English radicals as a flawed,

---

[1] Richard Holmes, *Coleridge: Early Visions* (London, 1989), pp. 59–88.
[2] Nicholas Roe, *Wordsworth and Coleridge: The Radical Years* (Oxford, 1988), pp. 113–15, 180, 211–12. Another very useful and detailed, intellectual history of Pantisocracy is provided by J. R. MacGillivray, 'The Pantisocracy Scheme and Its Immediate Background', *Studies in English by Members of University College* [of Toronto], ed. M. W. Wallace (Toronto, 1931), pp. 131–69.

but noble, revolutionary hero, having led a bold mutiny against the tyrannical Captain Bligh and subsequently departed with his comrades on board the *Bounty* for a voyage of discovery and settlement in uncharted waters. To Coleridge and Southey, the exotic islands of the South Pacific seemed to offer a safe haven for revolutionary enthusiasm and an ideal terrain for the theoretical projection of Pantisocracy.

On a more concrete level of historical experience, the Pantisocracy scheme may be regarded as a fairly typical example of European expansionism, intellectually justified by an ideology of political equality and religious freedom, yet grounded at a more unconscious level in an economics of colonial exploitation. Coleridge and Southey aim to establish a 'colony' in the 'back settlements' of Pennsylvania, an area that is optimistically portrayed as temptingly virginal land, yet is known to be pre-occupied by hostile Indians, fierce tigers, slithering serpents, bloodthirsty mosquitoes, and escaped African slaves.[3] Internally, Pantisocracy is riven by the ominously alluring presence of a more intimate Other, the 'females' who are inconsistently represented as fully empowered equals or as recalcitrant vessels of ignorance and corruption, malignant Eves who portend the destruction of these innocent American Adams.

What Pantisocracy seeks to escape – the terrors and dilemmas of European history – it instead reinscribes within the text of its own geo-political unconscious. Although Coleridge claims to be 'wisely forgetful' of such threatening issues, Pantisocracy, nevertheless, witnesses the return of the political repressed, particularly in its reinscription of the rigid class structure that had been the target of relentless, political critique among republicans in England and France.[4] Coleridge's bitter quarrel with Southey over the propriety of bringing servants with them to America vividly illustrates the precariousness of the egalitarian ideal that was the formally declared political rationale for Pantisocracy.

---

[3] In a letter of 22 September 1794, Thomas Poole writes: 'Their opinion was that they should settle in a delightful part of the new back settlements; that each man would labor two or three hours in a day, the produce of which labor would, they imagine, be more than sufficient to support the colony.' Margaret E. Sandford, *Thomas Poole and His Friends*, 2 vols. (London, 1888), I, p. 97.

[4] The phrase 'wisely forgetful' occurs in the poem 'Pantisocracy', *The Collected Letters of Samuel Taylor Coleridge*, ed. Earl L. Griggs, 6 vols. (Oxford, 1956–71), I, p. 104. Hereafter cited as *Letters*.

'THE MOST DELIGHTFUL THEORY OF AN ISLAND PEOPLED BY MEN'

The idea of establishing a utopian community in some remote, uncivilized region was entertained by Southey even before his first meeting with Coleridge in June 1794. In February 1793, Southey sought to imagine a distant island that would be exempt from the economic injustice of contemporary society:

Why is there not some corner of the world where wealth is useless! . . . Is humanity so very vicious that society cannot exist without so many artificial distinctions linked together as we are in the great chain? Why should the extremity of the chain be neglected? At this moment I could form the most delightful theory of an island peopled by men who should be Xtians not Philosophers and where Vice only should be contemptible. Virtue only honourable where all should be convenient without luxury all satisfied without profusion.[5]

For Southey, the geographic location of this island is less important than its utter remoteness from the 'artificial distinctions' of the British class system. Southey's theoretical utopia will allow everyone to share in 'luxury' by eliminating class distinctions and by establishing a communal bond of fellowship among a select group of virtuous men. The main historical prototype for such an alternative society is mentioned in the next sentence of Southey's letter:

If the *Bounty* mutineers had not behaved so cruelly to their officers I should have been the last to condemn them. Otaheitia independant of its women had many inducements not only for the sailor but the philosopher. He might cultivate his own ground and trust himself and friends for his defence— he might be truly happy in himself and his happiness would be increased by communicating it to others. He might introduce the advantages and yet avoid the vices of cultivated society.[6]

Southey refers here to the events of the mutiny on the *Bounty*, rendered famous by the publication of Captain Bligh's *Narrative* in 1790 and by the capture and court martial of the mutineers in 1792. Before their capture, the mutineers had established a settlement on Tahiti and were enjoying its sybaritic splendours. Like many of his friends in the English radical movement, Southey sympathized deeply with the mutineers in their desperate attempt to escape the

[5] *New Letters of Robert Southey*, ed. Kenneth Curry, 2 vols. (New York, 1965), I, p. 19. Hereafter cited as *New Letters*.
[6] Ibid., I, p. 19.

tyranny of Captain Bligh; their mutiny (which occurred in 1789) was regarded as an English equivalent of the Fall of the Bastille. The mutineers, after being captured on the island of Tahiti and returned to England aboard the *Pandora*, were closely questioned by the wealthy and influential relatives of Fletcher Christian, their ringleader, who had evaded capture and sailed off into parts unknown on board the *Bounty*. Their testimony formed the basis for a pamphlet issued in 1794 by Edward Christian, the brother of the mutineer; he sought to exonerate Fletcher Christian by blackening the reputation of Captain Bligh.

Southey reveals the main source of his information about the *Bounty* mutiny in a letter of 1809, in which he explains why he called Captain Bligh 'notorious' in a recent *Quarterly Review* article on the South Sea Missions:

I called Captain Bligh *notorious* as the only way in which I could imply that he was a thorough rascal. It was an act of self-controul not to accompany the sentence with a bitter sarcasm, saying the Missionaries had a lucky escape, for his unendurable tyranny might have driven more Christians to desperation. I know a great deal of that affair of the *Bounty* from James Losh, who with Professor Christian (Poor Fletcher C's brother) went to the mutineers that were brought home, and collected their testimony concerning all the circumstances which led to it.[7]

James Losh was a Cambridge radical of the circle of William Frend. Southey may have been acquainted with him as early as 1793, when he first expressed interest in the *Bounty* affair, and Southey's deep admiration for Fletcher Christian (and corresponding contempt for Bligh) reflects a radical political reading of these historical events. For Southey, the idyllic settlement established by the *Bounty* mutineers on Tahiti, as described by James Losh, provided an attractive model for his own aspiration toward an ideal society.

For Coleridge, who was also well acquainted with Losh, the most imaginatively appealing aspect of the *Bounty* narrative was not the settlement on Tahiti, but the 'Adventures of CHRISTIAN, the mutineer', as Coleridge described the topic for a possible narrative work in about December 1795.[8] Fletcher Christian had sailed off into the

---

[7] Ibid., 1, p. 519. In this letter, Southey reports the rumour 'that Fletcher C[hristian] was within these few years in England and at his fathers house', and he asserts that 'if every man had his due Bligh would have had the halter instead of the poor fellows whom we brought from Taheite'. Southey returns to the topic of Christian's alleged presence in England in a subsequent letter (*New Letters*, 1, p. 521).

[8] Number 22 in a list of 'My Works', in *The Notebooks of Samuel Taylor Coleridge*, ed. Kathleen

vast Pacific Ocean in 1790, and his whereabouts remained a total mystery until the discovery of the Pitcairn Island settlement in 1808; but the purpose of Christian's final voyage was clearly recorded in the Court-Martial *Appendix* published by his brother. Christian asked his comrades to set him adrift in the *Bounty* so that he could seek refuge from his burden of revolutionary guilt:

I desire no one to stay with me, but I have one favour to request, that you will grant me the ship, tie the foresail, and give me a few gallons of water, and leave me to run before the wind, and I shall land upon the first island the ship drives to. I have done such an act that I cannot stay at Otaheite. I will never live where I may be carried home in disgrace to my family.[9]

When Christian found some shipmates to accompany him on this final voyage, he made the following proposal:

that they should go and seek an island, not before discovered, where they were not likely to be found, and having run the ship aground, and taken out every thing of value, and scuttled and broke up the ship, they should endeavour to make a settlement.[10]

The prospect of making a 'settlement' on a remote, uncharted island is evidently what appealed most strongly to Coleridge in the 'Adventures of CHRISTIAN, the mutineer', and the Pantisocracy project found its original inspiration in this revolutionary voyage of escape and colonization in the uncharted waters of the South Pacific.

Another account of Pacific exploration that contributed substantially to the genesis of Pantisocracy was George Keate's *Account of the Pelew Islands*.[11] Since I have elsewhere described the influence of this

Coburn, 5 vols. (Princeton, 1957–), I, p. 174, dated by the editor ?Dec 1795–Jan 1796. Hereafter cited as *Notebooks*. On the radical Cambridge circle that included Coleridge, William Frend, and James Losh, see Roe, *Wordsworth and Coleridge*, p. 19. Coleridge praises James Losh in a letter of February 1797, *Letters*, I, p. 308.

9   *Minutes of the Court-Martial held at Portsmouth, August 12, 1792, on Ten Persons Charged with Mutiny on Board His Majesty's Ship Bounty with an APPENDIX containing a full account of the real Causes and Circumstances of that unhappy transaction, the most material of which have been withheld from the public* (London, 1794; reprinted Melbourne, Australia, 1952), p. 73. These *Minutes* were transcribed from notes taken by Stephen Barney, attorney for the defence; the *Appendix* was written by Edward Christian, brother of the mutineer. John Livingston Lowes, *The Road to Xanadu: A Study in the Ways of the Imagination* (Boston, 1927; reprinted Princeton, 1986) discusses Coleridge's response to the mutiny on the *Bounty*, pp. 26–27 and 424 n.125. C. S. Wilkinson, in *The Wake of the Bounty* (London, 1953), argues that the Ancient Mariner's voyage is patterned after the voyage of the *Bounty*. On Wordsworth's involvement with Edward Christian, see Geoff Sanborn, 'The Madness of Mutiny: Wordsworth, the *Bounty* and *The Borderers*', *The Wordsworth Circle*, 23 (1992), pp. 35–42.

10   Christian, *Appendix*, p. 73.

11   George Keate, *An Account of the Pelew Islands, Situated in the Western Part of the Pacific Ocean. Composed from the Journals and Communications of Captain Henry Wilson, and some of His Officers,*

account on Coleridge, I will only summarize my findings here.[12] Keate tells the story of Captain Henry Wilson and the crew of the *Antelope*, a merchant vessel belonging to the British East India Company. During the summer of 1783, the *Antelope* was shipwrecked in the Pelew or Palos Islands, a remote chain in the Western Pacific. The survivors were warmly welcomed to the islands and visited with great ceremony by the local king, Abba Thulle. The king was particularly impressed by the fire power of the English muskets, cannon, and swivel guns, and he prevailed upon some of Captain Wilson's men to accompany him on military raids against neigh-bouring islands, where their muskets did 'great execution' upon his enemies.[13] After constructing a small sloop from the remains of their vessel, the English castaways bid a reluctant farewell to their generous hosts. Abba Thulle sent his son Lee Boo as an emissary to England with the departing seamen. Lee Boo travelled safely to England, but upon his arrival he contracted smallpox and died. The East India Company erected an elaborate monument over his grave in Rotherhithe churchyard; its inscription describes the circum-stances of his journey to England and ends with an affecting epitaph: 'Stop, Reader, stop! – let NATURE claim a Tear– / A Prince of *Mine*, LEE BOO, lies bury'd here'.[14]

The sad story of Lee Boo exercised a strong effect upon the poetic sensibility of Coleridge and his contemporaries. William Lisle Bowles, in the 1794 edition of his *Sonnets*, included a poem entitled 'Abba Thule', a dramatic monologue depicting the sorrow of the king waiting hopelessly for the return of his son.[15] Coleridge was deeply impressed by this poem; he praises it in a letter of 22 July 1794 as a poem of 'marked beauties'.[16] Bowles acknowledges Keate's account of the Pelew Islands on the title page of 'Abba Thule', and this reference may have encouraged Coleridge to consult that account, or at least to refresh his memory of the remote, idyllic paradise described in its pages. Coleridge's interest in the Pelew Island narrative is apparent in a poem of September 1794, 'To a Young Lady with a Poem on the French Revolution', which recalls

---

Who in August 1783, were there Shipwrecked, in the Antelope, a Packet Belonging to the Honourable East India Company (London, 1788).

[12] James C. McKusick, '"That Silent Sea": Coleridge, Lee Boo, and the Exploration of the South Pacific', *The Wordsworth Circle*, 24 (1993), pp. 102–6.

[13] Keate, *An Account*, p. 139.   [14] Ibid., p. 361.

[15] William Lisle Bowles, *Sonnets, with Other Poems*, 3rd edn (Bath, 1794).

[16] Coleridge, *Letters*, I, p. 94.

the tears that Coleridge shed at the grave of Lee Boo: 'My soul amid
the pensive twilight gloom / Mourn'd with the breeze, O Lee Boo!
o'er thy tomb'.[17] The death of Lee Boo evidently stands for the
inevitable destruction of innocence when it comes into contact with
a corrupt and decadent society.

For Coleridge, as for Southey, the initial appeal of Pantisocracy
was its offer of escape from British tyranny to an exotic paradise
resembling the tropical islands described by South Sea explorers
since the time of Cook. In his sonnet entitled 'Pantisocracy', first
recorded in a letter of 18 September 1794, Coleridge envisions an
ocean voyage away from decadent, European culture to an innocent,
pastoral retreat:

> No more my Visionary Soul shall dwell
> On Joys, that were! No more endure to weigh
> The Shame and Anguish of the evil Day,
> Wisely forgetful! O'er the Ocean swell
> Sublime of Hope I seek the cottag'd Dell,
> Where Virtue calm with careless step may stray,
> And dancing to the moonlight Roundelay
> The Wizard Passions weave an holy Spell.[18]

Southey, the addressee of this letter, is no doubt intended to read
these lines as an allusion to their intended emigration to the shores of
the Susquehanna River; but the fundamental object of their voyage
will be to exempt themselves from the entanglements and perplexities
of civilized life, becoming 'wisely forgetful' of revolutionary violence
while also achieving a greater degree of economic self-sufficiency.
The 'moonlight Roundelay' is reminiscent of the native dances
witnessed by such explorers as Bougainville and Cook on Tahiti, and
this phrase may recall the erotic associations of that island paradise,
where Fletcher Christian and his comrades found sexual satisfaction
in the eager arms of their Tahitian paramours. Only in such an
arcadian setting, where sexual promiscuity is not tainted with guilt, is
it possible that 'Virtue calm with careless step may stray'.

---

[17] *The Complete Poetical Works of Samuel Taylor Coleridge*, ed. Ernest Hartley Coleridge, 2 vols.
(Oxford, 1912), I, p. 64. In *The Watchman* (1 March 1796), Coleridge adds the following note
to this passage: 'Lee Boo, son of Abba Thule, chief of the Pelew Islands. He came over to
England with Captain Wilson, died of the small pox, and is buried in Greenwich Churchyard.' *The Watchman*, ed. Lewis Patton (Princeton, 1970), p. 27. When Coleridge reprinted
this note in the 1796 edition of his *Poems*, he added the phrase: 'See Keate's Account.' *Poems
on Various Subjects* (London, 1796), p. 37n.

[18] Coleridge, *Letters*, I, p. 104; also printed in *Poetical Works*, I, p. 68.

Coleridge was reading a great variety of exotic travel accounts in 1794, when he was seeking to discover a suitable locale for the Pantisocracy scheme. Along with the *Bounty* narratives and Keate's *Account,* he was reading the voyages of Cook, Dampier, and Hakluyt, the African explorations of James Bruce, and an assortment of American travel accounts. All of these accounts record the experience of colonial encounter between British explorers and indigenous peoples; such encounters typically entail an awareness of cultural and economic differences that provide the European observer with a comfortable sense of his own superiority, even when the 'primitive' circumstances of indigenous life are represented as idyllic. For Coleridge, however, the innate superiority of the European perspective is no longer taken for granted, and his desire to become 'wisely forgetful' in the pantisocratic paradise is motivated, in part, by his guilty knowledge of the destruction visited upon indigenous cultures by European settlers. From the banks of the Susquehanna to the shores of Tahiti, virgin land is made available for economic improvement only by the conquest of the peoples whom the explorers had portrayed as noble savages. Coleridge chooses to be 'wisely forgetful' of the colonial cruelty entailed by Pantisocracy because its hidden human cost is perhaps greater, and certainly more widespread and enduring, than that of the Terror in France which causes him such 'Anguish and Shame'. In struggling to articulate his utopian scheme, Coleridge was tempted to represent its location as a primeval wilderness devoid of inhabitants, although he was well aware of the violent history of encounter between Europeans and the indigenous peoples of the New World.

Coleridge's awareness of this violent history is most apparent in a passage from *Conciones ad Populum* (1795) describing the invasion of the Wyoming Valley by Loyalist troops in 1778, and the massacre of its peaceful inhabitants by mercenary Indians allied with the British. The Wyoming Valley, located on the Susquehanna River in northeastern Pennsylvania, was one of the most remote and isolated settlements at the time of the American War of Independence; Coleridge describes it as a paradisal refuge of agrarian bliss:

What the wisdom of Agur wished, the inhabitants of Wyoming enjoyed – they had neither Riches nor Poverty: their climate was soft and salubrious, and their fertile soil asked of these blissful Settlers as much labor only for their sustenance, as would have been otherwise convenient for their health. The Fiend, whose name was Ambition, leapt over into this Paradise – Hellhounds laid it waste. *English* Generals invited the Indians 'to banquet on blood': the savage Indians led by an Englishman attacked it. Universal massacre ensued. The Houses were destroyed: the Corn Fields burnt: and where under the broad Maple trees innocent Children used to play at noontide, there the Drinkers of human Blood, and the Feasters on human Flesh were seen in horrid circles, counting their scalps and anticipating their gains. The English Court bought Scalps at a fixed price![19]

Coleridge makes it clear that the 'savage Indians' are just as much the innocent victims of British tyranny as the American settlers, whose 'holy Rebellion' brought down this hideous onslaught. Less clear, but still discernible in his lurid prose style, is Coleridge's realization that the process of colonial settlement is intrinsically violent, since it necessarily involves the displacement of indigenous peoples. Every colonial endeavour, no matter how lofty its ideals, will eventually be forced to confront the consequences of this unsavoury reality.

'THE BOOK OF PANTISOCRACY'

The Book of Pantisocracy was first conceived by Southey and Coleridge as a foundational document for their emigrant community. As Coleridge described it in a letter of 29 August 1794, it would set forth 'their political creed, and the arguments by which they support and elucidate it', along with 'the code of contracts necessary for the internal regulation of the society; all of which will of course be submitted to the improvements and approbation of each component member'.[20] The most likely startingpoint for this intended Book of Pantisocracy was the pastoral escapism of Rousseau, whose essential argument, that man's inherently good nature is inevitably corrupted by civilization, provides the main premise for Pantisocracy, which seeks to make men good by removing all inducements to evil.

The unwritten Book of Pantisocracy became the earliest version of Coleridge's primary enabling fiction, his lifelong aspiration to write a philosophical *Magnum Opus*; and although this book was originally conceived as a social contract of the legalistic type envisioned by

---

[19] Coleridge, *Lectures 1795: On Politics and Religion*, ed. Lewis Patton and Peter Mann (Princeton, 1971), pp. 56–57. Hereafter cited as *Lectures 1795*. This massacre was the historical basis of Thomas Campbell's popular poem, *Gertrude of Wyoming* (London, 1809).

[20] Coleridge, *Letters*, I, p. 97.

Rousseau, it eventually developed into a more extended treatise that would challenge the major philosophers of the day. By October 1794, Coleridge was describing his treatise in rather ambitious terms: 'In the book of Pantisocracy I hope to have comprised all that is good in Godwin – of whom and of whose book I will write more fully in my next letter.'[21] Coleridge refers to William Godwin's *Political Justice* (1793), which provided a philosophical foundation for Pantisocracy in its melioristic view of social progress; Godwin firmly rejected revolutionary violence, but he remained optimistic about the possibility of evolutionary change in the social order. *Political Justice* was an especially seminal text for Southey, who endorsed it in a letter of December 1793. In September 1794, Southey declared himself a complete Godwinian, although Godwin's critique of marriage and his advocacy of free love might not have appealed to the sexually puritanical Southey, at whose insistence the pantisocratic adventurers were to be paired like Noachic animals, two and two, in connubial bliss aboard the American Ark. David Hartley's *Observations on Man* (1749) could have provided Coleridge with a more systematic psychological basis for his intended treatise, since Hartley regarded human consciousness as a straightforward association of ideas; he affirmed that people were capable of becoming disinterested moral agents if only they were provided, from an early age, with the right sensory stimuli. Pantisocracy, likewise, envisaged the establishment of virtue, not through the old, failed methods of moral exhortation and retributive justice, but through the simple and effective expedient of abolishing all individual property. Such 'Aspheterism' (as Coleridge termed it) would irrevocably remove any material incentive for men to do evil.

In developing a practical scheme for daily life in their utopian community, Coleridge may have consulted Keate's *Account of the Pelew Islands*. The main, political doctrine of Pantisocracy, 'the equal government of all', went hand in hand with the economic doctrine of Aspheterism, 'the generalization of individual property'; and the Pelew islands could provide a working model for both principles.[22] Keate describes the democratic process that evolved among the English castaways: they freely elected a leader whose decisions were

[21] Ibid., I, p. 115.
[22] Letter to Thomas Southey, 7 Sept 1794, in *New Letters*, I, p. 75. Coleridge first uses the words 'Pantocracy' [sic] and 'aspheterized' in a letter to Southey, 6 July 1794, in *Letters*, I, p. 84.

subject to ratification by majority vote.[23] Keate also describes the egalitarian arrangements among the Pelew Islanders in a section entitled 'PROPERTY'. According to Keate, 'the natives only possessed a property in their work and labour, but no absolute one in the soil, of which the king appeared to be the general proprietor'.[24] Through the equal apportionment of property among his subjects, the king ensured that no landed class could lord it over landless peasants; and the result was, in Keate's view, an agrarian utopia:

Every family occupied some land for their maintenance, necessity imposed this labour on them; and the portion of time which they could spare from providing for their natural wants, passed in the exercise of such little arts, as, while they kept them industrious and active, administered to their convenience and comfort.[25]

This is Aspheterism in its ideal form, with communal property arrangements imposing an equal burden of labour upon all members of society, while preventing economic exploitation and allowing leisure time for the development of individual talents. Keate describes the harmonious society that resulted from these egalitarian values:

And whilst a mild government, and an affectionate confidence, linked their little state in bonds of harmony, gentleness of manners was the natural result, and fixed a brotherly and disinterested intercourse among one another.[26]

Coleridge could easily envision a similar arrangement on the banks of the Susquehanna, although he was soon to discover that such arrangements are easier to establish in theory than in practice. The egalitarian ideal of brotherly love might easily give way to sibling rivalry, and the concept of male bonding failed to address the role that women should play in the daily life of the community.

The role of women in Pantisocracy remained intensely problematic. Whether women could be trusted to behave themselves, even in the absence of temptation, was an issue that would later contribute to the total unravelling of the Pantisocracy scheme. At the outset, however, Coleridge was deeply impressed by the egalitarian feminism of Mary Wollstonecraft, as expressed in her *Vindication of the*

---

[23] Keate, *An Account*, pp. 76–77. Keate states that 'when a merchant-ship is wrecked, all authority immediately ceases, and every individual is at full liberty to shift for himself' (p. 77n).

[24] Ibid., p. 297.   [25] Ibid., p. 297.   [26] Ibid., p. 334.

Rights of Woman (1792). He approvingly cites Wollstonecraft in *The Watchman* (1796) as an advocate of woman's intellectual and physical equality with man. In this *Watchman* essay on the early Germanic tribes, Coleridge discovers a primitive analogue to his own utopian scheme, since these people (according to Mallet's *Northern Antiquities*) accepted women as trusted companions within a broadly democratic form of social organization. 'The women of Germany were the free and equal companions of their husbands; they were treated by them with esteem and confidence, and consulted on every occasion of importance'.[27] These Germanic tribes were revolutionary insurgents against the Roman empire; Coleridge stresses their bold, warlike nature, which exerted itself to combat Roman tyranny and defend the freedom and autonomy of their native land. Drawing upon the work of Edward Gibbon, Coleridge regards the early Germanic society as a strenuous, self-sufficient alternative to the corruption and decadence of Rome. In the Book of Pantisocracy, women would doubtless have been exhorted to a lofty ideal of strength and self-sufficiency, although in practical terms their role in the community might, nevertheless, have been limited to the domestic sphere.

On his walking tour of Wales, in July 1794, Coleridge encountered a rural population that seemed to present another such primitive alternative to the dominant, imperial culture; he found the Welsh people bold, jovial, uninhibited, and eagerly responsive to his advocacy of democratic principles.[28] His awareness of liberal alternatives to the decadent urban culture of London, continued to grow during his first visit to Bristol in August 1794, where he discovered among the local intelligentsia (and especially in Thomas Poole) an unaccustomed tolerance for his radical ways of thought. During this visit, Coleridge also developed an intense appreciation for the poetry of Thomas Chatterton, whose pseudo-archaic *Rowley Poems* (1777) portray medieval Bristol at the height of its commercial and literary prowess. In the 'Monody on the Death of Chatterton', first published in September 1794, Coleridge praises Chatterton's remarkable powers of invention, hails him as a friend of liberty, and

---

[27] Coleridge, *Watchman*, p. 90.
[28] This Welsh walking tour is described in Coleridge, *Letters*, I, pp. 87–95. Coleridge's experience of the Welsh people was not entirely positive, and he later rejected Southey's suggestion that they set up their farming community in Wales (*Letters*, I, pp. 132 and 150). John Thelwall (in 1798) and Percy Shelley (in 1812) briefly settled in Wales, but soon came to regret it.

offers to include him among his chosen companions in pantisocratic exile.[29]

As an intellectual enterprise, Pantisocracy emerges from a Georgic ethos of redemptive labour in a remote yet idyllic setting. Like Virgil's hardworking farmers, the Pantisocrats would seek to establish their fraternal community in virtuous exile from the centre of imperial power. A more proximate, historical paradigm was provided by the Quaker community already well established in America; Eugenia Logan has shown how *The Journal of John Woolman*, which depicted the peaceful agrarian society of the Quakers in Pennsylvania, could have provided Coleridge with a working model for his scheme of an egalitarian community in exile.[30] In the aftermath of the American Revolution, the United States offered a safe haven for dissenting religious and political communities of all kinds. As an escapist response to the imperial dominance of Britain, Pantisocracy could flourish in the imaginary space of the republican American landscape as Coleridge constructed it from contemporary travel accounts.

The American traveller who exerted the most direct influence upon Coleridge was Joseph Priestley, an exiled radical Unitarian, who actually sought to establish a utopian community on the banks of the Susquehanna. Priestley openly declared his intention to provide refuge for the expected exodus of freedom-loving Britons who would emigrate to the New World in the wake of reactionary violence; had they joined him, Coleridge and Southey would have been among the vanguard of those pioneering free-thinkers who sought to establish a radical alternative to the corrupt society of England.[31] Acting on behalf of Priestley, Thomas Cooper described the Susquehanna as an ideal location for settlement in *Some Information Respecting America* (1794), a shrewd promotional tract that helped convince Coleridge and Southey to follow in Priestley's footsteps.[32]

---

[29] The octave of the 'Pantisocracy' sonnet was incorporated in the 'Monody on the Death of Chatterton', version of 1796 and later; this poem envisions Chatterton as the resident poet of the pantisocratic community. Coleridge, *Poetical Works*, I, pp. 130–31.

[30] Sister Eugenia Logan, 'Coleridge's Scheme of Pantisocracy and American Travel Accounts', *PMLA*, 45 (1930), p. 1078. For further discussion of refugee colonies in Pennsylvania, see Virginia M. Swartz, 'Xanadu on the Susquehannah – Almost: The Pantisocracy of Coleridge and Southey', *Pennsylvania English*, 12 (1986), pp. 19–29.

[31] Holmes, *Coleridge: Early Visions*, p. 90.

[32] Logan, 'Coleridge's Scheme of Pantisocracy', p. 1074, n. 31.

By late October 1794, the Book of Pantisocracy was becoming an ever more grandiose and unworkable treatise, and Coleridge was forced to confront the growing disjunction between his ideal conception of the community and the flawed compromise that had emerged from Southey's generous propensity for taking on board the American Ark a seemingly endless series of dependents and hangers-on. Coleridge was especially concerned that the narrow-mindedness and prejudice of these additional members might contaminate the intellectual purity of the entire community. In a letter of 23 October 1794, Coleridge asks Southey: 'But *must* our System be thus necessarily imperfect? I ask the question that I may know whether or not I should write the Book of Pantisocracy.'[33] Southey eventually quarrelled with Coleridge and abandoned the Pantisocracy scheme; but Coleridge still aspired to write the projected philosophical treatise.

As Coleridge continued to equip himself for the daunting philosophical task of writing the Book of Pantisocracy, he lost his initial enthusiasm for the crude, psychological materialism of Hartley and turned instead to the subjective idealism of George Berkeley. In a notebook entry of about March 1796, long after the breakdown of his collaboration with Southey, Coleridge still included among a list of '*My Works*' the intended treatise on 'Pantisocracy, or a practical Essay on the abolition of Individual Property'.[34] In another version of this list, Coleridge projected his 'Hymns to the Elements', which would culminate in 'a sublime enumeration of all the charms or Tremendities of Nature – then a bold avowal of Berkley's System!!!!!'[35] Although the relevance of Berkeley's philosophy to the Book of Pantisocracy is not immediately apparent, it seems likely that Coleridge knew of Berkeley's plan to establish a theological seminary in the New World. Berkeley's colonial project bears a distinct geographic resemblance to that of the Pantisocrats; he intends to establish a divinity school in the remote island of Bermuda, safe from marauding savages and from the allurements of maritime commerce, self-sustaining in all material needs, with a serene atmosphere conducive to quiet study and meditation. Unlike the free-thinking symposium planned by Coleridge, however, Berkeley's seminary is projected upon a strictly authoritative and hierarchical model of education, intended 'to convert the Negroes of our

---

[33] Coleridge, *Letters*, I, p. 119.
[34] Coleridge, *Notebooks* I, p. 161, dated by the editor circa February-March 1796.
[35] Ibid., p. 74.

plantations' so that they would 'become better Slaves by being Christians', and to brainwash 'the Children of savage *Americans*' into an unquestioning acceptance of Christianity and Western values.[36] The Pantisocrats would presumably have taken a more progressive approach to the education of their children.

'OYSTERIZED BY A TIGER'

The pantisocratic pioneers anticipated certain difficulties in coping with the external environment of their community. The most frightful threats were imagined by Southey, who returns obsessively to scenes of encounter with ferocious beasts and hostile Indians. In a 'reverie' of December 1793, Southey envisions himself as an American Adam whose garden is invaded by snakes, tigers, and cannibals:

Fancy only me in America; imagine my ground uncultivated since the creation, and see me wielding the axe, now to cut down the tree, and now the snakes that nestled in it. . . . So thus your friend will realize the romance of Cowley, and even outdo the seclusion of Rousseau; till at last comes an ill-looking Indian with a tomahawk, and scalps me, – a most melancholy proof that society is very bad, and that I shall have done very little to improve it! So vanity, vanity will come from my lips, and poor Southey will either be cooked for a Cherokee, or oysterized by a tiger.[37]

Again, in a letter of 22 August 1794, Southey foresees himself as the victim of hostile Indians: 'Should the resolution of others fail, Coleridge and I will go together, and either find repose in an Indian wig-wam – or from an Indian tomahawk'.[38] Such stereotypical scenes of encounter with the colonial Other clearly embody an element of humorous self-caricature, but they also allow Southey to express a profound sense of anxiety in the face of the unknown American wilderness.

Coleridge shared this colonial anxiety, although he was less inclined to such melodramatic expressions of it. In September 1794, he spent several evenings in company with an American land agent, seeking assurances that the Susquehanna Valley enjoyed 'security from hostile Indians'. He also reported that the land agent 'never

---

[36] 'A Proposal for the better supplying of Churches in our foreign Plantations' (1725), in *The Works of George Berkeley, Bishop of Cloyne*, ed. A. A. Luce and T. E. Jessop, 9 vols. (London, 1948–57), VII, pp. 346–47.

[37] *Letters of Robert Southey: A Selection*, ed. Maurice H. Fitzgerald (London, 1912), p. 4.

[38] *New Letters*, I, p. 70.

saw a *Byson* in his life – but has heard of them . . . – The Musquitos
are not so bad as our Gnats – and after you have been there a little
while, they don't trouble you much'.[39] Coleridge's inquiries emerge
from a practical concern with the natural resources available in
Pennsylvania, but on another level they reveal his awareness of the
New World as a place already pre-occupied by its original inhabitants, and his underlying anxiety about 'trouble' with Indians, bison,
and mosquitos.

As the Pantisocracy scheme began to take definite shape, Southey
learned to cope with his anxieties about the colonial Other by
incorporating them within a cultural framework of rhetorical figures
and biblical archetypes. In a letter of 3 September 1794, he imagines
himself as Adam in *Paradise Lost*, setting forth to conquer an
unknown world in the security of providential guidance:

Like Adam I may 'drop some natural tears – but dry them soon'. Past
sorrows will be obliterated in anticipating future pleasure. When Coleridge
and I are sawing down a tree we shall discuss metaphysics; criticise poetry
when hunting a buffalo, and write sonnets whilst following the plough.[40]

Here again, Southey's jocular tone betrays an underlying anxiety of
colonial encounter, and he perhaps unwittingly reveals the discursive
paradigm that will enable the Pantisocrats to establish imperial
dominance over the uncanny otherness of the American landscape.
The primeval forest will be deconstructed by Western metaphysics;
the buffalo will be decimated by literary criticism; and the virgin
land will be reconfigured by poetic tropes. Language will provide an
invincible means of mastery over the colonial Other.

'THE MINDS OF OUR WOMEN'

The problematic presence of women among the Pantisocrats drove
them to extremes of erotic fantasy and patriarchal terror. Shortly
after meeting Coleridge and hearing the full details of the Pantisocracy scheme, Thomas Poole cannily observed: 'The regulations
relating to the females strike them as the most difficult; whether the
marriage contract shall be dissolved if agreeable to one or both
parties, and many other circumstances, are not yet determined.'[41]

---

[39] Coleridge, *Letters*, I, p. 99.
[40] *New Letters*, I, p. 72. Southey quotes Milton, *Paradise Lost*, xii, line 645.
[41] Sandford, *Thomas Poole and His Friends*, I, p. 97.

The view that the 'females' needed to be 'regulated' was common to both of the principal Pantisocrats, and it eventually became an extremely vexed issue between them. Southey was always the more prim and virginal of the two men, while Coleridge, during his college years, was said to be more 'promiscuous', although the precise, biographical details of this alleged behaviour have never been established. In private conversation, Coleridge stated 'that Southey was a virgin, and sternly "converted" him back from sexual promiscuity'.[42] It was Southey who held firmly to the view that each of the twelve Pantisocrats should be accompanied by his wife to the New World; no single men need apply, although in Coleridge's case Southey was willing to procure a spouse if needed. (Robert Lovell had already married Mary Fricker in 1794, and Southey was secretly engaged to Edith Fricker; it would make a very nice family arrangement indeed if Coleridge were to marry Sarah Fricker. Southey eventually set up housekeeping with all three Fricker sisters in Keswick, following the death of Lovell in 1796 and Coleridge's departure to Malta in 1804.)

Coleridge possibly entertained sexual fantasies about the pantisocratic community; if all goods were held in common, why not share the wives as well? From a Godwinian perspective, the marriage contract was just another corrupt, social institution, and to a roving bachelor like Coleridge, the sight of 'a number of fine Women bathing promiscuously with men and boys – *perfectly* naked!' doubtless held a certain erotic appeal.[43] Like these nude Welsh bathers, the Pantisocrats might seek to recapture a primitive or Edenic, sexual innocence by divesting themselves of cumbersome garments: 'But seriously speaking, where sexual Distinctions are least observed, Men & women live together in greatest purity. Concealment sets the Imagination a working, and, as it were, *cantharidizes* our desires.'[44] This prospective, American Adam could look forward to 'promiscuous' nude bathing in the pristine waters of the Susquehanna, and if he were excessively aroused, he might always calm himself with the reflection that such practices were conducive to the 'greatest purity' in sexual relations.

Eventually, however, Coleridge accepted Southey's decision to allow only married couples on board the American Ark. For

[42] Holmes, *Coleridge: Early Visions*, p. 63, citing Bodleian MS Abinger C604/3.
[43] Coleridge, *Letters*, I, p. 93.   [44] Ibid., p. 93.

Southey, the presence of the 'females' would exert a softening influence, a gentle corrective to the harsh, masculine energy needed to hack farmland out of the pathless wilderness. In a letter of September 1794, Southey gloats possessively about the virtues of the Fricker sisters, and he exults in the way they will establish a homosocial bond between the two men: 'Our females are beautiful amiable and accomplished – and I shall then call Coleridge my brother in the real sense of the word.'[45] An underlying theme in the attitudes of both men is the idea that women offer a virgin terrain that needs to be civilized, domesticated, and filled with useful knowledge. Coleridge exhorts Southey 'to be strengthening the minds of the Women and stimulating them to literary Acquirements'.[46] Mere intellectual assent to the doctrines of Pantisocracy is not enough: 'The *Heart* should have *fed* upon the *truth*, as Insects on a Leaf – till it be tinged with the colour, and shew it's food in every the minutest fibre'.[47] He is writing the Book of Pantisocracy as a foundational text for the entire community, but he intends it especially as 'an advantage to the *Minds* of our Women'.[48] This view of 'our Women' as empty vessels for masculine wisdom exists in uneasy tension with the more positive conception of women as active partners in the pantisocratic enterprise.

As their plans developed, these two bachelors began to feel a distinct anxiety about the prospect of uncontrolled females prowling in the midst of their 'patriarchal' community.[49] Their wives, lacking sophisticated, university education, might fail to grasp the intellectual attraction of subsistence farming in the American wilderness, and they might even yearn for the 'individual Comforts' of England; therefore, it would be each man's duty to ensure that the women were immersed in the 'generous enthusiasm of Benevolence' and 'saturated with the Divinity of Truth'. Coleridge worried that 'in the present state of their minds, . . . the *Mothers* will tinge the Mind of the Infants with prejudications'.[50] Coleridge's anxiety about the 'regulations relating to the females' became even more extreme when Southey proposed the addition of two elderly widows, Mrs.

---

[45] *New Letters*, I, p. 72.   [46] Coleridge, *Letters*, I, p. 119.   [47] Ibid., p. 115.
[48] Ibid., p. 115.
[49] Coleridge uses the term 'patriarchal' to describe Pantisocracy in *The Friend*, ed. Barbara E. Rooke (Princeton, 1969), I, p. 223: 'Our little society, in its second generation was to have combined the innocence of the patriarchal age with the knowledge and genuine refinements of European culture.'
[50] Coleridge, *Letters*, I, p. 119.

Southey and Mrs. Fricker, to their ideal community. '*That* Mrs Fricker – we shall have her teaching the Infants *Christianity*, – I mean, that mongrel whelp that goes under it's name – teaching them by stealth in some ague-fit of Superstition!'[51] The serpent in the pantisocratic garden will be a woman. Coleridge repeated to Southey the 'prophecy' of a Cambridge acquaintance that 'your *women* [will lack] sufficient strength of mind, liberality of heart, or vigilance of Attention – *They* will spoil it!'[52]

Such overt misogyny is clearly in conflict with the more generous ideal of female equality and self-sufficiency that Coleridge admired in the work of Mary Wollstonecraft, and its stubborn persistence within the discourse of Pantisocracy suggests that Coleridge's elaborate scheme was in danger of foundering upon an internal contradiction. If women are to become the fully empowered intellectual companions of men, they must be granted an equal degree of autonomy and freedom. Yet the underlying colonial paradigm of Pantisocracy, and specifically its conception of America as an untrammelled virgin landscape, necessarily presents women with a far more limited range of behavioural options. If they refuse to be meek, submissive brides, they threaten to become devouring, Geraldine-like serpents. Coleridge found himself unable to resolve these conflicts, or even to confront them openly, and the Book of Pantisocracy remained unwritten.

'THE PEACEFUL INHABITANTS OF A FERTILE SOIL'

An even more fundamental contradiction within the project of Pantisocracy became apparent when Southey suggested to Coleridge, in October 1794, that they bring labourers with them from England to do the heavy farming work. From Southey's point of view, these labourers would enjoy perfect 'equality' with the rest of the community: 'Let them dine with us and be treated with as much equality as they would wish – but perform that part of Labor for which their Education has fitted them.'[53] But for Coleridge, the creation of an indentured servant class was incompatible with the egalitarian ideal of Pantisocracy, and he objected very strongly to the proposal: '*Southey* should not have written this Sentence – my Friend,

---

[51] Ibid., p. 123.   [52] Ibid., p. 123.
[53] Southey, letter of October 1794, cited by Coleridge, *Letters*, I, p. 113.

my noble and high-souled Friend should have said – to his Dependents – Be my Slaves – and ye shall be my Equals.'[54] Coleridge
could not abide the hypocrisy of treating the servants as 'equals'
while making them do all the hard work; from his point of view, this
situation would be the moral equivalent of slavery:

> To be employed in the Toil of the Field while *We* are pursuing philosophical
> Studies – can Earldoms or Emperorships boast so huge an Inequality? Is
> there a human Being of so torpid a Nature, as that placed in our Society he
> would not feel it? – A *willing* Slave is the worst of Slaves – His *Soul* is a
> Slave.[55]

Coleridge regarded this issue as absolutely fundamental to the
conception of Pantisocracy; indeed, if Southey persisted in his
intention to bring servants, Coleridge felt it would be impossible to
write the Book of Pantisocracy: 'I can not describe our System in
circumstances *not* true: – nor can I *omit* any circumstances that *are*
true. Can I *defend* all that are *now* true? Is it not a pity, that a System
so impregnable in itself should be thus blasted?'[56] It was this issue,
more than any other, that led to the final quarrel between the two
men and the ultimate breakdown of their utopian scheme.

Coleridge's indignant response to Southey's proposal might seem
to suggest that it was an incongruous addition to an otherwise
perfect system; but, in fact, this proposal merely brought into view
an inconsistency that had been lurking in their project from the very
beginning. In his American 'reverie' of December 1793, Southey
imagines himself ensconced in a rustic cottage with 'my only
companion some poor negro whom I have bought on purpose to
emancipate'.[57] Southey's concept of 'emancipation' is curiously
paradoxical; it entails the purchase of another human being, not to
set him free, but in order that he may serve as a companion in the
shared effort of taming the wilderness. The relevant literary arche-
type would be Robinson Crusoe and his man Friday, who was so
grateful at being 'rescued' that he agreed to serve as Crusoe's slave
for the rest of the narrative. Southey's 'poor negro' appears to share
a similar fate; and thus it seems that Southey's concept of Pantisocracy always envisaged the existence of a clandestine, servant class,
comprised of 'these Unequal Equals – these helot Egalité-s', as
Coleridge contemptuously called them.[58] While it is possible to

[54] Coleridge, *Letters*, i, p. 113.   [55] Ibid., p. 122.   [56] Ibid., p. 120.
[57] *Letters of Robert Southey: A Selection*, p. 4.   [58] Coleridge, *Letters*, i, p. 114.

regard this argument as merely the result of a misunderstanding between the two men, it might more accurately be conceived as a profound contradiction in the colonial project of Pantisocracy, which seeks to escape the corrupt society of Europe but cannot avoid reinscribing the existing hierarchies of race, gender, and social class within its own imaginary community.

As his political consciousness developed through the 1790s, Coleridge became more generally aware of the destructive effects of the European, colonial project in remote parts of the world. His evolving attitude toward the conquest of indigenous peoples is apparent in his *Lecture on the Slave Trade*, delivered in Bristol on 16 June 1795.[59] In this lecture, Coleridge denounces the unspeakable cruelty of the African slave-trade, its enormous, human cost in the suffering and death of millions of slaves, captured in tribal warfare and transported to the West Indies, and its genocidal destruction of the African tribes; he also denounces the misery and death of British seamen on these harsh voyages.

As his lecture on the slave-trade approaches its rhetorical climax, Coleridge evokes an idyllic scene of communal existence in the remote parts of Africa; this passage is of special interest because it attributes to these indigenous people all of the cultural values that the failed Pantisocracy scheme was supposed to provide:

The Africans, who are situated beyond the contagion of European vice – are innocent and happy – the peaceful inhabitants of a fertile soil, they cultivate their fields in common and reap the crop as the common property of all. Each family like the peasants in some parts of Europe, spins weaves, sews, hunts, fishes and makes basket fishing tackle & the implements of agriculture, and this variety of employment gives an acuteness of intellect to the negro which the mechanic whom the division of Labour condemns to one simple operation is precluded from attaining.[60]

Coleridge derived his information on Africa from a book entitled *An Essay on Colonization*; this passage evidently caught his eye because it suggested to him that the idyllic community intended by Pantisocracy, no matter how unattainable by sophisticated Europeans, might

---

[59] Coleridge, *Lectures 1795*, pp. 231–51. Coleridge later revised and published this lecture in *The Watchman* (25 March 1796), pp. 130–40. The slave-trade and its possible relevance to 'The Rime of the Ancient Mariner' is examined by J. R. Ebbatson, 'Coleridge's Mariner and the Rights of Man', *Studies in Romanticism*, 11 (1972), pp. 171–206.

[60] Coleridge, *Lectures 1795*, p. 240. The editor notes that this passage, in Southey's hand, derives from C. B. Wadström, *An Essay on Colonization* (1794–95), which Coleridge had borrowed from the Bristol library.

actually exist among the indigenous peoples of the world. As a colonial project, Pantisocracy inevitably foundered under the weight of its internal contradictions; but as an ideal of equality among people of diverse social class and ethnic origin, it would survive as one of the most enduring legacies of the Romantic imagination.

CHAPTER 8

Darkness visible? Race and representation in Bristol abolitionist poetry, 1770–1810

Alan Richardson

At the very time when Romanticists are at last beginning to address issues of race, particularly the relation between Romantic-era culture and the formation of modern racist categories, 'race' has widely come under attack as a viable critical term.[1] Although the debate among theorists and scholars of African-American literature over the status of 'race' has been simmering for over a decade now, it has recently received new impetus (and animus) through an exchange in *The Black Scholar* initiated by Jon Michael Spencer's polemical attack on what he calls 'the postmodern conspiracy to explode racial identity'.[2] Spencer is responding in part to Kwame Anthony Appiah's critique, developed throughout *In My Father's House* (1992), of the notion of a 'racial essence' as itself implicated in the history of racism and grounded in an ultimately self-defeating 'biologizing of what *is* culture, ideology'. The 'truth is', Appiah states, 'that there are no races'.[3] For Spencer, Appiah's position undermines attempts to foster a 'self-reconciliatory sense of racial pride' and the 'quest for racial equity'; for Molefi Kete Asante, it even supports the 'demonization of African identity'.[4] Walter Benn Michaels extends the debate to take in 'cultural identity' and the claims of 'cultural' criticism generally, both of which depend, for Michaels, on the 'earlier notion of racial identity' deconstructed by Appiah: rather than offering a critique of racism, the 'modern

[1] A shorter version of this chapter appeared under a slightly different title in *The Wordsworth Circle* for 1996; I thank the editor, Marilyn Gaull, for her careful reading and for permission to reprint material from the earlier version.
[2] Jon Michael Spencer, 'Trends of Opposition to Multiculturalism', *The Black Scholar*, 23 (1993), pp. 2–5 (p. 2).
[3] Kwame Anthony Appiah, *In My Father's House: Africa in the Philosophy of Culture* (New York, 1992), pp. 13, 30, 45.
[4] Spencer, 'Trends of Opposition', p. 5; Molefi Kete Asante, 'Racing to Leave the Race: Black Postmodernists Off-Track', *The Black Scholar*, 23 (1993), pp. 50–51 (p. 51).

concept of culture' is itself 'a form of racism'.[5] Diana Fuss, on the other hand, holds that 'race' remains a viable, usefully flexible, and critically efficacious term, arguing that we can continue to 'work with "race" as a political concept *knowing* it is a biological fiction', and seconding Houston Baker's contention that a position – such as Appiah's – that dismantles 'race' as a biological category but fails to account for its 'continuing political efficacy' remains inadequate.[6]

My purpose here is not to engage in the debate on 'race' and culture, but rather to keep the contours of that debate in mind while examining the representation of race in the critical years 1770–1810 (from just before the Somerset decision in 1772 to just after the passing of the Slave Trade Bill in 1807) in the abolitionist poetry of four writers closely associated with Bristol: Thomas Chatterton, Hannah More, Anne Yearsley, and Robert Southey. The current revaluation of race as a conceptual category serves to remind us that race has been from the beginning an ideological construct, 'contradictory, disruptive and already deconstructed' as Robert Young has recently argued.[7] Even within a forty-year period in one English slaving port, the representation of race is most remarkable for its mutability and lack of coherence. During these years, as modern racial categories were being formulated, notions of race remained fluid, frequently at odds, and continually subject to further transformation under pressure from social struggles over the legal status of slaves, the legitimacy of the slave-trade, and the relation of skin colour to both of these issues.[8] Although conventional accounts of British Romanticism have shown little interest in the slave-trade (dominated by Britain during this period), colonial slavery, or the Abolition movement, these were unquestionably among the most pressing public issues of the late eighteenth and early nineteenth centuries.[9] It would have been highly unlikely for any but the most

[5] Walter Benn Michaels, 'Race into Culture: A Critical Genealogy of Cultural Identity', *Critical Inquiry*, 18 (1992), pp. 655–85 (pp. 658, 683). Cf. Robert Young's contention that 'culture has always been racially constructed' in *Colonial Desire: Hybridity in Theory, Culture, and Race* (London, 1995), p. 54.

[6] Diana Fuss, *Essentially Speaking: Feminism, Nature and Difference* (New York, 1989), p. 91.

[7] Young, *Colonial Desire*, p. 27.

[8] Anthony J. Barker, *The African Link: British Attitudes to the Negro in the Era of the Atlantic Slave Trade, 1550–1807* (London, 1978).

[9] See Robin Blackburn, *The Overthrow of Colonial Slavery, 1776–1848* (London, 1988) and Linda Colley, *Britons: Forging the Nation, 1707–1807* (New Haven, 1992) for relevant accounts of the historical background. Two helpful early studies of anti-slavery and British literature, long disregarded by Romanticists, are Wylie Sypher, *Guinea's Captive Kings: British Anti-Slavery*

isolated Briton to remain unaware of the slave-trade debate in the wake of the massive Abolition campaign of 1788–89, and difficult not to ponder one's own stand on and potential implication in the colonial slave system at a time when sugaring one's tea had become a politically significant act and the Abolitionist emblem had become ubiquitous, adorning hairpins and snuff boxes, bracelets and (of course) tea sets.[10] The Abolitionist campaign forced the average British citizen at least to consider connections between his or her daily life and the politics and economics of a growing colonial and mercantile empire.

Such considerations would have been still more pressing in Bristol where, as a phrase common by the early nineteenth century had it, 'every brick in the city had been cemented with a slave's blood'.[11] Bristol had become Britain's second largest city in the early eighteenth century through trading in 'slaves and sugar'; by the 1770s, however, it had been overtaken by Liverpool as 'Europe's chief slaving town' and, by the 1780s Bristol's share in the slave-trade was falling off significantly.[12] Toward the end of the century Bristol had all of the taint of the slave-trade and a rapidly diminishing share of the profit. The atrocities of the Middle Passage had become the 'talk of Bristol' when Clarkson began collecting evidence for the Abolition campaign in the 1780s: Bristol merchant seamen had lost their callousness and had to get themselves (or be made) 'dead drunk before they would sign on' with a slaver. At the same time, slaving and West-Indian planter interests had become so deeply entrenched in Bristol's political and economic hierarchy (the two overlapping groups could boast at least one mayor from among their numbers and had helped establish the local banking industry) that church bells were rung throughout the city and fireworks set off when Wilberforce's Abolition Bill failed in 1791.[13] For the Bristol poet, the

Literature of the xviii Century (Chapel Hill, 1969) and Eva Beatrice Dykes, *The Negro in English Romantic Thought: A Study in Sympathy for the Oppressed* (Washington, 1942); a recent study that represents the current renewal of interest in these topics is Joan Baum, *Mind-Forg'd Manacles: Slavery and the English Romantic Poets* (North Haven, 1994).

[10] Blackburn, *The Overthrow of Colonial Slavery*, p. 139; see also Hugh Honour, *The Image of the Black in Western Art* vol. iv: *From the American Revolution to World War I*, part 1: *Slaves and Liberators* (Cambridge, Massachusetts, 1989), pp. 62–66.

[11] Peter Fryer, *Staying Power: The History of Black People in Britain Since 1504* (Atlantic Highlands, 1984), p. 33.

[12] Ibid., pp. 33, 69; Angus Calder, *Revolutionary Empire: The Rise of the English-Speaking Empires from the Fifteenth Century to the 1780s* (New York, 1981), p. 631.

[13] Fryer, *Staying Power*, pp. 38–40, 56–57, 69.

slave-trade was an all but unavoidable theme and Africa was at once an exotic and uncannily familiar locale.

By beginning this brief and necessarily selective survey of Bristol anti-slavery poems with the 'pre-Romantic' Chatterton, I hope to throw into relief the connections between modern racist ideologies and the literary discourses generally termed 'Romantic' raised by students of racism from Leon Poliakov to Martin Bernal. It is generally agreed that racism in its modern form – what Appiah calls 'racialism,' others 'scientific' or 'pseudo-scientific' racism, and Robin Blackburn simply the 'new racism' – emerges in Britain in the late eighteenth and early nineteenth centuries, the very 'period' conventionally associated with Romanticism.[14] How much should be made, particularly by those engaged in redefining and re-evaluating Romanticism, of this coincidence? Increasing British domination of the slave-trade, the reliance on slave labour in the 'sugar islands', anxieties inspired by slave revolts (including the successful revolution led by slaves in Haiti), and the increasingly paternalist tenor of nineteenth-century British imperialist ideology have all been seen as contexts for the emergence of modern racism and racial categories without reference to Romanticism.[15] Other scholars, however, have found Romantic discourse to be at least complicit in the 'new racism', citing the emphasis on 'blood', 'soil', and climate associated with Rousseau, Herder, and Wordsworth, Walter Scott's popularization of a racialized philosophy of history, and conceptions of 'inbred national character and genius' found throughout European Romantic writing.[16] More recently, Laura Doyle has delineated an emergent 'racial-patriarchal rhetoric' within canonical Romanticism that anticipates the racialization of national identity within nine-

[14] Appiah, *In My Father's House*, p. 13; Nancy L. Stepan, *The Idea of Race in Science: Great Britain 1800–1960* (London, 1982), pp. 1–19; George M. Frederickson, *The Black Image in the White Mind: The Debate on Afro-American Character and Destiny, 1817–1914* (New York, 1971), p. ix; Blackburn, *The Overthrow of Colonial Slavery*, pp. 154–56; Young, *Colonial Desire*, pp. 91–92.

[15] P. J. Marshall and Glyndwr Williams, *The Great Map of Mankind: British Perceptions of the World in the Age of Enlightenment* (London, 1982), p. 228; Dorothy Hammond and Alta Jablow, *The Africa That Never Was: Four Centuries of British Writing About Africa* (New York, 1970), pp. 21–26; James Walvin, *England, Slaves, and Freedom, 1776–1838* (Jackson, 1986), p. 77; C. A. Bayly, *Imperial Meridian: The British Empire and the World, 1780–1830* (London, 1989), p. 109.

[16] Martin Bernal, *Black Athena: The Afroasiatic Roots of Classical Civilization*, vol. I: *The Fabrication of Ancient Greece 1785–1985* (New Brunswick, New Jersey, 1987), pp. 28, 204–6; Benedict Anderson, *Imagined Communities: Reflections on the Origin and Spread of Nationalism*, 2nd edn (London, 1991), p. 60; Leon Poliakov, *The Aryan Myth: A History of Racist and Nationalist Ideas in Europe*, tr. Edmund Howard (New York, 1974), p. 50; Frederickson, *The Black Image*, p. 97; Young, *Colonial Desire*, p. 42.

teenth-century eugenics, and David Lloyd has found a 'certain congruence' between the privileging of symbol over allegory in Romantic theories of literature and the shift in 'post-Enlightenment' theories of race from a 'system of arbitrary marks to the ascription of natural signs'.[17]

If Romantic discourse naturalizes nation and race, however, Enlightenment discourse manifests racist tendencies of its own. Historians of racism have generally contrasted the crude 'ethnocentrism' of pre-Enlightenment, European representations of non-European groups with the ways in which racial difference becomes regularized and hierarchized within the classificatory schemes, characteristic of Enlightenment thought.[18] Notorious expressions of eighteenth-century, cultural racism, such as David Hume's, or of proto-'scientific' racism such as Edward Long's, however, may be extreme and unrepresentative, as Anthony Barker argues throughout *The African Link*. Winthrop Jordan concurs that, until the end of the century, the tradition of Christian universalism constituted a 'rock-hard shelf' of belief in the full humanity of Africans, and that the 'handful of assertions to the contrary were not taken seriously'.[19] Whereas some historians have seen Enlightenment secularism as eroding this core belief in a shared human identity beneath the accident of physiological difference, others have, to the contrary, read Enlightenment universalism as corroborating and helping to maintain it.[20] Indeed, the convergence of Enlightenment conceptions of a universal human essence and a relativistic approach to cultural differences could, on occasion, give rise to remarkably non-Eurocentric arguments against notions of white racial superiority, although such arguments were generally qualified in one manner or another.

[17] Laura Doyle, *Bordering on the Body: The Racial Matrix of Modern Fiction and Culture* (New York, 1994), p. 69; David Lloyd, 'Race Under Representation', *Oxford Literary Review*, 13 (1991), pp. 62–93 (p. 90).

[18] Winthrop D. Jordan, *White Over Black: American Attitudes Toward the Negro, 1550–1812* (Chapel Hill, 1968), p. 25; Nicholas Hudson, 'From "Nation" to "Race": The Origin of Racial Classification in Eighteenth-Century Thought', Eighteenth-Century Studies, 29 (1996), pp. 247–64.

[19] Jordan, *White Over Black*, pp. 230–31.

[20] Ibid., p. 217 and David Brion Davis, *The Problem of Slavery in Western Culture* (Ithaca, 1966), p. 446, as opposed to Barker, *The African Link*, p. 198 and Frederickson, *The Black Image*, p. 97. Young has recently raised the stakes of this debate by pitting the 'radical egalitarian' implications of Enlightenment universalism against the overvaluation of 'difference' found in nineteenth-century – and contemporary – cultural theory (pp. 32–33, 91–92).

In *The Theory of Moral Sentiments* (1759), for example, Adam Smith rehearses an argument that, conceptions of beauty being relative to 'different climates' and 'different customs', a white complexion is legitimately considered a 'shocking deformity upon the coast of Guinea', whereas 'thick lips and a flat nose are a beauty'; but this argument, attributed to the 'learned Jesuit', Buffier, is one that Smith cannot quite bring himself to endorse.[21] In a paper for *The Idler* of the same year, Sir Joshua Reynolds argues that habit and custom make, 'in a sense, white black, and black white': 'It is custom alone determines our preference of the colour of the Europeans to the Aethiopians, and they, for the same reason, prefer their own colour to ours.'[22] Yet for Reynolds (as also for Buffier in Smith's paraphrase) this proposition depends upon seeing the 'black and white nations' as at least 'different species' if not 'different kinds', suggesting how Enlightenment relativism may eventually become twisted to support the 'biological' racism of the nineteenth century. A speech, reprinted in *The Gentleman's Magazine* for January, 1735, allegedly by a 'Free Negro' of one of the 'most considerable' West Indian colonies, contends that vaunted white 'superiority' proceeds from 'Education and Accident, not Difference of Genius':

What wild imaginary Superiority of Dignity has their sickly *whiteness* to boast of, when compared with our Majestic Glossiness! If there's Merit in Delicacy, we have Skins as soft as their velvets: In Manliness, consider your Shape, your Strength, and your Movement! All easier, firmer, and more graceful. Let a *White* Man expose his feeble Face to the Winds; or Heat at High-Noon, as we do. Will he bear it too, as we do? No: he will be sick; pale and red, by Turns; be haggard and Sun-burnt.[23]

Chatterton lent a markedly similar rhetoric to the black speakers of his *African Eclogues* (1770). While the tacit acceptance of European, cultural superiority ('Education') points to problems we will encounter in Chatterton as well, the willingness of Smith, Reynolds, and the writer in *The Gentleman's Magazine* to at least entertain a relativist argument against white racial superiority contrasts markedly with the dubious speculations of a Romantic author like Coleridge, who retails the myth that tortured slaves find comfort in

[21] Adam Smith, *The Theory of Moral Sentiments*, eds. D. D. Raphael and A. L. Macfie (Indianapolis, 1982), p. 199.

[22] Sir Joshua Reynolds, letter to *The Idler*, 10 November 1759, in Samuel Johnson, *The Idler and The Adventurer*, eds. W. J. Bate, John M. Bullitt, and L. F. Powell (New Haven, 1963), p. 257.

[23] 'The SPEECH of *Moses Bon Saam*, a Free Negro, to the revolted Slaves in one of the most considerable Colonies of the *West Indies*', *The Gentleman's Magazine*, 5 (1735), p. 21.

the eventual whiteness of their scars (symptomatic of their 'Love of *white*' generally) in support of 'permanent Principles of *Beauty* as distinguishable from Association'.[24] One might also contrast the well-known repugnance of both Coleridge and Charles Lamb to stage representations of Othello as a '*coal-black* Moor' or 'barbarous Negro' with Samuel Johnson's supreme indifference to skin colour in *Rasselas*, which makes so little of the blackness of its Abyssinians (cognate, of course, with Reynolds' 'Aethiopians') that readers scarcely ever register it at all.[25]

Chatterton is often called a 'pre-Romantic' rather than Enlightenment writer, and his *African Eclogues* have been read accordingly as prefiguring the 'great Romantics'.[26] However, Chatterton's attempt to imagine an African perspective and his reversal of the conventional Eurocentric connotations of black and white situate the Eclogues in close relation to the relativist discourse of his own cultural moment. Chatterton, as biographers invariably point out in relation to these poems, would have had 'actual sight' of African slaves on the Bristol quays, where merchant seamen would openly sell their 'privilege Negroes', one of the perquisites of the slave-trade.[27] Nevertheless, the three *African Eclogues* (along with Chatterton's 'African Song') tend to be discussed (when at all) in relation to literary Orientalism, as imitations of Collins' *Persian Eclogues* and anticipations of Coleridge's 'Kubla Khan'. Not only does the first of the Eclogues, 'Heccar and Gaira', position itself overtly as a critique of the slave-trade, however, but anti-'white' references occur throughout the poems, and Chatterton's concomitant revaluation of 'black' – at a time when blackness and slavery had become 'virtually

---

[24] *The Notebooks of Samuel Taylor Coleridge*, ed. Kathleen Coburn, 5 vols (London and Princeton, 1957–), II, p. 2,604; see also J. H. Haeger, 'Coleridge's Speculations on Race,' *Studies in Romanticism*, 13 (1974), pp. 333–57 and Deirdre Coleman, 'Conspicuous Consumption: White Abolitionism and English Women's Protest Writing in the 1790s,' *ELH*, 61 (1994), pp. 341–62 (p. 358). Coleridge's later pronouncements on race contrast markedly with, though do not necessarily contradict, his early and continued support of the abolition movement (including lecturing against the slave-trade in Bristol): for nuanced discussions, see Patrick J. Keane, *Coleridge's Submerged Politics: The Ancient Mariner and Robinson Crusoe* (Columbia and London, 1994).

[25] Charles Lamb, 'On the Tragedies of Shakespeare, Considered with Reference to their Fitness for Stage Representation', *The Works of Charles and Mary Lamb*, ed. E. V. Lucas, 7 vols (London, 1903–05), I, p. 108; Samuel Taylor Coleridge, *Lectures 1808–1819 On Literature*, ed. R. A. Foakes, 2 vols. (Princeton, 1987), I, p. 55, II, p. 314.

[26] E. H. W. Meyerstein, *A Life of Thomas Chatterton* (London, 1930), p. 357.

[27] Ibid., p. 19; Fryer, *Staying Power*, p. 59.

synonymous'[28] – makes an implicit anti-slavery statement of its own.

The black African speakers of 'Heccar and Gaira' see the whiteness of the European slavers who harry their coast as alien, sickly, demonic. For Heccar the 'Children of the Wave whose palid race / Views the faint Sun display a languid face'; Gaira describes the 'Daemons' who carried off his beloved as the 'palid shadows of the Azure Waves', pale yet unsunned, the white negative of light.[29] In implicit contrast, Gaira praises Cawna's 'sable Charms':

> Cawna the Pride of Afric's sultry Vales
> Soft, as the cooling Murmur of the Gales
> Majestic as the many colour'd Snake
> Trailing his Glorys thro' the blossom'd brake
> Black as the glossy Rocks where Eascal roars
> Foaming thro' sandy Wastes to Jagirs Shores.
> ('Heccar and Gaira', 1, p. 434, lines 51–56)

'Soft', 'glossy', and above all 'black' recur as the chief attributes of beauty throughout the African poems. Reynolds had suggested in *The Idler* that an Aethiopian painter, depicting the 'goddess of beauty', would 'represent her black';[30] blackness is one of the 'godlike charms' of the beloved in 'An African Song':

> Black is that skin as winter's skies;
> Sparkling and bright those rolling eyes,
> As is the venom'd snake.
> ('An African Song', 1, p. 663, lines 41–43)

The snake simile occurring in both passages suggests Chatterton's attempt to imagine not only a non-European but a non-Christian perspective in these poems, though it may also rely on a traditional connection (going back to *Exodus*) between Africa and snake worship.

Indeed, if Chatterton succeeds in the African poems in challenging his readers' association of blackness with slavery, he does so at the price of confirming an equally widespread eighteenth-century association between blackness and 'savagery'.[31] Chatterton's 'black Archers of the Wilds' ('Heccar and Gaira') hunt exotic game, fight with 'white warriors' or with other blacks using javelins and arrows, make love, perform ritual dances, sing 'warsongs' and hold quasi-

---

[28] Barker, *The African Link*, p. 60; see also Jordan, *White Over Black*, p. 11.
[29] My text for Chatterton's poetry is *The Complete Works of Thomas Chatterton*, ed. Donald S. Taylor, 2 vols (Oxford, 1971).
[30] Reynolds, Letter to *The Idler*, p. 257.
[31] Barker, *The African Link*, p. 78.

pastoral dialogues. In terms of the 'four-stage' theory of cultural development so effectively disseminated by Smith and other Scottish Enlightenment writers, in the second half of the eighteenth century, Chatterton's Africans, dwelling 'Where nature in her strongest vigor smiles' ('Narva and Mored'), remain in the hunting 'stage' – the lowest, to be succeeded by pastoralism, agriculture, and finally commerce.[32] Climate, rather than race, accounts for the black African's status at the bottom of the scale of human progress, although a potential linkage between climate and race is ominously latent throughout eighteenth-century discourse.[33] 'Furious, wild, and young' ('The Death of Nicou'), Chatterton's ideal African is a noble savage, rather than the cultural equal represented by the '*bon ethiopien*' of an earlier European discourse (recalled by *Rasselas*);[34] he evokes less an alternative civilization than an alternative *to* civilization. Chatterton's empathy with the enslaved Africans he would have seen on Bristol's wharves may in part have proceeded from his own sense of marginalization as an impoverished clerk and his animus against the Bristol commercial culture that he at once felt victimized by, scornful of, and (as the posthumous son of a school-master) pointedly excluded from.[35] His empathy, however, stops well short of full recognition, lapsing instead into an escapism and exoticism still more extravagant than the idealized medievalism of the Rowley poems. Chatterton can, in the context of assailing the slave-trade, entertain a perspective that inverts the Eurocentric values of white and black, but he can represent African culture only in starkly primitivist terms.

In Hannah More's *Slavery, A Poem* (1788), the link between climate and biological race, latent within so much eighteenth-century writing, begins to become manifest.[36] More writes as a social reformer and Evangelical critic of abuses like the slave-trade who remains, nevertheless, deeply committed to the reigning political order, a pioneering professional woman writer and activist, yet, also,

---

[32] Ronald L. Meek, *Social Science and the Ignoble Savage* (Cambridge, 1976).

[33] Marshall and Williams, *The Great Map of Mankind*, pp. 245–48, 275–76; see also Young's discussion of Herder, *Colonial Desire*, pp. 38–40.

[34] Henri Baudet, *Paradise on Earth: Some Thoughts on European Images of Non-European Man*, tr. Elizabeth Wentholt (New Haven, 1965), pp. 14–20.

[35] For recent revaluations of Chatterton in relation to his Bristol context and to issues of class identity, see the special issue of *Angeleki*, 1 (1993/1994), *Narratives of Forgery*, ed. Nick Groom, particularly the essays by Jonathan Barry and John Goodridge.

[36] My text for More's *Slavery* (cited by line number) is *Women Romantic Poets 1785–1832: An Anthology*, ed. Jennifer Breen (London, 1992), pp. 10–20.

a 'father's daughter' bent on ameliorating the status quo, the better to maintain it.[37] Her opening invocation of 'Liberty' as an 'intellectual sun' – 'While the chill North with thy bright beam is blest, / Why should fell darkness half the South invest' (lines 15–16) – seems to promise an Enlightenment critique of slavery in terms of 'human rights' (line 305), but as the poem proceeds the 'darkness' of the 'South' becomes interwoven with the blackness of the 'sable race' (line 76). With its ultimate appeal to Christian sentiment over secular argument, More's poem, as Donna Landry notes, undermines its Enlightenment rhetoric with an anti-rational appeal to faith; Wylie Sypher compares its 'sentimental, or even sensational' appeal to experience and feeling with the 'counter-rationalistic' propensities of Burke and Wordsworth.[38] More's verses also evoke tendencies within Romantic rhetoric – perhaps surprisingly, given recent attempts to differentiate women's writing of the period from (canonical, male) 'Romanticism' – in their intensification of the trope of 'African savagery' and their insistent connection between 'darkness' or blackness and 'rude', 'luxuriant' African 'energy', the 'wild vigour of a savage root' (lines 87–90).[39] As an index of the poem's ambivalence, these epithets appear immediately following a brief, apparently relativist, argument against judging from the 'casual colour of a skin', yet More's incipient racialism leaves its mark even on those lines: 'is mind / Degraded by the form to which it's joined?' (lines 80–83). At once casual and degrading, the African's skin implies a low position in a racialized scheme of human culture, with Africa itself already represented (again in contrast to the explicit argument) as the dark continent, 'quenched in total night' (line 20). Similarly, the very terms with which More argues for the African's essential humanity throw her claim into question: 'Though dark and savage, ignorant and blind, / They claim the common privilege of kind' (lines 165–66). 'Dark' cannot be mitigated here as an incidental antonym for a racially neutral 'enlightened', as the African's 'darker skin!' has been given emphasis three lines previously. The slave's skin colour, Africa's 'fell darkness' (note that 'fell' nominally signifies skin

---

[37] See Beth Kowaleski-Wallace, *Their Father's Daughters: Hannah More, Maria Edgeworth, and Patriarchal Complicity* (New York, 1991).

[38] Donna Landry, *The Muses of Resistance: Laboring-class Women's Poetry in Britain, 1739–1796* (Cambridge, 1990), pp. 238–39; Sypher, *Guinea's Captive Kings*, pp. 194–95.

[39] These tendencies were neither monolithic nor unchallenged within the Romantic corpus itself, as I have argued in relation to Blake's 'The Little Black Boy' in *Literature, Education, and Romanticism: Reading as Social Practice, 1780–1832* (Cambridge, 1994), pp. 153–66.

or pelt) and the unchristened African's 'mental night' (line 241) all converge in a rhetoric of black savagery, characteristic of More's writing and prevalent within Romantic-era writing on slavery, by 'Romantics' as well as others, by anti-slavery writers, as well as apologists for the trade and colonial slavery.[40]

More's rhetoric also concurs with much canonical, Romantic writing as it veers from Enlightened universalism toward British nationalism.[41] In keeping with its ambivalent tenor, *Slavery* at times dismisses the trope of climate on which it tacitly depends ('In every nature, every clime the same' [line 146]) and attempts to reverse the savagery trope as well (the European slaver is a 'Barbarian' [line 163] or 'White Savage' [line 249]). But as this last epithet implies, the slave-trade is problematic, precisely because it threatens to under-mine the distinction between 'White' and 'Savage' on which the British redemption of Africa through Christianization and 'fair Commerce' (line 173) is founded.[42] Boasting only the simplest 'arts' (line 158) and lacking the cultural and historical memory which writing (the 'recording page') would give them (line 103), 'untutored' Africans must look to Britain not simply for guidance and civilization but even to give voice to their wrongs (line 193). Heroes of British stock – the explorer Cook and the settler Penn – are cited as models of 'mild' and 'peaceful' colonization (lines 279, 288), in contrast to the cruel and relatively barbarous Spanish (line 258). Britain, 'where the soul of Freedom reigns' (line 295), will seal its right to lead and civilize the world by unilaterally abolishing the slave-trade, abolition serving to buttress, rather than weaken, a British empire based on trade and benign colonization. Through the luminous writing (the 'shining page' [line 305]) of its abolition statute, and through a repetition of God's originary decree, 'Let there be light', Britain will assume its leading and God-given role in enlightening the 'dusky myriads' of 'benighted' Africans (lines 345–56). Two years after publishing *Slavery*, More wrote to Horace Walpole of her indignation

---

[40] Ibid., pp. 156–58.

[41] Marlon B. Ross, 'Romancing the Nation-State: The Poetics of Romantic Nationalism', *Macropolitics of Nineteenth-Century Literature: Nationalism, Exoticism, Imperialism*, ed. Jonathan Arac and Harriet Ritvo (Philadelphia, 1991), pp. 56–85; cf. Peter Thorslev's remark, after quoting Wordsworth on Burke, that the 'Romantic ideology, for all its enthusiasm for infinite variety and transcendence, was at its core concrete, experiential, and nationalist', 'German Romantic Idealism', *The Cambridge Companion to British Romanticism*, ed. Stuart Curran (Cambridge, 1993), p. 89.

[42] This is a distinction that other Evangelical educationalists also strove to maintain, as Moira Ferguson demonstrates in her chapter in this volume.

at learning that – 'at my city of Bristol' – a 'poor negro girl' was forcibly returned to a ship bound for the West Indies; had she known in time, she might have played a redemptive role herself, 'buying' the girl with help from her wealthier friends 'if the cost had been considerable'.[43]

Ann Yearsley, a poor working woman from a suburb of Bristol, did become More's protégée for a time and benefited from her talent at raising subscriptions, but Yearsley came to resent More's patronage and may have written her own anti-slavery work of 1788 in competition with her former mentor. Yearsley's *A Poem on the Inhumanity of the Slave-Trade* begins and ends with apostrophes to Bristol, assuming a 'local' and 'civic' position in contrast to More's nationalistic and Christian stance.[44] If the reactionary, often anti-feminist, More has proved something of an embarrassment to recent attempts to construct a coherent female or 'feminine' tradition out of the welter of Romantic-era texts by women writers, Yearsley has proved attractive due to her double alterity as a woman of the labouring class. Her representation of the slave has been found refreshingly particularized as opposed to More's dehumanizing abstraction, based on conscious 'class' identification rather than the 'repressed' identification that contributes to the 'othering' of the black subject in More's 'Anglo-Africanist' discourse.[45] And Yearsley's critique of 'Custom' (which renders class and gender oppression no less seemingly 'natural' than slavery) has been read as a call to resistance that contrasts markedly with the condemnation of mob violence with which More anxiously qualifies the invocation of 'Liberty' (not to be confused with its evil twin, 'Mad Liberty') that begins her abolitionist poem (line 25).[46] Yearsley's representation of the slave has also been linked with that of More, however, in its stock assumption of the slave's 'savagery' as it registers and attempts to recuperate the 'threat of cultural difference'.[47] Ironically, Yearsley had named *herself* a 'savage' in her first collection of poems, published under More's aegis, portraying herself as in need of More's ('Stella's') illumination,

---

[43] William Roberts, *Memoirs of the Life and Correspondence of Mrs. Hannah More*, 2 vols. (New York, 1835), I, p. 354; cited by Sypher, *Guinea's Captive Kings*, p. 83.

[44] Landry, *The Muses of Resistance*, p. 238.

[45] Moira Ferguson, *Subject to Others: British Women Writers and Colonial Slavery, 1760–1834* (London and New York, 1992), pp. 153, 164, 170.

[46] Landry, *The Muses of Resistance*, p. 238; Ferguson, *Subject to Others*, pp. 170–72.

[47] Ferguson, *Subject to Others*, p. 171; Landry, *The Muses of Resistance*, p. 238.

her mind as a den of 'native darkness'.[48] Asserting her independence from More by producing an abolitionist work of her own, Yearsley simultaneously projects the 'savage' character she had adopted to please More (and with which More eventually came to taunt her) onto a native other, who is seemingly both African and not African, and whose racial status is significantly vague.

The romantic couple at the centre of Yearsley's sentimental narrative, the enslaved Luco and his 'artless' lover Incilanda (line 25), may indeed be named and individuated in comparison with More's 'abstract formula of "a slave"', but they belong to no one identifiable location or community.[49] Yearsley herself calls Luco (the 'dingy youth' [line 52]) an 'Indian' at several points, presumably (as Sypher supposes) an aborigine of the Americas, but Moira Ferguson is also justified in describing Luco as an 'African'.[50] Though Luco and Incilanda are (apparently) natives of a 'cane' bearing isle that the sun 'embrowns' (lines 127–32) – that is, a yet uncolonized West-Indian island – the belief of Luco's father (cognate with the 'inky sire' of line 40?)[51] that slaves will be released by 'his country's gods' after death is one typically attributed in this period to Africans (line 174). In a note to line 209, 'Indians' are cited as using the word 'buckera', a term for whites current among slaves of African origin. Later in the text, the punitive amputation of an 'Indian' slave's limb is glossed in the notes by an anecdote recounting the same punishment inflicted on a 'Negro', more specifically a 'Coromantin' (line 345). The text vacillates throughout between assigning its represented slaves an African or Caribbean origin, collapsing the two exotic regions into an undifferentiated 'barb'rous' (line 317) or 'wild' (line 148) space of 'dingy' natives vulnerable to the incursions of European slavers.

This confusion should not be attributed to Yearsley's supposed limitations as a self-educated (or, as Southey would have it, 'un-educated') poet.[52] Rather, confusion between 'Indians' and black

---

[48] Alan Richardson, *Literature, Education, and Romanticism: Reading as Social Practice, 1780–1832* (Cambridge, 1994), pp. 252–53.

[49] Ferguson, *Subject to Others*, p. 166.

[50] Sypher, *Guinea's Captive Kings*, p. 199; Ferguson, *Subject to Others*, p. 170. Yearsley's *A Poem on the Inhumanity of the Slave-Trade* (cited by line number) is included in *First Feminists: British Women Writers 1578–1799*, ed. Moira Ferguson (Bloomington, 1989), pp. 386–96.

[51] 'Inky sire' is my emendation for the unlikely 'inky fire' (evidently based on a mistranscription of the elongated first-position 's') in Ferguson's text.

[52] Southey included Yearsley in his *Lives and Works of the Uneducated Poets*, first published as an introduction to the *Attempts in Verse, by John Jones, an old Servant* in 1831.

Africans is common throughout anti-slavery writing, and sub-Saharan Africa tended in this period to be thought of as an '*annexe*' of the sugar islands, the two regions linked in the popular mind through the Atlantic slave-trade.[53] But Yearsley's lack of geo-political specificity, if common, nevertheless signals a parochial tendency to lump together various non-white, 'alien' groups into a single 'savage' category, defined simply by its racial and cultural otherness. Such thinking is seen at its most pernicious in Yearsley's depiction of Luco's bereaved father reproaching his African gods on his Indian isle:

> he shuts out
> The soft, fallacious gleam of hope, and turns
> Within upon his mind: horrid and dark
> Are his wild, unenlighten'd pow'rs: no ray
> Of forc'd philosophy to calm his soul,
> But all the anarchy of wounded nature.   (lines 168–73)

The native's mind is, at least in the 'savage' state, no less dark than his 'dingy' or 'inky' skin, no less wild than his 'clime'. Yearsley had learned from More to link such terms as dark, wild, and unenligh-tened, and had dutifully turned this rhetoric on herself in the period of literary homage that she soon came to regret ('she descended in calling me a savage, nor would she have had the temerity to do it, had I not given myself that name').[54] Beginning the *Poem on the Inhumanity of the Slave-Trade* with a disclaimer requesting 'Bristol' to fill out the poet's 'rustic thought' and 'crude ideas' (lines 10–11), Yearsley goes on to negate her imputed wildness as an 'uneducated poet' by projecting it onto her racially different (yet undifferentiated) subject. Racial difference or 'darkness' facilitates the transfer of the burden of savagery from the 'native genius' to the native other.

Yearsley's problematic status as 'uneducated' poet, her first-hand experience of class oppression, and her local allegiances to Clifton and Bristol, rather than London, all serve, however, to differentiate her Abolitionist stance from that of More. In breaking with More and the Blue-stocking culture represented by her, Yearsley turned from a self-consciously feminine version of the patron-client relation to solidarity with other marginalized poets; her second volume

---

[53] Sypher, *Guinea's Captive Kings*, pp. 105–06; Marshall and Williams, *The Great Map of Mankind*, p. 227.
[54] Yearsley's preface to *Poems on Various Subjects*, reprinted in *First Feminists*, ed. Ferguson, p. 385.

includes an address to a fellow 'Unlettered Poet' and an elegy on Chatterton, exemplar of 'hapless Genius . . . by Pride opprest'. In contrast to More, Yearsley recognizes the value of oral 'traditions' among the unlettered people (or peoples) she represents (line 193) and epitomizes written law not in the 'shining page' that might repeal the slave-trade but in the 'iron pen' that codifies it (line 107). 'English law' is criticized more generally as the law of a 'few' in an unreformed and unrepresentative senate (line 383); in place of More's nationalism, Yearsley contrasts the pure commercialism of the British slave holder to the greater concern for the slave's 'spirit' exhibited by the Spaniard and even 'Mussulman' (lines 322–30). In a phrase anticipating the 'mind-forg'd manacles' of Blake (another self-educated poet), Yearsley writes that due to his 'avarice' the Briton is himself enslaved by the 'fetters of his mind' (line 397), hardly in a position to enlighten the heathen until 'enlarged' by 'social love' (line 414). Yet her representation of racial and cultural difference is no less insidious than that of her erstwhile mentor, as its very indistinctness leaves it less open to challenge on empirical grounds and all too readily extendible to other 'barb'rous' groups, from the Amerindian to the 'wildest Arab' (lines 317–20).

Among Southey's various humanitarian projects, in the late 1790s, were a personal campaign to persuade his various acquaintances to leave off sugar, and an edition of Chatterton's works to benefit the poet's niece and sister.[55] Southey's 'Poems Concerning the Slave Trade' (1794–98), particularly the six sonnets published together in his 1797 *Poems*, at times recall Chatterton, in their opposition of 'Pale tyrant' and 'sable brother' (Sonnet III) and their characterization of the slaver as a 'pale fiend' (Sonnet I; in later revisions a 'white, cadaverous fiend').[56] But Southey's attempt to reproduce a radical Enlightenment critique of slavery (the 1797 *Poems* also included the 'Botany Bay Eclogues' and a tribute to Mary Wollstonecraft) for the most part founders on his apparent inability to represent a black subject without setting off the negative associations with blackness

[55] Geoffrey Carnall, *Robert Southey and His Age: The Development of a Conservative Mind* (Oxford, 1960), p. 52. For a particularly rich and complex discussion of the ideology and imagery of the sugar boycott and of Southey's early anti-slavery poetry, see Timothy Morton's chapter in this volume.

[56] My text for Southey's sonnets and 'To the Genius of Africa' is the facsimile edition of *Poems, 1797*, introduced by Jonathan Wordsworth (Oxford, 1989); my text for Southey's other poems (and for the later textual variants in the sonnets) is *Poetical Works of Robert Southey* (New York, 1839).

which had become so deeply engrained in British discourse by the
end of the eighteenth century. Chatterton's strategy of reversing the
valences of white and black seems no longer quite workable, despite
Southey's gesture towards it. In the other four sonnets, colour is not
mentioned, save for a reference to 'gay negroes' in Sonnet IV and to
'Freedom's pale spectre' in Sonnet V: Southey seems finally unable
to resist either the blandishments of African pastoralism or the
association of freedom with whiteness (implicit throughout More's
Slavery as well). His anti-slavery poems are for the most part abstract
even in comparison with More, avoiding representation of their
black subjects *as* black and producing instead a series of stock (but
oddly colourless) Abolitionist figures – the bereaved lover, the sinking
slave ship, the scourged, the weeping, and the dying slave.[57]

In his poems of the 1790s, Southey can imagine the spectacle of
successful slave insurrection, celebrating the Haitian revolution in
'To the Genius of Africa' (in contrast to his horrified contemporaries)
and warning, in his preface to the sonnets, that with abolitionist
legislation and the sugar boycott both having failed, opponents of
the trade must put their faith either in maple sugar or in the
'vindictive justice of the Africans'. Ultimately, though, an increasingly conservative Southey will turn instead to the heroic portrayal
of a white subject in his 1810 verses on Lord Grenville (a capstone to
the anti-slavery poems), acting on behalf of an 'Afric' whose only
function in the poem is to sing Grenville's praise.[58] Black resistance,
however abstract (and however lightened by freedom's pallor),
proves too charged a subject for poetic representation, and Grenville
(who oversaw the final passing of abolitionist legislation in 1806–07)
becomes a figure for British justice and England's 'ancient liberty'
restored.[59] Heralding the new world order that will displace Napoleon's 'upstart tyranny' with a system of world commerce dominated
by Britain, Southey envisions the entire African continent filled with
undying gratitude for Grenville and England ('Afric with all her

---

[57] Cf. Morton, who finds that the 'voices of the slaves seem unavailable, or tantalizingly out of
reach' in Sonnet III; Morton, however, argues persuasively for a more 'radically unstable'
reading of the sonnets than the one sketched out here and places more emphasis than I am
willing to on their 'revolutionary suggestiveness'.

[58] For a helpful account of Southey's changing political allegiances in their historical context
(particularly the crisis years of 1810–1811), see Carnall, *Robert Southey*, pp. 120–70.

[59] Slave resistance is represented in fiction and on the stage in this period only to be
demonized and wishfully dismissed, as I have argued in 'Romantic Voodoo: Obeah and
British Culture, 1797–1807', *Studies in Romanticism*, 32 (1993), pp. 3–28.

tongues will speak of thee'), Abolition once more redeployed in the
cause of British nationalism and trade imperialism. Southey's fitful,
but unconvincing, attempt to return to an Enlightened anti-racism
in the sonnets (qualified, as usual, by the characterization of Africa
as 'savage' [Sonnet 1]) and his abstract but radical evocation of black
self-determination in 'To the Genius of Africa' yield, seemingly
inevitably, to expressions of Romantic nationalism and the relegation
of Africans to the role of grateful chorus.

Given Southey's inability to convincingly represent a black subject
in his abolitionist verse, it is noteworthy that the only one of the
'Poems Concerning the Slave Trade' to generate much human
interest or pathos features not an oppressed African slave but a guilt-
ridden English seaman. Set in a Bristol 'cow-house', 'The Sailor,
Who Had Served in the Slave Trade' (1798) retells, in ballad form, a
narrative of the type Clarkson had been collecting in and around
Bristol a decade before, portraying in all its Satanic intensity ('every
place is Hell!') the psychic torment incurred by a sailor who had
flogged a 'sulky' woman to death during the Middle Passage. The
story of a mariner who has 'done a cursed thing' at sea in an
atmosphere of shrieks and groans, who has lived ever since in a
restless agony of guilt, and who on returning home tells his tale in
vague hope of absolution, Southey's ballad clearly asks to be read as
a gloss on Coleridge's recently composed 'Ancyent Marinere',
announcing its affinities from the very first line ('It was a Christian
minister. . . .'). Once having read the ballads – one a defining text of
canonical British Romanticism and the other a 'topical' or 'ephem-
eral' work by a now 'minor' poet – in tandem, it becomes difficult,
thereafter, as several commentators have attested, to detach the
psychological guilt and horror described to such seemingly universal
effect in Coleridge's 'Ancyent Marinere' from the material,
economic, and political context made overt by Southey's companion
piece.[60] This is not to suggest that we simply reinterpret Coleridge's
ballad as a cryptic response to the slave-trade, but rather that

---

[60] There is a long (though, until recently, neglected) tradition of placing these two poems into
juxtaposition, beginning with Sypher, *Guinea's Captive Kings*, pp. 218–19, and Dykes, *The
Negro in English Romantic Thought*, pp. 81–82, and including Malcolm Ware, 'Coleridge's
"Spectre-Bark": A Slave Ship?', *Philological Quarterly*, 40 (1961), pp. 589–93 and Chris
Rubenstein, 'A New Identity for the Mariner? A Further Exploration of "The Rime of the
Ancyent Marinere"', *The Coleridge Bulletin*, 3 (1990), pp. 16–29. More detailed comparisons
can be found in Baum, *Mind Forg'd Manacles*, pp. 48–54 and Keane, *Coleridge's Submerged
Politics*, pp. 157–59.

attending to the context of slavery, colonialism, and the construction of racial difference may not only cause us to revive long-forgotten texts by marginalized writers, but also to read the canon in a markedly different, more historically engaged manner.

Reading Romantic-era texts with an awareness of the concomitant rise of modern racism and racial categories does not only give us a different 'Romanticism', however; it also gives us an object lesson in the pitfalls of analyzing 'race' without regard to a particular historical and cultural context. Paul Gilroy's exhortation to 'compare and evaluate the different historical situations in which "race" has become politically pertinent' takes on still more weight when dealing with historical situations in which the concept of 'race' is not simply in flux and subject to competing definitions, but is still very much in the process of formation.[61] Chatterton's attempt to invert the aesthetic and moral valences of 'black' and 'white', More's confounding of intellectual 'darkness' and dark pigmentation, Yearsley's positing of a 'savage' other whose racial status is at once indefinite and overdetermined, and Southey's vacillation over the question of racial difference at a time when racism is becoming endemic to pro- and anti-slavery ideologies alike, imply not so much different attitudes toward or perspectives on 'race' but divergent and internally unstable schemas from within and among which 'race' is only beginning to emerge in its modern (and currently contested) sense. So marked a degree of divergence and instability is all the more striking in texts by Bristol writers, who would have had first-hand exposure to African and Caribbean slaves and former slaves (More's 'poor negro girl') and who would have been steeped in the oral as well as written discourses growing out of the slave-trade and the abolition movement (Southey's overheard confession in the 'cow-house').

It seems evident that the literary discourses we group together for convenience under the banner of 'Romanticism', particularly in their mutually reinforcing naturalizing and nationalizing tendencies and their 'passion for ethnicity', helped to precipitate the emergence of modern racism.[62] What precisely to make of that historical conjunction, however, remains open to debate and will depend on localized and particularized studies in addition to the broader

---

[61] Paul Gilroy, 'There Ain't No Black in the Union Jack': The Cultural Politics of Race and Nation (Chicago, 1991), p. 38; see also Fuss, Essentially Speaking, p. 92.
[62] Young, Colonial Desire, p. 42.

historical and theoretical perspectives being developed by scholars like Laura Doyle and David Lloyd.[63] If the construction of race is a crucial topic within Romantic-era writing, as I hope to have indicated here, 'race', nevertheless, remains so slippery and vexed a term that it will need to be constantly rearticulated and will continue to resist generalization. Understood *as* a construct, however, race has a critical role to play in revaluations of late eighteenth- and early nineteenth-century, British culture and in our attempts to re-situate Romantic writing in its contemporary historical and political contexts.

[63] See note 17 above.

CHAPTER 9

Fictional constructions of Liberated Africans: Mary Butt Sherwood

Moira Ferguson

Mary Butt Sherwood was not a Romantic. She was, however, one of that school of Evangelical writers and educationalists which achieved popularity and influence during the period.[1] It was in relation to this school that the Romantics defined themselves when discussing morally improving literature in general, and missionary work in particular.[2] Sherwood's *Little Henry and his Bearer*, an educational children's story set in India, where she lived for years as an officer's wife, was one of the era's most popular tales of colonial life. It is not principally, however, Sherwood's representation of India and its colonial servants that I wish to discuss in this essay but the story she wrote after briefly visiting Africa, *Dazee, The Re-captured Negro* (1821).[3] This story, set in Sierra Leone, exhibits both the spiritual viewpoint and the colonialist attitudes, which Sherwood had acquired in India, where she had become an Evangelical missionary, called 'the most intense moralist of them all'.[4] Yet it also, I shall argue, briefly casts doubt upon the values it seeks to uphold, as it puts words into the

[1] Two main sources for Mary Martha Butt Sherwood's biography are *The Life of Mrs. Sherwood, Chiefly Autobiographical, with extracts from Mr. Sherwood's Journal During His Imprisonment in France and Residence in India*, edited by her Daughter, Sophia Kelley (London, 1857); and *The Life and Times of Mrs. Sherwood (1775–1851) From the Diaries of Captain and Mrs. Sherwood*, ed. F. J. Harvey Darton (London, 1910).

[2] For Southey's support of Evangelical and Dissenting missionary societies see his article on the *Transactions of the Missionary Society in the South Sea Islands* for the *Quarterly Review*, 2 (1809), pp. 24–61, and his review of *Periodical Accounts relative to the Baptist Missionary Society*, *Quarterly Review*, 1 (1809), pp. 193–226. Coleridge's more qualified support is expressed in his letters. See *Collected Letters of S. T. Coleridge*, ed. E. L. Griggs, 6 vols. (Oxford, 1956–71), III, p. 35. See also Hazlitt's essay on William Wilberforce in *The Spirit of the Age* (in *The Complete Works of William Hazlitt*, ed. P. P. Howe, 21 vols. (London, 1930–34)). See also De Quincey's sketch of Hannah More, in *The Collected Writings of Thomas De Quincey*, ed. David Masson, 14 vols. (Edinburgh, 1889–90), XIV.

[3] Mary Butt Sherwood, *The Re-captured Negro* (Boston, 1821). Henceforth cited by page number in the text.

[4] Helen Wolter, 'Give the Children Something Good to Read', *Christianity Today*, 24 (1980), p. 28.

mouth of the liberated slave, whose conversion to Christianity it narrates.

I begin with an examination of Sherwood's development in India of the religious principles which shaped her representations of indigenous peoples there and, later, in Africa. By the turn of the century, Mary Butt Sherwood was publishing short stories that inculcated religious principles. Sherwood said of her first book that it had 'religion for its object', and this claim remained true for every book she wrote. Even the giants and dwarves in Sarah Fielding's harmless *The Little Female Academy*, Sherwood averred, would morally corrupt children:

Since fanciful productions of this sort can never be rendered generally useful it has been thought proper to suppress [them] . . . substituting in their place such appropriate relations as seemed more likely to conduce to juvenile edification.[5]

In 1803, Mary Butt married her cousin Henry Sherwood, an army officer who was appointed paymaster of his regiment the following year. Not long after the birth of their first child, the couple were ordered to India for eleven years.[6]

In Cawnpore, Mary Sherwood met the Evangelical missionary, Henry Martyn, who was to become a major religious influence in her life.[7] She seems to have undergone an informal, religious conversion. Certainly, she embraced an even stricter Evangelical agenda. She turned to writing pious, even rigid, propaganda for use in Indian schools for missionary converts and British children. Her brief stories appeared in several books and magazines, especially after she became closely allied with Martyn's teachings.[8] In 1815, she

---

[5] Constantia Meigs, Anne Thaxter Eaton, Elisabeth Nesbitt, and Ruth Hall Viguers, *A Critical History of Children's Literature: A Survey of Children's Books in English*, rev. edn (London, 1969), p. 81.

[6] To give a sense of Mary Sherwood's pro-Evangelical and Eurocentric gaze in India, I quote her description of Hindu women in Dinapore: 'The women in and about Dinapore, that is, the Hindoos, are the very dirtiest I ever saw in India. Their dress consists of a single web of coarse cotton, gathered by the hand on the hips, and brought round the lower part of the person, so as to form a scanty petticoat; then so manoeuvred as to cover one arm, the back, and the lower part of one side under the arm, and finally carried over the head forming a veil. This is a most beautiful arrangement of drapery for a picture or statue, or for a young and delicate girl; but for the old and the ugly, most disgusting' (*The Life of Mrs. Sherwood*, p. 287).

[7] For Mary Sherwood's meeting with Henry Martyn, 'that simple-hearted and holy young man', see *The Life of Mrs. Sherwood*, p. 317.

[8] *The Life and Times of Mrs. Sherwood (1775-1851)*, pp. 334-35.

composed *Little Henry and His Bearer*, a tale that rivalled *Uncle Tom's Cabin* in popularity, becoming the accepted construction for white Britons of 'how India was'. One hundred editions were published in the next seventy years.[9] Sherwood viewed the popular reaction to *Henry and His Bearer* as a divine sign that she should continue her authorial endeavours:

When I was known to be the person sought [who wrote the tale] my lionship commenced, and I began to pay the penalty for my greatness by finding myself sought after and being obliged to endure much talking to. . . . High encouragement was being held out to me to write for children. So the Almighty orders our ways and gives us power to walk in them.[10]

Pursuing spiritual duties in India, she became assiduous about introducing people to scriptures:

Before we left Cawnpore we received a parcel of New Testaments in Hindustani from the Calcutta Press. In coming up from Calcutta to Cawnpore we had brought the first strawberries up the country from the Botanic Gardens; in going from Cawnpore to Meerut we carried up the first Hindustani Testament to the Province of Delhi.[11]

Sherwood's texts match her fervent commitment to Evangelical ideas and her colonial vision.[12] The freedom or emancipation of the soul is her principal concern. In a tale entitled *Emancipation*,[13] freedom is represented as a spiritual possibility that has no specific overlapping with colonial slavery, except in a moral sense. At the end of the tale, the formerly unenlightened and rascally protagonist, Penson, repents and sees the light:

This closed that happy day . . . Neither is it the least benefit for which we have to praise the Lord, that we are all set free from that absurd system of liberality by which every bond of society is broken through, and every ancient and sacred obligation dissolved; by which the wife is emancipated from the dominion of her husband, the child from that of the parent, the servant from that of his master, and the members of the Established Church from the authority of the legal rulers of the empire.[14]

In its single-minded focus on religion, Sherwood's daily living resembled her writings. Her experiences on the journey home from

---

[9] Ibid., p. 373.   [10] Ibid., p. 414.   [11] Ibid., p. 392.
[12] For information about Mary Sherwood's Eurocentric cultural role in India, see Pat Barr, *The Memsahibs* (London, 1976); J. K. Stanford, *Ladies in the Sun. The Memsahibs' India, 1790–1860* (London, 1962); Kenneth Ballhatchet, *Race, Sex and Class Under the Raj: Imperial Attitudes and Policies and Their Critics, 1793–1905* (London, 1980).
[13] Mary Butt Sherwood, *Emancipation* (London, 1829).   [14] Ibid., p. 150.

India in 1816 provide a telling example. As she testifies, religion was so constantly on her mind that when she discovered that a 'black Ayah' had drawn 'a Hindu god on deck and made poojah (worship) to it', and then made Sherwood's children worship it alongside hers, she became enraged.[15] It was on this voyage that she briefly visited Africa for the only time, stopping at Cape Colony; her description of the event reveals her belief in 'natural' hierarchy among people, the Christian duty involved in helping 'lower' races, the primacy of Anglo-Saxon physiognomy and complexion. In these attitudes she was influenced by Evangelical and colonialist beliefs about indigenous peoples, which she had acquired in India, but also by the exoticism of fashionable Orientalist texts, as a reference to the 'Persian Tales' (the *Thousand and One Days*) reveals. Here an imagined and textualized Orient, constructed by European translators, shapes her view of peoples in Africa:

I only went on shore once, taking the children that they might be able to say that they had been in Africa. The town looked altogether English to me. The small houses and glass windows seeming nothing but toys. The European inhabitants, such as I saw, looked quite second-rate. The streets abounded with Hottentot servants, dressed according to the homeliest European fashions. The Hottentots may vie for beauty with the Chinese, and on the whole would certainly be preferred in that island of the Indian Seas, of which we read in the 'Persian Tales,' where deformity is accounted the perfection of loveliness. The Hottentot is swarthy and peculiarly ill-formed, the women being much like their sheep; what is most ugly about them is the absolute failure of the bridge of the nose, so that their two little nostrils appear like holes in their faces. Before the English took the Cape, these servants were slaves, living in one family from generation to generation, and becoming deeply attached. When liberty was given to them, they were all dismissed, and went away; but lo and behold, the next morning they were most of them found sitting on the steps of their old masters' doors, and begging to be taken in again; and taken in they were.[16]

On the return of the freed 'Hottentots' or Khoikhoi people, she remarks:

The Dutch at the Cape brought this fact forward as an argument for slavery, forgetting that from the prevalence of slavery for so many years

---

[15] *The Life of Mrs. Sherwood*, p. 479.
[16] Ibid., p. 420. Sherwood refers to 'The Story of Prince Seyd el Mulouk' in *The Persian and Turkish Tales, Compleat, translated formerly from those languages into French by M. Petis de la Croix*, tr. Dr King, 4th edn, 2 vols. (London, 1739). The Prince is disgusted by the black princess's 'Nose turn'd up, . . . wide Mouth, great Lips, and Teeth the Colour of Amber' (I, p. 318).

these poor people had no homes to go to. Much might be said on both sides, but unjustifiable as slavery is, and wholly incompatible with Christianity, may it not be used by Almighty God for some good purpose?[17]

Sherwood, then, equates paganism with racial difference; hence, the spiritual necessity of converting Africans, despite their inferiority. A letter of 17 May 1826 to the Dissenter, Mary Ann Rawson, concerning a request to contribute to an anti-slavery anthology, displays Sherwood's views on empire most clearly:[18]

Perhaps the knowledge I have acquired abroad of the characters and general habits of the Africans and other half civilized persons makes me see the more danger in interfering with them than I should otherwise be, that our exertions should at present be chiefly devoted to the promotion of their spiritual and intellectual good.[19]

Three years later she reiterated this point of view when she shied from promoting emancipation: 'the matter [she said] is too high for me'.

Sherwood's proselytizing mission in India helps to explain her foray into fiction in *The Re-Captured Negro*.[20] With no direct know-ledge of Sierra Leone, having visited Africa only for a few hours on her return from India, Sherwood, nevertheless, believed that she was an appropriate conduit of knowledge about its inhabitants. The heroic Dazee of the tale may be Sherwood's tribute at one remove to her religious mentor in India, Henry Martyn, in that Dazee resembles a character in a story that Henry Martyn told to the Sherwoods.[21]

Written after her return to England, Sherwood's tale provides a model of Christian conversion, especially of drawing children into the Christian fold. Not long after its publication, Sherwood helped

---

[17] *The Life and Times of Mrs. Sherwood (1775–1851)*, p. 420.

[18] Mary Anne Rawson, *The Bow in the Cloud, or the Negro's Memorial*, ed. Mrs. [Mary Anne] Rawson (London, 1831). *The Bow in the Cloud* (1831), the anthology that Rawson was assembling, constituted a powerful collective statement by male and female abolitionists about slave emancipation. Eternal salvation, conversion, and the sanctity of motherhood were major themes, as well as some unquestioned attitudes of superiority toward slaves, particularly telling in a decade marked by a high incidence of West Indian slave resistance.

[19] Moira Ferguson, *Subject to Others: British Women Writers and Colonial Slavery, 1760–1834* (London and New York, 1992), pp. 268, 272. This information about the replies of Mary Anne Sherwood and Barbara Hofland to Mary Anne Rawson can be found in pre-publication handwritten notes to the manuscript of *The Bow in the Cloud*, available at the John Rylands Memorial Library, Manchester.

[20] *The Life and Times of Mrs. Sherwood (1775–1851)*, pp. 493–96.

[21] Ibid., p. 341ff. Dazee resembles, it has been suggested, Sabat in Martyn's story.

to establish a Ladies' branch of the Missionary Society at Worcester and then met William Wilberforce. They agreed that spiritual salvation was the paramount concern of all humans, that worldly affairs were inconsequential:

It is no part of their citizenship in heaven. No doubt the African natives are deprived of natural rights, refused law and justice, cruelly oppressed. These are worldly matters. They have no permanent importance . . . The Africans should be submissive and contented, endure their unfortunate lot. . . . Mrs. More pointed all this out to the Mendip miners and the Spitalfields weavers. No Evangelical principle is more clearly established than that suffering is better than discontent. In how much more comforting a position eternally speaking are the Africans than their oppressors![22]

Thus *The Recaptured Negro* appeared when the lot of suffering Africans had provoked Evangelical and national debate.[23] Its setting, Sierra Leone, had become the destination, after the abolition of the slave-trade, of Africans who had been illegally smuggled into slavery and subsequently freed.[24] These freed slaves, sent to be educated in the 'free colony' of Sierra Leone, rather than returned to their place of origin, were known as Liberated Africans or recaptured negroes.[25] They joined black expatriates from Nova Scotia (known

---

[22] William Wilberforce in, *The Life and Times of Mrs. Sherwood (1775–1851)*, pp. 439–42. See also William Baker, 'William Wilberforce on the Idea of Negro Inferiority', *Journal of the History of Ideas*, 31 (1970), pp. 433–40; Ford K. Brown, *Fathers of the Victorians* (Cambridge, 1961), pp. 379–80.

[23] See, for example, 'Instructions to Naval Officers, Emigration Agents and Commanders of Emigration Transports', and 'Origin of Liberated Africans Introduced into the West Indies', Appendixes 4 and 6 in Johnson U. J. Asiegbu, *Slavery and the Politics of Liberation, 1787–1861: A Study of Liberated African Emigration and British Anti-Slavery Policy* (London, 1969), pp. 170–77; pp. 189–214. See also John Peterson, *Province of Freedom: A History of Sierra Leone, 1787–1870* (Evanston, 1969), pp. 45–188.

[24] For information on Sierra Leone, see Christopher Fyfe, *A History of Sierra Leone* (Oxford, 1962), p. 35; G. T. Stride and Caroline Ifka, *Peoples and Empires of West Africa. West Africa in History, 1000–1800* (Sunbury-on-Thames, Middlesex, 1971); Joe A. D. Alie, *A New History of Sierra Leone* (London, 1990); Peterson, *Province of Freedom*, pp. 26–27. Note also that the persistent plans to colonize the land were tied to abolitionist agitation in Britain. Preparatory to the St. George's Bay Company receiving its new charter, the noted abolitionist, Thomas Clarkson, on tour around England in 1791, had informed audiences that about two thousand acres of sugar-cane would be grown in Sierra Leone with free, not enslaved, labour. This crop would cut the price of West-Indian sugar in half. Eventually Britain would be trading with free Africans in Sierra Leone. Philip D. Curtin, *The Image of Africa: British Ideas and Action, 1780–1850* (London and Madison, 1964), p. 106.

[25] For Liberated Africans, see Michael Craton, *Sinews of Empire: A Short History of British Slavery* (Garden City, 1974), p. 265; Asiegbu, *Slavery*, p. 23. Carelessly undertaken registrations of Liberated Africans were a problem. See Richard Meyer-Heiselberg, 'Research Report No. 1: Notes for Liberated Africans, Dept. in the Archives at Fourah Bay College, Freetown' (Upsala, 1967), quoted in Asiegbu, *Slavery*, p. 24; see also Fyfe, *A History*, p. 114; Christopher

as Black Loyalists because they had fought on the British side in the American revolution in order to emancipate themselves) and former Jamaican maroons, in a settlement increasingly subject, after 1814, to missionary activity.[26] With reassigned British names, the Liberated Africans were sent to settlement villages and invited to choose jobs. They could enlist in British regiments, join the navy, or be apprenticed. The Anglican Church Missionary Society (C M S) established a Christian institution where freed children could be taught and trained for jobs as farmers, teachers, or missionaries. The C M S, however, found it well-nigh impossible to recruit missionaries to go to Sierra Leone for a variety of reasons. Among them, the high rate of tropical disease and mortality was well-known and no successful system had yet been devised for educating the people liberated from slave ships. Furthermore, the difficulty of building a successful mission severely compounded by the fact that liberated Africans shared no common language. Each spoke the language of his or her tribe that in turn was not understood by English-speaking administrators. At that time, the conversion of Liberated Africans was a primary colonial concern.

Sherwood opens the tale by characterizing Sierra Leone from an Evangelical perspective while praising the abolitionists who had helped to found it:

Sierra Leone is a settlement, which was formed towards the end of the last century by certain benevolent English gentlemen on the coast of Africa, in order to afford an asylum for such of the captive negroes as should be retaken from the holds of slave-vessels, or in other ways delivered from the hands of their barbarous masters. (p. 3)

The young, male protagonist, Dazee, is 'a native of the country on the western coast of Africa, lying north of Sierra Leone' (p. 3). The simplicity of his life marks its 'primitive' state:

The hut in which Dazee was born, like most other African buildings, was composed of thick posts, . . . the intermediate spaces being filled up with twigs. The only furniture of this dwelling was a few mats and *cloths* to sleep on, an iron pot, a kettle for water, and a small chest for clothes. (p. 5)

Fyfe, *Sierra Leone Inheritance* (London, 1964), pp. 131–32; and Curtin, *The Image of Africa*, p. 157.

[26] Viscountess Knutsford, *Life and Letters of Zachary Macaulay* (London, 1900), p. 18. For information about Black Loyalists, see Ellen Gibson Wilson, *The Loyal Blacks* (New York, 1976); see also C. H. Fyfe, 'Thomas Peters. History and Legend', *Sierra Leone Studies*, NS 1 (December 1953), pp. 4–13. For the relationship between black expatriates who arrived in Sierra Leone from Nova Scotia and former Jamaican maroons, see Fyfe, *A History*, p. 104.

This seemingly idyllic (though pagan and simple) life is soon shattered. Dazee's father was enslaved one morning as he fished 'and never returned'. Since that time, Dazee finds himself drawn toward males 'with an erect mien and open countenance . . . as to a father'. Dazee's sister, nursing at the breast of a grief-stricken mother, 'pined away till she died' (p. 6). The miserable situation of this family, the authorial 'we' points out, was intensified by their lack of 'all the sweet consolations of religion. How can they be supported by the heathens who are destitute of these consolations?' (p. 7) Such losses having grafted the mother-son bond more firmly, the enslaved Dazee remembers his mother's stories that her parents told her; the memory of a strong, oral tradition resonates. She blamed the disappearance of her husband on evil spirits and witches.

At fourteen, after Dazee is captured and removed from the village by men from a different nation, he beseeches his captors, who 'seemed not to understand the exact meaning of his request' to let him see his mother. Put aboard ship, shut down under hatches, he is prevented by a boatman from plunging overboard. Sherwood elaborates on the horror of the hold that encloses Dazee:

Abodes without light, against whose hollow sides the green waves of the raging ocean continually dash themselves – abodes, which are never refreshed by the pure air of heaven; but which are constantly filled with noxious smells and an insufferable marine odour. (p. 22)

The boatman's threats are not 'in the dialect of his [Dazee's] own country' and Dazee sadly bids farewell to the hills of his fathers and to his mother (pp. 15–16).

Dazee prays to 'his mother, his beloved mother, his native country' (p. 17), whereupon a British sailor strikes him to make him stop his invocation, causing him to lapse into a feverish, semi-conscious state. During this lull, he envisions his beautiful, native land and his mother's face transformed into that of a corpse. He dreams of his local river, now running 'with streams of liquid fire'. The fever induces an unconscious realization in Dazee that his past was steeped in immorality, that his mother subscribed to 'dead' beliefs; he, himself, teetered on the edge of spiritual bankruptcy. Hence his dream of a dangerous river, a stream which might burn (immoral?) people to death. Witches, devils and evil spirits fuse with Dazee's morbid imaginings.

Sherwood describes how Dazee's fever subsides and how he and the other smuggled slaves are 'liberated' from the ship and removed to the 'free colony' of Sierra Leone. Here she endorses contemporary Evangelical efforts to prevent, by force, the slave trading which had been made illegal by the Abolition Act of 1807. Following the Act, she notes,

certain captains of ships were still found wicked enough to carry on this trade. . . . On this discovery, a certain set of pious and humane persons formed themselves into a society, under whose direction ships were sent out to seize upon such vessels as were engaged in this unlawful course; to restore liberty to the captives; and to bring their captors to deserved punishment. (p. 26)

Sherwood then explains why liberated Africans could not be returned to their countries but were domiciled willy-nilly in the colony that Britain had tried to establish:

But, whereas it was found impossible to reinstate each individual captive in his own respective village and family, on account of the great danger and difficulty of travelling in Africa; the British government directed that such negroes as might be found in the captured slave-vessels should be carried to the settlement of Sierra Leone. (pp. 26–27)

According to Sherwood, the administrators of the settlement would donate some land to the captured Africans who had just arrived from another country on the continent and were in the process of being physically freed. Along with land, they would receive

materials for building; and . . . also provided with means of instruction, with ministers, and with places of worship – by which means, many are now taught to know the true God, who would otherwise have remained in a state of total ignorance. (pp. 26–28)

Next, Sherwood introduces the issue of a quasi-system of apprentice-ship involving Liberated Africans. Because the people were unpro-tected when they arrived, people offered to house them and then used them illegally as workers or indentured servants. Since records were loosely kept, some of those workers were being subjected to a form of slavery about which they had no recourse. This use of forced labour in Sierra Leone was stirring up a controversy in London where humanitarians were being branded as hypocrites:

[They] practiced slavery [i.e. apprenticeship] in Africa while trying to deny it to the West Indian planters. The controversy ran through the whole decade of the 1810's before it finally died away. It did nothing to stop the practice of apprenticeship in Sierra Leone, but it did serve as a warning that schemes for the 'civilization' of Africa through forced labor would be sure to meet a powerful and diverse opposition in Britain.[27]

Sherwood's tale offsets these critiques and offers a new more positive, Evangelical gloss on corrupt practices. She goes on: 'On board one of these ships was a certain missionary – a Mr. W— , who was going to Africa in order to devote his life to the instruction of its ignorant inhabitants' (p. 32). In the Evangelical scheme, such missionaries were compensating for European 'crimes' committed in Africa in the name of Christianity. These religious educators could help to cancel or offset such corruption. Mr. W— makes sure that Dazee is immediately 'washed to get rid of the filth which he had contacted in the slave-vessel' (pp. 32–33). Lightly modelled on Henry Martyn, Mr. W— educates Dazee about his former state of spiritual darkness and his future duties as a Christian.[28] The fact that Sherwood knew about derisive responses to missionaries in India is an unknown variable in Mr. W—'s discourse.

A man who understands both Dazee's unspecified native tongue and English helps Mr. W— communicate Calvinist doctrine to Dazee. The ex-slave quickly learns about the Edenic Fall, natural depravity, rewards and punishments; to Mr. W—'s delight, he catches on quickly. Evangelical ideas seem – the text implies – like a game to him, to be played, mastered, and regurgitated. Nonetheless, he still longs for his 'poor mother'. The fact that he articulates this longing 'in his own tongue' marks the fact that he has, spiritually speaking, far to go (p. 50). If he were more 'civilized', he would recognize the superiority of English. He also transfers to Mr. W— 'that affection which till that time had been wholly confined to his mother' (p. 36). Mr. W— places Dazee in a beautiful school for boys, with newly cultivated gardens all around. These gardens are metonymic of Dazee himself: 'for their general improvement and comfort and they should all learn the English tongue as a common medium of intercourse' (p. 40).

Through Christian practice, Dazee gradually transforms himself. He comes to represent the assimilated Other; he substitutes an obedient citizen for the conventional West African stereotype. In other words, Dazee functions as a foil to that native who is usually

---

[27] For illicit labour practices, see Curtin, *The Image of Africa*, p. 275.
[28] *The Life and Times of Mrs. Sherwood (1775–1851)*, p. xx.

described as 'indolent, dull, treacherous, and childish'.[29] According
to David Killingray, West Africans were most commonly characterized as 'lazy, superstitious, brutal, cruel, barbaric, stupid, bloodthirsty.'[30] Like a garden of flowers, Dazee will flourish if he becomes
a Christian, whereas his mother lies still buried in dark soil. Gardens
symbolize self-cultivation. As Dazee becomes a more ardent Christian, he understands the need for weeding and pruning, for bright-
ening the world and leaving a permanent trace behind. His
gardening will signify God's kindness, his grateful and active co-
operation with nature. In conjunction with this harmony in nature,
Dazee becomes a fine and literate pupil who learns hymns, some
agriculture, and garden management. He becomes 'like' a British
citizen, or at least someone to whom a British readership can relate.

Unsurprisingly, Evangelical beliefs exercise a powerful and wholesome influence. But he still feels the effect of that earlier trauma.
Several years after his conversion, he informs Mr. W—:

'I do pray; every day I pray for my mother,' replied the young man. 'She
nurse me when I a child – she too kind – she very much cry when she no
find me, I know. Oh, my poor mother!' (pp. 42–43)

Collapsing in 'an agony of grief and tears', Dazee confesses that
finding his mother has been constantly preying on his mind.
Common in societies harmoniously bound by extended family units,
his actions are in line with the Ten Commandments; Dazee's quest,
that is, enhances his spiritual cachet. Many of the Liberated Africans
in the Freetown King's Yard were hopeful of finding relatives, quite
frequently their mother.[31]

When Dazee's mother eventually arrives in Sierra Leone as a re-
captured slave, Dazee flies 'like lightning' to the missionary room
when he hears she might be there: 'He stole . . . softly round the
room . . . stepped gently forward, [spoke] in his native tongue with
all that warmth of attachment, [using the] tender appelation of
mother' (pp. 52–54). Dazee's delicate reaction, his quiet almost-
stalking of his mother and his bestowing evident affection on her at
the final recognition marks Dazee as a dependent child, even a

---

[29] Syed Hassein Alatas, *The Myth of the Lazy Native. A Study of the Image of the Malays, Filipinos and
Javanese from the 16th to the 20th century and its function in the ideology of colonial capitalism* (London,
1977), p. 112.

[30] David Killingray, *A Plague of Europeans. Westerners in Africa Since the Fifteenth Century*
(Harmondsworth, 1973), pp. 6, 56 and passim.

[31] Peterson, *Province of Freedom*, p. 194.

'feminized' figure. He resembles many protagonists in eighteenth-
and nineteenth-century women's novels, who are Christ-like in their
gentleness and benevolence. Embodying a mix of male and female
qualities, Dazee exemplifies a certain ambiguity about power. In this
respect, Dazee's character reflects a prominent trope in British
representations of India – the 'androgyny' of Indian men: 'By
characterizing the entire Indian race as feminine – that is, weak –
colonial ideology put [British] patriarchy in the service of imperialism.'[32] By contrast, as soon as Dazee assumes the missionary role, he
acts somewhat differently. That is, he rather high-handedly, even
brutally, tries to introduce his mother to Christianity:

It would be impossible to describe the joy of the young negro when, at last,
he saw his poor mother a little recovering, and stretching out her withered
hand in order to draw him towards her. She began to talk rapidly, and to
shew a *greegree*, or charm, which she had always carried about her, and
which, she said, she was sure had brought her good luck in the end. But her
son, breaking the string from her neck, and throwing it from him with
disdain, sought, without loss of time, to give her the first religious
instruction of which she was capable. (pp. 56–57)

This act of Dazee's, in violently pulling the necklace off his mother's
neck, is often included as an illustrated plate in the text. Sherwood
intends this act – it seems – to signify Dazee's Evangelical ardour at
white heat. In frightening his mother with such violence, moreover,
he mimics the brutality of slavers. He replicates his own traumas.
And to push replication even further, does he also reproduce or re-
channel suppressed feelings about his psychological-ideological cap-
tivity? At one level, Sherwood foregrounds the violence of European
intervention in African lives in the name of freedom. Yet the fact
that intimidation persists in the mother's life and that she cannot live
in a psychologically secure state goes unmentioned. After removing
the necklace, Dazee takes his weak, emaciated mother to his house,
carrying her 'tenderly . . . to his little dwelling, where he laid her on
his own bed in the inner apartment' (p. 57).

At this point, Dazee's conflicts emerge even more clearly. He still
deeply loves his mother. European interference, however, has rendered him a mimic son. He ventriloquizes the civilizing (and

---

[32] See Janaki Nair, 'Uncovering the Zenana. Visions of Indian Womanhood in English-
women's Writings, 1813–1940', *Expanding the Boundaries of Women's History. Essays on Women in
the Third World*, ed. Cheryl Johnson-Odim and Margaret Strobel (Bloomington and
Indianapolis, 1992), p. 28.

Evangelical) mission – making people accept Christian values at all costs. After explaining the goodness of white people's activities, he informs her 'that by the divine help she might be taught the true religion, and might receive help from God to give up her *greegrees*, and her idols, with all the other abominations and absurdities of heathenism' (p. 62). When he is close by his mother, without any Europeans present, he becomes the Dazee who longs for womb-like comfort.

To match his refashioned relationship to his mother, Dazee's language becomes miraculously grammar perfect.[33] Even the pidgin English in which he formerly spoke has transformed itself. Christianity has fostered a new understanding. Dazee can now enact the Christian imperative down to and in perfect English. His mother's response about 'the great spirit of the woods' incites Dazee's contempt: 'He assured her that he feared no evil spirit of any description, knowing that all spirits were at the command of the one great God, and that no spirit had any power to injure the true followers of that God' (p. 63). Once again, supercilious attitudes toward Africans thread their way through Dazee's discourse. Sherwood's spokesman, he models a future, African statesman, desirable to the British. Whether he will succumb to or sabotage their demands provides a point of radical indeterminacy.

The rest of the story constitutes a diatribe against African religion and culture under the guise of converting Dazee's mother: 'all was as yet very dark and confused to her understanding'. Perhaps this final section constitutes Sherwood's personalized vision of how the Sierra Leone colony should look, peopled by Evangelical converts. Fashioning a new textual Sierra Leone, she imagines it 'out loud' for the British reading public. Through the figure of the mother, Dazee's natal culture is ridiculed and textually dissolved, such an eradication mandatory in a text of Christian propaganda. Sherwood fears 'paganism' for its social alternative, encoded as a disruption of 'the realm of affective ties'.[34] The tale ends neatly – or so it seems. Slowly Dazee's mother grasps the significance of Dazee's beliefs: 'Though not able to comprehend the whole of his address to the Almighty, notwithstanding its being made in her own language, yet

---

[33] Mary Louise Pratt, *Imperial Eyes. Travel Writing and Transculturation* (London and New York, 1992), p. 52.
[34] Nancy Armstrong quoted in Mary Jean Corbett, 'Feminine Authorship and Spiritual Authority in Victorian Women Writers' Autobiographies', *Women's Studies*, 18 (1990), p. 21.

she understood enough to be tenderly touched.' (p. 69) After this 'he led her out to see his garden, and the hut or cabin he had built in remembrance of that in which he had spent his infancy' (p. 70).

Here, at some level, the fictional characters enact a buried, historical knowledge. To return to what they crave of that former idyllic harmony, they must accept what has been forced on them in the interim. Given their palpable vulnerability, they can scarcely ignore or overtly sabotage British colonialism. Through their acceptance of the Christian paradigm, the mother-son unit has at least a chance of growing together. Dazee ends by warning his mother that

the men of our village are idolaters, and their understandings are darkened by a vile and cruel superstition. They lie under the terrors of witchcraft, and the fear of evil spirits, from which we are delivered in this place, where the Sun of Righteousness arises and shines upon us with healing in his wings. Barbarous slave-dealers, also, frequent our country; while the white men in this place devote their lives to the comfort and happiness of such rescued captives as ourselves. (pp. 70–71)

Such overstatement about African culture belies an insecurity and a fear of future resistance. Even though Dazee became a convert years ago, intimidation still hovers:

Her pious son labored incessantly in this great work in which he could receive no material assistance from the missionaries until his mother began to understand somewhat of the English language. (pp. 71–72)

As Europeans see it, Dazee is responsible for African culture and its negativity. A final act of colonial treachery unwittingly highlighted by Sherwood, this intimidation is represented as an efficacious recommendation in the service of conversion. After Dazee's mother is converted, the author steps in for a final address:

It pleased the Lord, however, in his good time, to bless the efforts of Dazee for the spiritual welfare of his beloved parent; and the author has great pleasure in reporting, that, after residing little more than two years in the station, she gave such satisfactory evidence of a change of heart, that it was thought proper to receive her into the church, by the administration of holy baptism. (p. 72)

Sherwood's tale about Africa proffers a moral code to live by, and Dazee's scrupulous surveillance of his mother, Sherwood implies, will persist. He has become a permanent Christian soldier.[35]

---

[35] For this point in another context, see Benedict Anderson, *Imagined Communities: Reflections on the Origin and Spread of Nationalism* (New York, 1983).

The timing of Sherwood's tale is no coincidence. Her ardent
Evangelical beliefs, Wilberforce's enthusiasm, her departure from
India, and the consequent cessation of tales about the subcontinent
– all inspired and spurred her on. Specifically, she wrote *The Re-
captured Negro* after she returned to England and Wilberforce requested her to 'tell me about . . . the heathen, all you know – let me
hear it'.[36] In prioritizing conversion, Sherwood includes the familiar
matrix of references that characterized anti-slavery tracts: family
fracture, Christianity, good and bad Africans as well as good and
bad Europeans, and patriotism. The notable absence is any discourse about emancipation itself, although, arguably, that discourse
is implied, regardless of what Sherwood explicitly states.

The Re-captured Negro re-enacts a white fantasy about post-abolition
in Africa in which Africans themselves are configured as malleable
objects; it produces a colonial discourse about Africa that re-enacts
Sherwood's abruptly terminated texts about India. Sherwood shows
the new nation at work. Ideologically blinkering her audience, she
constructs a seemingly workable – though narrow and incomplete –
community of believers. Her erasures are evident but a reading
public could, and probably did, assume that this narrative was one
facet of the society being brought to birth.

Thus, this odd eruption of a West African narrative in Sherwood's
corpus partly stems from colonial nostalgia. It fills an emotional
vacuum, expressing her grief at being deprived of a topic and a
subcontinent whose land and people she was used to expropriating
at will. Sherwood's representations of West Africa serve a complex
purpose, partly religious, partly economic and personal, but decisively national and colonial.[37]

By maintaining the colonized subject as an obedient and proper
subject (object) of investigation, women like Sherwood were cultural
proponents of British foreign policy. Offering readers a textual place
that is 'obviously intelligible' from which to view the 'subject',[38] Sherwood sites her audience on the side (in the ideology) of colonialism. The
narrator offers an identification with her/his 'gaze' for the reader:[39]

---

[36] Wilberforce in, *The Life and Times of Mrs. Sherwood (1775–1851)*, pp. 439–42.
[37] Nair, 'Uncovering', p. 26.
[38] Catherine Belsey, 'Constructing the Subject. Deconstructing the Text', in *Feminist Criticism
and Social Change: Sex, Class and Race in Literature and Culture*, ed. Judith Newton and Deborah
Rosenfelt (New York, 1985), p. 45.
[39] Ibid., p. 53.

In an Althusserian sense this colonial ideology is a deliberate obfuscation, nothing less than a system of representations (discourses, images, myths) . . . but imagery [too] in that it discourages a full understanding of . . . conditions of existence.[40]

For colonial purposes, Sherwood encodes the new possibility of a liberated African society as part of the 'white man's burden' – a people to be fed, clothed, taught, and generally taken care of. Often uncomprehending, since the native tongue of Liberated Africans is never English, the repatriated people are treated as children, as limited/liminal cultural beings. Their transportation from one drastic experience to another, in the guise of objectified, barterable beings, never surfaces as a serious issue.

For personal reasons too, Sherwood does not deviate from her principles since they constitute a blanket permission to write. Her commitment brands her work as necessary and her self-representation as noble, despite the almost unladylike boldness required for publication. In Mary Jean Corbett's words,

the religious woman writer reduces the risk of entering discourse by appealing to values, specifically religious ones, that require her self-effacement even as they invest her with a voice to which other Evangelical Christians will listen.[41]

Sherwood's political representation notwithstanding, however, through the popular, hegemonic discourse of 'Evangelese', an embedded narrative about Africans and self-assertion insistently inflects the text. This veiled subtext disrupts the spiritual message when Christianity, for example, threatens to separate Dazee from his mother. Such privileging of religion over maternality is fleetingly questioned. The presence of Africans, whether silent or not, further reveals textual fissures that assail Sherwood's seemingly inviolable, moral position. Not to put too fine a point on it, were it not for Dazee's coincidental reconciliation with his mother, the tale would reveal the extent to which the colony of Sierra Leone destroyed African family life and denied individuals the constant use of their 'first' language. Unwittingly, Sherwood kept pushing at and beyond the text's political limits. Simultaneously, she adopted a traditional Evangelical stance as an architect of conversion and empire, as a colonizer with assumed rights.

[40] Ibid., p. 46.   [41] Mary Jean Corbett, 'Feminine Authorship', p. 20.

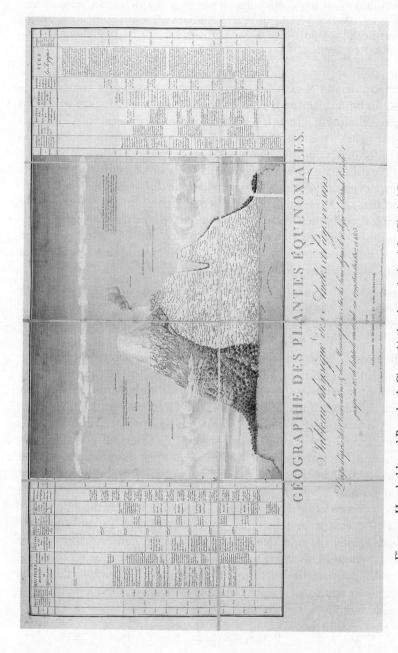

Figure 1. Humboldt and Bonplerd, *Géographie des plantes équinoxiales* (*Physical Portrait of the Tropics*)

CHAPTER 10

'Wandering through Eblis'; absorption and containment in Romantic exoticism[1]

Nigel Leask

THE PHYSICAL PORTRAIT OF THE TROPICS

Alexander von Humboldt's huge engraving of the Ecuadorian mountains Chimborazo and Cotopaxi – considered to be the highest in the world – and of the vertical ecology of the Andes, was published in 1807 as the frontispiece to the first volume of his monumental *Voyage en Amerique*, entitled *Essai sur la géographie des plantes, accompagné d'un tableau physique des pays équinoxiales*.[2] Humboldt's 'Physical Portrait of the Tropics' offers an extreme, but, nevertheless instructive case of the problems of exotic representation in the Romantic period, and of the contradiction between aesthetic affect and topographical information in mediating the non-European world to a European public, greedy for such images of its distant Others. On the one hand, the 'Physical Portrait' solicits an *aesthetic* response to Chimborazo, the partial ascent of which in 1802 had been, perhaps, the most celebrated episode in Humboldt's five-year expedition to Spanish America. Like the best eighteenth-century landscape traveller-artists, Humboldt claimed to have sketched Chimborazo 'on the spot'; his field sketches, suffused with his own affective response to the sublimity of the mountain, provided the basis for further published engravings in his celebrated *Vues des Cordillères*, translated into English by Helen Maria Williams and published in 1814 as *Researches concerning the Institutions and Monuments of the Ancient Inhabitants of America, with Descriptions and Views of Some of the most Striking Scenes in the Cordilleras*.

But unlike the Chimborazo of the *Vues des Cordillères*, the mountain's depiction, in the 'Physical Portrait of the Tropics' plate, went

---

[1] My title refers to the Halls of Eblis in William Beckford's novel *Vathek* (1786).
[2] Alexander von Humboldt, *Voyage en Amerique* (Paris, 1807).

beyond the picturesque or the sublime. The whole right half of the
mountain's surface has been cut away in order to present a *tabula
rasa* upon which to record the Linnaean names of plants growing at
different altitudes, entailing a sudden transition from figurative to
cartographic representation. Moreover, the huge fold-out image of
the mountains is itself framed by sixteen columns or tables which
present 'all the phenomena that the surface of our planet present to
the observer – the general result of five years in the tropics'.[3] For
example, column three from the left gives the comparative elevation
of other celebrated mountains in metres; column five, types of
agriculture practised at different altitudes; column seven the blue-
ness of the sky, measured with Saussure's cyanometer; column
eleven the chemical composition of the atmosphere, measured with
Volta's eudiometer; and column fifteen the geological structure at
different altitudes. Humboldt's 'Physical Portrait of the Tropics'
represents an encyclopedic digest of information about the tropics,
in the guise of an image, a sort of informational hypertext, which
confounds the spatial and temporal disciplines of aesthetic looking.
Humboldt's attempt to combine subjective and objective representation of the Tropics – the *way we feel* about the external world is as
much a part of its meaning as what we can measure or know about it
– is described by Mary Louise Pratt as an attempt 'to reframe
bourgeois subjectivity, heading off its sundering of objectivist and
subjectivist strategies, science and sentiment, information and experience . . . he proposed to Europeans a new kind of planetary
consciousness'.[4]

At the same time, Pratt is in accord with post-colonial critics like
Gayatri Spivak who read such totalizing projects as acts of 'epistemological violence' wrought upon the non-European world in the
interests of European, imperial expansion.[5] Notwithstanding the fact
that Humboldt's 'rediscovery' of Spanish America made an important contribution to emergent nineteenth-century creole nationalist
ideologies and to the complex post-colonial cultures of 'independent'
Latin America, it bears all the tell-tale marks of Euro-imperialism.

---

[3] Quoted in Michael Dettelbach, 'Global Physics and Aesthetic Empire: Humboldt's Physical
Portrait of the Tropics', in *Visions of Empire: Voyages, Botany and Representations of Nature*, eds.
David Miller and Peter Reill (Cambridge, 1996), p. 269.
[4] Mary Louise Pratt, *Imperial Eyes: Travel Writing and Transculturation* (London and New York,
1992), p. 119.
[5] See Gayatri Chakravorty Spivak, 'Can the Subaltern Speak?', in *Marxism and the Interpretation
of Culture*, eds. Cary Nelson and Lawrence Grossberg (London, 1988), pp. 271–313; passim.

For example, in the instance before us, indigenous plant nomenclatures and indigenous accounts of the coherence of the Andean eco-system are forced into a globalized, Linnaean taxonomy and, thereby, made subject to European bio-imperialism, foreshadowing the deculturization and deterritorialization of colonized peoples in the capitalist 'modernization' movements of the nineteenth and twentieth centuries. Nor is this 'epistemological violence' limited to the natural environment; ethnographic representations of the period frequently empty landscapes of indigenous inhabitants (as in the present example), or else typify their cultural attributes as fixed essences frozen in a primordial antiquity.

How does the sort of totalizing representation of the Tropics, of which Humboldt's image is an (extreme) example, impact upon Romantic poetics? Robert Southey paid a high tribute to Humboldt when he wrote 'He is among travellers what Wordsworth is among poets. The extent of his knowledge and the perfect command which he has of it are truly suprising; and with this he unites a painter's eye and a poet's feelings.'[6] Wordsworth's poetry characteristically creates a sense of unity by interiorizing landscape and distancing detail, a process aptly exemplified in 'Lines written . . . a few miles above Tintern Abbey' (1798). As Barbara Maria Stafford writes, 'the Romantic quest ultimately leads, not unidirectionally out into the blank plains, dense forests, or nebulous skies of a beckoning or unknown land, but back into the tangled self'.[7] In this light the exotic mannerism of Coleridge's dream-landscape in 'Kubla Khan' (albeit inspired by Samuel Purchas's Renaissance travelogue) seems more characteristic of Romantic, exotic representation than Humboldt's 'Physical Portrait of the Tropics', and certainly has no trouble achieving *formal* unity, whatever the exegetical problems which arise from it. In the essay which follows, I want, however, to suggest that, perhaps after all, Humboldt does represent a better paradigm for Romantic exoticism than 'Kubla Khan', and that a discursive tension between subjectivist and objectivist strategies of representation, perfectly illustrated by the aporetic superimposition of Humboldt's scholarly graffiti onto the blank surface of the sublime

[6] *New Letters of Robert Southey*, ed. Kenneth Curry, 2 vols (New York and London, 1965), II, p. 231; 19 December 1821.
[7] Barbara Maria Stafford, *Voyage into Substance: Art, Science, Nature and the Illustrated Travel Account 1760–1840* (Cambridge, Massachusetts and London, 1984), p. 444.

mountain, frequently disrupts the unity of exotic images and narratives in the period.

What then is at stake in this tension between an 'absorptive', figural realism and the distancing, epistemological command in exotic representations like the 'Physical Portrait', and to what extent is it reproduced in literary as well as visual accounts? In an attempt to answer this question, I will draw upon the work of art historians like Michael Fried (from whom I have borrowed, out of context, the notion of 'absorption'), Barbara Stafford and Bernard Smith, as well as upon the popular panoramic displays of the Romantic period. I do so in order to suggest some ways in which problems arising from exotic visual representation might help us understand analogous problems in the case of literary exoticism, exemplified in this essay by the Romantic Orientalism of Southey, Byron and Sir William Jones. I choose this particular grouping of poets, rather than the 'internalized' exoticism of 'Kubla Khan', because I want to push the link between 'scientific exploration' and Romantic poetry further than Barbara Stafford, for whom the link is mainly metaphorical, a question of contextual or stylistic innovation.[8] A glance at the dense footnotes of (for example) *Thalaba the Destroyer*, *The Corsair* or *Lalla Rookh* will reveal a much more literal dependence upon the 'scientific' travel narrative on the part of the poets than Stafford seems to allow, in exotic narrative poems which differ somewhat from the 'dream-like Orient' of 'Kubla Khan'. The totalizing project revealed by these footnotes and the depth of ethnographic detail which they underwrite may well be a vestige of the Renaissance notion of epic as a compendium of universal science[9]; although as I will suggest below they also represent a new Romantic aesthetic of cultural particularism. What is of most interest here is poetic *affect*; namely, the actual discrepancy, rather than desired unity, between poetic text and annotation. I will argue that the absorptive pull of the exotic visual image or allusion – exemplified, but not of course exhausted, by the *panoramic* image – is constantly checked and qualified by a globalizing, descriptive discourse which draws the viewer/reader away from dangerous proximity to the image, in order to inscribe him/her in a position of epistemological power; nothing other than the commanding vision of imperialist objectivity. The aporetic

---

[8] Ibid., p. 444.

[9] See Stuart Curran, *Poetic Form and British Romanticism* (New York, 1986), pp. 180–81.

eruption of Linnaean graffiti on the surface of Humboldt's Chimborazo (as well as the 'Physical Portrait's' 'framing' columns) is in this respect analogous to the role of the scholarly footnote which constantly disrupts the reader's concentration in the exotic poems of Southey or Moore.

EXOTICISM, ORIENTALISM, AND THE PANORAMIC DISPLAY

Like the souvenir described by Susan Stewart in her provocative essay *On Longing*, the Romantic exotic image is not simply an object appearing out of context, a distant object surviving incongruously in present space; rather, its function is to envelope or absorb the present or familiar within the distant or unfamiliar.[10] The Romantic exotic image, like the souvenir, *solicits a grounding narrative*. In this respect, it differs markedly from the exotic 'curiosity' of an earlier period which, in departing from the aesthetic norm, really served to consolidate neoclassical notions of a standard of taste. James Bunn has linked the exotic curio to the aesthetics of British Mercantilism in the period 1688–1763; 'since each curio has been remaindered from its originating environs, it no longer signifies in a figure/ ground relationship such as Heidegger's *The Origin of the Work of Art*, which sets forth the earth as it discloses itself. In a curio cabinet, each cultural remnant has a circumscribed allusiveness among a collection of others.'[11] It is precisely the holistic figure/ground relationship denied by the curio which we saw Humboldt's 'Physical Portrait of the Tropics' attempting to represent. Harriet Guest describes the transformation from the mercantilist curio to Romantic exoticism in her essay on tattooing, 'Curiously Marked'; '[eighteenth-century] exoticism ... inscribes its object with an accultural illegibility, isolated from any coherence of origin. Exoticised subjects are characterised as sports, marked as singular tokens lacking any significance beyond that of a fragmentary and unrepresentative (because unrepresent*able*) insularity.' In contrast, exoticism of a later period (described by Guest, with a nod to Edward Said, as 'Orientalism') brings a context with it; 'assimilat[ing] its objects to a

---

[10] Adapted from Susan Stewart, *On Longing: Narratives of the Miniature, the Gigantic, the Souvenir, the Collection* (Baltimore and London, 1986), p. 151.

[11] James Bunn, 'The Aesthetics of British Mercantilism', *New Literary History*, 11:2 (Winter 1980), pp. 303–21 (p. 304).

generalised homogeneity, a wealth of inscrutable detail that it is the perquisite of the knowing European to articulate'.[12]

Building on Guest's useful distinction here, I want to suggest that the figure/ground relationship axiomatic to Romantic exoticism was closely linked to the rise of new technologies and genres of aesthetic illusionism – new and 'all-embracing' ways of seeing and telling – coterminous with a more systematic exploration and codification of the colonial, contact zone, entailing a corresponding rejection of mercantilist-style 'collecting'. This made it possible, for the first time, for the artist to absorb or 'find a home' for the metropolitan spectator in a particularized, exotic scene, rather than demarcating off the exotic object as a decontextualized 'curiosity'. The effect of this not only troubled the prospective command of neoclassical and picturesque aesthetics, constructed through generalized subject-matter, perspectival distancing and framing, but also permitted, in David Bunn's words, 'a rival indigenous semiotics . . . to assert itself'.[13] The new figure/ground relationship effected a trans-formation in the cultural imagining of space: as a writer in the *Repository of Arts* put it in 1826, 'What between steam-boats and panoramic exhibitions, we are every day not only informed of, but actually brought into contact with remote objects.'[14] The shift from a mercantilist to a colonialist phase of imperialist ideology was productive of a new relationship between the metropolitan spectator and the exotic – now, often, in the strict sense, *colonial* – image. The inversion from curio to absorptive exoticism, in the first half of the nineteenth century, is exemplified in the development of eighteenth-century theatrical scenography and topographical painting, with the difference that theatricality has now been erased; the spectator is here identified with the actor and placed, as it were, within the proscenium. We can see an early example of this in Philip de Loutherbourg's scenographic 'Egyptian Hall', constructed at William Beckford's seat, Fonthill Abbey, in 1781, for an expensive private party, a weekend of 'romantic villagiatura'. De Louther-

---

[12] Harriet Guest, 'Curiously Marked: Tattooing, Masculinity, and Nationality in 18th Century British Perceptions of the South Pacific', in *Painting and the Politics of Culture. New Essays on British Art 1700–1850*, ed. John Barrell (Oxford, 1992), p. 102.

[13] David Bunn, ' "Our Wattled Cot": Mercantile and Domestic Spaces in Thomas Pringle's African Landscapes', in *Landscape and Power*, ed. W. J. T. Mitchell (Chicago and London, 1994), p.128.

[14] Quoted in Ralph Hyde, *Panoramania: The Art and Entertainment of the 'All-Embracing' View* (London, 1988), p. 37.

bourg's spectacular scenography, based on careful study of Egyptian archaeology, would inspire Beckford's celebrated description of the 'Halls of Eblis' in his Oriental romance *Vathek* (about which I will have more to say below), published five years later, in 1786. Here, the shock of representational novelty, the exotic *verisimilitude* of de Loutherbourg's imagery, is characteristically mediated through the 'transgressive' genre of romance.[15] This is how Beckford later described the Egyptian Hall, and his absorption into the scenery through which he was wandering;

I still feel warmed and irradiated by the recollections of that strange, necromantic light which Loutherbourg had thrown over what absolutely appeared a realm of Fairy, or rather, perhaps, a Demon temple deep beneath the earth set apart for tremendous mysteries . . . the glowing haze investing every object, the mystic look, the vastness, the intricacy of this vaulted labyrinth, occasioned so bewildering an effect that it became impossible for any one to define – at that moment – where he stood, where he had been, or to whither he was wandering . . . it was in short the realization of romance in its most extravagant intensity.[16]

The absorptive 'pull' of de Loutherbourg's scenery (his illusionistic *Eidophusikon*, also invented in 1781, and his magnificent stage-scenery for O'Keefe's 1785 pantomime *Omai; or a Voyage round the World*, described by Bernard Smith, seem to have had a similar effect[17]) would soon have to compete with the huge panoramas of Robert Barker, William Daniell and Robert Ker Porter, Charles Marshall's *Kineorama* and, most spectacularly of all, Louis Daguerre's diorama. Although by no means all the panoramic images of the Romantic age were exotic, Asian cities like Madras, Constantinople, Calcutta, Banares, as well as archaeological sites like Karnac, Thebes, Balbek and 'subterraneous temples in Hindoostan' were particularly popular.

[15] An analogous 'rhetoric of evocation', developing simultaneously in the field of historical and antiquarian representation, has been explored in the work of Stephen Bann, which I have found tremendously suggestive in preparing the present chapter. See Bann's 'Sense of the Past: Image, Text, and the Object in the Formation of Historical Consciousness in Nineteenth-Century Britain', in *The New Historicism*, ed. H. Aram Veeser (London and New York, 1989), p.105, and his *The Clothing of Clio: A Study of the Representation of History in Nineteenth-Century Britain and France* (Cambridge, 1984).

[16] Cited in William Beckford, *Vathek*, ed. with introduction by Roger Lonsdale (Oxford, 1970), pp. xi-xii.

[17] Cf Bernard Smith, *European Vision and the South Pacific, 1768–1850*, 2nd edn (New Haven and London, 1985), pp. 114–18 for a full account of *Omai* and of de Loutherbourg's stage designs.

Robert Ker Porter's imperialist panorama, *The Storming of Seringa-patam*, has been provocatively discussed by William H. Galperin in *The Return of the Visible in British Romanticism*, one of the few critical discussions of panoramic representation in the period, and to which my present remarks are indebted.[18] Here, the serene pastoralism of the Daniell's picturesque views of India is transmogrified into a huge, imperial battlefield. The documentary and ethnographical detail of Ker Porter's panorama was its great strength, particularly when compared with scenographical representations of the same event. The storming of Seringapatam, in 1799, produced a wave of Tipu dramas over the next thirty years, climaxing with a big Easter Monday production at Astley's, in 1829, characterized by grave, ethnographical misrepresentation, or what Denys Forrest calls 'the whole rag-bag of pseudo-Orientalism and pseudo-history'. The black hole of Calcutta was relocated in Mysore and Hyder Ali's court was set against a backdrop of 'the Ganges by Moonlight'.[19] In stark contrast, Ker Porter's panorama of the *Storming* was 120 feet long, covering 2,550 square feet of canvas, stretched around three-quarters of a circle, one of the biggest paintings ever executed. According to the *Times* of 26 April 1800, it was 'designed from the most authentic and correct information, relative to the Scenery of the Place, the Costume of the Soldiery, and the various circum-stances of the Attack . . . Explanatory Descriptions will be given at the Exhibition Room'.[20]

Part of the sensational appeal of the massive panorama, with its mobile, circulating audience, was the sacrifice of a picturesque framing technique, its replacement by the 360° canvas, and a proliferation of minute and apparently accidental particulars. The panorama thus made a decisive break with the framing devices of theatricality, as shared by scenography and picturesque painting. One contemporary described how in the panorama, 'the top and bottom of the picture are connected by the framework of the gallery; thus to the spectator, having no object with which to compare those represented in the picture, they appear in their natural dimensions, and, with the aid of aerial perspective, an almost infinite space and distance can be represented with a degree of illusion quite won-

---

[18] William H. Galperin, *The Return of the Visible in British Romanticism* (Baltimore, 1993).
[19] Denys Forrest, *The Tiger of Mysore: The Life and Death of Tipu Sultan* (London, 1970), p. 319.
[20] Cited in Galperin, *The Return of the Visible*, p. 50.

derful'.[21] The panorama's illusionistic recreation of natural effects, the abolition of this frame and the effect of 'perspectival relativism' which nullified a commanding, viewing position (placing the spectator as it were 'within' the scene, without any external point of visual comparison), embodied a novel relationship between the spectator and the exotic object, demanding a radical revision of viewing dispositions. Disruption of the spectator's aesthetic command in this manner and the suspension of a point of comparison bear more than a passing resemblance to the aesthetics of the sublime as formulated by Kant and other influential theorists of the Romantic period. 'Sublimity', as a term of art, however, is seldom encountered in descriptions of panoramic viewings, presumably on account 'of the panorama's low 'cultural capital' as a highly commodified version of landscape aesthetics, and a privatized *substitute* for aristocratic or imperial travel. The panorama is the apotheosis of the eighteenth-century tradition of topographical painting, prevented, inasmuch as it was considered to be a *mechanical*, representational practice, from participating in the sort of gentlemanly 'republic of taste' described by John Barrell in *The Political Theory of Painting*.[22] As the painter Constable commented, 'great principles are neither expected nor looked for in this mode of describing nature', and (in relation to the diorama) 'it is without the pale of Art because its object is deception – Claude's never was – or any other great landscape painter's'.[23] Wordsworth similarly dismissed the panorama's 'mimic sights that ape / The absolute presence of reality' in Book 7 of the *Prelude*, (1805, VII, lines 248–49; 261–64) – a sort of troubling, early nineteenth-century version of 'virtual reality'.

The only control exerted over panoramic viewing seems to have been (as it were) extrinsic to the act of perceptual engagement, namely the preparatory lectures or explanatory pamphlets offered to the public which served as 'guides' or 'keys' to the exotic vista. (We might contrast this with Humboldt's disruptive incorporation of botanical nomenclature into the figural image itself in the 'Physical Portrait of the Tropics'.) The fact that in viewing panoramas the

---

[21] F. W. Fairholt's description in *A Dictionary of Terms in Art* (London, 1854) quoted in Martin Meisel, *Realizations: Narrative, Pictorial and Theatrical Arts in 19th Century England* (Princeton, 1983), p. 61. Meisel describes the influence of panoramic viewing upon the structure of Dickens' novels.

[22] See John Barrell, *The Political Theory of Painting from Reynolds to Hazlitt: 'The Body of the Public'* (New Haven and London, 1986).

[23] Constable, *Correspondence*, II, p. 34; VI, p. 134. Quoted in Hyde, *Panoramania*, p. 28.

spectators moved about the circular viewing platform meant that they needed instruction in how to 'read' the 360° panoramic surface. Like the copious footnotes to Romantic Orientalist poems by Robert Southey, Lord Byron or Tom Moore, the descriptive pamphlet sold by the Barkers and other entrepreneurs sought to translate the vertiginous 'shock' of the panorama into ethnological or historical information, often with an ideological (imperialist, pious or patriotic) bent, not always evident within the viewing experience itself. Significantly, the first panoramic representation of an Oriental city, Barker's 1801 *Constantinople* at the Leicester Square Rotunda, also saw the beginning of this practice of annotation; a descriptive booklet was on sale for the price of sixpence which 'contained not only further descriptions of the numbered objects (the keyed prints were included), but also a general historical background, facts on native manners and costumes, and a wealth of interesting anecdotes [manifesting] a growing concern for completeness and educational value'.[24]

The panorama presents us with a clear (although clear because extreme) example of the absorptive quality of the exotic image in the Romantic period: it also provides an opportunity for combining the approaches of art historians like Michael Fried and Barbara Stafford in theorizing the construction of absorptive spectatorship in relation to exotic images. For Stafford, in her magisterial *Voyage into Substance*, the 'scientific' style characteristic of the travel-account is marked by *enargeia* (vivid description, devoid of metaphor and pathos) rather than the more literary *energeia* (forceful writing, appealing to the imagination to 'supplement what the external signs indicate only in part').[25] Here a conventional, neoclassical aesthetic (idealizing a plethora of particulars into 'a unified structure of generalisation') is nullified by the singularity or otherness of the phenomena observed. 'When the traveller . . . looks at, not over, the natural object [or cultural sign], he is no longer a spectator, he cannot become anything except what he beholds.'[26] Stafford's lack of interest, however, in eighteenth-century conventions of viewing tends to place emphasis upon the physical object rather than the 'object-disposition' of the viewer, as if such a pure, transparent gaze were at all

---

[24] Hyde, *Panoramania*, p. 36.
[25] Stafford, *Voyage into Substance*, p. 48.
[26] Barbara Stafford, 'Toward Romantic Landscape Perception: Illustrated Travels and The Rise of "Singularity" as an Aesthetic Category', *Art Quarterly*, NS 1 (1977), p. 114.

possible. But *Voyage into Substance* can be usefully read in tandem with Michael Fried's classic study of late eighteenth-century French painting, *Absorption and Theatricality*. Fried's account of the complexities of visual representation and, particularly, of absorption is far more nuanced than Stafford's, although he refuses to develop the historical context which her study might (at least in part) be seen to provide. On the basis of writings on art by Diderot and other contemporary French critics, the second part of Fried's study reconstructs an Enlightenment notion of the beholder's *absorption* in minor genres, such as pastoral and topographical painting. In contrast to Stafford, Fried is alert to the politics of genre which predetermined that absorptive representations were judged to possess little cultural capital. He describes how, in order to *detheatricalize* the experience of viewing, the fiction of the beholder's physical presence within the painting 'by means of an almost magical recreation of the effect of nature itself'[27] decisively broke with the picturesque aesthetic of Claude or Salvator Rosa. In 'pastoral' or exotic, topographical paintings a sort of perspectival relativism was achieved by the depiction of numerous points of view which 'ma[de] it virtually impossible for the beholder to grasp the scene as a single instantaneously apprehensible whole'; thereby dissolving 'the imaginary fixity of his position in front of the canvas'.[28] Of particular interest here is Fried's linkage of perceptual absorption with subject-dissolution in the new genres of visual representation, typified by theatrical scenography, exotic, topographical painting and panoramic displays.

'COSTUME-POETRY' VERSUS HIGH ROMANTIC THEORY

In the remainder of this chapter I want to shift from discussion of visual to literary representations of exotic subject-matter. The absorptive strangeness of the exotic image or allusion, like the vertiginous, viewing experience of the panoramas discussed above, called for footnoting, which at once guaranteed the authenticity of

---

[27] Michael Fried, *Absorption and Theatricality: Painting and Beholder in the Age of Diderot* (Berkeley, Los Angeles and London, 1980), p. 228. This occurs in the context of a discussion of the connections between de Loutherbourg's earlier 'absorptive' landscape paintings and his invention in 1781 of the *Eidophusikon*, a miniature theatre without actors that foreshadowed, in some respects, the dioramas of the early nineteenth century.

[28] Ibid., p. 134.

the allusion, whilst at the same time reassuring the metropolitan reader that it was both culturally legible and translatable. Of course, the footnote would have been unnecessary were it not for the aesthetic of particularism which had become axiomatic to Romantic exotic and (particularly in relation to the writings of Sir Walter Scott) antiquarian representations. It is not difficult to find a bridge between the 'sister arts' in discussing the new representational techniques of Romantic exoticism and the analogies between terms of art like 'typical landscape' and 'poetic costume'. The word 'costume' appears repeatedly in late eighteenth-century and Romantic poetics, a technical term which critics had derived – via eighteenth-century French channels – from the Italian 'costume', employed by painters since the Renaissance to describe 'guise or habit in artistic representations'; what we might prefer to call *setting* rather than mere clothing.[29] Neoclassical aesthetics had been hostile to 'costume' on the grounds that it jeopardized the 'grandeur of generality', and Dr Johnson had famously praised Shakespeare because of his sublime indifference to costume; 'His story requires Romans or Kings, but he thinks only on men.'[30] The craze for 'typicality' and 'costume' caused heated controversy in the field of travel-writing and poetry as well as in the visual arts; travel writers and painters might just as well be criticized for being unfaithful to the object, *insufficiently* particular, as over-particular. John Hawkesworth was censured for 'ghosting' Cook's first voyage, in 1773, by melding several first-hand narratives into 'a single first-person account, full of his own embellishments'.[31] Hawkesworth's 'sentimentalist' rendering of Cook's voyage was rejected by purist advocates of 'typicality' like George Forster (who had accompanied Captain Cook and later became Humboldt's mentor).

Bernard Smith has discussed the shortcomings of Anna Seward's celebrated *Elegy on Captain Cook* (1780) compared to Zoffany's painting *The Death of Cook* (1795), commenting that 'the conjunction of classical mythology and exotic naturalism was more incongruous in poetry than in painting'.[32] But a more ambitious, literary engagement with exotic 'costume' in the immediate pre-Romantic period is

---

[29] *Oxford English Dictionary* under 'costume'.
[30] 'Preface to Shakespeare' in *Selected Writings of Samuel Johnson*, ed. Patrick Crutwell (Harmondsworth, 1968), p. 266.
[31] Pratt, *Imperial Eyes*, p. 88.
[32] Smith, *European Vision*, p. 119.

represented by Sir William Jones's *Hindoo Hymns*, the first of which was published in the *Asiatic Miscellany* in 1784. The *Hymns*, in accordance with Jones's desideratum in his *Essay on the Poetry of the Eastern Nations* (1772), sought to regenerate the stale, neoclassical canon of European poetry 'with a new set of images and similitudes . . . which future scholars might explain and future poets might imitate'.[33] However, whilst Jones's *Hymns* enriched English poetry with a new, Hindu 'costume' and imagery, they stopped short of imitating Oriental poetic form (as well as the more 'extravagant' aspects of Hindu mythology), thereby establishing an acceptable, because adequately generalized, paradigm for future exotic poetry. Although the *Hymns* sought to 'explain and adorn the mythological fictions of the Hindus',[34] they did so by incorporating them as a sort of 'imperial heraldry' into the European poetic canon: to this end the cultural particularism of Hindu 'costume' was mediated by the poetic vehicle of the Pindaric or Miltonic Ode.[35] This wasn't simply to promote Hindu religion and culture in an uncritical and partisan manner, however: safely located within the timelessness of a classical ideal, Jones's vision of Indian culture (particularly attractive to us in the light of subsequent British denigration), nonetheless, exemplifies the ethnocentric strategy described by Fabian as 'the denial of coevalness' to non-European cultures.[36] Jones's *Hindoo Hymns* participated in his scholarly and administrative 'reconstruction' of an Upanishadic, golden age and in the Hindu cultural renaissance which he considered it to be Britain's historical mission to accomplish, as justification for her colonial and commercial presence in the sub-continent. It is interesting to note that Jones's *Hindoo Hymns* were warmly received by the *Monthly* and *Critical Reviews* in 1787,[37] in contrast (as we will see below) to the universally negative, critical reception of Southey's *Curse of Kehama* twenty-four years later.

Just as Cook's voyages had inspired a new visual curiosity in the arts, the work of William Jones and other members of the Asiatick Society working in the colonial, contact zone disseminated a wealth

---

[33] 'Essay on the Poetry of the Eastern Nations', in *Poetical Works of Sir William Jones*, 2 vols (London, 1807), II, p. 228.

[34] Lord Teignmouth, *Memoirs of the Life, Writings and Correspondence of Sir William Jones* (London, 1807), p. 333.

[35] See Michael Franklin, 'Accessing India', p. 48 in this volume.

[36] See Johannes Fabian, *Time and the Other: How Anthropology Makes its Object* (New York, 1983).

[37] See John Drew, *India and the Romantic Imagination* (Delhi, 1987), p. 76, for a discussion of the contemporary reception of Jones's *Hymns*.

of new information about Eastern cultures from the mid-1780s, upon
which metropolitan poets could draw for accurate 'costume'. By
1813, in the wake of Southey's Orientalist romances, *Thalaba the
Destroyer* (1801), and *The Curse of Kehama* (1810), Byron was advising
the poet Tom Moore to 'Stick to the East . . . the North, South, and
West have all been exhausted . . . the public are Orientalizing.'[38]
British expansion in Asia and the fashion for exotic 'costume' made
Orientalist poetry financially lucrative. Although Byron later came
to regret the 'false stilted trashy style' of the *Turkish Tales*,[39] he
boasted in *Beppo* of the facility with which he could throw off 'A
Grecian, Syrian or Assyrian Tale; / and sell you, mix'd with Western
sentimentalism, / Some samples of the finest Orientalism'.[40] Byron
had hit upon the formula for a more popular and lucrative style of
Oriental poetry than that produced by Jones or Robert Southey.

Despite, or perhaps because of, the meteoric commercial success
of the 'costume poetry' of Byron and Moore (Southey's Oriental
romances – described by Byron as 'Southey's unsaleables'[41] – were
less widely read), it was quickly dropped from the literary canon of
'high Romanticism'. This can be taken to exemplify the enduring
relegation of the exotic 'curio' to a lowly status in the aesthetic
hierarchy, analogous to the 'cheap' and transient shock of the exotic
panorama compared to the moral dignity of the academic history-
painting. Although it has a longer history than the rise of ethnological realism in the mid-eighteenth century, the critical subordina-
tion of *enargeia* to *energeia* survived intact into the theoretical
deliberations of 'high romanticism', closely intertwined with disdain
for the populism and commercialism of 'costume poetry'. Even in
Coleridge's celebrated distinction between Fancy and Imagination
in the 1817 *Biographia Literaria*, we might discern an attempt to
incorporate a particularist aesthetic into Coleridge's theory of
Imagination *in a subordinate position*, whilst at the same time acknowledging the undeniable impact of particularist 'costume' upon contemporary poetry. Whereas Imagination, under the tutelage of the
conscious will 'struggles to idealize and to unify', reconciling 'the
sense of novelty and freshness, with old and familiar objects' (note
the exclusion of exotic or *un*familiar object here), Fancy (like

---

[38] *Letters and Journals of Lord Byron*, ed. Leslie Marchand, 12 vols (London 1973–82), III, p. 101.
[39] Ibid., VII, p. 182.
[40] *Byron: Poetical Works*, ed. Frederick Page, corrected by John Jump (Oxford, 1970), p. 629.
[41] *Byron's Letters and Journals*, III, p. 101.

'costume', with its 'phenomenal' provenance) 'has no other counters
to play with, but fixities and definites' [42] – one might say *marked*
cultural types. Coleridge as author of 'Kubla Khan' was doubtless
fully aware of the seductive powers of the exotic image, although as I
mentioned above, he seems, as a poet, to have been more attracted
to the supernatural topos – with its unifying effect of dream-like
intensity – than to particularized topography. In *Biographia Literaria*,
chapter 14, Coleridge reflected upon the agreed division of labour in
the 1798 *Lyrical Ballads* between Wordsworth's projected aim of
'giving the charm of novelty to things of every day' and his own
attempts imaginatively to 'realise' the supernatural; 'procuring for
these shadows of imagination that willing suspension of disbelief for
the moment, which constitutes poetic faith'.[43] As Coleridge grew
further from his Gothic experiments of the late 1790s, famously
failing to complete *Christabel,* he evidently came to prefer Words-
worthian imaginative realism to his own former 'supernaturalism'.
In the *Biographia,* Coleridge relegates the shock of novelty from the
dangerous margin of a Fanciful alterity to the 'safe centre' of
Imagination and Will, subordinating the former to the latter, within
a secure aesthetic hierarchy. The fact that Coleridge shows so *much*
consideration to Fancy (given its lowly, epistemological pedigree)
testifies both to the undeniable impact of alterity upon romantic art,
as well as to the author of 'Kubla Khan' and the 'Ancient Mariner' 's
own lifelong fascination with travel literature. The prestige of
Coleridge's distinction has become almost axiomatic to English
criticism, but this has, paradoxically, occluded a vital component of
the Romantic culture, to which it was a frustrated response.

Writing in his Ravenna journal in January 1821, Lord Byron took
umbrage with Thomas Campbell's neoclassical remark that 'no
reader cares any more about the characteristic manners of [William
Collins' *Oriental Eclogues*] than about the authenticity of the Tale of
Troy'. 'Tis false' thundered an irate Byron 'we *do* care about the
authenticity of the tale of Troy . . . The secret of Tom Campbell's
defence of inaccuracy of costume and description is, that his [1809
poem] *Gertrude of Wyoming* . . . has no more locality in common with
Pennsylvania than with Penmanmaur. It is notoriously full of grossly
false scenery, as all Americans declare, though they praise parts of

[42] S. T. Coleridge, *Biographia Literaria*, ed. James Engell and W. Jackson Bate, 2 vols. (Princeton and London, 1983), I, p. 304; II, p. 17; I, p. 30.
[43] Ibid., II, pp. 6–7.

the poem.'[44] Despite his later regrets about the populist 'costume' of
the *Turkish Tales*, in a letter of 23 August 1821, Byron still needed to
insist that the description of Oriental furniture in Canto III of *Don
Juan* was meticulously copied both from the latest travel accounts of
the Levant and 'the rest from my own observation' during his own
Levantine tour. Byron, the gentleman-traveller, insisted (rather
defensively) that 'no writer ever borrowed less, or made his materials
more his own' [Ibid], a fact which his reviewers duly appreciated.[45]

In a footnote to *The Giaour*, Byron paid tribute to his Orientalist
precursor William Beckford and his 1786 novel *Vathek;* 'for correct-
ness of costume, beauty of description, and power of imagination,
Vathek far surpasses all European imitations; and bears such marks of
originality, that those who have visited the East will find some
difficulty in believing it to be more than a translation'.[46] Byron was
probably right to see *Vathek* (rather than the 'classical' Orientalism of
Jones's Hindu Hymns) as the really innovative, literary manifestation
of Romantic exoticism. Beckford's novel represented a watershed
between the old and the new styles, largely on account of its
preference for cultural *typicality* over neoclassical *generality*. The
preference was underlined by the detailed notes explicating its
Oriental costume supplied by Beckford's tutor the Reverend Samuel
Henley. Inspired, as we saw above, by de Loutherbourg's stage-
wizardry, Beckford had sought to transform the conventional
eighteenth-century Oriental tale associated with Johnson or Voltaire
by means of a playfully 'primitive' style, authenticated (like one of de
Loutherbourg's sets) by an unprecedented realism of costume.
Henley, in many ways, seems to have played de Loutherbourg to
Beckford's O'Keefe, however, for example admonishing the author
in a letter of 12 April 1785; 'Surely for instance Vathek mistaking the
tattered awnings and chintzes for large flowers – would be better
expressed by *palampores* instead of *chintzes*'.[47] Palampores it would be,
as a generalized and rather dated chinoiserie gave way to a more
ethnographically informed, middle-Eastern costume. Henley's
superb notes to *Vathek* set the standard for the notes to the Oriental
epics of Southey, Byron and Moore, drawing upon the (rapidly
augmenting) archive of Oriental learning. The fact that Beckford

---

[44] *Byron's Letters and Journals*, VIII, pp. 21–22.
[45] Ibid., VIII, p. 186.
[46] *Byron: Poetical Works*, p. 895.
[47] Cited in Beckford, *Vathek*, p. 138.

remained unconvinced by Henley's documentation reveals the novelty of a practice that would become a standard feature of Romantic 'costume poetry'. 'Notes are certainly necessary', he wrote to Henley in 1785, '& the dissertation I myself should very much approve, but fear the world might imagine I fancied myself the author, not of an Arabian tale, but an Epic poem.'[48] Henley's 'institutionalized' Orientalism is here evidently at work, recuperating the exotic text from its cultural illegibility, its low aesthetic status as curio.

Lionel Gossman has remarked upon the banishment of otherness to the notes and margins of Romantic, historical texts; 'it was in the historian's notes, one could say, that the Other was given a sanctuary and protection from the appropriating energy of the historical narrative'.[49] Southey hoped that the notes to his *History of Portugal* would 'draw off all quaintness' from the text, which he boasted was 'plain as a Doric building'.[50] In the case of Orientalist fiction and poetry, one finds a similar phenomenon but with the terms reversed. Here the fictional *narrative* transcribes otherness whilst the *notes* translate it into the ethnological or historiographical discourse of the same. But the exotic image or allusion in the poetic narrative and the explanatory footnote, running like a parallel text alongside, beneath, or after the poem, exist in a kind of intimate co-dependency (it is significant that later nineteenth-century editions of the poetry of Southey and Moore frequently omit the footnotes altogether). In this connection, it is worth considering Percy Shelley's comment in a letter of 1821 to his cousin Tom Medwin, referring to a collection of the latter's Indian poems which he had been sent to edit; 'The only general error seems to me to be the employment of Indian words, in the body of the piece, and the relegation of their meaning to the notes. Strictly, I imagine, every expression in a poem ought to be an intelligible picture. But this practice, though foreign to that of the great poets of former times, is so highly admired by our contemporaries that I can hardly counsel you to dissent.'[51] Shelley's Horatian strictures about the 'pictureability' of the poetic image

---

[48] Cited in the introduction to *Vathek*, p. xvi.

[49] Lionel Gossman, 'History as Decipherment: Romantic Historiography and the Discovery of the Other', *New Literary History*, 18:1 (Autumn 1986), p. 41. Thanks to Phil Connoll for this reference.

[50] *Life and Correspondence of Robert Southey*, ed. Rev. Charles Cuthbert Southey, 6 vols. (London, 1849–1850), II, p. 133.

[51] *Collected Letters of P. B. Shelley*, ed. Frederick L. Jones, 2 vols. (Oxford, 1964), II, p. 183.

reflect his own avoidance of exotic 'costume' and notes alike in his own Oriental poems like *Alastor* and *The Revolt of Islam*. Shelley here expresses a version of the 'high Romantic' relegation of costume poetry. Like Coleridge in 'Kubla Khan', he seeks to suppress the cultural specificity of his sources in order to create vivid 'dream-landscapes' consistent with his ideological goal of cultural universalism, as I have argued in relation to his reworking of Lady Morgan's Orientalist novel, *The Missionary*, in his *Alastor* and *The Revolt of Islam*.[52]

ORIENTALISTS AND REVIEWERS: ABSORPTION AND CONTAINMENT

In the concluding section of my essay, I want to survey some of the reactions of contemporary reviewers (rather than 'high' Romantic theorists like Coleridge and Shelley) to the Oriental 'costume poetry' of Byron and Southey. Francis Jeffrey's response to Byron's *Turkish Tales* represents the paradigm of an 'acceptable' mediation of the Oriental image, which can be instructively compared with critical responses to Southey's Oriental epics, which failed the test. In his 1814 review of the *Corsair* and *Bride of Abydos*, in the *Edinburgh Review*, Jeffrey lavished praise upon Byron's 'moral sublimity', the result of his formulaic blending of exotic manners and costume with the heroics of 'Western sentimentalism'. Unimpressed by the poet's claims to first-hand experience of the Orient, Jeffrey described how Byron had been obliged (like Southey and Scott) to 'go out of his own age and country in quest of the . . . indispensable ingredients' for passionate poetry. Byron's lot 'has fallen among the Turks and Arabs of the Mediterranean; – ruffians and desperadoes, certainly . . . but capable of great redemption in the hands of a poet of genius by being placed within the enchanted circle of antient Greece, and preserving among them so many vestiges of Roman pride and magnificence'.[53] Byron's 'Middle East' represents for Jeffrey an allowable, threshold area where the threat of the absorptive, Oriental image is framed and moderated by its contiguity to a gentlemanly classical and civic setting.

In advising Tom Moore to 'stick to the East' in his future poetic

---

[52] Nigel Leask, *British Romantic Writers and the East: Anxieties of Empire* (Cambridge, 1992), pp. 115–18; pp. 126–29.
[53] *Edinburgh Review* (April, 1814), p. 202.

endeavours, Byron had warned him off the sort of poetic Orientalism typified by Robert Southey's 'unsaleables'. These '[Southey]
has contrived to spoil by adopting only [the] more outrageous
fictions' of the East.[54] Byron was referring to Southey's two Oriental
epics, *Thalaba the Destroyer* (1801) and *The Curse of Kehama* (1810), which
sought a literal implementation of William Jones's desideratum of
introducing 'a new set of images and similitudes' borrowed from 'the
principal writings of the Asiaticks' (see note 33 above). Javed Majeed
has described Southey as acting 'as though he were in a laboratory
of cultures, experimenting with and constructing different cultural
identities'.[55] But, unlike the poetry of Jones, Byron and Moore,
Southey's work broke a number of representational codes, as we
shall see. It might, therefore be seen to occupy an extreme – and
(judging from contemporary reviews) evidently unallowable – point
in the schema of poetic Orientalism in the Romantic period. The
shifting, episodic narrative structure, the exotic machinery and
terminology and the apparatus of footnotes in Southey's poem are
not fundamentally different from Beckford or Moore. But Southey,
at work in his 'laboratory of cultures', was not interested in 'Western
sentimentalism' or ironic qualification of the Oriental allusion,
preferring to 'transcribe' rather than translate not only the imagery
and costume but also the 'grotesque' style of Oriental, poetic
mythology. Southey's negative effect on contemporary reviewers is
ironic given the 'official', Evangelical and imperialist aims which he
expressed as the ostensible goal of his Orientalist poems; his alterity
is, thus, certainly not a conscious strategy but rather a symptom of
the ideological contradictions which riddle his work in the
1800–1810 period. Technical innovation and formal poetic experi-
mentation in what might be called the 'panoramic mode' compromise the Anglocentric and imperialist discourse in whose service the
poems are enrolled.

I want to suggest here that the contemporary perception of
Southey as a poet who had been 'engulfed' by the Orient is closely
linked to his style of representation, more 'panoramic' than any of
his fellow poets, and, like the panorama or pantomimic display,
relegated by contemporary critics to a lowly place on the aesthetic
scale. (Curiously enough, Southey, himself, saw 'grand pantomime

---

[54] *Byron's Letters and Journals*, III, p. 101.
[55] Javed Majeed, *Ungoverned Imaginings: James Mill's 'History of British India' and Orientalism*
(Oxford, 1992), p. 53.

scenes' in *Thalaba*, although he 'knew not how they were to be brought together').[56] Contemporary reviewers of the Arabic *Thalaba* and the Hindu *Kehama* often insinuated that Southey had gone over to the 'other' side, while at the same time confessing to their own (transitory) ravishment. The *Monthly Magazine* for January 1802 described *Thalaba's* 'versatile instantaneity of pantomime scenery, from the blasted wilderness to caverns of flame; from bowers of paradise, to cities of jewels . . . figures, motley, strange, causing palpitation, dance before the eye, and thwart the anxious grasp'.[57] Jeffrey's celebrated attack on *Thalaba*, in the first number of the *Edinburgh Review* in October 1802, was more negative, decrying Southey's 'wild and extravagant fictions', likened to 'the exhibition of a harlequin farce', lacking any rational principle in its choice and succession of incidents. For Jeffrey, the interest of this sort of Orientalism (in marked contrast to Byron's) 'expires with its novelty; and attention is frequently exhausted, even before curiosity is gratified'.[58] Even Southey's friend, William Taylor, tellingly described *Thalaba*, in *The Critical Review* of December 1803, as 'a gallery of successive pictures . . . the personages, like the figures of landscape-painters, are often almost lost in the scene: they appear as the episodical or accessory objects'. Southey's costume and settings had absorbed the moral interest of character and action. Like so many reviewers of Orientalist poetry in this period, Taylor derived his critical vocabulary from the technology of scenic illusionism; the characters 'burst into luminousness, like figures in a phantasmagoria; and before one can ask, Whence and whither dost thou fly? another springs before us more mysterious and awful'. Making Southey's poem sound like de Loutherbourg's *Eidophusikon*, with its 'Various Imitations of Natural Phenomena, represented by moving pictures',[59] Taylor found the overall effect of *Thalaba* to be 'like theatrical representation reversed: the places seem the realities, the actors the fictitious existences'.[60]

Southey's treatment of the 'monstrous' Hindu pantheon in *Kehama* also begged to be described in the language of scenic illusionism. An unsigned review of June 1811 in a short-lived journal called the

[56] *New Letters*, I, p. 384, 12 May 1808.
[57] Lionel Madden, ed., *Robert Southey: The Critical Heritage* (London, 1972), p. 66.
[58] Ibid., p. 81.
[59] See Fried, *Absorption and Theatricality*, p. 228.
[60] Madden, *The Critical Heritage*, p. 92.

Literary Panorama, described *Kehama* as 'a series of shifting pictures
. . . to do them justice demands conceptions of immense magnificence; colours of superlative brilliance; a canvas of endless extent: in
fact, a PANORAMA'.[61] True to its title, the *Literary Panorama*
applauded Southey for having achieved this aim, seeking to describe
his absorptive 'panoramic' aesthetics in terms of the Burkean
sublime (although, interestingly, without explicitly using the term
itself). Southey had successfully expressed 'in the most suitable and
energetic terms the images which agitate his mind . . . his descriptions are so charming, so powerful, so delightful, or so tremendous,
that we are engrossed by the incident under our perusal, and
willingly endeavour to suspend our recollection of the incongruities
by which it was introduced or to which it leads'.[62] As I argued
above, this sort of suspension of comparison was characteristic of
panoramic viewing, with its analogon of sublime affect.

According to most reviewers, however, Southey's fault was precisely to have represented the incongruities of the Orient without the
distancing device of 'Western sentimentalism'. Southey's poetry
seemed to be dignifying Hindu mythology with the representational
and devotional apparatus of Christian, and Miltonic epic, despite
the fact that his footnotes constantly condemned Hindu religious
practices. The cultural 'costume' of *Kehama* was simply not translatable. As the *Monthly Mirror* put it in February 1811, 'Mr Southey will
never acquire the fame, which his poem is capable of conferring,
until he obtains readers who reverence and adore his deities; and
that time can never come until *The Curse of Kehama* is translated into
Hindoostanee'.[63] Even the poem's copious footnotes seem here to have
added to the illusionistic effect of the text rather than framing and
translating it for the imperial reader as intended, rendering it more,
rather than less, bizarre. Southey had wrongly presumed that his
notes would provide an adequate *cordon sanitaire* for his exotic,
mythological monsters, thereby translating the readers' absorption
into productive knowledge.

Southey seems to have been brought to heel by the critical
onslaught on his Oriental epics. His next major work, *Roderick the
Last of the Goths* (1814), dealt with the war against the Moors in Spain.
It was as if Southey sought once and for all to purge himself of the
Orient, which had so damaged his reputation, by mediating it with

---

[61] Ibid., p. 146.   [62] Ibid.   [63] Ibid., p. 134.

the 'safe' discourse of Christian chivalry. In his 1838 preface to
Kehama in his *Collected Poems*, he sought (rather disingenuously) to
meet Jeffrey's most damaging charges by insisting that, although 'the
spirit of the poem was Indian, . . . there was nothing Oriental in the
style. I had learnt the language of our own great masters and the
great poets of antiquity.'[64] In reviews and poems, he praised
missionary attempts to convert the Hindus to Protestantism. Part of
this ascendant missionary project, as Gauri Viswanathan has shown
in her recent study, *Masks of Conquest*,[65] was to render English
literature a focal point of the nineteenth-century, colonial curriculum
in educating Indian students. But it certainly wouldn't be works like
Southey's *Kehama* which were presented for study in Bengali class-
rooms.

Finally, how did the critical assault on 'absorptive' representations
of colonized peoples and places effect a later nineteenth-century
literature of empire? One brief example must suffice, Phillip
Meadows Taylor's popular Indian novel of 1839 entitled *Confessions of
a Thug*.[66] In terms of its meticulous ethnological realism and
'costume', *Confessions of a Thug* can easily be mistaken for a late
product of Romantic Orientalism. However, Meadows Taylor
(whilst undoubtedly paying homage to Thomas De Quincey in his
choice of title) casts his narrator as an Indian Thug confessing to a
silent English police officer the multiple murders he has committed
in the name of the goddess Kali. If the metaphorical affiliation of
Southey's writing is with the *panorama*, with its abolition of subject/
object distinctions and vertiginous lack of a framing perspective,
Meadows Taylor's novel is affiliated rather with Bentham's *panopticon*.
The *panopticon* is an ordering of visual representation in which
aesthetic absorption has been replaced, as John Bender argues in
Imagining the Penitentiary, 'by the isolation of both spectator and
captive within an impersonal, narratively ordered field of moral
sentiment and conscience'.[67] Patrick Brantlinger has commented
upon the way in which the reader of Meadows Taylor's novel
identifies with the silent English interlocutor, rather than the richly
characterized Thug and the gruesome 'typicality' of his monologue;

---

[64] Southey *Poetical Works*, p. xv.

[65] Gauri Viswanathan, *Masks of Conquest: Literary Study and British Rule in India* (London, 1989).

[66] Phillip Meadows Taylor, *Confessions of a Thug*, with a new preface by Nick Mirsky (Oxford,
1986).

[67] John Bender, *Imagining the Penitentiary* (Chicago and London, 1987), p. 231.

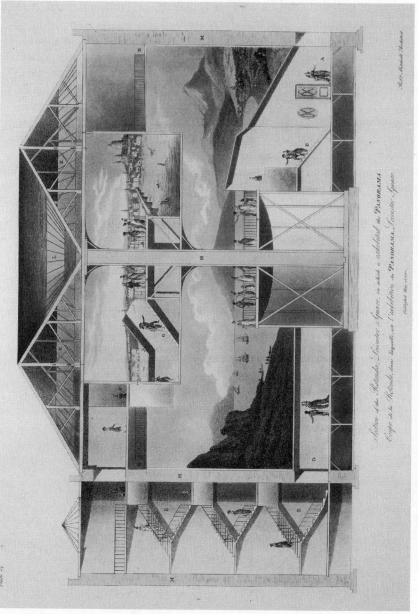

Plate 14

Section of the Rotunda, Leicester Square, in which is exhibited the PANORAMA

Coupe de la Rotonde, dans laquelle est l'exhibition du PANORAMA, Leicester Square.

Published May 1801.

Robt. Mitchell, Architect.

Figure 2. Robert Mitchell, *Plans and Views in Perspective of Buildings Erected in England and Scotland*, Plate no. 14: 'A section of the Rotunda in Leicester Square'.

the former epitomizing 'the perfect Benthamite policeman, an ideal
figure of imperial discipline and surveillance, or "panopticism", to
use Foucault's term'.[68] The transformation of panorama into panopticon here emblematizes the changing representation of the exotic
object in the period which my essay charts, perhaps already foreshadowed in the Linnaean graffiti, erupting onto the figurative
surface of Humboldt's 'Physical Portrait of the Tropics' with which I
began. As ethnological 'costume' becomes the disciplinary preserve
of a professionalized, colonial anthropology, a host of new scientific
and geographical languages divide up exotic nature in the terms of
specialized disciplines, more or less voided of concerns with aesthetics and public discourse. Meanwhile the nineteenth-century
legacy of high Romanticism psychologizes and internalizes the
'voyage into substance', converting what we have seen as the
originally *contentious* discourse of 'pure imagination' into a dominant,
literary norm. Arising in the brief lacuna between the generic
triviality of the eighteenth-century Oriental tale and the rise of
scientific anthropology, the age of the literary footnote draws to an
unlamented close.

[68] Patrick Brantlinger, *Rule of Darkness: British Literature and Imperialism, 1830–1914* (Ithaca and
London, 1988), p. 88. In his *History of British India*, James Mill suggested that 'the Panopticon
penitentiary house, invented and described by Mr Bentham' '(he later called it a hospital
for the mind)' so well adapted to the exigencies of every community, would, with
extraordinary advantage, apply itself to the extraordinary circumstances of Bengal'. *History
of British India*, abridged with introduction by William Thomas (Chicago and London,
1956), p. 574.

CHAPTER 11

The Isle of Devils: the Jamaican journal of M. G. Lewis

D. L. Macdonald

Matthew Gregory Lewis was not only the author of *The Monk* (1796), the most sensational of Gothic novels, and of *The Castle Spectre* (1797), the most successful of Gothic melodramas, but also a member of a class that now seems almost mythical but was then taken for granted: the liberal slave-owner. He came of age during the great social and political struggle that led to the abolition of the slave-trade and the emancipation of the British slaves (the Abolition Society was founded when he was twelve), and when his father died, in 1812, he inherited two Jamaican sugar estates, six or seven hundred human beings, and the problem of slavery.

Lewis's solution to this problem seems to us ambiguous. He was not an emancipationist. He did consider freeing his slaves, if not during his life then in his will, and he consulted William Wilberforce on the subject.[1] He came, however, to a melancholy conclusion:

Every man of humanity must wish that slavery, even in its best and most mitigated form, had never found a legal sanction, and must regret that its system is now so incorporated with the welfare of Great Britain as well as of Jamaica, as to make its extirpation an absolute impossibility, without the certainty of producing worse mischiefs than the one which we annihilate.[2]

Lewis was, however, an abolitionist. He was elected to Parliament in 1796 (after the war with France had brought to an end the first phase of the struggle to abolish the slave-trade) and resigned his seat in 1802 (before the beginning of the second phase that culminated in

---

[1] *The Correspondence of William Wilberforce*, ed. Robert Isaac Wilberforce and Samuel Wilberforce, 2 vols. (London, 1840), II, pp. 383–84.

[2] Matthew Gregory Lewis, *Journal of a West India Proprietor, Kept During a Residence in the Island of Jamaica* (London, 1834), p. 402. Further references to this work are given after quotations in the text.

the Abolition Act of 1807), but he supported the campaign in a number of ways. *The Castle Spectre* includes the anachronistic but striking figure of Hassan, an African who has been enslaved and brought to medieval Wales. Far from being a voiceless Other, Hassan is given to lamenting his lot in long speeches, strongly marked by the rhetoric of the sublime; far from being an abstract and idealized figure like the speaker of Cowper's 'The Negro's Complaint', he has a history (made up mostly of oppression) and a vivid personality (devoted mostly to his desire for revenge):

I have been dragged from my native land, from a wife who was every thing to me, to whom I was every thing! Twenty years have elapsed since these Christians tore me away: they trampled upon my heart, mocked my despair, and, when in frantic terms I raved of Samba [his wife], laughed, and wondered how a negro's soul could feel![3]

To avenge himself, he devotes himself enthusiastically to the nefarious schemes of his master, the villain of the play: in a paradox characteristic of Lewis's treatment of slavery, the slave realizes that the best way to punish his master is to obey him.

If, as J. R. Oldfield argues, the 'docility and tenderness' of African characters 'had become almost stereotypical' on the London stage,[4] Hassan's passionate protest must have come as a shock. The political significance of the character was not lost either on the censor, John Larpent, who ordered some of his speeches (including this one) to be cut in performance,[5] or on the reviewers. The radical *Analytical Review*, though doubtful about the dramatic propriety of the character, was pleased

with the sentiments, that Mr. L., with the opportunity of Hassan, discovers on the subject of that dreadful trade, which constitutes the shame and the guilt of Britain; which execrated by the just, and reprobated by the intelligent, is yet effectually supported by the short-sighted and the corrupt; and which our devoted country seems resolute to hold with it's last grasp . . .[6]

The conservative *Monthly Visitor* thought that Lewis had actually intended to defend, not just the abolition campaign, but even

---

[3] Matthew Gregory Lewis, *The Castle Spectre: A Drama* (London, 1798), p. 13.

[4] 'The "Ties of Soft Humanity": Slavery and Race in British Drama, 1760–1800', *Huntington Library Quarterly*, 56 (1993), pp. 1–14 (p. 12).

[5] *Seven Gothic Dramas, 1789–1825*, ed. Jeffrey N. Cox (Athens, Ohio, 1992), p. 161, n. 36.

[6] Review of *The Castle Spectre*, by Matthew Gregory Lewis, *Analytical Review*, 28 (1798), pp. 179–91 (p. 182).

uprisings like the Haitian revolution: to 'justify the blacks, in their execution of black gratitude, and black vengeance'.[7]

Lewis made two trips to Jamaica, in 1815–16 and in 1817–18, to visit his plantations and if possible to improve the living and working conditions of his slaves. On his first voyage out, the ship was becalmed. Lewis was philosophical: 'whether we have sailed slowly or rapidly, when a day is once over, I am just as much nearer advanced towards "that bourne," . . . towards which the whole of our existence forms but one continued journey' (p. 41).[8] Lewis passed the time partly in writing a long, narrative poem, 'The Isle of Devils'; on his return voyage, he copied it into his *Journal of a West India Proprietor* (published posthumously in 1834). The testimony of a man who was both uncomfortably aware of his own implication in the institution of slavery and an eye-witness of its practices, the *Journal* is one of the most revealing documents of the Romantic period.

Lewis claimed to have a low opinion of 'The Isle of Devils', but he evidently felt it was worth preserving (*Journal*, p. 260). It ends with a debate between the narrator and a dissatisfied listener over the fate of its heroine, Irza. The listener asks: 'and did her days thus creep / So sad, so slow, till came the long last sleep?' In his reply, the narrator repeats the metaphor of the journey to death and adopts the tone of Christian resignation Lewis used in describing his own journey:

> Ah! what avails it, since they ne'er can last,
> If gay or sad our span of days be past?
> Pray, mortals, pray, in sickness or in pain,
> Not long nor blest to live, but pure from stain.
> A life of pleasure, and a life of woe,
> When both are past, the difference who can show?
> But all can tell, how wide apart in price
> A life of virtue, and a life of vice.
>   Then still, sad Irza, tread your thorny way,
> Since life must end, and merits ne'er decay.
>
>   (*Journal*, pp. 288–89)

---

[7] Review of *The Castle Spectre*, by Matthew Gregory Lewis, *Monthly Visitor*, 3 (1798), pp. 105–8 (p. 108).

[8] For Lewis and temporality, see D. L. Macdonald, 'Juvenal in the 1790s: The Imitation and the Plot of History', *Transactions of the North-West Society for Eighteenth-Century Studies*, 18 (1989–90), pp. 183–92, and 'The Erotic Sublime: The Marvellous in *The Monk*', *English Studies in Canada*, 18 (1992), pp. 273–86.

Whatever one makes of this argument, Irza's fate has certainly been harsh enough to provoke the listener's protest. She is shipwrecked on a desert island, where she is held prisoner in a cave, and repeatedly raped, by a demon.[9] When her lover, who has also been ship-wrecked, tries to rescue her, the demon brains him. She bears the demon two sons, one monstrous and one human; when she is finally rescued, the abandoned demon kills their children, and commits suicide, before her eyes. She spends the rest of her life in a convent, in penance and good works.

Strangely enough, this fantastic and horrible poem, written on the way to Jamaica and copied on the way home, provides an allegorical frame for all the impressions of the island that Lewis recorded in his *Journal*, which is otherwise a realistic, cheerful, and (within limits) humane document. For the 'demon-king' of the poem is clearly a black slave, as re-created by the guilty and fearful fantasy of a white slave-owner. He recalls the devil who appears at the climax of *The Monk*, who is doubly black: 'A *swarthy darkness* spread itself over his gigantic form'.[10] Most of the time, he behaves with a servility reminiscent of Crusoe's Friday: 'Humbly, slowly crept he near [Irza], / Then kissed the earth, his club before her laid, / And of his neck her footstool would have made' (*Journal*, p. 272). This servility is interrupted by the stereotypical acts of slave rebellion: the brutal murder of a white man and the rape of a white woman. The results of the rape seem to be a denial, in fantasy, of the possibility of racial mixture, a subject in which Lewis took, in reality, a keen interest (*Journal*, pp. 106–07, 171–72). And the demon's suicide suggests that the slave, however savage and rebellious, cannot survive without his master.

The ethnographer, James Clifford, has argued that ethnography is inherently allegorical; the same point could be made about travel writing generally (and especially about travel writing with ethno-graphic pretensions, like Lewis's *Journal*). Ethnographers and other

---

[9] The rape of Irza, by a demon, in a cave, is reminiscent of the rape of Antonia, by the demon-assisted Ambrosio, in the catacombs, at the climax of *The Monk*, but there is a significant difference in presentation. The rape scene in the novel is focalized through the rapist and structured pornographically; Antonia has recovered from her sleeping potion so that she can struggle enticingly (see Macdonald, 'The Erotic Sublime'). Almost the whole of the poem, however, is focalized through the victim, and since she is unconscious when the demon rapes her, the act is not represented at all.

[10] Matthew Gregory Lewis, *The Monk*, ed. Louis F. Peck, introduced by John Berryman (New York, 1952), p. 412 (emphasis added).

travellers come to terms with new experiences by turning them into allegories of familiar concepts. Clifford argues that travellers tend to assume that appearances need to be interpreted; whatever the content of these interpretations may be, the interpretative process itself is essentially reassuring, because it portrays the strange as 'meaningful within a common network of symbols'.[11]

Lewis allegorizes his experiences on board ship and in Jamaica in several different ways. A number of short, neoclassical poems included in the journal turn specific incidents into specific symbols. In 'Landing', the pleasant sound of a woman's voice after nearly two months in the all-male ambience of the ship becomes a sentimental symbol for the general superiority of women over men (*Journal*, pp. 71–73). In 'The Runaway', a runaway slave becomes a symbolic victim of feminine perfidy. 'Missy Sally', who leads him astray, recalls the temptress Matilda of *The Monk*, but also the unfortunate Irza of 'The Isle of Devils', for she is a 'lilly white girl', and her whiteness reduces him to a servility like that of the 'demon-king'. At the end of the poem, he begs his master's wife to intercede for him:

> 'Missy, you cheeks so red, so white;
>> Missy, you eyes like diamond shine!
> Missy, you Massa's sole delight,
>> And Lilly Sally, him was mine!
> Him say – "Come, Peter, mid me go!" –
> Could me refuse him? Could me say "no?" –
> Poor Peter – "no" him could no say!
> So Peter, Peter ran away!' –

His master accepts this excuse and ends the poem with a warning against white women, a misogynist inversion of 'The Little Black Boy': 'Though fair without, they're foul within; / Their heart is black, though white their skin' (*Journal*, pp. 120–21). In 'The Humming Bird' and 'The Flying Fish', flowers and flying fish become symbols of justly punished feminine presumption and unchastity (*Journal*, pp. 210–11, 246–49). These symbolic moments certainly reveal a preoccupation with sexual relations in a slave society; a tendency to think of gender, as well as race, in terms of binary opposites; and a drive, reminiscent of Ambrosio's, to penetrate beneath the white skin of femininity and uncover its heart of darkness. Considering Lewis's Gothic background, however, it is not

---

[11] 'On Ethnographic Allegory', in *Writing Culture: The Poetics and Politics of Ethnography*, ed. James Clifford and George E. Marcus (Berkeley, 1986), pp. 98–121 (pp. 99, 101).

surprising that only the concepts of death, damnation, and the demonic are invoked frequently and methodically enough to create the coherent network of symbols, characteristic of allegory proper.

Lewis can conceptualize even the most pleasant experiences in terms of death. On a trip to Montego Bay, he is struck by 'the fragrance of the Sweet-wood, and of several other scented trees, but above all, of the delicious Logwood'; these scents remind him of 'the buxom Air, imbalm'd / With odours', which Satan, in *Paradise Lost*, promises to his children Sin and Death if they will follow him to Eden (*Journal*, p. 66).[12] If Jamaica is a paradise, it is a doomed one; within a page, Lewis is discussing the local snakes.

The abundance and excellence of the local fish make him wish for 'the company of Queen Atygatis of Scythia, who was so particularly fond of fish, that she prohibited all her subjects from eating it on pain of death, through fear that there might not be enough left for her majesty'.[13] Lewis's train of thought leads him through Henry I, who died of a surfeit of lampreys, to Frederick the Great, who 'might have prolonged his existence, if he could but have resisted the fascination of an eel-pye; but the charm was too strong for him, and, like his great-grandmother of all, he ate and died'. (As forbidden foods which were also somewhat serpentine, Henry's lampreys and Frederick's eel pie were both temptations and tempters.) Lewis meditates on the two fatal appetites:

And now, which had to resist the most difficult temptation, Frederic or Eve? *She* longed to experience pleasures yet untasted, and which she fancied to be exquisite: *he* . . . pined after known pleasures, and which he knew to be good; *she* was the dupe of imagination; *he* fell a victim to established habit. (*Journal*, pp. 104–5)[14]

Like all allegorizing travellers, Lewis is somewhere between the two: he is experiencing pleasures yet untasted, but his imagination falls victim to established habits. These imaginative habits are deathly

---

[12] See *Paradise Lost*, II, lines 842–43, in *The Complete Poetry of John Milton*, ed. John T. Shawcross, revised edition (Garden City, 1971).

[13] Lewis seems to be thinking of Atargatis, who was not a Scythian queen but a Syrian goddess, in fact the subject of *The Syrian Goddess*, a work attributed to Lucian. Fish were sacred to her, and she was worshipped in Phoenicia, under the name Derceto, in the form of a woman with the tail of a fish. See Lucian, *The Syrian Goddess (De Dea Syria)*, ed. and tr. Harold W. Attridge and Robert A. Oden (Missoula, 1976), pp. 21–23. This rather vague reference is one example of how Lewis's account of the West Indies is informed by Orientalism.

[14] For the story of Frederick the Great, see Honoré Gabriel Riqueti, Comte de Mirabeau, *Memoirs of the Courts of Berlin and St. Petersburg*, anonymous translation (New York, 1910), p. 40.

ones: whether he is the dining companion of Queen Atygatis or a surfeited English king (which, as an English slave-owner, he somewhat resembles), he is doomed.

Less surprisingly, he also conceptualizes unpleasant experiences in terms of death. The road to Spanish Town is so rough as to make him 'envy the Mahometan women, who, having no souls at all, could not possibly have them jolted out of their bodies' (*Journal*, p. 159). The road between his estates runs along the sea-shore; two of his horses are frightened by the waves: 'one of them actually fell down into the water, while the off-wheel of the curricle flew up into the air, and thus it remained suspended, balancing backwards and forwards, like Mahomet's coffin' (p. 360).[15] Returning from this journey, Lewis stops for the night at a convenient estate and has 'supper with the musquitoes,–"not where I ate, but where I was eaten"', like Polonius (p. 375).[16] It is common enough for travellers to speak of being eaten alive; it must be more unusual to compare the experience to that of decomposition after death.

Europeans have usually had more than decomposition to look forward to after death; Lewis's allegory draws on both classical and Christian religion for concepts of the afterlife. The difficulty of eating and drinking during a storm at sea makes Lewis think of a famous classical punishment: 'We drink our tea exactly as Tantalus did in the infernal regions; we keep bobbing at the basin for half an hour together without being able to get a drop' (*Journal*, p. 11). Many travellers compared the lots of the Jamaican slaves with those of English labourers, and many slave-owners decided that the slaves were better off; Lewis characteristically put the comparison in terms of life after death: 'if I were now standing on the banks of Virgil's Lethe, with a goblet of the waters of oblivion in my hand, and asked whether I chose to enter life anew as an English labourer or a Jamaica negro, I should have no hesitation in preferring the latter' (*Journal*, p. 101).[17]

---

[15] The Orientalist belief that Islam denied that women had souls was widespread enough in Europe to be proverbial; so was the bizarre rumour that Mohammed's body had been encased in an iron coffin and suspended in mid-air by means of powerful magnets fixed to the roof of the great mosque in Mecca – evidently a post-mortem pseudo-miracle illustrating the belief that Mohammed was an imposter; see Edward W. Said, *Orientalism* (New York, 1978), pp. 65–66, 72.

[16] See *Hamlet*, IV, iii, line 19, ed. Willard Farnham, in *William Shakespeare: The Complete Works*, ed. Alfred Harbage (Baltimore, 1969).

[17] See *The Aeneid of Virgil*, ed. R. D. Williams, 2 vols. (London, 1972), Book VI, lines 748–51.

References to the Christian after-life, especially to the Christian hell, are more numerous. The tropical climate reminded Lewis of an old joke about a courtier who died and went to hell. When the devil politely asked him how he found his new home, he replied politely: 'not at all disagreeable, by any manner of means, Mr. Devil, upon my word and honour! Rather *warm*, to be sure' (*Journal*, p. 38). On his first departure from Jamaica, Lewis, himself something of a courtier, gave his slaves a holiday and asked them to drink the health of the Duchess of York. Their enthusiastic response recalled that of Milton's devils at the sight of Satan's standard: 'the negroes cheered with such a shout as might have "rent hell's concave"' (*Journal*, p. 237). The mood of the Miltonic passage is, in fact, distinctly mixed: the devils, who have just emerged from the fiery gulf, appear 'with looks / Down cast and damp, yet such wherein appear'd / Obscure some glimpse of joy'; Satan's own countenance wears a 'Like doubtful hue', and he only gradually manages to cheer up the troops.[18] The slaves' enthusiasm for the Duchess of York may well have been equally forced.

On his second voyage out, Lewis was becalmed even sooner and even longer than on his first. Three weeks after his departure, he was still in the English Channel, and his philosophical resignation began to wear thin: 'Here we are, still riding at anchor, with no better consolation than that of Klopstock's half-devil Abadonna; the consciousness that others are deeper damned than ourselves': another ship had left three weeks before them and was still becalmed (*Journal*, p. 312).[19] Lewis's identification with the half-damned Abadonna, like the mixed feelings of his Miltonic quotation, seems appropriate to the difficult position of the liberal slave-owner. The calm was suddenly succeeded by three weeks of storm, at the end of which Lewis reflected: 'I had often heard talk of "a hell upon earth," and now I have a perfect idea of "a hell upon water." It must be precisely our vessel during the last three weeks.' (p. 312) A major purpose of this second trip was to inspect his eastern estate, which he

---

[18] *Paradise Lost*, I, lines 522–43. Lewis, about to leave Jamaica, may also be thinking of the similar shout that greets Satan's announcement of his intention to escape from hell, *Paradise Lost*, II, lines 514–20.

[19] Abadonna is a repentant devil in the second canto of *Der Messias*; when Satan announces his plan to kill the Messiah, Abadonna objects: 'Yes, SATAN, I will speak, that the heavy judgments of the ETERNAL may more lightly fall on me than on thee.' Friedrich Gottlieb Klopstock, *The Messiah*, tr. Mary and Joseph Collyer, 2 vols. (London, 1763), I, p. 86.

had not had time to visit on his first: 'here I expected to find a perfect paradise, and I found a perfect hell' (p. 365).

Lewis himself plays a surprising variety of roles in his allegory of death and damnation. He is in an Edenic world, threatened, but not yet entered, by Sin and Death; he is journeying towards death; he is sentenced to death by Queen Atygatis or sentences himself to death by eating a surfeit of fish; he is at the point of death, with his soul jolted out of his body; he has passed the point of death, like Mahomet in his coffin or Polonius feeding the worms. He is about to be reborn, like one of Virgil's purified dead, or half-damned like Klopstock's Abadonna, or damned like Tantalus or the courtier, or like Milton's Satan, inspiring a cheer that would tear hell's concave.

Since Lewis was travelling to Jamaica in order to inspect his plantations and his slaves, his allegorization of the exotic is not likely to have been politically innocent. Lewis even expresses an uneasy awareness of the politics of his allegory – which, however, he could not transcend – through his uneasy humour. The political tenor of the allegory is obvious enough. Jamaica is an isle of devils because it is an island inhabited largely by black slaves. Lewis's discourse is shaped, not by the pseudo-scientific racism of the Enlightenment, but by an older, religious racism that sees in blackness a sign of the curse of Canaan (Genesis 9. 20–25), and of the diabolical.[20] (Lewis's characteristic mode is Gothic fantasy, not science fiction.)[21] In *Some Years Travels into Divers Parts of Africa* (fourth edition 1677), Thomas Herbert remarks that the natives 'in colour so in condition are little other than Devils incarnate'.[22] In Defoe's *Captain Singleton* (1720), the hero and his comrades, marooned on Madagascar, decide not to raid the natives for provisions, because they are 'loath to bring down a whole Nation of Devils upon [themselves] at once'; later, on the African mainland, they grow bolder and fight a battle against a 'Black Army' of 'Devils'.[23] In *A Tour in the United States of America* (1784), John Ferdinand Smyth complains that he once had to share a

[20] D. L. Macdonald, 'Pre-Romantic and Romantic Abolitionism: Cowper and Blake', *European Romantic Review*, 4 (1993–94), pp. 163–82 (pp. 175–76).

[21] For a discussion of pseudo-scientific racism in contemporary science fiction, see Mary Wollstonecraft Shelley, *Frankenstein; or, The Modern Prometheus*, ed. Marilyn Butler (London, 1993), pp. xxx, xxxiv–xli.

[22] Quoted in Winthrop D. Jordan, *White over Black: American Attitudes Toward the Negro, 1550–1812* (Chapel Hill, 1968), p. 24.

[23] Daniel Defoe, *The Life, Adventures, and Pyracies of the Famous Captain Singleton*, ed. Shiv K. Kumar (London, 1969), pp. 21, 75–78.

cabin with 'a parcel of nasty black devils'.[24] The very casualness of Smyth's tone suggests how automatic the association between blacks and devils has become.[25] Thomas Phillips, a seventeenth-century slave-trader, thought that the Africans returned the compliment: 'the blacks . . . say, the devil is white'. If Phillips was right, one can only add that the Africans, unlike the Europeans, had good reasons for their opinion.[26]

The devil is not only black; he is also a sort of slave-owner;[27] this paradox may partly account for the unsettling variability of roles in Lewis's allegory – for his uneasy assumption of the role of Milton's Satan. The roles are already variable – even reversible – in *The Monk*. Matilda assures Ambrosio that there is no danger involved in dealing with the devil. She has done so herself, and reports: 'I saw the daemon obedient to my orders: I saw him trembling at my frown; and found that, instead of selling my soul to a master, my courage had purchased for myself a slave': the results of her experiment have been the reverse of what she feared.[28] She is lying, of course; by the end of the novel, the roles have been reversed again, and the hapless Ambrosio finds himself enslaved to the devil – that is, damned.

Lewis's slaves seem to have perceived the allegorical relation between their condition and damnation, a concept to which they had been introduced by Christian missionaries. A slave catechism devised at about this time by John Shipman (who based it on Wesley's *Instructions for Children*) explains it:

> What sort of place is hell?
> A dark, bottomless pit full of brimstone.

---

[24] Quoted in Jordan, *White over Black*, p. 256.

[25] Olaudah Equiano quotes three times from *Paradise Lost* in the chapter of his autobiography devoted to a survey of the slavery system, and only once elsewhere in the book; all four quotations identify the black slaves (and Equiano, in particular) with Milton's devils. There is some evidence that Equiano, distressingly but unsurprisingly, had internalized the racism of his masters; but, since the quotations all emphasize the sufferings of the devils, and their continued resistance, it is possible that this devout Anglican may have been, like Blake's Milton, of the devil's party without knowing it. See *The Interesting Narrative of the Life of Olaudah Equiano, or Gustavus Vassa, the African, Written by Himself* (London and New York, 1969), pp. 93, 107, 120, 127; Milton, *Paradise Lost*, I, line 175; I, lines 65–68; II, lines 616–18; II, lines 332–40.

[26] Quoted in Katharine M. Rogers, 'Fact and Fiction in Aphra Behn's *Oroonoko*', *Studies in the Novel*, 20 (1988), pp. 1–15 (p. 9). The warning against white women with black hearts at the end of 'The Runaway' may effect something like this reversal – or simply displace the demonic from the racial to the sexual Other.

[27] Jordan, *White over Black*, p. 55.   [28] Lewis, *The Monk*, p. 265.

Will both [the] souls and bodies [of the damned] be tormented?
Yes, every part of them at once.

Who will be their tormentors?
Their own conscience, the devils and one another.

How long will their torments last?
Forever.[29]

Lewis was amused to overhear one of his slaves accuse another of being so lazy 'that instead of being a slave upon Cornwall estate, he was only fit to be the slave of the devil' (*Journal*, p. 344). In 1808, a British missionary to the Windward Islands had drawn much the same contrast: 'it is neither my business nor in my power to deliver [the slaves] from the bondage of men. I have always considered it my duty to endeavour thro' divine assistance to direct the poor negroes, how they may be delivered from the bondage of sin and Satan.'[30] In both cases, of course, the contrast is actually grounded on an analogy between the two types of bondage. One slave convert said that hell was where 'twenty thousand driba [drivers] . . . poke you wid fire stick'.[31]

When the slaves began to reflect more seriously on the missionaries' message, and on the parallels between slavery and damnation, the consequences were less amusing:

One poor negro, on one of my own estates, told the overseer that he knew himself to be so great a sinner that nothing could save him from the devil's clutches, even for a few hours, except singing hymns; and he kept singing so incessantly day and night, that at length terror and want of sleep turned his brain, and the wretch died raving mad. (*Journal*, p. 174)

Jamaica was an island of death as well as an isle of devils, and for similar reasons. As Orlando Patterson argues, slavery 'always originated (or was conceived of as having originated) as a substitute for death, usually violent death'; it was a sort of living death or, as Patterson calls it, 'social death'.[32] Patterson distinguishes between two forms of social death. In the first and perhaps most common form, the slave was supposed to have lost the right to life by being

---

[29] Quoted in Mary Turner, *Slaves and Missionaries: The Disintegration of Jamaican Slave Society, 1787–1834* (Urbana, 1982), p. 78.

[30] Quoted in Michael Craton, *Testing the Chains: Resistance to Slavery in the British West Indies* (Ithaca, 1982), p. 246.

[31] Quoted in Turner, *Slaves and Missionaries*, p. 78.

[32] Orlando Patterson, *Slavery and Social Death: A Comparative Study* (Cambridge, Massachusetts, 1982), p. 5; see also Orlando Patterson, *Freedom* (New York, 1991–), I, p. 10.

taken prisoner in a war. In *Leviathan* (1651), Hobbes declined to decide whether *Servant* was 'derived from *Servire*, to Serve, or from *Servare*, to Save': the implication of the second etymology was that the slave was a slave by virtue of having been saved, spared from slaughter. This form of slavery was as much a deferral of death as a substitute for it: 'he that hath Quarter', Hobbes declared, 'hath not his life given, but deferred till farther deliberation; For it is not an yeelding on condition of life, but to discretion' – the discretion of the victor, the master.[33] In the second form of social death, the slave lost the right to life by being convicted of a capital crime. According to Locke's *Two Treatises of Government* (1689–90), this form of slavery is also essentially a deferral of death: if someone has 'forfeited his own Life, by some Act that deserves Death; he, to whom he has forfeited it, may (when he has him in his Power) delay to take it, and make use of him to his own Service, and he does him no injury by it'. To Locke, the deferral of death was at the discretion of the slave as well as of the master: 'For, whenever he finds the hardship of his Slavery out-weigh the value of his Life, 'tis in his Power, by resisting the Will of his Master, to draw on himself the Death he desires'.[34] The famous analysis in the *Phenomenology of Spirit* (1807) is closer to Hobbes than to Locke, since it is set at the origin of society, before there were such things as capital crimes; but Hegel is consistent with both his predecessors in calling the slave a 'consciousness in the form of *thinghood*', or, in Alexandre Kojève's paraphrase, 'a living corpse'.[35]

Whether or not the Jamaican slaves thought they were living corpses, they were aware that their masters did. Lewis's own slaves still sang a song about the brutal, former proprietor of a nearby estate, who used to avoid the expense of feeding sick and aging slaves by having them thrown into a gully, to be eaten by the vultures while they were still alive (*Journal*, pp. 322–24). Lewis himself did not explicitly refer to his slaves as living corpses, but he came close to it in thinking of them (if only occasionally) as virtually inanimate chattels, and he was acutely conscious of their mortality, for which he thought that the slaves themselves were largely responsible. He

---

[33] Thomas Hobbes, *Leviathan*, ed. Richard Tuck (Cambridge, 1991), p. 141.
[34] John Locke, *Two Treatises of Government*, ed. Peter Laslett, 2nd edn (Cambridge, 1967), p. 302.
[35] Georg Wilhelm Friedrich Hegel, *Phenomenology of Spirit*, tr. A. V. Miller, foreword and notes by J. N. Findlay (Oxford, 1977), p. 115; Alexandre Kojève, *Introduction to the Reading of Hegel: Lectures on the 'Phenomenology of Spirit'*, assembled by Raymond Queneau, ed. Allan Bloom, tr. James H. Nichols (New York, 1969), p. 16.

blamed the high rate of infant mortality on the carelessness of the mothers and their prejudices against such medical advances as immersing newborn infants in cold water to protect them from tetanus (*Journal*, pp. 97, 321). Slaves who survived to adulthood found a variety of means of self-destruction: they stabbed each other in quarrels over women (*Journal*, pp. 199, 234); they ran away and contracted palsy from sleeping in the rain (*Journal*, pp. 209–10, 223–24); they put spells on each other (*Journal*, pp. 94, 350–57); they ate fatal quantities of dirt (*Journal*, p. 327); if accused unjustly, they committed suicide (pp. 385–86); they made themselves sick by over-indulging at each other's funerals (p. 327). Even when no-one was at fault, they were vulnerable to disease and to the fatalities of everyday life. 'Whether it be the climate not agreeing with their African blood (genuine or inherited), or whether it be from some defect in their general formation', Lewis concluded sadly, 'certainly negroes seem to hold their lives upon a very precarious tenure' (*Journal*, p. 331). He does not seem to have wondered whether it might be from some defect in their living and working conditions.

Masters held their lives on a similarly (though not equally) precarious tenure. While in Jamaica, Lewis lived in fear of a slave uprising like the one in French St Domingue; plans for such an uprising were actually detected during his first visit: 'Above a thousand persons were engaged in the plot, three hundred of whom had been regularly sworn to assist in it with all the usual accompanying ceremonies of drinking human blood, eating earth from graves, &c.' (*Journal*, p. 225). They had planned to kill all the whites on the island and found an African kingdom. This conspiracy followed smaller ones in 1806 and 1808; it was, itself, followed by further unrest in 1819, 1823, and 1824, and finally by the Baptist War of 1831–32, which led to the deaths of fourteen whites and some 540 slaves, and which may have hastened the Emancipation Act of 1833.[36]

Even without the support of a conspiracy, the slaves were believed to be unpleasantly prone to murder their masters. One of the 'worst faults' of 'the negro character', according to Lewis, was 'the facility with which they are frequently induced to poison to the right hand and to the left'; he ascribed this bad habit to 'their ignorance of a future state, which makes them dread no punishment hereafter for

---

[36] Craton, *Testing the Chains*, pp. 291, 293–94.

themselves, and look with but little respect on human life in others'
(*Journal*, pp. 148–50). Faced with a danger to his class, Lewis was
prepared to overlook the danger, to the slaves, of religious instruction.
The real reason for their propensity to poison seems not to have been
their lack of religious beliefs but their retention of the West African
belief that misfortunes such as slavery were the result of witchcraft,
and that poison was an effective antidote to witchcraft.[37] During his
first visit, Lewis attended the trial of a fifteen-year-old girl who had
put corrosive sublimate (mercuric chloride) in her master's brandy-
and-water. She was executed; the master lingered for two years and
died during Lewis's second visit – as much, Lewis suspected, from
the brandy as from the poison (*Journal*, p. 397).

Non-human dangers were equally sinister. The bad roads not only
made him envy Mahometan women and think of Mahomet in his
coffin, they also were the scene of two near-fatal accidents on trips
between his two estates. Most sinister of all was disease, especially
yellow fever, which was then believed to be highly contagious. One
of the occasional poems included in the *Journal* is a prayer to the
'tropic Genius', which explicitly describes Jamaica as an isle of devils
– the devils of disease:

> Let not thy strange diseases prey
> On my life; but scare from my couch away
> The yellow Plague's imps; and safe let me rest
> From that dread black demon, who racks the breast . . .
>
> (*Journal*, p. 23)

If Lewis refers to yellow fever as the 'yellow Plague', then the 'black
demon, who racks the breast', in the next line, is presumably the
plague proper, the Black Death, in its severe, pneumonic form.
Calling the Black Death a black demon identifies the two key concepts
in Lewis's allegory; it brings together the Christian idea of the Devil as
a black slave-owner and the Hegelian characterization of death as
'the absolute Lord' or master.[38] These particular aspects of the
deadliness of Jamaica were direct consequences of colonialism: yellow
fever, a West African disease, would have been imported along with
the slaves.[39] The plague would have come with the shipboard rats.

---

[37] Craton, *Testing the Chains*, pp. 27–28, 46.

[38] Hegel, *Phenomenology of Spirit*, p. 117. Hegel himself encountered the absolute lord in the
form of Asiatic cholera.

[39] Alfred W. Crosby, *Ecological Imperialism: The Biological Expansion of Europe, 900–1900*
(Cambridge, 1986), pp. 140, 198.

On his second trip, Lewis heard that yellow fever was 'committing terrible ravages' among the white population (p. 331). On one of his trips about the island, he was disturbed to find that he had spent the night in an inn where two travellers had recently died of yellow fever, and a third was still dying of it (pp. 378–79). Although Lewis was wrong to believe that yellow fever was contagious, he was right to be concerned. Our best information concerning the danger of disease in Jamaica comes from a survey commissioned by the War Office in 1836, which concluded that of the British soldiers stationed in Jamaica between 1817 and 1836, 12.13% per year died of disease; during yellow fever epidemics, the rate could be as high as 30.7% – though for officers, to whom Lewis should probably be compared, it averaged only 8.34%. Of those who caught yellow fever, 75% died.[40]

Like Lewis's concern about slave mortality, these fears for his personal safety seem to have been both a cause and an effect of his allegory of death: he tended to allegorize his Jamaican experiences in terms of death because he thought Jamaica really was a deadly place, both for himself and for his slaves; and his Gothic imagination predisposed him to find the island deadly. The Gothic imagination itself, with its recurrent fantasies of domination and revolt, was shaped by the debate over slavery and abolition.

Lewis managed to be as philosophical about the prospect of dying in Jamaica as about his delays in getting there:

If I could be contented to *live* in Jamaica, I am still more certain, that it is the only agreeable place for me to die in; for I have got a family mausoleum, which looks for all the world like the theatrical representation of the 'tomb of all the Capulets.' Its outside is most plentifully decorated 'with sculptured stones,'–

'Arms, angels, epitaphs, and bones'.

Within is a tomb of the purest white marble, raised on a platform of ebony; the building, which is surmounted by a statue of Time, with his scythe and hour-glass, stands in the very heart of an orange grove, now in full bearing; and the whole scene this morning looked so cool, so tranquil, and so gay, and is so perfectly divested of all vestiges of dissolution, that the sight of it quite gave me an appetite for being buried. (*Journal*, p. 102)[41]

---

[40] Peter Burroughs, 'The Human Cost of Imperial Defence in the Early Victorian Age', *Victorian Studies*, 24 (1980–81), pp. 7–32 (pp. 14–15, 17).

[41] When I visited the tomb in 1992, it was completely ruinous, and almost completely buried in garbage: understandably enough, the woman who lived next to it did not cherish this relic of her colonial heritage. As I took photographs of it, she asked me if I would take it away.

Lewis's allusion to the *Liebestod* of *Romeo and Juliet* recalls the rape and murder of Antonia and the live burial of Agnes in *The Monk*, which are grotesque parodies of it. The 'appetite for being buried' which the tomb provokes in Lewis recalls the necrophilia of his novel; it also suggests guilt, as if the slave-owner recognized that his plantation would be a suitable place to die. He was tempted to follow his grandfather's example and ask for his body to be shipped back to Jamaica for burial.

Lewis died of yellow fever on his second voyage home, in 1818. The Tropic Genius had refused to hear his prayer. His friends and relatives promptly inverted the rhetorical strategy of his *Journal*, allegorizing his death by spreading rumours about it. The composer Michael Kelly heard (erroneously) that Lewis had entertained his slaves with a private performance of *The Castle Spectre*: 'they were delighted, but of all parts which struck them, that which delighted them most was the character of Hassan, the black'. Inspired by this treat, and by an 'indulgence, which they were not prepared to feel or appreciate', they

petitioned him to emancipate them. He told them, that during his lifetime it could not be done, but gave them a solemn promise, that at his *death*, they should have their freedom. Alas! it was a fatal promise for him, for on the passage homeward he died; it has been said, by poison, administered by three of his favourite black brethren, whom he was bringing to England to make free British subjects of, and who, thinking that by killing their master they should gain their promised liberty; in return for all his liberal treatment, put an end to his existence at the first favourable opportunity.

The political point of this anecdote, as a warning against tempering authority with liberality, is obvious; not surprisingly, it seems to have been current in Jamaica.[42] Granting the slave a voice was dangerous enough in a drama performed for a metropolitan audience; allowing the slaves, themselves, to hear that voice might not only justify a slave revolt (as the *Monthly Visitor* had complained) but provoke one. The social anxiety expressed in the anecdote found its clearest expression in the anti-literacy laws and other controls on knowledge in the slave colonies.[43] The same anxiety may have influenced the

---

[42] *Reminiscences of Michael Kelly*, 2 vols. (London, 1826), II, pp. 142–43; see also [Margaret Baron-Wilson], *The Life and Correspondence of M. G. Lewis*, 2 vols. (London, 1839), II, pp. 235–36.

[43] Kari J. Winter, *Subjects of Slavery, Agents of Change: Women and Power in Gothic Novels and Slave Narratives, 1790–1865* (Athens, Georgia and London, 1992), pp. 32–33, 77–78.

fate of Lewis's *Journal*: *The Monk* had been expurgated in 1798; so had the speeches of Hassan; the *Journal*, though clearly written for publication, was not published until 1834, sixteen years after Lewis's death – and one year after the emancipation of his slaves. Lewis seems to have begun and ended his writing career by telling his compatriots more than they wanted to know about their bad consciences, and their bad dreams.

CHAPTER 12

Indian Jugglers: Hazlitt, Romantic Orientalism and the difference of view

John Whale[1]

It is seeing with the eyes of others, hearing with their ears, and pinning our faith on their understandings. The learned man prides himself in the knowledge of names, and dates, not of men or things. He thinks and cares nothing about his next-door neighbours, but he is deeply read in the tribes and casts of the Hindoos and Calmuc Tartars.

(Hazlitt: 'On the Ignorance of the Learned')[2]

I

Recent work on the relationship between early nineteenth-century Orientalism and Romantic literary texts has successfully challenged and extended Said's definition of a monolithic construction of 'the Orient' by deploying psychoanalytic models of interpretation and imperialism. By giving psychoanalysis the status of a metaphorical economy, critics, such as John Barrell and Nigel Leask, have been able to articulate and display the various forms of the imaginary, whilst maintaining a committed concern for an underlying material, social reality.[3] By taking 'anxiety' as his startingpoint, Leask focuses on the instability within Romantic constructions of 'the East' and he is able to expose the variety of impulses within Romantic Orient-alism which are simultaneously collusive with and critical of the hegemony of imperialism. The interrelationship between British culture and its construction of 'the East' mixes absorption and dominance with identification and differentiation so that, as others have pointed out, there is a profound ambivalence at the heart of the

[1] I would like to thank my colleague Shirley Chew for her help in the writing of this chapter.
[2] In *The Complete Works of William Hazlitt*, ed. P.P. Howe, 21 vols (London and Toronto, 1931), VIII, p. 73; hereafter cited as *Works*.
[3] See John Barrell, *The Infection of Thomas De Quincey: A Psychopathology of Imperialism* (New Haven and London, 1991) and Nigel Leask, *British Romantic Writers and the East: Anxieties of Empire* (Cambridge, 1992).

Orientalist imagination as a result of the subject's 'inoculation' and the enzymic nature of change taking place in the colonial culture.[4] Although Leask begins with an example of the polymorphous and pervasive character of 'the Orient' within early nineteenth-century British culture, thereafter his main and appropriate concern is the traditional literary province of Romanticism.

My aim in this essay is to question, with a relatively modest example from the margins of the traditional canon, the ethical basis of Romantic aesthetics, particularly in its dependence on the emotion of sympathy and the faculty of imagination. I situate Hazlitt's essay 'The Indian Jugglers' in its theatrical context as it self-consciously aestheticizes a sign of 'the East'.[5] Hazlitt's essay is close to home in that it treats of a specific popular act within the metropolis of London, but it is still a direct result of colonial power. The case of the Indian jugglers presents, I hope, an interesting example of the assimilative and appropriative power of British, popular culture in the Regency period. That such a spectacle could take place at all in the heart of Regency London is testimony to the imperial power, which had already produced a well-developed and multifarious set of cultural practices by the early nineteenth century. That said, the material conditions of popular entertainment seem to have had a certain degree of power to mask the anxiety within what is, nevertheless, a sign of the Orient for British culture at large. Precisely because of the proliferation and mixture of signs within a popular theatre and the mixture of people within its audience,[6] the East might seem to figure here less as a sign of guilt or anxiety, than a source of pleasure. I also wish to suggest that there is a strangely paradoxical nature to this particular example of visual spectacle and physical performance. Clearly, to some extent, juggling effaces the

---

[4] The idea of 'enzymic change' is taken up by Leask, *British Romantic Writers and the East* (Cambridge, 1992), p.7 and is quoted from Stephen Greenblatt, *Marvellous Possessions: The Wonder of the New World* (Oxford, 1991), p. 4 where he writes of the need for representational modes to recognize that 'individuals and cultures tend to have fantastically powerful assimilative media that work like enzymes to change the ideological composition of foreign bodies. These foreign bodies do not disappear altogether, but they are drawn into what Homi Bhabha terms the inbetween, the zone of intersection.'

[5] For an alternative reading of Hazlitt's essay see David Bromwich, *Hazlitt: The Mind of a Critic* (New York and Oxford, 1983), pp. 351–55.

[6] According to Gillian Russell: 'While other places of entertainment – the assembly room, the pleasure garden, the race-ground, or the circulation library – were being clearly demarcated as the public spaces of the polite and the genteel, to the exclusion of the lower orders, the theatre remained socially heterogeneous in its audience composition.' See: *The Theatres of War: Performance, Politics, and Society, 1793–1815* (Oxford, 1995), p. 112.

recognition of difference. At the same time as triumphing over the limits of the body, it triumphs over an overdetermined awareness of ethnic difference. But when the body makes itself known, so difference becomes apparent, and the body's colour becomes once again the determining sign of cultural classification and racial identity. When it does so, as we shall see, it exposes the cognitive precariousness of imaginative sympathy.[7]

The act of juggling provides an opportunity for examining Hazlitt's problematic intersection between the Romantic sublime and Regency 'popular' culture. In his own terms, it is a question of redrawing the boundaries between the 'vulgar' and 'the learned'. As Hazlitt's writing negotiates mechanical perfection and sublime transcendence, it offers, I think, a fascinating anatomy of the Romantic aesthetic's relationship to the body and the ethical instability of its claim to truth.

II

Fakirs, snake-charmers, and jugglers fascinated many British travellers to the Indian sub-continent in the early nineteenth century.[8] Troupes of jugglers made frequent visits to London in the first two decades of the century and they were spectacular successes, playing to enthusiastic crowds in Pall Mall and in popular theatres such as the Olympic in Newcastle Street, the Strand.[9] Clearly, part of the thrill enjoyed by these audiences was the thought of sharing in the experience of travellers to the East and of seeing at first-hand the accounts of Indian culture which circulated in books such as Edward Moor's *Hindu Pantheon* and Emma Roberts's *Travels.*[10] A claim to authenticity is evident in the theatre notices and advertisements for the tours of Indian jugglers in 1819 and 1820, but it is not the

---

[7] For an enthusiastic account of Hazlitt's imaginative sympathy as an enabling form of historicism see Jonathan Bate, *Shakespearian Constitutions: Politics, Theatre, Criticism, 1730–1830* (Oxford, 1989), pp. 129–84.

[8] See Pratapaditya Pal and Vidya Dehejia, eds., *From Merchants to Emperors: British Artists and India, 1757–1930* (Ithaca and London, 1986), pp. 138–40 and, more generally, pp. 97–152. See also H. K. Kaul, *Traveller's India: An Anthology* (Delhi, 1979), pp. 123–35.

[9] That such popularity was not unique is evident from Michael Duffy's *The Englishman and the Foreigner* (London, 1986) in which he reports that: 'London was gripped with a Cossack-mania when two Cossacks appeared in full costume in April 1813'; and that they subsequently became prominent in popular prints.

[10] See Edward Moor, *Hindu Pantheon* (London, 1810) and Emma Roberts *Oriental Scenes, Dramatic Sketches and Tales, with other Poems* (Calcutta, 1830; London, 1832).

juggling so much as a featured 'Dimma' or 'Deema Dance' which is signalled as ethnographically definitive, being described as 'original' in the *Morning Chronicle's* advertisement for the Adelphi Theatre's production of 'a new Divertisement called MAHOMET' in November 1820; and in the Olympic's claim that: 'The celebrated Deema Dance will be performed for the first time during the Pantomime by a native Mahometan.'[11] From these examples it is clear that authenticity was part of the commercial competition between the illegitimate popular theatres in London at the time. There was a self-generating aspect to such popular phenomena, especially when they were supported, not just by commercial exploitation of rarity, but by fashion.

Despite this concern for and exploitation of authenticity in the consumption of the exotic, the theatrical context in which the Indian Jugglers performed is remarkable for its heterogeneity rather than its purity. Popular theatres such as the Olympic, the Surrey, the Adelphi, and the Coburg specialized in the mixed nature of their performances. A contract between proprietor and actor at the Olympic, dated 1815, suggests how this variety might have impacted upon the individual performer. The terms of a 'Memorandum of Agreement' between Robert William Elliston, proprietor of the Olympic Theatre, and actors in the company, contract them to play on demand in any of the following: 'Burlettas, Melo-Drames, After-pieces, Chorusses, Masks, Ballets, Preludes, Interludes, Processions, Spectacles, Pantomimes, Dances and other Performances'.[12]

This kind of mixed theatrical context provided the setting for the Indian jugglers in the tour of 1819 which involved the celebrated Ramo Samee, so-called chief of the Indian Jugglers. Even at the apparent peak of its popularity, the act could be staged as a special feature within the melodrame *Don Juan*. (In the case of Ramo Samee

---

[11] References are to the British Museum's *A collection of cuttings from newspapers, etc., relating to the Olympic Theatre, from 1805 to 1841*, MS NOTES. 2 vols (1805–1841) Theatre Cuttings 47 & 48.

[12] Minor theatres such as the Surrey and the Olympic were severely restricted by the Stage Licensing Act of 1737 and other supplementary licensing statutes of 1752 and 1755. According to John Russell Stephens: 'In order to satisfy the terms of their licences, which forbade encroachment on the preserves of the patent houses in legitimate drama, the minor theatres, if they submitted manuscripts for official approval at all, were obliged to describe them as "burlettas". The term was quite as tricky to define for contemporaries . . . as it is for modern historians of the theatre.' (*The Censorship of English Drama, 1824–1901* (Cambridge, 1980), p. 80.) See also L. W. Conolly, *The Censorship of English Drama, 1737–1824* (San Marino, 1976).

there is a progression from anonymity to personality, or even celebrity.)

If the popular theatres presented the Indian Jugglers in a cultural context which was peculiarly mixed, the same can be said of its audiences. In the 1813 tour, when performances took place up to six times a day at 87 Pall Mall at a cost of 3s, the popular and commercial impetus for the success of the act was provided by an invitation to perform in front of the Prince Regent and Ministers at Carlton House. And at the Olympic Theatre in 1819, the audiences included numerous members of fashionable society.

It is, of course, difficult to know what range of response there was within these audiences and whether they were particularly marked by imperialist anxieties. The most culturally defined and negative response to the jugglers I have encountered is generated by liberal taste. In a letter in *The Examiner* for 1815, a self-styled 'patron of the liberal arts' takes issue with the description of a 'superior set of jugglers' and argues for European pre-eminence in the face of this dextrous threat from the East. There is even perhaps a peculiar inversion of identity in his plea for 'native merit'.[13] The force of the cultural differentiation here becomes evident when, only three weeks later, *The Examiner* also published a letter, addressed to 'Members of Parliament, the Prince and the Nation' and 'the Committee for the Waterloo Monument', which, faced with the threat of foreign talent available in the rich hoard of artistic spoils taken from defeated Napoleonic France, argues against the idea of a Museum of '*Foreign Paintings* (however exquisite), but wholly and solely for one of *Native Productions*'.[14] This case exemplifies the facility with which the perspectives of cultural identification can be changed. The Other becomes fluid and flexible as we move between the categories of foreign, British, European and the implicitly Eastern.

Paradoxically, it is in the most positive responses to the jugglers that we can find the most complex response to this particular conjunction of culture and identity. In James Green's (1771–1834) watercolour, exhibited at the Royal Academy in 1814, 'the focus is on the extraordinary elegant standing figure of the juggler whose companions are a sword swallower, a young boy, and a group of wriggling snakes'.[15] Similarly, in accounts of the performances in

[13] *The Examiner*, no. 416, 17 December 1815, p. 813.
[14] *The Examiner*, no. 418, 31 December 1815, p. 843.
[15] Pal and Dehejia, eds., *From Merchants to Emperors: British Artists and India, 1757–1930*, p. 140.

1820, the terms of public response revolve around 'astonishment', 'admiration' and 'beauty', and they are coupled with a peculiarly unthreatening familiarity, evident in the following review from 26 November:

The performances of that man are of the most incredible description: he plays with four balls, which he keeps up whirling with the greatest velocity round his head at the same time, yet never hitting one another, and never falling from the hand of the performer. The Indian speaks very good English, and tells the spectators from time to time what he is about to do. A tube, which he presents to them, he calls 'his gun'. He then balances on his nose a small tree, on the branches of which eight or ten images of birds are placed; kneeling with this tree so balanced, he introduces the tube into his mouth, and then shoots peas from it at the birds, which he brings down in regular succession . . . He performs another very beautiful feat, in which he makes and unmakes an elegant little toy, while the parts are all balanced in the most exquisite nicety. A heavy cannon-ball he throws from his arm to his back, and from his back to his arm, and then plays with it as if it were a shuttlecock and his back a battledore. His exhibition concludes with the insertion of a piece of iron (somewhat like a sword) down his throat; this he calls his 'supper', but professes 'not to like it so well as a mutton chop'. He, however, puts it almost out of sight, kneeling; rises with it still in his chest, and throws it down on the stage so as to satisfy every one that no deception is practised. He is a very good looking man; his pleasantries excite laughter, but his astonishing dexterity, which, even from seeing we can hardly believe, call forth the loudest tokens of admiration and reiterated plaudits from all parts of the House. (British Museum, Cuttings, Theatre Cuttings 47 and 48)

Although one reviewer refers to the sword-swallowing as the '*chef d'œuvre* of the marvellous' which is 'done with so much ease as to prevent any pain to spectators' (17 November 1820), it is this part of the act which actually generates most unease and which breaks the spell of astonishment produced by the mesmeric facility of juggling.[16]

---

[16] See also Edward Braddon's account of sword-swallowing and bird-swallowing in the 1870s which speaks of 'the only emotion, besides disgust' being 'envy of the juggler's capacity for taking pills': 'As for some of the feats of Indian Jugglers, they are totally destitute of any element of conjuring. Take, for example, that which is possibly best known to fame – the sword-swallowing performance. No sleight of hand or artful machinery is exhibited in this; there is literally no deception: the juggler throws his head back so as to obtain a reasonably straight course of some eighteen inches from his thorax downwards, and then, employing so much of his internal economy as a scabbard, inserts therein the instrument that is accepted as a sword – that is to say, an instrument closely resembling the pinless and edgeless cutlass of the British sailor or bandit of melodrama. The performance is, in short, an uncomfortable one for all concerned, but not otherwise remarkable.' *Thirty Years of Shikar* (Edinburgh, 1895), pp. 338–39; quoted in *Traveller's India*, pp. 132–36.

Here, the body obtrudes upon the scene, interrupting the dazzling surface of continuous motion with a threatening spectacle of interiority and appetite. Graceful taste is disrupted by the prospect of the physical body making itself known in the penetrative act of sword-swallowing. And, as we have seen, the threat of familiarity is compounded by the juggler referring to the sword as his 'supper'. This, as one might expect, is also the point at which the response to the jugglers becomes explicitly gendered. His 'introducing a foot of cold steel into his stomach' generates a thrill which belongs as much, one suspects, to the *Morning Chronicle's* reporter as it does to the women who figure in his description: 'one of them plunges a sword down his throat to the delight of the ladies who have not *delicate nerves*'.[17] Hazlitt, too, as we shall see, is quick to dissociate himself from a part of the act which so vulgarly reminds us of the body: 'As to the swallowing of the sword, the police ought to interfere to prevent it.'[18]

III

Coming forward and seating himself on the ground in his white dress and tightened turban, the chief of the Indian Jugglers begins with tossing up two brass balls, which is what any of us could do, and concludes with keeping up four at the same time, which is what none of us could do to save our lives, nor if we were to take our whole lives to do it in . . . To catch four balls in succession in less than a second of time, and deliver them back so as to return with seeming consciousness to the hand again, to make them revolve round him at certain intervals, like the planets in their sphere, to make them chase one another like sparkles of fire, or shoot up like flowers or meteors, to throw them behind his back and twine them round his neck like ribbons or like serpents, to do what appears an impossibility, and to do it with all the ease, the grace, the carelessness imaginable, to laugh at, to play with the glittering mockeries, to follow them with his eye as if he could fascinate them with its lambent fire, or as he had only to see that they kept time with the music on the stage – there is something in all this which he who does not admire may be quite sure he never really admired any thing in the whole course of his life. It is skill surmounting difficulty, and beauty triumphing over skill. (*Works*, VIII, pp. 77–78)

In the face of the Indian jugglers, Hazlitt the essayist is moved to admiration and beauty. He is then humbled and shamed. The first

[17] *The Morning Chronicle*, 7 July 1813.
[18] Hazlitt, *Works*, VIII, p. 78.

reaction is one of humanistic apostrophe: 'Man, thou art a wonderful animal, and thy ways past finding out!'[19] This is soon followed
by a seemingly self-defeated exclamation as Hazlitt is prompted to a
competitive mode of comparison which induces a state of anguished
introspection: 'What abortions are these essays!'[20] The restorative
capacity of the essay turns on this fraught self-consciousness. From
this point onwards, I will argue, the essay readjusts itself in order to
find solace within elegiac limitations.

In this way, the performance of the Indian jugglers provides the
spring-board for a definition of a distinction between genius and
talent. And as we might expect from the Romantic essayist, the
difference rests on what is perfectible and what is not. Mechanical
arts can be measured. They are a question of success or failure and
can be tested visually. The activity of genius, on the other hand, can
never be brought to perfection and exists, as Hazlitt admits, in the
more confusing and relativistic arena of opinion and aesthetics. His
description of genius is characterized by mixture and mediation
rather than direct visual apprehension: 'The more ethereal, more
refined and sublime part of art is the seeing nature through the
medium of sentiment and passion, as each object is a symbol of the
affections and a link in the chain of our endless being.'[21] In stressing
the limit of visual perception, Hazlitt's text enacts a familiar
Romantic preference for the unseen over the seen, the visionary over
the merely visual; but it also draws attention to the limits of
imagination itself. Despite his reference to an emotional and perspectival form of the sublime, Hazlitt offers an illustration of
mediation rather than transcendence. He never quite cuts himself
free from mimesis.

'The Indian Jugglers', the title of one of Hazlitt's most famous
essays, is plural and, as a result, anonymous. This is appropriate, for
the kind of mechanical skill which the 'Indian juggler' brings to
stylish perfection, according to Hazlitt's description, is infinitely
repeatable. It lacks that singular imprint of individuality which
comes, paradoxically, from failure. As in some other forms of
Romantic creativity, Hazlitt's aesthetic actually makes a virtue out of
failure, and his essay moves, characteristically, from abjection to a
celebration of genius before returning with an appropriate sense of
limit to an appreciation of physical skill and dexterity which takes

---

[19] Ibid., pp. 77–78.   [20] Ibid., p. 79.   [21] Ibid., pp. 82–83.

the form of an obituary on the hand fives-player John Cavanagh. According to Hazlitt: 'He who takes to playing at fives is twice young. He feels neither the past nor future "in the instant".'[22] In many ways, the significance of Hazlitt's whole essay lies in its appreciation of temporality: the limit placed on human performances whether they be concerned with ethereal genius or mechanical perfection. This is its function as an essay – an attempt or trial – which mirrors the impossibility of moving beyond its capacity. As if to demonstrate the strategic materiality of his writing, Hazlitt redeploys his own previously published obituary on Cavanagh, thereby also illustrating the professional journalist's need to make a virtue out of necessity.

In this way, Hazlitt's essay mediates popular entertainment and aesthetic theory. Although the essay may seem to move from the mechanical feats of the Indian jugglers to a definition of genius, by the end, it is the seeing through the 'medium of sentiment and passion' which is pitted humanistically against the ravages of time. The 'endless chain of our being' is measured against death, and the essayist's description of the Indian jugglers is itself an act of imagination, a manifestation of historical consciousness which cannot defeat or transcend time, merely show an awareness of it. We are now able to translate the limitation of Hazlitt's humility in the face of the Indian juggler – 'The utmost I can pretend to is to write a description of what this fellow can do'[23] – into a sign of powerful mediation.

The Indian jugglers are thus assimilated into the complex cultural mix of Hazlitt's text. Popular entertainment in the Olympic Theatre is not simply a stepping-stone to the main event of the idealizing imagination; it shares the same situation and is subject to the same limitations. His definition of genius is sandwiched between a spectacular manifestation of popular Orientalism and the individualized celebrity of the manly, Regency sportsman. This essay, provocatively, seemingly indiscriminately, combines Indian jugglers, Richer, the rope-walker, Cavanagh, the fives-player, and Sir Joshua Reynolds, the Academician.

The return to physical performance in the essay, in the form of John Cavanagh, registers the conflict at its heart. Although it is confidently stated that the test of greatness is the page of history:

---

[22] Ibid., p. 87.   [23] Ibid., p. 79.

'Nothing can be said to be great that has a distinct limit, or that borders on something evidently greater than itself'[24] and that: 'No act terminating in itself constitutes greatness';[25] Hazlitt's own medium of the essay gives the power of greatness – communicated through passion – to Cavanagh. As a result, Hazlitt's essay does not simply lend the power of polite culture to the popular and what might be thought of as transitory and vulgar. More problematically, and more interestingly, Hazlitt's text finds itself situated by an act of mediation, which is not transcendent.

This conflict between different ways of seeing, between the physical and the metaphysical, is evident in the responses generated in Hazlitt the essayist by the Indian jugglers. Only a few pages later this has turned into a wary scepticism based on cultural and religious difference:

If the Juggler were told that by flinging himself under the wheels of the Juggernaut, when this idol issues forth on a gaudy day, he would immediately be transported into Paradise, he might believe it, and nobody could disprove it. So the Brahmans may say what they please on that subject, may build up dogmas and mysteries without end, and not be detected: but their ingenious countryman cannot persuade the frequenters of the Olympic Theatre that he performs a number of astonishing feats without actually giving proofs of what he says. (*Works*, VIII, p. 81)

Here Hazlitt's sense of cultural difference serves to differentiate the Brahmans from the jugglers in order to support the self-centred nature of the mechanical. At the same time, however, he reinforces a stereotypical vision of Indian religion as dangerous, even barbaric, superstition. At this point in the essay, the jugglers are in danger of losing their Indian identity. In so far as they are endorsed by Hazlitt's sense of the mechanical, which is rooted in the material world, they forfeit their cultural particularity. Defined as mechanical, the jugglers also lose the imprint of identity and the possibility of historical self-consciousness. At this moment, for Hazlitt, 'India' conveniently images the threat of religion and the death of the body. It enables him to rehearse a familiar movement between the horrors of irrational superstition and the facelessness of the mere body. This sudden intrusion of self-conscious, cultural difference confirms, along with other key aspects of the essay, a sense of elegiac limitation, linked to an unnerving uncertainty over the after-life.

[24] Ibid., p. 84.   [25] Ibid., p. 85.

In this way Hazlitt's sceptical empiricism resists Eastern religion as much as it does abstraction or abstruse metaphysical speculation. As we have seen, he is wary of cutting loose into the extremes of the sublime. And when this empiricism is linked, as it often is in Hazlitt's writing, with a poetics of sympathy and imagination, it proves to be a difficult combination. One of its toughest tests is in response to the increasingly powerful modes of utilitarian thought which draw on the works of Bentham and Malthus. And in the case of James Mill's *History of British India* utilitarianism and imperialism are inextricably linked in a text which, perhaps even more significantly for Hazlitt, wages war on the epistemology of imagination.[26]

In his essay 'On Reason and Imagination' in *The Plain Speaker,* Hazlitt argues passionately for the role of imagination in the face of contemporary demographic and social theorists such as Malthus and Bentham. The essay is one of his classic definitions of the humanizing power of sympathy. Working from the characteristically aggressive premise that: 'I hate people who have no notion of any thing but generalities, and forms, and creeds, and naked propositions, even worse than I dislike those who cannot for the soul of them arrive at the comprehension of an abstract idea';[27] Hazlitt proceeds to defend the imagination's capacity to imbue particularity with morality. His version of the imagination must mediate between abstract generalities and particularities, but because of the prevailing mode of political economy: 'We have been so used to count by millions of late, that we think the units that compose them nothing; and are so prone to trace remote principles, that we neglect the immediate results';[28] it finds itself, somewhat surprisingly, on the side of facts.

For these contextual reasons and because of his inveterate empiricism, Hazlitt bases his argument on the primacy of reality: 'There is no language, no description that can strictly come up to the truth and force of reality; all we have to do, is to guide our descriptions and conclusions by the reality.'[29] He then proceeds to locate truth in powerful feeling: 'Passion, in short, is the essence, the chief ingre-

---

[26] For an analysis of James Mill's puritanical mistrust of 'susceptible imaginations' see Javed Majeed, *Ungoverned Imaginings: James Mill's 'History of British India' and Orientalism* (Oxford, 1992), pp. 162–79.

[27] Hazlitt, *Works,* XII, p. 44.

[28] Ibid., p. 53.

[29] Ibid., p. 45.

dient in moral truth; and the warmth of passion is sure to kindle the light of imagination on the objects around it.'[30] What might have thus appeared to be a stark conjunction of subjective and objective is soon dissolved: 'where our own interests are concerned, or where we are sincere in our profession of regard, the pretended distinction between sound judgement and lively imagination is quickly done away with'.[31]

Significantly, the two examples which Hazlitt uses to illustrate the force of his humanist argument both turn on cultural difference. In keeping with his impassioned liberalism, the first concerns the slave-trade, where he encounters no problem in quoting and endorsing the following powerful words from the relatively recently published *The Memoirs of Granville Sharp*: 'if any one takes away the character of Black people, that man injures Black people all over the world; and when he has once taken away their character, there is nothing he may not do to Black people ever after'.[32]

The second example, which is brought to bear against James Mill and what he disparagingly refers to as 'Mr Bentham's artificial ethical scales',[33] brings us conveniently back to the conjunction of London and India:

one of this school of thinkers declares that he was qualified to write a better History of India from having never been there than if he had, as the last might lead to local distinctions or party-prejudices; that is to say, that he could describe a country better at second-hand than from original observation, or that from having seen no one object, place, or person, he could do ampler justice to the whole. It might be maintained, much on the same principle, that an artist would paint a better likeness of a person after he was dead, from description or different sketches of the face, than from having seen the individual living man. On the contrary, I humbly conceive that the seeing half a dozen wandering Lascars in the streets of London gives one a better idea of the soul of India, the cradle of the world, and (as it were) garden of the sun, than all the charts, records, and statistical reports that can be sent over, even under the classical administration of Mr Canning. *Ex uno omnes.* One Hindoo differs more from a citizen of London

---

[30] Ibid., p. 46.
[31] Ibid., p. 47.
[32] Ibid., p. 49. See also Prince Hoare, *Memoirs of Granville Sharp Esq., Composed from his own Manuscripts, Authentic Documents in the Possession of His Family and of the African Institution* (London, 1810); and for a brief account of Sharp's significance in the anti-slavery campaigns of the 1770s see Moira Ferguson, *Subject to Others: British Women Writers of Colonial Slavery, 1760–1834* (New York and London, 1992), pp. 168–70, 221–23.
[33] Hazlitt, *Works*, XII, p. 50.

than he does from all other Hindoos; and by seeing the two first, man to man, you know comparatively and essentially what they are, nation to nation. By a very few specimens you fix the great leading differences, which are nearly the same throughout. Any one thing is a better representative of its kind, than all the words and definitions in the world can be. The sum total is indeed different from the particulars; but it is not easy to guess at any general result, without some previous induction of particulars and appeal to experience. (*Works*, XII, p. 51)

When we are referred to the 'soul', 'the cradle of the world', and the 'garden of the sun', it is clear that 'India' here is a sign of the Romantic imagination which is being deployed to fend off the threat of a burgeoning utilitarianism represented by 'charts, records, and statistical reports'. And in its attack on the new demographic 'science' it reveals some of its own limitations. Whereas the committed libertarianism of Hazlitt's quotation from *The Memoirs of Granville Sharp* insistently couples 'Black' with 'people' and thereby generates a universal humanism; Hazlitt's definition of difference on the streets of London finds itself in danger of invoking an unwelcome taxonomy of natural history: a potentially dehumanizing discourse of 'specimens' and 'kind'. There is also a downgrading of language and representation here, which matches the anger vented on the learned in the epigraph with which I began this essay. Given Hazlitt's dependence on the power of sympathetic passion to bridge the gap between particularity and abstraction, it is difficult to imagine the passion or interest which generates the need for cultural difference. Hazlitt's committed liberalism finds an understandable and manifest passion in the case of the slave-trade, but the need to move from the 'wandering Lascars of the streets of London' seems to be seriously under-motivated. One of the problems with the metonymic exchange at the heart of these examples – which suggests that the part equals (or stands in for) the whole – is that it is not susceptible, I think, to such a reversal. Is the symbolic force of the passage from *The Memoirs of Granville Sharp* really equivalent to Hazlitt's description of the visual cognition of racial difference on the streets of London?

In any case, interpretation of such a passage is fraught with problems, precisely because of such loaded inversions. Typically, Hazlitt's subscription to what appears to be a simplistic, visual epistemology is complicated by his line of attack. Apparently against the force of his own aggression, his argument seems to endorse rather than to oppose a perversely myopic vision of India from 'home'. However, Hazlitt's appeal to the streets of London, like his enjoyment of the illegitimate theatres, makes another kind of difference apparent: the peculiarly English struggle to define the limits of 'vulgarity'. The challenge of reading Hazlitt is to see the workings of liberal imagination inextricably linked to bad feeling. Hazlitt's view from home is not made in the name of utilitarian scientific impartiality; it operates within the affect of partisanship, reassessing the very nature of sympathy and hatred.

IV

According to the artist William Bewick, the lectures of Sir Anthony Carlisle, Professor of Anatomy at the Royal Academy, were popular performances which contained some rather theatrical demonstrations, and he recalls how Hazlitt was driven to attend after having heard the Professor speak provocatively of 'the uselessness of poetry':

He therefore requested me to take him to hear one of his anatomical lectures, delivered to the students of the Academy. I consequently accompanied him on the appointed evening to Somerset House. This celebrated surgeon generally treated the artists, his hearers, with some exhibition of novelty or interest, and his lectures were always crowded. Once he had six or eight naked Life-guardsmen going through their sword experience, exhibiting the varied muscular action of the body. On another occasion he had some Indian or Chinese jugglers, performing their feats of agility, showing the flexibility of their joints, and what suppleness training may produce in the frame of man. On the evening I speak of, the lecturer, when speaking of the emotions and passions of the mind, handed round upon a dinner-plate the brain of a man, and on another a human heart. As these severally came to Hazlitt for observation, and to be passed round, he shrank back in sensitive horror, closed his eyes, turned away his pale, shuddering countenance, and appeared to those near him to be in a swooning state. I was glad, however, after a little while to observe him rally, when he whispered in nervous accents, 'Of what use can all this be to artists? Surely the bones and muscles might be sufficient.'[34]

An anecdote at Hazlitt's expense, but one which provides further illustration of the way in which his aesthetics of mediation and limit are interestingly situated between corporeality and sublimity. As he recoils in 'sensitive horror' at the sight of internal organs, but

---

[34] *Life and Letters of William Bewick (Artist)*, ed. Thomas Landseer (Wakefield, 1978; first published 1871 in two volumes), I, pp. 141–42.

steadies himself sufficiently to appreciate the benefits of 'bones and muscles', Hazlitt's taste is defined in terms of a problematic proximity to the body which recalls his threatened response to the sword-swallowing act of the Indian jugglers.

If this kind of reflex or recoil of disgust captures Hazlitt's vulnerability in the face of something a little too close to home, his radical empiricism in the face of the Indian jugglers also demonstrates, I think, the challenging forcefulness of his strategic irritability. Hazlitt's provocative returns home, evident in his switch from Mill's disinterested utility to the streets of London, in his attack on the scholar 'who cares nothing about his next-door neighbours . . . but is deeply read in the tribes and casts of the Hindoos and Calmuc Tartars', and in his populist appeals to the eyes of the audience in the Olympic theatre, provide a tough testing-ground for defining the limits of imaginative knowledge and liberal sympathy.

Instead of envisaging the interaction between the Romantic imagination and drama as an exclusively private affair, evidence once more of the power of an idealizing or transcendent imagination which produces a psychological theatre of the mind, Hazlitt's presentation of the spectacle of the Indian jugglers resists such an easy and powerful process of internalization. Hazlitt finds himself uncomfortably situated between historical consciousness and the moment, between the 'vulgar' and 'the learned'.

CHAPTER 13

'Some samples of the finest Orientalism': Byronic Philhellenism and proto-Zionism at the time of the Congress of Vienna

Caroline Franklin

Oh that I had the art of easy writing
What should be easy reading! could I scale
Parnassus, where the Muses sit inditing
Those pretty poems never known to fail,
How quickly would I print (the world delighting)
A Grecian, Syrian, or Assyrian tale;
And sell you, mix'd with western sentimentalism,
Some samples of the finest Orientalism!

Byron, *Beppo*, 51

Taking their cue from self-mockery such as this, critics wanting to debunk the romantic image of the poet who gave his life for the Greek revolution of 1824 have often portrayed Byron as a self-promoting purveyor of fashionable Orientalist fantasy, who cynically stuck to the East as 'the only poetical policy'.[1] Of course, Byron's self-conscious deconstruction of his own Romantic Orientalism prefigured modern scepticism like Edward Said's famous definition of Orientalism as 'the corporate institution for dealing with the Orient' operating as a Western style for 'dominating, restructuring, and having authority over the Orient'.[2] But as Byron also consistently denounced imperialism throughout his verse, he has proved a trickier writer to fit into the binary model of Said's thesis than government polemicists like Byron's bête noire, Robert Southey. The Poet Laureate expressed a low opinion of both western Orientalists and the Indian and the middle-eastern literature which they studied

---

[1] *Letters and Journals of Lord Byron*, ed. Leslie Marchand, 12 vols. (London, 1973–82), III, p. 68. Henceforth referred to as *Byron's Letters and Journals*. Critics who emphasize the way Byron's Oriental tales cater for popular taste include Paul West, *Byron and the Spoiler's Art* (London, 1960); Andrew Rutherford, *Byron: A Critical Study* (Edinburgh, 1961); Philip W. Martin, *Byron: A Poet Before His Public* (Cambridge, 1982); and Jerome Christensen, *Lord Byron's Strength: Romantic Writing and Commercial Society* (Baltimore, 1993).

[2] Edward W. Said, *Orientalism* (London, 1978), p. 3.

in notes to his verse romances on the Eastern mythology and stylistic motifs he had utilized.[3] The Utilitarians of the next generation would go much further. The theoretical project of James Mill's *The History of British India* (1817) was no less than 'to emancipate India from its own culture'.[4]

In fact, Byron's self-satire and Southey's professed contempt for Oriental literature can both be seen, with hindsight, as defensive strategies. Paradoxically, their very scoffing testifies to the overwhelming importance for the development of British Romanticism of Europe's fascination with the East. Modernity had come into being with the decentring of theology by Renaissance Christendom's revaluation of the ancient, pagan cultures it had superseded. By the eighteenth century, the era of neoclassicism faded as a second shock of Enlightenment was experienced. Eurocentricity, itself, was challenged by the rediscovery of the ancient civilizations of India and the East, whose impact was so great that Raymond Schwab termed it 'the Oriental Renaissance'.[5]

Said's seminal essay performed a useful task in foregrounding the ideological implications and utilitarian usefulness to Western colonialism of Orientalist scholarship, which earlier writers like Schwab had understated. Nevertheless, Said's Foucauldian model is too monolithic. It could be argued that the very notion of the dichotomy between 'East' and 'West' as having appertained throughout history is itself a product of nineteenth-century historiography. The Victorian ruling class, educated in the classics, had identified ancient Greece with Europe, and so interpreted Herodotus' account of the wars between the Greek cities devoted to trade and those under the influence of the feudal 'barbarians' (Persians) as the first of many clashes between civilized Hellenic freedom and barbaric Eastern

---

[3] 'A waste of ornament and labour characterizes all the works of the Orientalists . . . The little of their literature that has reached us is equally worthless. Our *barbarian* scholars have called Ferdusi the Oriental Homer. . . . To make this Iliad of the East, as they have sacrilegiously styled it, a good poem, would be realizing the dreams of alchemy, and transmuting lead into gold.' *The Poetical Works of Robert Southey, Collected by Himself*, 10 vols. (London, 1846), IV, p. 29. Compare Macaulay's famous remark that 'a single shelf of a good European library was worth the whole native literature of India and Arabia'. *Education Minute* of 2 February 1835, quoted by David Kopf, *British Orientalism and the Bengal Renaissance: The Dynamics of Indian Modernization, 1773–1835* (Berkeley and Los Angeles, 1969), p. 249.

[4] Javed Majeed, *Ungoverned Imaginings: James Mill's 'The History of British India' and Orientalism* (Oxford, 1992), p. 127.

[5] Raymond Schwab, *The Oriental Renaissance: Europe's Rediscovery of India and the East, 1660–1880*, tr. Gene Patterson-Black and Victor Reinking (New York, 1984).

despotism.[6] This reading of history as a struggle between a notional 'East' and 'West' gave a comforting sense of continuity to the imperialist project in which nineteenth-century Britons found themselves engaged.

Though the development of scholarly Orientalism in the eighteenth and nineteenth centuries certainly had connections first with European mercantilist expansion and then the assertion of colonial power, the writing of the East was not always utilitarian or a mode of metaphorical domination. Literature functioned – as always – as the site in which contesting ideologies were imagined in struggle, and which could effect changes in perception of the workings of power. Amongst the variety of voices within British representations of the East, Byron's distinctiveness consisted in the rhetoric of a sceptical critique of imperialism, alternating with the discourse of sentimental nationalism. Both texts to be considered here, the Oriental tale, *The Siege of Corinth* (1816) and *Hebrew Melodies* (1815), a collection of Biblical lyrics written for Jewish liturgical music and traditional airs arranged by the young composer Isaac Nathan, were published when Europe's boundaries were being redrawn with the defeat of Napoleon, and both configure the slippery relationships between religion and patriotism.

Two years earlier, Byron's publication of his first Oriental romance, *The Giaour*, had coincided with parliament's review of the Charter of the East India Company and debate over whether missionaries should be allowed to preach Christianity in India. The eponymous 'Giaour', or infidel, unexpectedly turns out to be a decadent Westerner seen from the Islamic point of view. In *The Corsair* (1814), the European anti-hero disguises himself as an Islamic holy man, and in *The Siege of Corinth* (1816), the Western protagonist becomes an Islamic convert fighting for the Turks. At a time when conversion of the Eastern 'pagans' had become a justification for colonialism, these ironic narrative poems experiment with point of view to confound readerly expectations.

Since the growth of the Evangelical movement in the 1790s, British Protestantism had taken a newly hostile stance towards Asian religions. The official policy of the East India Company had

---

[6] Raghavan Iyer, 'The Glass Curtain between Asia and Europe', in *The Glass Curtain Between Asia and Europe*, ed. Raghavan Iyer (London, 1965), p. 14. See also Martin Bernal, *Black Athena: The Afroasiatic Roots of Classical Civilisation*, 2 vols. (London, 1987–91), I, Chapters 6 and 7.

previously been toleration of the indigenous religious and cultural practices of the subcontinent. Not only had pragmatism suggested that missionaries would unnecessarily antagonize the local populations, but eighteenth-century relativists viewed proselytism as inherently wrong. Indeed, many Britons in India, inspired by Sir William Jones and Warren Hastings, studied and revered Oriental civilization. The hawkish Anglicists (dominated by Evangelicals and supported by Southey) were now opposing these scholarly Orientalists, who continued to argue that Indian education should appertain as opposed to an imposed Europeanization. The Orientalists lost the argument and a new phase began in the history of British India. It could be said that a line had been crossed: that Britain now saw herself as a colonial power, rather than merely a trading nation.

The dialogue within British imperialism was not simply between politically conservative Evangelicals and Whiggish Orientalists. The Evangelicals' dismissive view of Asian religion as mere superstition was matched by the development of a secular call for the reform of the feudal institutions of Asia, by Utilitarians influenced by the ideas of the philosophical radical, Jeremy Bentham. Byron was therefore writing at a time when Orientalist Enlightenment relativism was being consciously challenged by a movement emanating from both right and left which espoused an openly Eurocentric and Christianizing ideology. He had Minerva send this message to Britain:

> 'Look to the East, where Ganges' swarthy race
> Shall shake your tyrant empire to its base;
> Lo! there rebellion rears her ghastly head,
> And glares the Nemesis of native dead;
> Till Indus rolls a deep purpureal flood
> And claims his long arrear of northern blood.
> So may ye perish! Pallas, when she gave
> Your free-born rights, forbade ye to enslave'.
>
> *The Curse of Minerva* (lines 221–28)

Byron differentiated between economic colonialism, which left the civil rights of the indigenous population in place (as by the British East India Company in India pre-1813), and wholesale, foreign incursion, settlement and direct rule, which converts 'subjects' to 'slaves'. In 1812, he even grudgingly praised Britain in contrasting the fate of her colonial subjects with the degradation of the Greeks under the Turks:

The Greeks will never be independent; they will never be sovereigns as heretofore, and God forbid they ever should! but they may be subjects without being slaves. Our colonies are not independent, but they are free and industrious, and such may Greece be hereafter. At present, like the Catholics of Ireland and the Jews throughout the world, and other such cudgelled and heterodox people, they suffer all the moral and physical ills that can afflict humanity.[7]

Marilyn Butler asserts that Byron's resistance to the changing character of British imperialism was conservative in comparison with the 'progressive' Southey and Utilitarian Mill, whose 'writing on India is centrally concerned with its transformation'.[8] Nigel Leask also comments: 'One of the great ironies of early nineteenth-century liberal imperialism was the manner in which it employed enlightenment attacks on the tyranny and priestcraft of the ancien régime to justify the conquest of non-European societies and culture.' He suggests this entrapped an aristocratic Whig like Byron in an ideological cul-de-sac, wishing to affirm enthusiasm neither for popular radicalism nor empire, yet isolated in his 'quixotic' recourse to the 'classical ideal as a foundation for both political and poetical practice'.[9] Byron was a republican rather than a democrat, and Malcolm Kelsall compares his political outlook, changeable though it was, to that of the Foxite or Jacobin Whigs.[10]

Such comments illuminate the political impasse of Byron, the man. However, Byronism was a literary phenomenon too wide-ranging to be solely attributable to the inspiration of Byron himself, and the ideological significance of Byron's poetry is not reducible to his conscious political views. Byronic Romanticism emanated from a sentimentalist strand of Enlightenment liberalism distinct from that of the rationalists, Bentham, Ricardo and Marx, and its mythic importance was to be hugely influential in the development of nationalism, not only in Europe but also later in the independence movements of her colonies. Bertrand Russell considered Byronism so significant in the development of nationalism that he devoted an

---

[7] *Lord Byron: The Complete Poetical Works*, ed. Jerome J. McGann, 7 vols. (Oxford, 1980–91), II, p. 201. All references to Byron's poetry except *Hebrew Melodies* are taken from this edition, henceforth abbreviated to *BCPW*.

[8] Marilyn Butler, 'Orientalism', in *The Penguin History of Literature: Vol. 5 The Romantic Period*, ed. David Pirie (London, 1994), pp. 446–47.

[9] Nigel Leask, *British Romantic Writers and the East: Anxieties of Empire* (Cambridge, 1992), pp. 24–25.

[10] Malcolm Kelsall, *Byron's Politics* (Brighton, 1987).

entire chapter of *History of Western Philosophy* to the poet.[11] The
aristocratic anarchism and idealization of national freedom in
Byron's poetry, like the ideas of Fichte, originated in revolt against
supra-national dynastic empires and would influence both Carlyle
and Nietzsche. Byronism, like some forms of imperialist thinking,
romanticized both the hero and traditional organic communities,
but the former, rather than seeing primitive countries as providing
opportunities for the entrepreneur, lamented their lost innocence
through colonization and the advance of industrialism.

In contrast to the cultural superiority asserted by the Utilitarians
and the relativism practised by the Enlightenment, Byronic Romanticism represented the most developed European civilizations in
history as decadent, and instead idealized the primitive past. *Childe
Harold's Pilgrimage* was also a profound elegy for the recurrent loss of
political freedom in the cycles or 'revolutions' of European history
throughout time. Byronic pessimism therefore deconstructed the
Whigs' and the radicals' view of history as progress, while also
attacking Burke's notion of the slow organic development of political
constitutions, by representing as tragic the restoration by the allies of
the ancien régime in 1815.

It is not necessary to ask how the rhetoric of a Whig noble
functioned as sufficiently oppositional in a nineteenth-century, political context to inspire European nationalist causes and to be
appropriated at home by radical publishers of Chartist propaganda.[12] It was just because Byron's discourse was so distinctly that
of the British ruling class that his critique of government policy was
so useful. Moreover, his class position enabled him uniquely to
challenge through insouciant romanticization of aristocratic libertinism the growing determination of the powerful Evangelical movement to reform both the British working classes and subject peoples
abroad.

The Siege of Corinth and *Hebrew Melodies* may be considered both as
symbolic meditations on the politics of imperialism and as discourse
oppositional to the Evangelical movement at home. (Said tends to
underestimate the self-reflexive aspect of Orientalism.) Byron's verse
romances demonstrate the sensationalist fascination with sexuality

---

[11] Bertrand Russell, *History of Western Philosophy and its connection with Political and Social
Circumstances from the earliest times to the present day* (London, 1946), pp. 667, 774–80.
[12] See N. Stephen Bauer, 'Romantic Poets and Radical Journalists', *Neuphilologische Mitteilungen*,
79 (1978), pp. 266–75.

and violence of popular Oriental Gothic. However, his dramatiza-
tion of Judaeo-Christian themes in the Biblical poetry should be seen
as a complementary aspect of Byron's Orientalism – the subject-
matter reflects that revisionary search for the semitic origins of
European culture, which had been, since the Reformation, a motive
for turning to the East, arguably of equal importance to imperial
conquest. In contrast with Arnold later in the century, Byron
emphasized the barbaric in representing the modern Greeks, and
stressed the semitic aspect of the Judaeo-Christian tradition.

In the early nineteenth century, both Greeks and Jews were
distinguished as peoples only in terms of their religion: the 'Greeks'
being a heterogeneous group of Romaic populations criss-crossed by
tribal loyalties and rivalries, and the Jews of the diaspora having
settled and become almost indistinguishable from their fellow-
citizens throughout much of the world. These dispossessed peoples
become representative for the poet of the abstract concept of a
'nation' separate from statehood. Byron's Orientalist poetry of 1815
focuses particularly on the dual role which religion plays in the
process of colonization. *The Siege of Corinth* is a savage denunciation
of the way religious institutions, whether Islamic or Christian,
underwrite imperialist expansion and the destruction of rival
empires. In contrast, the personae of *Hebrew Melodies* express religion
as intense, personal emotion which sanctifies a sense of place
through the individual's mystical apprehension of Nature. In conquered lands, religious traditions thus foster group memories, which
may be transformed into a sentimental patriotism based on cultural
identity. This is comparable with the ideas of Herder but should be
distinguished from nationalism defined as a belief in the borders of
the nation state.

Jews and Greeks both presented a symbolic cause of lost freedom:
a particularly poignant subject at this, the time of the Congress of
Vienna (1814–15). Napoleon was deposed on 3 April 1814, and his
empire was to be disposed of by the 'Holy Alliance' of Austria,
Prussia, Russia, and Great Britain. The map of Europe was redrawn
in the hope of establishing a balance of power between various
imperial and dynastic interests, and with no regard to the concept of
nationalism, which was still in its infancy for much of Europe. In the
settlement of 1815, Germany was still a loose confederation of states;
Italy was fragmented, but mainly parcelled out to the Hapsburgs;
Norway was ruled by Sweden; Holland incorporated Belgium, and

so on. The relationship between imperialism and nationalism was seen in Whiggish rhetoric as a simple opposition or choice (as made in 1813 by Britain with regard to her role in India, for example). In fact, the two terms are inextricably connected. The Burkean model of the ancient English kingdom, organically developing over time, implies political and economic growth, and Britain's role indeed enlarged from trade with Eastern lands to encompassing them. Likewise, the concept of the self-created nation state, enshrined in the French revolution, had led directly to that country's messianic mission to create others by conquest on the Roman model. Yet both the British and the Napoleonic empires, which developed out of nationalism, paradoxically, went on to produce nationalist aspirations in their colonies, through the latter's reaction to exploitation or incursion. Byronism, especially in its fascination with the Napoleonic Byronic hero and Romantic individualism, explored both the danger and attraction of the Rousseauistic republic: a ruthless yet charismatic leader whose militaristic power is derived directly from the citizens' consent, with no mediating social or constitutional structures. When thrown into heroic relief by the poet's death in 1824, Byronism was to become a source of inspiration to revolutionary liberal and nationalist movements, especially in Germany, Italy, Greece and Poland.

Byron's Philhellenism and Zionism were distanced from the immediate political situation of Europe, being safely Utopian dreams of emancipation etched against the traditional Western Other of Islamic empire, for the Turks controlled both Greece and Palestine. However, both Byronic nationalist ideals were, therefore, in opposition to British foreign policy which since 1791 had been to prop up the declining Ottoman Empire in order to keep open the route to India, and prevent the ambitions of Napoleonic France, Russia and Austria of extending their influence to the Mediterranean. The Congress of Vienna was the first time the Eastern Question was formally discussed between the great powers, and Britain unsuccessfully tried to instigate a proposal to guarantee the integrity of Turkey.

Byron's Romantic Philhellenist poetry, inspired by his travels to the Levant in 1809–11, adopted many of the conventional motifs of popular Orientalism, in which the Ottoman Empire had long been regarded as the epitome of despotism. He cited Knolles, Cantemir, D'Herbelot, De Tott, Lady Mary Wortley Montagu, Chardin, Hyde,

Sir William Jones, Scott's *Arabian Nights*, Beckford's *Vathek*, and many more. In imaginative recreations of the harem, in *The Giaour*, *The Bride of Abydos* and *The Corsair*, the traditional stereotype of Oriental woman as a sexual slave evokes pathos. While her Turkish master uses and disposes of the Greek odalisque, emblem of her colonized country, the Byronic hero of the Oriental tales – owning allegiance to no monarchy – aligns with the desire of European Philhellenes to intervene and 'liberate' Greece. The Byronic adventure of rescuing the Greek slave necessitates the erotic fantasy of entering the harem, and entails a form of vicarious identification with its master. I have argued elsewhere that the harem functions in Byron's poetry not merely as a conventional image of Eastern Imperialism, but as an example of the libido-driven psychology of all empire-building.[13] This psycho-sexual analysis of colonialism would be pointedly universalized in the juxtaposition of the Turkish and Russian monarchs in *Don Juan*, when man and woman, Easterner and Westerner, are shown to share the power-hungry desire for possessing concubines and armies and the same ability to effeminize their subjects.

In *Childe Harold's Pilgrimage* the hero was a jaded libertine, who 'through Sin's long labyrinth had run' (*Childe Harold's Pilgrimage*, I, line 37), but placing the aristocratic Byronic heroes of the tales which followed in an Oriental setting made them seem comparatively more saviours than exploiters of women; observers not consumers of decadent Eastern luxury; autocratic yet in opposition to the despotism of Turkey. Conrad's uxoriousness, teetotalism and vegetarianism are emphasized to an almost bathetic extent (I, lines 67–76; 285–308; 422–30; II, lines 123–26; III, lines 550–54). The Byronic hero is famously monogamous, but still functions as a sexual threat by taking a woman from her father or husband, or committing incest. In *Don Juan* the most famous libertine of all is condoned through sentimentalism and humour, as being good-hearted in acquiescing to women's lust for him. Such formulations obviously challenged conventional, bourgeois ideology, which whether politically conservative or radical concurred in fearing the power and stigmatizing the decadence of the aristocratic and court culture of

---

[13] I have dealt with the sexual politics of Byron's Oriental poetry more fully in *Byron's Heroines* (Oxford, 1992), Chapter 3; and 'Juan's Sea Changes: Class, Race and Gender in Byron's *Don Juan*' in *Don Juan*, ed. Nigel Wood, Theory in Practice Series (Buckingham, 1993), pp. 56–89.

the ancien régime. Nevertheless, the poems wooed a huge readership by simultaneously suggesting the Utopian ideals of the libertine controlled by woman and the aristocrat at the service of the people. In his preface to *A Vision of Judgement*, Southey was to denounce Byronism specifically for its dangerous appeal to women and the working classes.

In *The Siege of Corinth*, however, the theme of the harem is now abandoned, along with direct representation of the Greek insurgents themselves, leaving the stark outline of the Western natural leader etched against the evocative landscape. For the first time, the Byronic hero fights on the Ottoman side. His attempted abduction of a woman takes place in a battle between the Venetian and the Turkish empires, and one of considerable historical significance. The date, 1815, not only meant the reimposition of Hapsburg and Bourbon rule on Europe, but also marked the centenary of the re-establishment of Turkish sovereignty in Greece after a period of Venetian rule.

> A hundred years have rolled away
> Since he [Coumourgi] refixed the Moslem's sway
>
> (lines 106–7)

So strategically important was the city that the capture of the citadel, Acro-Corinthus, in 1715, had led the way to the surrender or defeat of all the other Venetian fortresses in the Peloponnesus, and swiftly to the Turkish capture of the whole territory. The combination of this fact with Corinth's prominence in classical history, especially as the Greek headquarters in the Persian war, made the city's name particularly evocative for Philhellenists. These comprised classically educated Europeans and Greek ex-patriots of the diaspora living in the West, for the indigenous Romaic population neither knew nor cared about its classical heritage. Byron's friend, the antiquarian William Haygarth, had already singled out the name of Corinth as a rallying call to the would-be liberators of the country:

> Hard is his heart, O Corinth! who beholds
> Thee bow'd to dust, nor sheds one pitying tear.
>
> *Greece* (1814)[14]

Recapturing the citadel would have both a propagandist and a

---

[14] Quoted by Terence Spencer, *'Fair Greece, Sad Relic': Literary Philhellenism from Shakespeare to Byron* (London, 1954), p. 283.

strategic importance. After noting that British engineers had surveyed the isthmus to determine the practicality of its defence,
Haygarth called for intervention:

> And yet thou art not cast for ever down;
> Thro' the dark night of time the muse beholds
> Thy glory's second morn; thy lofty rock
> Gilded by liberty's returning day,
> Shall be the point to which awakening Greece
> Shall turn her anxious eye.   *Greece* (1814)

Corinth symbolized another significant, defining moment in the
history of Greece – the founding of the Christian church there by
St Paul, which marked the beginning of the change from pagan
Hellenism to Romaic culture. Byron was almost certainly inspired
by Goethe's Philhellenist poem *Die Braut von Korinth*, a prose
translation of which he would have found in Madame de Staël's *De
l'Allemagne*, a work he admired, and which had been brought out by
his publisher Murray in 1813, after the French edition was pulped
by Napoleon on the grounds that it was anti-French.[15] Goethe's
verse romance was based on a Roman legend, and set at the time
of the Christian conversion of the city. It told the story of a pagan
youth visited unexpectedly by the maid he had hoped to marry
before her parents forbade the match on account of their conversion to Christianity, and ordered their daughter to take the veil. As
in Byron's tale, the words of the young woman are ambiguous, and
the hero fails to realize that she is a ghost. But Goethe's revenant
becomes vampiric, illustrating the life-denying creed of Christianity
draining the spirit of the Hellenic civilization. In the year of the
'Holy Alliance' of sovereigns, Byron was also driven to satirize
Christianity, which sought to mystify the role of the monarch as
based, according to the Czar, 'upon the sublime truths which the
Holy religion of Our saviour teaches'.[16] Byron's focus here is less
on Goethe's theme of Christian sexual repression than the way by
which, in Christianity and Islam alike, the threat of punishment
and the promise of rewards in the afterlife are still harnessed to
inspire armies to outdo each other in brutal militarism. The

---

[15] See my note, 'The influence of Madame de Staël's account of Goethe's *Die Braut von Korinth*
in *De l'Allemagne* on the heroine of Byron's *The Siege of Corinth*', in *Notes and Queries*, New
Series 35:3 (September, 1988), pp. 307–10.
[16] Quoted by Harold Nicolson, *The Congress of Vienna: A Study in Allied Unity, 1812–1822*
(London, 1946), p. 252.

followers of the Caligula-like, Turkish Grand Vizier, Coumourgi, urge each other on with:

> . . . the loud fanatic boast
> To plant the crescent o'er the cross,
> Or risk a life with little loss,
> Secure in paradise to be
> By Houris loved immortally.
>
> *Siege of Corinth* (lines 252–56)

The aged Minotti, representative of the now degenerate (lines 84–85) Christian republic of Venice, seems no less bloodthirsty, having dispatched 'more than a human hecatomb' (line 763).

His daughter represents the soul of Venice, for possession of which the Doge's representative, Minotti, and the reformer turned renegade, Alp, struggle, though ironically we find that her future is already doomed. Into the mouth of the ghost of this pious Catholic virgin is put the offer of (heavenly) reunion and eternal life if Alp will only turn from Islam back to Christianity. Francesca appears to him seated in a ruined, classical temple, and her image thus suggests the claim of Venice to combine the best of the classical republican and Christian traditions, a claim to be reiterated by the nineteenth-century empire of Britain, also based on maritime trade and describing its colonizing as the spread of freedom. Keeping his eye on the moon, associated with the pagan deity Diana rather than the Christian Mary, Alp refuses to be saved. The fact that he believed he would be rewarded by earthly marriage with his beloved Francesca as well as by the redemption of his soul, makes Alp's defiance an emphatic repudiation of both social bonds and Christian orthodoxy, imaged as the feminine principle. This anticipates the reiterated refusals of the metaphysical rebel, Manfred, in the drama of the following year, to be reconciled with any cultural concept of deity, and the resulting separation from his female counterpart Astarte as he faces death without the comfort of an after-life.

Minotti is obviously associated with the wrathful God of the Old Testament, the common heritage of both these warring religions deriving from Judaism, as he stands at the altar making the sign of the cross while lighting the gunpowder to blow up his pagan enemies, even though he will also destroy his own side. The narrator, with a black humour which sickened Byron's contemporary readers, pointed out that the shards of human flesh, which thus literally reached heaven, were too much of an inextricable mixture to be divided:

> Christian or Moslem, which be they?
> Let their mothers see and say!
> *Siege of Corinth* (lines 996–97)

The unregarded icon of the Virgin and her child, representing New Testament pacifism, which shines down on Minotti, continues to smile helplessly on the scene of carnage (lines 904–14). Like the eternal snow on Delphi, which represents Alp's dream of Freedom in his meditation on classical Greece (lines 313–78), this static image of feminine purity represents an ideal, remote from the actual here and now of masculine power on earth. Both Venetians, Alp and Minotti are fallen though titanic heroes, for the latter also scorns saving his earthly and eternal life (line 807), and both are professional soldiers rather than defenders of their homelands (lines 257–58). They are forced to act out their chosen roles in an impossible situation, exhibiting physical bravery in unworthy causes. The characterization of both the Byronic hero and his antagonist demonstrates the Romantic emphasis on the will to power, and the formidable potentiality of the individual to shape the events of history for good or for evil.

The tragic story of Alp cannot but allude to the potent image of Napoleon in its suggestion that personal vanity combined with frustrated idealism immersed him in mere militarism. Although a superb soldier who declares himself the enemy of legitimacy and orthodox Christianity, Alp fails to restore true, republican freedom to his native Venice, and out of personal egotism, is instrumental in replacing one colonial regime with a worse tyranny in Greece. The exotic glamour, with which Alp is invested, even as an anti-hero, testifies to the strength of the poet's disappointment that Napoleon's example had failed to renew and revitalize the British, aristocratic philosophy of rebellion which Byron inherited from the exhausted, Whig tradition.

Hebrew Melodies might be assumed to be an uncharacteristic work, in contrast with *The Siege*, but Byron's Presbyterian upbringing had inculcated a love and thorough knowledge of the scriptures. In his *Compendium of Biblical Usage in the Poetry of Lord Byron*, Travis Looper has tabulated 1,704 allusions, of which two-thirds were to the Old

Testament.[17] Byronic Orientalism challenged Evangelicalism not only by giving new literary life to libertinism, but also by invading its own territory and bringing a defamiliarizing, primitivist vision to the Bible in *Hebrew Melodies, Cain* and *Heaven and Earth*. Elinor Shaffer points out that Romantic Hellenism included fascination with the historical context of the evolution of Christianity, as well as interest in Greek classical antiquity.[18] Throughout Byron's poetry, it is emphasized that Christianity is but one religious tradition among many that emanated from the East. In the notes to *The Bride of Abydos*, Byron commented: '. . . every allusion to any thing or personage in the Old Testament, such as the Ark, or Cain, is equally the privilege of Mussulman and Jew; indeed the former profess to be much better acquainted with the lives, true and fabulous, of the patriarchs, than is warranted by our own Sacred writ . . .' (*BCPW*, II, line 440). In *Hebrew Melodies*, the poet could not have been unaware that confining the biblical material of his lyrics to the Old Testament would smoke out the prejudices of the Christian reviewers. *The British Critic* much preferred *Palestine* by Reginald Heber, shortly to become the Bishop of Calcutta, and this review, like several others, was peppered with anti-semitism.[19] Opposition to the Anglicists and Evangelicalism with regard to British colonialism and bourgeois morality also shaped the themes of *Hebrew Melodies, Cain* and *Heaven and Earth*, the first of which examines romantically and the latter two sceptically the psychology of sectarianism. The subject of Noah's flood, in *Heaven and Earth*, is used for Byron's bitterest attack on the Calvinist concept of predestination and religious chauvinism of the type now fuelling missionary zeal.

The antiquarianism of the project to write lyrics to traditional Jewish tunes was also fashionable. Scottish, Irish and Welsh airs had been popular since the turn of the century – the concept of Britishness having been so well cemented by the Napoleonic wars that Celtic nationalism could be safely indulged. Thomas L. Ashton notes that Byron was not alone in tackling the Old Testament sublime: William Gardiner brought out *Sacred Melodies* (1812–15) and Thomas Moore eventually published his long-planned *Sacred Songs* in

---

[17] Travis Looper, *Byron and the Bible: A Compendium of Biblical Usage in the Poetry of Lord Byron* (New Jersey and London, 1978), pp. 284–88.

[18] E.S. Shaffer, *'Kubla Khan' and The Fall of Jerusalem: The Mythological School in Biblical Criticism and Secular Literature, 1770–1880* (Cambridge, 1975), p.14.

[19] *The Romantics Reviewed*, ed. Donald Reiman, Part B, 5 vols. (New York, 1972), I, p. 259.

1816; Sotheby, in 1807, and Smedley, in 1814, had both written poems entitled *Saul*.[20] Jews had also been featuring as sympathetic characters in drama and novels since the 1781 translation of Lessing's *Nathan the Wise*.[21]

Hebrew Melodies was resoundingly successful. Nathan's two lavish folios with music and Murray's edition of the lyrics alone both went into numerous editions in the poet's lifetime, despite the price of a guinea per volume being charged for the former. The paradox of Byronism was that the poetry provided the idealization of archaic, 'authentic' culture between the gilt-engraved covers of a luxury commodity of genteel literature, produced by a book trade expanding and mechanizing as the Industrial Revolution advanced. Herder had led the way in prizing the unique character of each people formed by its cultural history, influenced by Bishop Robert Lowth's *Lectures on the Sacred Poetry of the Hebrews* (1749–50), which for the first time treated the Bible in secular fashion as literature comparable to Homer.[22] Byron's *Hebrew Melodies* was the product of a comparable, primitivist impulse, opposing the progress, industrialization and science of modernity with the simple, spiritual values of an organic, Asian, tribal society. Many of the speakers dramatize a direct relationship with God – often through sense of place:

> There – where thy finger scorched the tablet stone!
> There – where thy shadow to thy people shone!
> 'On Jordan's banks' (lines 6–7)

These visionary believers testify to their communion with the divine:

> A spirit passed before me: I beheld
> The face of Immortality unveiled –
> Deep sleep came down on ev'ry eye save mine
> And there it stood, – all formless – but divine;
> 'From Job' (lines 1–4)

---

20 The edition of *Hebrew Melodies* used is that edited by Thomas L. Ashton (London, 1972). On Jewish themes in late eighteenth-century art, music and literature see Howard D. Weinbrot, *Britannia's Issue: The Rise of British Literature from Dryden to Ossian* (Cambridge, 1993), pp. 405–45.

21 Cecil Roth, *A History of the Jews in England* (Oxford, 1941), p. 242.

22 Herder exalted: 'the primitive periods when irrational elements predominated, barbarian and heroic ages, ages long distant in which language was elaborated and in which legends and myths were formed'. Herder inspired Goethe to study the Orient, and the latter declared: 'Here I want to penetrate to the first origin of human races, when they still received celestial mandates from God in terrestrial languages.' Herder and Goethe are both quoted by Schwab, *The Oriental Renaissance*, pp. 211–12.

As in folk poetry, the supernatural and the unexplained are part of life fatalistically experienced. Enemies of the Jewish people, archetypal Oriental despots like Herod and Belshazzar, or invading warriors like the wolf-like Assyrian, Sennacherib, may be mysteriously doomed at the height of their power. Even their own king Saul is brought low by the spectre of the prophet Samuel who prophesies his death:

> Earth yawned; he stood the centre of a cloud:
> Light changed its hue, retiring from his shroud.
> Death stood all glassy in his fixed eye;
> His hand was withered, and his veins were dry;
> His foot, in bony whiteness, glittered there,
> Shrunken and sinewless, and ghastly bare:
> From lips that moved not and unbreathing frame,
> Like caverned winds, the hollow accents came.
>
> 'Saul' (lines 5–12)

Saul is reminiscent of Napoleon, in that he is portrayed at the end of a life devoted to winning many victories against the Philistines, but now in the process of being overwhelmed by their superior forces, and his own mental disintegration. In 'Song of Saul' he redeems himself through dying nobly by his own hand, like the classical republican heroes on whom the Jacobins modelled themselves. Nathan quoted Byron as commenting, 'Napoleon would have ranked higher in future history, had he even like your venerable ancestor Saul, on mount Gilboa, or like a second Cato, fallen on his sword, and finished his mortal career at Waterloo.'[23]

Hebrew Melodies contributes to the Romantic elevation of the poet in its celebration of David accompanying the king to battle, and spontaneously expressing the events which would be handed down as the story of the nation. Behind the bard ideally synthesizing politics, poetry and religion, of course, stands Byron himself, who elegizes that Golden Age, but at the same time places himself in David's footsteps by composing lyrics for ancient, liturgical, Jewish music.[24]

---

[23] Isaac Nathan, *Fugitive Pieces and Reminiscences of Lord Byron* (London, 1829), p. 40.

[24] Byron wrote excitedly to Annabella that he was writing lyrics to 'the *real old undisputed Hebrew melodies,* which are beautiful and to which David & the prophets actually sang the "songs of Sion" . . .' *Byron's Letters and Journals,* IV, 220. The style and possible antiquity of the music is discussed by Francis L. Cohen, 'Hebrew Melody in the Concert Room', *Transactions of the Jewish Historical Society of England,* 2 (1896), pp. 7–13.

The harp the monarch minstrel swept,
The King of men, the loved of Heaven,
Which Music hallowed while she wept
O'er tones her heart of hearts had given
Redoubled be her tears, its chords are riven!

It softened men of iron mould,
It gave them virtues not their own;
No ear so dull, no soul so cold,
That felt not, fired not to the tone,
Till David's Lyre grew mightier than his throne!
                    'The Harp the Monarch Minstrel Swept' (lines 1–10)

Mystical apprehension of the immanence of God in nature crystallizes into nationalist sentiment as first the tribe evolves into a monarchy and then the land is swallowed by the Roman empire. Byron's ventriloquization of the Jews' feeling of helplessness and powerlessness to control their own destiny functions as sympathetic identification with all the peoples of Europe whose political fate was decided for them in 1815:

Oh! in the lightning let thy glance appear!
Sweep from his shiver'd hand the oppressor's spear:
How long by tyrants shall thy land be trod?
How long thy temple worshipless, Oh God?
                    'On Jordan's Banks' (lines 9–12)

Many of the *Hebrew Melodies* elegize a lost land and the passing of a way of life and worship now crushed. The emphasis on the countryside and its holy places – 'Jordan's banks', 'Sinai's steep', 'Salem's high places', Sion's 'once holy dome' – like the allusions to places where heroic deeds were done in classical times in the Oriental tales, suggests that shared culture and oppression shapes what the modern consciousness thinks of as a national identity. *Hebrew Melodies* expresses the Jews' desire to conserve that historical experience of the race, which exile only hardens into an idealized patriotism.

On Jordan's banks the Arabs' camels stray,
On Sion's hill the False One's votaries pray,
The Baal-adorer bows on Sinai's steep –
Yet there – even there – Oh God! thy thunders sleep;
                    'On Jordan's Banks' (lines 1–4)

There was a specific political context for this. *Hebrew Melodies* is an example of Christian proto-Zionism, an aspect of liberalism which preceded the emergence of Jewish Zionism in the later nineteenth century.[25] After a century of Enlightenment pleas for tolerance from Montesquieu, Rousseau, Mirabeau and Lessing, and the influence of Moses Mendelssohn, first the American constitution of 1789, then the French Revolutionary government of 1791 had led the way in granting civil rights to their Jewish citizens. Napoleon imposed equality for Jews in most of the lands he conquered – though these freedoms would be lost with the fall of the First Empire. Britain and the rest of Europe would not allow Jews full civil rights until the middle of the century. In 1795, the Evangelicals had established the London Society for the Promotion of Christianity among the Jews, sparking off a pamphlet war on the question of religious toleration and anti-semitism. On 14 July 1820, Byron's friend, the radical MP John Cam Hobhouse, unsuccessfully asked the House to review the disabilities forced on Jews. In 1807, Napoleon had convened the Great Sanhedrin in Paris to clarify whether the Jews should be regarded as a nation within a nation or individuals belonging to a religious sect, and the Jews were only too anxious to assert their loyalty in return for emancipation. In the early nineteenth century, the reform movement arose which sought to separate Judaism as a religion from its nationalist connotations, and rejected the belief in an eventual restoration of Palestine.

In Britain, the notion of actually restoring the Jews to Palestine had been advanced by thinkers like David Hartley, Richard Hurd, and Joseph Priestley in the latter half of the eighteenth century.[26] In addition, extreme Protestant British sects had since the English Revolution, read the Book of Revelation as predicting the restoration of the Jews to their homeland as a prelude to the second coming. Popular millennarians at the turn of the century, like Richard Brothers, believed that day was at hand and that Britain's destiny was to effect it. Byron mocked such Messianism, but, nevertheless, Presbyterianism had steeped him in the Dissenting

---

[25] See Ben Halpern, *The Idea of the Jewish State* (Cambridge, Massachusetts, 1961), pp. 252–54. For the contrary view that Zionism was implicit in Judaism from the time of the destruction of the temple, see Joseph Slater, 'Byron's *Hebrew Melodies*', *Studies in Philology*, 49 (1952), pp. 75–94 (p. 90); and Gordon Thomas, 'The Forging of an Enthusiasm: Byron and the *Hebrew Melodies*', *Neophilologus*, 75:4 (1991), pp. 626–36 (p. 631).

[26] Slater also cites William Hamilton Reid, *Causes and Consequences of the French Emperor's Conduct Towards the Jews* (London, 1807) and J. Bicheno, *The Restoration of the Jews* (London, 1807). Slater, 'Byron's *Hebrew Melodies*', p. 91.

tradition of identifying with the Jews as the Chosen People, resisting tyranny.

With hindsight, we can see that proto-Zionism can be compared to Philhellenism as an apparently Utopian ideal, which sometimes proved useful to European powers scheming to dismember the Ottoman empire. At the end of the eighteenth century, Russia unsuccessfully attempted to use the Jews as pawns in schemes of setting up a homeland, in order to dispossess the Turks of Palestine, while the French, on the other hand, had tried to encourage them to become new settlers if they would help to bolster up Turkish power.[27] Byron habitually connected the Greeks and the Jews in his mind as the scapegoats of the world: 'The Greeks have as small a chance of redemption from the Turks as the Jews have from mankind in general.'[28] He was perfectly aware of treating Philhellenism and proto-Zionism as symbolic nationalist causes, having no pretensions to seem a democrat, or even free of racial prejudice: 'I love the cause of liberty, which is that of the Greek nation, although I despise the present race of Greeks, even while I pity them . . . I am nearly reconciled to St. Paul, for he says, there is no difference between the Jews and the Greeks, and I am exactly of the same opinion, for the character of both is equally vile.'[29]

Interestingly, even before Nathan approached Byron with the idea for *Hebrew Melodies*, Byron had been inspired by the abdication of Napoleon, three days after Good Friday in 1814, to write 'Magdalen'. This bitter poem, spoken by the converted prostitute, describes the hatred of the mocking mob of Jews who crucified Jesus and prophesies that the whole race will be cursed. (The underlying, political allusion is, of course, to the revengeful Europeans on the downfall of Napoleon.) Here we see Byron utilizing traditional, Christian, anti-semitic myth:

---

[27] Halpern, *The Idea of the Jewish State*, p. 254. There were isolated examples of Western Jews settling in Palestine. In 1808–09 a party of Jews from eastern and central Europe, under the instigation of pupils of Rabbi Eliahu, the Gaon of Vilna, established a community in Safed. See David Vital, *The Origins of Zionism* (Oxford, 1975), p. 7. A year before the publication of the *Hebrew Melodies*, Byron himself received a letter requesting his assistance, when he next travelled abroad, in helping to transport a settlement of Jews in Abyssinia to Egypt on their way to settle in Palestine. See Ashton, *Byron's Hebrew Melodies*, p. 73.

[28] *BCPW*, II, p. 202.

[29] James Kennedy, *Conversations On Religion with Lord Byron and Others, Held in Cephalonia, A Short Time Previous to His Lordship's Death* (Philadelphia, 1833), p. 246.

> Tribes of self-sentence! ye shall suffer long,
> Through dark Milleniums of exiled grief
> The outcast slaves of sightless unbelief.
> Stung by all torture,– buffeted and sold –
> Racked by an idle lust of useless gold–
> Scourged – scorned – unloved – a name for every race
> To spit upon – the chosen of disgrace;
> A people nationless . . .   'Magdalen' (lines 14–21)

Of course, the conventional Christian notion of the Jews as a race cursed with unending exile would be transmuted in *Hebrew Melodies* into admiration and pity for their heroic defiance of tyrants and refusal to change. So 'Magdalen' is in complete contrast to 'Were my Bosom as False as Thou Deem'st it to Be', spoken by a recalcitrant Jew exiled from the Holy Land after the destruction of the temple in A.D. 70. That speaker's bitter sarcasm could equally be that of a modern member of the diaspora passionately answering an anti-semitic detractor:

> If the bad never triumph, then God is with thee!
> If the slave only sin, thou art spotless and free!
> If the Exile on earth is an Outcast on high,
> Live on in thy faith, but in mine I will die.   (lines 5–8)

Many Romantic writers were fascinated by the legend of the Wandering Jew, which had originated in the mediaeval myth of a person present at the Crucifixion who refused Jesus succour and was condemned to a living death of wandering until Judgement day.[30] Byron's versions of this symbol of obdurate and unrepentant rejection of Christian redemption (Cain, his descendants in *Heaven and Earth*, and to an extent of the dispossessed Jews of *Hebrew Melodies*) acquire the heroism of Promethean protest against the shackles of faith or a new dispensation.

Byron's Philhellenist and proto-Zionist poetry of 1814–15 fanta-sized the idea of the nation by focusing on dispossessed peoples. More than this, it suggested that the Greeks and the Jews were chosen peoples, whose ancestors had created the Hellenic and Hebraic bases of civilization, to whose pure springs it was necessary to return to regenerate Europe. While Scott and Southey's poetry had endorsed the unified British nation, which had been reciprocally formed by conquest of the Celts at home and colonialist rivalry with

---

[30] See Joseph Gaer, *The Legend of the Wandering Jew* (New York, 1961).

France abroad, their younger rival, in both politics and poetry, idealized a new notion of nationalism, arising out of *reaction* to imperialism. This was an ideal which found favour not with the first Western colonial powers of the early modern period – Spain, Portugal, Britain, and France – who were building empires in far-flung America, Asia, Australasia, but with the peoples still ruled by the remnants of European dynastic powers after the Congress of Vienna.

To supporters of the missionary work of the Evangelicals, like Southey, imperial conquest now provided a spiritual quest which compensated for the collapse of the supra-national unity of Christian Europe, which had once produced the crusades. Coleridge, too, when he rejected religious individualism, developed further the Burkean view of the national church as the corner-stone of national unity in structuring national culture through custom and tradition. Coleridge, with his hugely influential *On the Constitution of Church and State* (1830), Southey, with his history of the Church of England, *The Book of the Church* (1824), and even Wordsworth, with his *Ecclesiastical Sketches* (1822), may all be seen as contributing to the nationalist ideology which vindicated the Church of England's unifying role as fostering patriotism and social control at home and abroad.[31] Byron attacked the burgeoning Anglicanism of his poetical and political enemies, hostile as it was to Catholic emancipation and the cosmopolitanism favoured by liberals and dissenters.

Byron's own contribution to the debate derives from his contrasting belief in religious individualism. His scepticism of systems led him to dissect the links between religious institutions and imperialism, and to romanticize, instead, a mystical 'natural' communion with the spirit of place. He lamented the failure of the attempt to revive the republican ideal in the French revolution. The new republic had seen the birth of the first modern nation state, enshrined in the Declaration of the Rights of Man and the Citizen: 'The principle of sovereignty resides essentially in the Nation; no body of men, no individual, can exercise authority that does not emanate expressly from it.'[32] But Byron's poetry, written in reaction

---

[31] William Stafford, 'Religion and the Doctrine of Nationalism in England at the time of the French Revolution and Napoleonic Wars', in *Religion and National Identity: Papers read at the Nineteenth Summer Meeting of the Ecclesiastical History Society*, ed. Stuart Mews, *Studies in Church History*, 18 (Oxford, 1982), pp. 381–95.

[32] Elie Kedourie, *Nationalism* (London, 1960), p. 12.

to the imperialism which had resulted from both Napoleonic and British ambitions, sought to express the emotions of the dispossessed. Political theory is less important than sentiment in Byronism. As Hans Kohn comments, the sanctification of European nationalism was developed out of Old Testament mythology: 'The idea of a chosen people, the emphasis on a common stock of memory of the past and of hopes for the future, and finally national messianism'.[33] The Byronic combination of the re-validation of aristocratic leadership together with the championship of the Hebraic and Romaic underdogs of the Ottoman empire proved a potent combination in suggesting both the inherent superiority of a chosen people and the recognition of the struggle faced by oppressed classes or outcast races. The Romantic combination of aristocrat and 'folk' sets itself in opposition to the middle-class professionalization of colonial administration then taking place in the British Empire in India and elsewhere, appealing instead to a new stage in nationalism emerging not from the experience of exploration, but from the experience of being colonized.

---

[33] Hans Kohn, *Nationalism: Its Meaning and History* (New York and Cincinnati, 1965), quoted by Timothy Brennan, in 'The National Longing for Form' in *Nation and Narration* , ed. Homi K. Bhabha (London and New York, 1990), p. 59.

CHAPTER 14

'Once did she hold the gorgeous East in fee . . .':
Byron's Venice and Oriental Empire

Malcolm Kelsall

> Once did she hold the gorgeous East in fee;
> And was the safeguard of the West: the worth
> Of Venice did not fall below her birth,
> Venice the eldest Child of Liberty.
> She was a maiden City, bright and free;
> No guile seduced, no force could violate;
> And when she took unto herself a Mate,
> She must espouse the everlasting Sea.
> And what if she had seen those glories fade,
> Those titles vanish, and that strength decay;
> Yet shall some tribute of regret be paid
> When her long life hath reached its final day:
> Men are we, and must grieve when even the Shade
> Of that which once was great is passed away.

Wordsworth's sonnet 'On the Extinction of the Venetian Republic' (1802)[1] was addressed to Britain at war with Napoleon rather than the citizens of Venice. The celebration of a maritime empire as 'the safeguard of the West', and the invocation of that power as a 'Child of Liberty' had obvious patriotic implications. Hence the inclusion of the sonnet among the series dedicated to 'National Independence and Liberty'. These home thoughts from abroad were also a *memento mori*. The invocation by the sequence of 'The later Sidney, Marvel, Harrington . . . and others who called Milton friend' (Sonnet xv) was a warning 'lest we forget' the principles which made the British republic great. So, too, the ills of empire were now as plain in the new English *imperium* as they had become, ultimately, in the elder child of liberty, Venice:

---

[1] Text from *The Poetical Works of William Wordsworth*, ed. Thomas Hutchinson (Oxford, 1913). Subsequent quotations from Byron from *Lord Byron: The Complete Poetical Works*, ed. Jerome J. McGann, 7 vols (Oxford 1980–93).

and at this day,
If for Greece, Egypt, India, Africa,
Aught good were destined, thou wouldst step between.
England! all nations in this charge agree. . .

                              (Sonnet XXI, lines 6–9)

Wordsworth drew on the commonplaces of eighteenth-century history. 'Liberty', like empire, had taken a Westward progression through the millennia from Greece to Italy, and thence, according to Whig philosophy, to Britain (although there were some, like the Irishman James Barry, who claimed that the Westward progression now led to the newly-founded United States of America). More specifically, Venice and Britain were closely related typologically for both were imperial states whose power rested upon naval supremacy and whose wealth derived from Oriental trade; and each found precedent in the ideology and practice of ancient Rome. The association was flattering. Venice had been the greatest and longest lasting republic modern Europe had known; for Locke and Voltaire a 'living demonstration' of fundamental values.[2]

Thus, when Byron took Venice as his subject, he also took British history as his matter. Historical typology might extend to contemporary allegory. Otway's *Venice Preserved*, which was so influential in shaping Byron's representation of the Venetian republic, had invited identification of its characters as individuals in the Popish Plot, and Byron's own Venetian plays were inevitably drawn into the Queen Caroline affair and radical opposition to the Tory administration. Such 'constructive' reading of history was a commonplace of typology – one thinks of the use of Voltaire's *Brutus* in France, or Addison's *Cato* both in Britain and America – and is analogous to the radical purposes of 'new historicism' now. But Byron resisted the allegorical application of his Venetian texts. There is an important distinction between a general typology derived from the history of the rise and fall of empires, and the specific application of historical analogies for local, party-political advantage.

It is a distinction as relevant now as then. Since Edward Said's *Orientalism* (1978), it has become commonplace to view Byron's representation of Mediterranean culture as part of the discursive

---

[2] For discussion of the issue see Denis Cosgrove, 'The myth and the stones of Venice', *Journal of Historical Geography*, 8 (1987), pp. 145–69; Tony Tanner, *Venice Desired* (Oxford, 1992), p. 76; more generally see J. G. A. Pocock, *The Machiavellian Moment: Florentine Political Thought and the Atlantic Republican Tradition* (Princeton, 1975).

structure of British imperialism. But that history is read retrospectively from the instantaneous present. For modern, liberal, cultural
historians, such as Marilyn Butler and Nigel Leask,[3] discussion of
the empire in the East has become involved with the guilt of the
post-colonial West, and although Butler, in particular, has brilliantly
disintegrated the post-Foucauldian reading of British imperial
history as a hegemonic whole, the agenda remains that set by post-
colonial criticism. The 'culture of complaint'[4] places the liberal in a
position of apologetic retreat, and imperial history is constructively
read in terms of the critic's political objectives.

But the typological history of empires was concerned with the
exploration of repetitive patterns, and, thus, with the taxonomy of
things. For Byron, as for Wordsworth, the Venetian republic had
been the meeting place of Occident and Orient in direct imperial
and religious conflict. It was a frontier in a millennial struggle
between 'the Crescent' and 'the Cross' – as *The Siege of Corinth* puts it
(line 253). (So, even now in Europe in the late twentieth century the
siege of Sarajevo has repeated the issues of the siege of Corinth.) For
Byron and Wordsworth, Venice could not be a *locus* on which to
focus post-colonial guilt, for most of the Eastern Mediterranean was
still part of the Ottoman empire, and it is arguable that it was
'Islam'[5] which had been the major, imperial power of European
history. We know (but are significantly silent)[6] about processes of
conquest which encompassed much of the Ukraine, pressed to the
gates of Vienna, involved the eastern littoral of the Adriatic, and
thence, across the Mediterranean, spread into North Africa. Since
the 'Moors' penetrated deep into Spain, much of what we call 'the
West' was for centuries the rump of the Roman empire on the verge
of absorption by 'the East'. Thus, it is arguable that the very concept
of 'Europe' was generated by anti-colonial resistance, and it is
certain that a number of specific European national identities were
directly forged by anti-imperialism. Our current history of 'Orient-

---

[3] Nigel Leask, *British Romantic Writers and the East: Anxieties of Empire* (Cambridge, 1992); Marilyn
Butler, 'Orientalism' in *The Penguin History of English Literature: Vol. 5 The Romantic Period*, ed.
David Pirie (London, 1994).
[4] Edward W. Said, *Culture and Imperialism* (London, 1993), p. xxvii.
[5] Andrew Rutherford in the keynote paper at the 1994 Byron conference at Athens began to
lay the groundwork for a study of Byron and Mediterranean history, but scholarship has not
yet got to grips with Byron's reading about the long and intricate processes of colonialism in
the Mediterranean world.
[6] Said raises the issue in *Culture and Imperialism* only to pass by since there is 'special cultural
centrality' in western imperialism – an astonishing view of Islamic culture!

alism' starts so late in that process that we have lost the long perspective (and sense of irony) which Gibbon, Renan, or even Napoleon's Egyptologists brought to Mediterranean history.

In *Childe Harold*, Byron, in the tradition of typological history, picked out two crucial instances of the frontier wars between Cross and Crescent: the success of the Venetian fleet at Lepanto (near Missolonghi) in 1571, and the loss by Venice of Candia (1669) after long-protracted defence. They marked points of imperial rise and fall, and if 'History . . . Hath but *one* page' (*Childe Harold*, IV, lines 968–69), it concerns the rise and the decline and fall of empires ineluctably engaged in mutual conflict. States either exert their power, or they go under to those more powerful. Such a philosophy of history underlines the personal experience of the characters of *The Giaour*, for instance, where the Oriental point of view makes the Occident 'Other' – an alien threat to be exterminated or expelled and from which the race must be purged by the murder of the woman (who may bear an alien child). This is now known as 'ethnic cleansing' although the Western, secular term misses the religious dimension to the conflict. The occidental giaour displays a certain liberal guilt, from which the Muslim is free, but as Delacroix's painting of 'The Conflict of the Giaour and the Pasha' indicates, once West and East are locked in battle they are virtually indistinguishable.[7]

This neo-Machiavellian (or even neo-Darwinian) view of history as imperial conflict is vulnerable to the same criticism with which Marilyn Butler qualifies post-colonial critiques of British imperialism.[8] It is too imprecise to serve as a means of historical enquiry. If

---

[7] Gibreel/Sir Henry Diamond in Salman Rushdie's *The Satanic Verses* provide(s) a contemporary double, and Rushdie quotes Fanon: 'The native is an oppressed person whose permanent dream is to become the persecutor' (New York, 1988), p. 353.

[8] Butler, 'Orientalism'. I have been influenced by Homi K. Bhabha's discussion of liminality in 'DissemiNation: time, narrative, and the margins of the modern nation', in *Nation and Narration*, ed. Homi K. Bhabha (London, 1990), pp. 291–322; and Said's discussion of the 'hybrid' in *Culture and Imperialism*. More generally relevant are Lisa Lowe, *Critical Terrains: French and British Orientalisms* (Ithaca, 1991); Tzvetan Todorov, *On Human Diversity: Nationalism, Racism, and Exoticism in French Thought* (London, 1993); James Clifford, 'On Orientalism', in *The Predicament of Culture: Twentieth-Century Ethnography, Literature and Art* (Cambridge, Massachusetts, 1988); Homi K. Bhabha, 'The Other Question: the Stereotype and Colonial Discourse', in *The Location of Culture* (London, 1994); Martin Bernal, *Black Athena: The Afroasiatic Roots of Classical Civilization* (London, 1991). Robert Young, *White Mythologies: Writing History and the West* (London, 1990). But the principles of my argument are more fundamentally derived from the questions about symbiosis raised by August Schlegel's *Vorlesungen über dramatische Kunst und Literatur*; Friedrich Schlegel's *Geschicte der alten und neuen Literatur*, and Sismondi's *De la littérature du midi de l'Europe*.

history has only 'one page' it cannot distinguish a Tamerlane from an Akbar, or Ghengis Khan from Solyman the Magnificent. Or to turn to the briefly transitory (but spectacular) history of British imperialism, 'the empire' was never an ideologically homogeneous nor administratively hegemonic structure. The colonial settlement of the North American continent (the creation of the 'empire of liberty' as Jefferson called it) was a manifestly different process from the interposition of the East India Company among the previous colonial powers already settled on the Indian subcontinent. The British empire split along radical lines of ideological difference as early as 1776. In the West, a natural rights, 'post-colonial' ideology developed (for instance, in the writings of Jefferson and Paine); in the East, the claim was to be developed that the empire offered a more efficient, juster and more 'civilized' administration than earlier imperial settlers (so Macaulay and Mill argued). We are confronted, thus, with an extremely complex, variable, and even self-contra-dictory imperial process, and one which was contentious within, as well as challenged from without.

Byron and 'Byronism' are a relatively small but potent part of this diverse argument and praxis. It is difficult to place him exactly for although Byron (with his friend Scott) is one of the creative writers of his age most deeply imbued with history, there has been little specific enquiry into the nature of the history which he knew, and, thus, into the matrix (or matrices) he might have employed to seek to locate and to order the turmoil of competing, imperial histories in Europe, the Americas and the middle and far East. Yet, if we are to 'rethink historicism', one of our first tasks should be to read history. It is clear that the foundations of education for the ruling orders in Britain (and thus for Lord Byron) were in the literatures of classical imperialism. We need to begin in Greece and Rome. But the classical literatures were deeply divided about the nature of Hellenistic and Roman imperialism – as Jefferson's favoured authors Thucydides and Tacitus show. Thus a key text behind the *Weltanschmerz* of *Childe Harold* – Volney's *Ruins . . . of Empires* (1791) – in its opposition to imperial 'superstition' and 'tyranny' is, paradoxically, directly derived from classical and imperial sources. Likewise, in the 'empire of liberty' of the United States of America, Hamilton and Madison derived the anti-imperial arguments of *The Federalist* from Greek and Roman examples – but, for the Federalist administration, Volney was *persona non grata*. Or, in the Eastern empire, Sir William Jones and a substantial school of Oriental scholarship were to claim that the very origins of Western civilization lay in Oriental culture which Westernizers like Macaulay and Mill were set to extinguish. But there were more radical divides within Romantic historiography – the reactionary interpretation of history of Rousseauism (with its deep distrust of urbanization, commerce, industry, luxury and corruption); the progressive reading of Western civilization associated with writers like Adam Smith or Joel Barlow; or the conservatism of Hume, the organicism of Burke, the multiracialism of Herder.

These oppositional generalizations merely indicate the limitations of any overarching contextual generalizations, whether shaped in terms of an historicist 'Romantic ideology' or a modernist 'post-colonial theory'. Such props for enquiry are necessary, but are imperfect. Thus, in coming close to Byron, one needs, as far as possible, to jettison the kind of baggage with which terms like 'imperial' or 'colonial' are *now* loaded, and to remain aware how contested they were *then*. In the simplest and most empirical terms possible, for Byron *one* frontier between Occidental and Oriental imperialisms had been the Venetian republic. He would have understood both imperialisms as being ideological (religiously based), power structures (although he would not have put it that way). The extinction of the Venetian republic (1797) marked the transition of a former imperial power to colonial status (imposed by the hand of the new 'Tamerlane' as Byron called Napoleon).[9] Within this nexus, Byron's Venetian poems are a series of meditations on the extinction of the republic. They are both an attempt to understand the signification(s) of the decline and fall of the Venetian empire, and a series of explorations of the way history is understood and constructed through the archaeology of knowledge and the making of interpretative texts. Venice, for the Byronist, has the advantage as a *locus* that it is separable from Byron's own interposition in 'history' at Missolonghi. Romantic nationalism was one way to challenge imperial hegemony. But the subsequent history of nation states has its own post-colonial problems.

If these are the historical parameters in which Byron – the localized human subject – wrote at this time, in this place, yet these

---

[9] Letter to Sir Walter Scott, 4 May 1822. *Byron's Letters and Journals*, ed. Leslie A. Marchand, 13 vols. (London, 1973–94), IX, p. 155.

boundaries were not fixed even in a unitary text. Writing can itself be a process which unfixes, unsettles, destabilizes, transgresses. These potentialities are implicit in Byron's very entry into the topic 'Venice': 'I stood in Venice on the Bridge of Sighs; / A palace and a prison on each hand . . .' (*Childe Harold*, IV, lines 1–2). The 'palace' and the 'prison' need little elucidation as Romantic signifiers, whether one thinks of the historical use of the Bastille as the sign for the tyranny of the old order in Europe, or the mental prison of the 'mind-forged manacles' of Blake's spiritual history. Here, the palace and the prison are made one by the grammatical symbiosis. Thus, the imperial glory of the lion of St Mark (to adopt Byron's words) is intrinsically one with the incarceration of others and the imprisonment of the self. It is a trope as old as Stoicism where emperors are 'slaves' and only the *sapiens* is 'free', but Byron's reworking of the motif leaves the human subject bridging the palace/prison without a way out. The dilemma is that you either rule or are imprisoned, but the very rulers themselves are imprisoned by their own position. There is no existential 'liberty'.

But who is the 'I' on the bridge? He is, in general, one of the many pilgrims seeking some undefined shrine of transhistorical value; but also one whose very name – 'Childe Harold' – speaks a specific history. If Venice marks the frontier between Occidental and Oriental imperialism, the feudal name of the protagonist directly involves the speaker in the history of that conflict. The feudal warlords, who were the forefathers of the Spenserian 'childe', carved out their baronies by conquest in the West, and their military 'pilgrimage' then carried them eastward. The *Drang nach Ost* of Byron/Childe Harold is part of the same historical process, although Athens 'delivered', rather than Jerusalem, was to be Byron's ultimate objective. (The famous Homeric helmet he carried to Missolonghi alludes to an even earlier invasion of the Orient from the West). The history of imperialism was to write Byronism just as much as Byron wrote history.

These historical processes cannot be divided by crude distinction into a definitive Occident and Orient. The frontier was too fluid, moving in the eastern Mediterranean from Troy to Jerusalem, from Athens to Venice – the fall of Constantinople interpreted (in the West) as a crucial hinge. Colonizers and colonized are involved, thus, in diverse relationships over long periods of time and extended geographical space. It is a commonplace of post-colonial experience that the nascent nationalities, which the tide of imperialism leaves behind, are the inheritors of a deep sediment of colonial culture. But, conversely, colonial powers become imbued with their colonies.[10] So, in Venice, those cultures crudely distinguished as Occidental and Oriental self-evidently interpenetrate. 'Self-evidently' because the 'Orientalism' of the city is manifest in the very 'stones of Venice' – 'Fraught with the Orient spoil of many marbles' (*Marino Faliero*, IV, i, line 78) – and the stones, in Ruskinian phrase, provide 'the only reliable biography' of 'civilization'. The Ruskinian commonplace was to be taken up by Browning and Proust, and was already explicit in Byron's first reading of Venetian history through the iconography of architecture. The account of the Piazza San Marco in *Venice: A Fragment* describes

> a princely colonnade –
> And wrought around a princely place –
> Where the vast edifice displayed –
> Looks with its venerable face
> Over the far and subject sea
> Which makes the fearless isles so free:-
> And 'tis a strange and noble pile
> Pillared into many an aisle –
> Every pillar fair to see –
> Marble – Jasper – or Porphyry –
> The church of St. Mark – which stands hard by
> With fretted pinnacles on high –
> And cupola and minaret –
> More like the mosque of Orient lands –
> Than the fanes wherein we pray
> And Mary's blesséd likeness stands.   (lines 21–36)

The very banality of these lines makes obvious the commonplaces of ideology. The dichotomy between 'free' and 'subject', although less complex than the opening of *Childe Harold*, still remains paradoxical, for to be princely and 'free' is to hold someone else 'subject'. The subject here is 'the sea', which might mean no more than a Venetian equivalent of 'Britannia rule the waves', but it is also a displacement of the real, historical subject: Venice's conquests and colonies in the East. The oceanic, the illimitable, the Asiatic and the ultimately unsubjectable are in the metaphor, and are emergent in the descrip-

---

[10] See *Venice Desired* and also the discussion of the 'spatialization of historical time', in Simon During, 'Literature – Nationalism's other? The case for revision', in *Nation and Narration*, ed. Bhabha, pp. 138–53.

tion of San Marco which follows. The relics of the saint were part of
the spoils of the East brought by the republic from Muslim Alexan-
dria and are now enshrined under 'cupola and minaret / More like
the mosque of Orient lands . . .'. Byron's language is Orientalized
not only by the Eastern architectural terms but by the exotic stones:
marble, jasper and porphyry. The opposition between mosque and
blesséd Mary distinguishes ultimately (for the fragment ends here)
the virgin mother of God from Orientalism whose commonplace
signifiers include the sensual paradise of the Muslim religion, the
sexuality of the harem, and the whore of Babylon. Since these lines
are Byronic, what is here 'other' from Occidental religion is
undoubtedly desired, indeed desired more because a forbidden fruit.

These Occidental/Oriental signifiers are commonplace in commonplace verses. In *Childe Harold* the relationship between Occident
and Orient in Venice is more complex. The opening of Canto IV is
an exercise in syncretic history where Tyre, Venice and Britain are
seen as mutually related in their rise (and fall): '[Albion] the Ocean
queen should not / Abandon Ocean's children; in the fall / Of
Venice think of thine, despite thy watery wall' (IV, 17). It is the specific
historical role of Venice as 'Europe's bulwark 'gainst the Ottomite'
which is problematized by this parallel history, spelled out in the
simple, political opposition: 'Though making many slaves, herself
still free.' But *Childe Harold* is stranger and more troubling than the
'Fragment' in the patterns of contradictory history it establishes:

> She looks a sea Cybele, fresh from ocean,
> Rising with her tiara of proud towers
> At airy distance, with majestic motion,
> A ruler of the waters and their powers:
> And such she was; – her daughters had their dowers
> From spoils of nations, and the exhaustless East
> Pour'd in her lap all gems in sparkling showers.
> In purple she was robed, and of her feast
> Monarchs partook, and deem'd their dignity increas'd.
>
> (IV, 2)

The city is feminized here and in so doing Byron reverses the
traditional image of Venice as master of the sea annually taken as
the city's spouse by the mystic marriage of the Doge to the Adriatic
(stanza 11). The figure of Cybele should be read as one might read a
Spenserian allegory (these are Spenserian stanzas). She is an Asiatic
deity, worshipped first in Phrygia (according to Lemprière), whose

worship spread to Greece and whose statue was carried thence by Roman imperialism to Italy. Her history, therefore, is as much an account of the cultural colonization of the Occident by the Orient as of the spread of Western colonialism to the East. Lemprière's account is worth quoting at length:

In Phrygia the festivals of Cybele were observed with the greatest solemnity. Her priests, called Corybantes, Galli, etc., were not admitted in the service of the goddess without a previous mutilation [castration]. In the celebration of the festivals, they imitated the manners of madmen, and filled the air with dreadful shrieks and howlings, mixed with the confused noise of drums, tabrets, bucklers, and spears. This was in commemoration of the sorrow of Cybele for the loss of her favourite Atys. Cybele was generally represented as a robust woman, far advanced in her pregnancy, to intimate the fecundity of the earth. She held keys in her hand, and her head was crowned with rising turrets, and sometimes with the leaves of an oak. She sometimes appears riding in a chariot drawn by two tame lions; Atys follows by her side, carrying a ball in his hand, and supporting himself upon a fir tree, which is sacred to the goddess. Sometimes Cybele is represented with a sceptre in her hand, with her head covered with a tower. She is also seen with many breasts, to show that the earth gives aliments to all living creatures; and she generally carries two lions under her arms.

There is a clear iconography which links the traditional representation of the goddess to Venice. The 'tiara of proud towers' of which Byron writes is a formal attribute of the deity, and the lions of St Mark are as much her signifier as his. When Byron imagines the East as 'exhaustless' and 'pouring all gems in sparkling showers' into the lap of Venice, the fecundity of the Orient and the role of many-breasted Cybele as a fertility goddess are united. The castrated Atys who accompanies the goddess at her festivals is the equivalent of the subjected monarchs who partook of 'her feast' at Venice. The feminine, 'Oriental' principle is thus totally dominant, subjecting the male (who worships this subjection); exhaustless (as Cleopatra, to choose a more familiar Oriental signifier); and endlessly fertile. She is also a figure of overwhelming disorder. At her festivals men are driven mad, shrieking and howling in celebration of the deity.

Seen retrospectively, by way of Tanner and Said, the Cybele image suggests a process by which the Occident is overwhelmed by the sensuality and disorder of the Orient. *Death in Venice* is a *locus classicus*, but Mann's novella belongs to a period of late, imperial angst with Conrad's *Heart of Darkness* and Forster's Marabar caves. These writers possess a common awareness that the European nation states have assumed a role of world government totally beyond their capabilities (hence the brevity of European, imperial history) and are 'vanquished by their conquest' (to adapt Victor Hugo's lament for Napoleon's defeat in the East). The 'Other' is plural, universal, and hence overwhelming, and for the 'Self' to move outside its own culture is to risk dissolution. Hence, it may be, to counteract this threat, the excesses of ethnocentric nationalism, racial apartheid and Aryan *Reinheit*. But Byron's image of Cybele by comparison is positive. As Rome had done, so, too, Venice welcomes the deity; in similitude has become Cybele. One might call this (in a colonial context) 'hybridism'. So, as Byron tells his own story, his first images of Venice had been shaped by texts which emphasized the cultural diversity of the city, and he names 'the Jew' and 'the Moor' from Shakespeare. Both the semitic East and Muslim Africa found employment within the Venetian empire. As Lady Morgan had argued in a seminal text for Byronic Orientalism – *Woman: or, Ida of Athens* (1809) – ethnic diversity characterizes great commercial cities, and Byron, himself a citizen of a commercial empire, was himself to play out a carnival of diverse Orientalisms in Albania, Greece and Turkey, testing the boundaries of selfhood and nationality.

What the Byronic carnival embodies is the symbiosis in Mediterranean culture produced by the imperial conflict between 'East' and 'West' from Homeric times to Napoleon, and not resolved yet. At Athens he had recorded how pagan temple, Christian church and Muslim mosque all formed part of the site of the Acropolis, and had he travelled further east, Jerusalem would have provided him with typologically similar imagery and history at the Dome of the Rock. He himself was to die in a typical, ethnic conflict between Christian and Muslim. But if the poet is enclosed historically within this arena of perennial, imperial conflict, yet the potent image of Cybele, translated from East to West, received by both cultures, and celebrated as the very signifier of a great commercial city (as well as an imperial power) suggests another kind of historical process by which antagonistic cultures meld and are reconciled.

If the image of Cybele has crucial significance, one fundamental issue raised concerns the place of sexuality in imperial culture. Byron's early Oriental romances used the fantasies of female pulp fiction to explore the liberations of cross-cultural sexuality between Christian and Muslim in the stories of the giaour, Conrad and Alp, or even, *mutatis mutandis*, in *The Bride of Abydos*. The Oriental tragedy

Sardanapalus was set in the heartland of Asiatic imperialism in an empire created by Nimrod and Semiramis. The tragic colonial ruler, Sardanapalus, seeks to divest himself of this empire (in vain) recognizing (in Auden's phrase) 'we must love one another or die'. His love for the enslaved Greek woman, Myrrha, may be read as an allegory challenging Ottomite imperialism, and the love between Oriental and Occidental protagonists has affinities with the Shelleyan myth of *Prometheus Unbound*, although, unlike Shelley's cosmic creatures, monarch and slave cannot escape from the exigencies of history. The individual remains trapped in the imperial system.

Behind both Byron and Shelley lies the work of the most important British imperial poet of the Romantic era, Sir William Jones, one of only a handful of major writers at this time who had passed 'East of Suez'. The now almost forgotten Hymns to Hindu Deities are one of the most extraordinary outpourings of 'Oriental' sexuality in English. They deify sexuality as the loftiest expression of Hindu religion, link that religion to Mediterranean culture by a typological reading which identifies the deities of the East with the Pantheon of Greece and Rome, and fundamentally challenge the exclusivity, puritanism and patriarchal values of Christianity by portraying the feminine and the sexual as prime movers of the universal order. We know that much of the mythology of Shelley derives from Jones (as does the second part of Goethe's *Faust*). It is 'Asia' which leads Prometheus out of the old imperial order of Jupiter into the new order of universal love. But there still remains a dichotomy in Shelley between Jupiter (the Occident) and Asia (the Orient). It is this dichotomy which Jones denied. The 'Third Anniversary Discourse' to the Asiatick Society of Bengal has become a classic text for modern linguistics, but it is also a crucial text for imperial history. There Jones argues (albeit imprecisely) that the languages of Europe and the ancient Sanskrit of the East 'have sprung from some common source although that source no longer exists. The philological assumption that there was once a common Indo-European language has major cultural implications, for if a common language is a signifier of common nationality, then Occident and Orient are one. As Goethe put it in the *Westöstlicher Diwan*: '*Gottes ist der Orient! / Gottes ist der Okzident!*'[11] The subsequent division of the *Urvolk* turns the myth of the tower of Babel into a myth of

---

[11] *Talismane*, lines 1–2. *Goethe's Werke*, ed. Erich Trunz, 14 vols. (Münschen, 1978), II, 10.

colonialism, for 'Babel' is that cultural separation where 'East is East, and West is West, and never the twain shall meet . . .' (except when strong men meet in war).

This is a long excursus from the image of Byron's Venice as a 'sea Cybele', but the symbiosis between Occident and Orient at this military and commercial frontier-post between empires is an historical manifestation of that melding of cultures which Jones sought to move back towards an originary cultural unity. Venice, as it were, by its exposure to the East and by its colonies and commerce, is reaching back to the origins of things (just as on the Acropolis the different religious signifiers of paganism, Christianity and Islam are the colonialists' variants upon an original natural religion). In this context, what we call 'Byronism' becomes an attempt to escape existentially (in terms of the divided 'I' who stands in Venice) from the imperial divide of Mediterranean history and from a world post-Babel. This should not be interpreted in a crude biographical sense, for after Franklin and Wolfson we recognize the wider significations of the sexual politics of Byronism.[12] But now, as we probe at the historical meanings of Romantic Orientalism, one may suggest that for a reader of Jones, Shelley and Byron the mores of sexuality are intrinsic in defining culture, and that the historical divisions of a sexually defined original culture underlie the imperial conflicts of East and West. (If this is so, then the act of rape on which Forster's *A Passage to India* and Scott's *Raj Quartet* both hinge is not a mere enabler of plot, but part of a fundamental topos).

For this interpretation, the Venetian fabliau of *Beppo* is a crucial text. It is a variant on the topoi of one of the fundamental texts of British Orientalism: *Othello*. It stands to *Othello* as *The Miller's Tale* stands to *The Knight's Tale* in Chaucer. It challenges and subverts an imperialist ethos. Shakespeare's story is a tale of conflict on the frontier between Christian and Muslim in which the governorship of a key frontier-post is given to a mercenary condottiere – a man (like Byron's Alp) who has betrayed his own (Oriental) culture, but who does not belong to his adopted land. Hence the tragedy. Othello can command sufficient force to repel Muslim imperialism, but culturally

[12] Caroline Franklin, *Byron's Heroines* (Oxford, 1992); Susan Wolfson, ' "Their She Condition": Cross-Dressing and the Politics of Gender in *Don Juan*', *ELH*, 54 (1987), pp. 585–617, and ' "A Problem Few Dare Imitate": *Sardanapalus* and "Effeminate Character" ', *ELH*, 58 (1991), pp. 867–902. The special issue of *Studies in Romanticism*, 31 (Fall, 1992) is generally relevant.

he cannot adapt to the sexual mores of his host (Christian) culture. But that culture itself is divided between patriarchal authority and sexual transgression – as centred on the character of Desdemona and the contrary pulls of her duty to her father and love for her husband. Her (white, Christian, European) sexuality is further divided by the dichotomy between the virginal purity of Catholic Mariolatry and the seething cesspit of sexual licence which is ultimately the creation of Othello's 'Oriental' imagination. The subtitle, 'The Moor of Venice' expresses the cultural or sexual divisions which are ultimately unresolvable – hence the death of the protagonists.

In Byron the Othello story is given a comic resolution. In part this is by means of the substitution of 'the common man' – Beppo – for 'the tragic hero', and thus the pliable, commercial *mobilité* of the 'Turkey trader' for that of the honour-driven principle of a military hero. Like Lady Morgan, Byron here distinguishes between capitalism and imperialism, and in capitalism's favour. But more central to the comic resolution is the use of the Venetian carnival as the *locus* of the action. We know the signification of the carnivalesque as a mode of release, yet containment, of transgressive forces within culture, but here the transgression and tension is between cultures: the Occidental and the Oriental. When Beppo reappears he has the appearance of a Turk, and there is no means of telling whether he is a Westerner in carnival costume or (as Laura puts it) 'really, truly . . . a Turk' (line 729). Or, looked at in another way, the difference between cultures is only a form of carnival costuming which overlays a common humanity. The comic hero – the common man – has the *mobilité* and the tolerance to survive in any circumstances, and Laura's chatter about Turkish culture is indicative of how trivial are the differences between East and West:

> With any other women did you wive?
> Is't true they use their fingers for a fork?
> Well, that's the prettiest shawl – as I'm alive!
> You'll give it me? They say you eat no pork . . .
> (*Beppo* lines 730–33)

Beppo's ability to survive in any society and to trade between them is the human equivalent of the cultural symbiosis of the transfer of Cybele from East to West written in the stones of Venice. In describing Beppo's capacity, the Byronic term 'mobilité' has been preferred to Byron's own earlier use of 'cosmopolite'. Enlightenment cosmopolitanism was a unificatory movement which posited the common ground of a classic, humanist, European intelligentsia as a normative goal to which mankind was evolving (or, put another way, Byron's cosmopolitan Childe Harold never escapes from himself in all his travels). Our own term 'multiculturalism' may seem nearer the mark for Beppo, but in practice multiculturalism merely creates different national identities within a society.

Beppo has a parodic resemblance, rather, to that other well-experienced Mediterranean traveller and bridge between East and West: St Paul. Both are 'all things to all men' (even if with Beppo all things include Turkish whiskers and Venetian small clothes!). Yet one may add, in Paul's words, that by these diverse means one might 'save some'. In Beppo's case the means of salvation are not religious (for this would be divisive) but are toleration, a sense of humour, and, especially, an openness to diverse sexual practice, for sexuality is the ultimate and fundamental symbiosis which bridges the gap between races by returning the divided bloodstock of humanity to a common origin. In this he goes further than Paul, who was deeply suspicious of all forms of sexuality.

But this is only possible in Venice and in the carnival because Venice itself has, as it were, fallen out of Mediterranean history. It remains at the frontier between East and West, but it is no longer a contested frontier. It is as much a never never land as the South Sea island to which Torquil and Neuha flee in late Byronic romance. They mingle races but are only secure because hidden and disempowered. Those parts of the story of *Beppo* which lie outside the city remind the reader that imperial history is still contested. Beppo has been a slave in the Ottoman empire, and his capture at Troy reminds one that this East/West struggle goes back to the Grecian world. He has survived in that empire only in disguise. His tolerance is not theirs. The terms 'racist, imperialist . . . ethnocentric' which Edward Said has used pejoratively of the West might equally be aimed at the East.[13] Although *Beppo* is a crucial poem for the development of Byronism as a *modus vivendi* in a world at war, even the text of this carnivalesque poem cannot escape from the realities of imperial conflict.

[13] Said, *Orientalism*, p. 204. But in *Culture and Imperialism* Said represents his humanism as besieged from both sides.

The desire to escape is the strong motive behind *Venice: An Ode* which is Byron's farewell to the city:

> better be
> Where the extinguish'd Spartans still are free,
> In their proud charnel of Thermopylae,
> Than stagnate in our marsh, – or o'er the deep
> Fly, and one current to the ocean add,
> One spirit to the souls our fathers had,
> One freeman more, America, to thee!

> (lines 154–60)

The poem ends as uneasily poised as Childe Harold on the Bridge of Sighs, but now between the old ethnic conflict between Occident and Orient represented by death in the 'proud charnel of Thermopylae' and the desire to escape from the web of that history entirely by adding, as a late historical remnant, 'One freeman more, America, to thee!' The expropriation of Byron as a hero of Romantic nationalism subsequently closed the issue in favour of Greece, but in the context of Byron's Venetian poetry, the Romantic idealization of the newly born United States of America is his chosen ending. Without this ideal Occident (in fact, Britain's former western empire), Romantic Orientalism lacks its full historical context, and the New World in the West here, for Byron, is the only life-giving way to escape from the closed circuit of empire and colony of Mediterranean history.

This aspect of Romantic historiography has been little explored, in part because American, patriotic history has separated the United States from its role as a European power engaged within the Romantic *Weltordnung*, in part because the liberal guilt of British imperialism has looked East to India not West to the other half of the empire. But the American Declaration of Independence is arguably the primary document of Romantic politics (and, thus, the first document of modern post-colonialism). It was a demand for national self-determination, for 'the separate and equal station to which the laws of nature and of nature's God' entitle an autonomous people; and it was a proclamation of a universal, revolutionary principle based on 'self-evident' and 'inalienable rights', among which are 'life, liberty, and the pursuit of happiness'. Since these rights rest upon 'the laws of nature and of nature's God', the United States was free from the conflict between 'Crescent' and 'Cross' and the religious fundamentalisms which divided Oriental and Occidental imperialism in Europe. Moreover, as a constitutional league between thirteen, consenting, independent States, the new order in the West was idealized as an example of co-operative freedom utterly different from the imperial governments, Christian or Muslim, in the old world. Hence Jefferson's favoured, but paradoxical, description of the United States as 'the empire of liberty'. When Byron looked to America in *Venice: An Ode* in the dark days of the Holy Alliance, it was because the United States was perceived as the only free government to survive the cataclysm of the wars of Romantic revolution.

This is a myth, of course, as much as Wordsworth's celebration of Venice (at its fall) as 'the eldest Child of Liberty'. Closer experience of the racial tensions within America could be a disillusioning experience. But the American myth is another subject.[14] For Byron, as for migratory millions in the nineteenth century, it was an enabling, ideal history. George Washington was for him perhaps the only hero who did not turn out a 'pagod' (like Bonaparte). *Venice: An Ode* is the expression of a poet who claims now to be tired of the stagnation of a carnival culture out of history (and of the fripperies of his own Morganesque Orientalism). He is seeking some means to influence the world away from the 'barbarian' towards 'liberty', or a new beginning outside the dichotomy of the old imperial order. The *Ode* is a gestural poem, but there was little for an individual to do given the power and the longevity of the old conflict in which he himself eventually fell. But entry into that conflict – a place in the 'charnel' of Thermopylae – is not the preferred ending to the *Ode*.

Ultimately death at the 'holy and sacred' town[15] of Missolonghi, fighting for the Occident against the Orient may be preferable to death in Venice overwhelmed, like von Aschenbach, by an imaginary East. But the Venetian poems provide a dark prologue to Byron's last 'pilgrimage' to Greece. Missolonghi, like the Venetian republic in its power, was then on the frontier between 'Cross' and 'Crescent'. One thinks of other frontline cities, Corinth and Ismael from Byron's own poems; or Jerusalem and Sarajevo from ancient and modern history. Or one might consider, like Childe Harold, the Acropolis – that imperial shrine to Periclean hubris, shattered by a Venetian shell

---

[14] I hope to discuss these issues further in my forthcoming *Jefferson and the Iconography of Romanticism* (Macmillan).

[15] So Missolonghi was described in the welcome to delegates of the 1994 Byron conference at Athens (at which a shorter version of this chapter was delivered).

falling upon a Turkish arsenal. Byron never found an answerable
style to express his commitment to a two thousand year war. That
war continues, as does the struggle represented by this discourse, to
find fitting words to describe these things.

CHAPTER 15

The plague of imperial desire: Montesquieu, Gibbon, Brougham, and Mary Shelley's The Last Man

Joseph W. Lew

The Last Man (1824), Mary Shelley's third published and fourth written novel, is impure. Most obviously, this is true of the novel's subject matter: a bubonic-type plague which wipes out the entire human race with the exception of the title character, Lionel Verney. This 'impurity' is transgressive (literally, 'a going beyond or over a limit or boundary'), the result of a fatal and extremely contagious crossing of boundaries. In anthropological terms, it is about 'dirt', which Mary Douglas defines as 'things out of place';[1] perhaps symptomatic of this contagion, the novel seemed 'dirty': *The Monthly Review* called it 'The offspring of a diseased imagination, and of a most polluted taste', while *Blackwood's* termed it an 'abortion'.[2] The novel's filth, or to use its own term, its 'corruption', operates, as I hope to show, on many levels; and this corruption is not merely thematic or even overdetermined, but is intrinsic to the novel, part of its very 'conception'.

One of the levels on which corruption is conceived in the novel concerns Lord Byron. The character of Lord Raymond, a Byron figure, experiences passion in 'strange fits' as he alternates between his political ambitions, his love for Lionel's sister, and his infatuation with a Greek woman, Evadne. The Shelley circle held Byron responsible for the death of his daughter Allegra in a notoriously unhealthy, Italian convent and for blighting the future of Claire Claremont. Byron abandoned another mistress in order to join the struggle for Greek independence. For Mary Shelley, Byron's recent behaviour was not aberrant, but deeply and disturbingly consistent. In her novel, what appears to be the long domestic preamble to the

---

[1] Mary Douglas, *Purity and Danger* (New York, 1970).
[2] Morton Paley, '*The Last Man*: Apocalypse without Millennium', in *The Other Mary Shelley: Beyond Frankenstein*, ed. Audrey A. Fisch, Anne K. Mellor, and Esther H. Schor (New York, 1993), pp. 107–23.

appearance of the plague underscores the artificiality of the line which supposedly separates the 'personal' from the 'political'. The plague-infection which Lord Raymond, in attacking Constantinople, looses upon the world has already, in a metaphoric sense, corrupted him.[3]

The early reviewers found the novel's narrative logic, as well as its subject matter, to show a corrupt imagination at work. Why should Lord Raymond's perversion of the Greek War for Independence into a war for empire be the proximate cause of the destruction of Constantinople and the dispersal of a plague which will destroy humankind? Crime and punishment are scarcely proportionate. The novel repeatedly insists that the plague has been ravaging Asia with unaccustomed ferocity long before Lord Raymond's army besieges Constantinople – insistences themselves undermined by the powerful account of Lord Raymond's entrance into the uncannily silent city and the explosion that destroys both Lord and city. To content ourselves with the obvious, autobiographical explanation – that Shelley was at work on *The Last Man* when she heard of Byron's death – denies Shelley artistic control over this text. Moreover, stopping with the autobiographical has little explanatory value: it cannot account for Shelley's marvellous transformation of Byron's rather inglorious death at Missolonghi, nor does it begin to explain why it is this character's death in this very specific way which allows (and on some level even causes) the plague to be introduced into Europe. My explanation takes me on a circuitous journey through *The Last Man's* literary antecedents, historical accounts and political economy. I shall examine writings by Montesquieu, Gibbon, and Brougham, prominent eighteenth-century theorists of corruption, despotism, and imperialism, in order to elucidate Shelley's specific-ally Romantic anxieties about the dangers of Oriental 'infection' for individual bodies and for the body politic.

---

[3] The Byronic figure of Lord Raymond indicates that, as Anne K. Mellor argues in her provocatively titled 'Why Women Didn't Like Romanticism: The Views of Jane Austen and Mary Shelley', in *The Romantics and Us: Essays on Literature and Culture*, ed. Gene W. Ruoff (New Brunswick, 1990), pp. 274–87, women writers were deeply disturbed by the effects of what Jerome J. McGann called the Romantic Ideology upon women in particular and the world in general.

I

Two immediate precursors for Mary Shelley's conflation of physical and political corruption are from her own circle. Byron ended his *The Vision of Judgment* with an image of the damnation of Robert Southey, who falls to the bottom of hell but quickly rises again, 'for all corrupted things are buoy'd like corks, / By their own rotten-ness'.[4] More pointed and pertinent still is Percy's 1819 play, *The Cenci*. Cenci rapes his daughter hoping 'to poison and corrupt her soul' (IV, i, lines 44–45). Cenci imagines how 'her spirit shall approach the throne of God / Plague-spotted with my curses. I will make / Body and soul a monstrous lump of ruin' – Beatrice's beautiful young body transformed by her father's syphilitic em-braces. He hopes to have impregnated his daughter and that the offspring might 'grow, day by day, more wicked and deformed' (IV, i, lines 145–51).[5]

As Fisch points out, Mary Shelley's choice of plague may have been influenced by the westward progression of cholera which 'reportedly began in India'.[6] Yet there were literary precedents as well. In *Volpone*, the plague is said to have its origin in Syria; ships are quarantined in Venice until they are proven not to carry plague. In Defoe's *A Journal of the Plague Year* (the novel on which *The Last Man* is partly modelled), H. F. reports having

heard, in ordinary discourse, that the plague was returned again in Holland; for it had been very violent there, and particularly at Amsterdam and Rotterdam, in the year 1663, whither, they say, it was brought, some said from Italy, others from the Levant, among some goods, which were brought home by their Turkey fleet; others said it was brought from Candia; others from Cyprus.[7]

Important here are the 'Turkish' origins: the Levant, the 'Turkey fleet,' Candia (better known to us as Crete, which was in the process of being wrested from Venice by the Ottomans as the result of a twenty-five year war), Cyprus (taken, again from Venice, by the Ottomans in the sixteenth century). Plague or the Black Death was

[4] *Lord Byron: The Complete Poetical Works*, ed. Jerome J. McGann, 7 vols. (Oxford, 1980–91), VI, p. 345.

[5] *Shelley's Poetry and Prose*, ed. Donald Reiman (New York and London, 1977).

[6] Audrey A. Fisch, 'AIDS, Deconstruction', in *The Other Mary Shelley*, eds. Fisch, Mellor, and Schor, p. 270.

[7] Daniel Defoe, *A Journal of the Plague Year* (New York, 1960), p. 11.

epidemic in Europe, but was widely believed to be endemic to Constantinople, Syria, and Egypt. For H. F., the 'corruption' of the plague is primarily, if not exclusively, physical: with the exception of the possibility of its being imported with 'some goods' (probably luxury cloth such as silk), there are no moral or political overtones – in other words, the plague is not a metaphor.

These precedents, however, locate the source of infection in a much vaguer Orient. Mary Shelley's choice of 'Constantinople' (which had ceased to exist in 1453; on finally conquering the city, the Ottomans changed its name to 'Istanbul') needs to be explained. Western reluctance to accept the name 'Istanbul' accompanied and was symptomatic of Western refusal to accept the legitimacy of the Ottoman dynasty and empire. Although calling the Ottoman Empire the 'Old Man of Europe' was a nineteenth-century phenomenon, fantasies of overthrowing Ottoman rule recurred with great frequency, and can be dated back to the reception in Western Europe of the news of the fall of Constantinople.

'Constantinople' is itself a name change: Constantine I built his city on the site of the ancient city of Byzantium. Constantinople was Greek, but not part of the Greece worshipped by Romantic Philhellenes.[8] The new capital symbolized a significant re-orienting of the empire. Straddling the Bosphorus, the New Rome dominated the trade routes between the Black Sea and the Mediterranean and between Asia and Europe. If, as was believed in the first century and reported by Gibbon, Roman greatness was undermined by the importation of Oriental luxuries, religions, and political ideologies, this re-orienting of the empire intensified the process. While adopting Greek as its language, the later emperors adapted Persian court ceremonies. Centuries before its conquest by the Ottomans (and certainly by the time of the Crusades), Constantinople was considered, in the West, as the Oriental capital of an Oriental empire (the phrase 'Oriental despotism' would be an eighteenth-century coinage).

Gibbon's attribution of Roman decline to Eastern corruption was familiar to Mary Shelley and her contemporaries. But Gibbon's *Decline and Fall* is itself shaped by eighteenth-century developments in political economy. Central to this development is the thought of

---

[8] Timothy Webb, *English Romantic Hellenism, 1700–1824* (New York, 1982).

Montesquieu.[9] The equation of the physical, moral, and political meanings of 'corruption' was a reinvention or rediscovery of the seventeenth and eighteenth centuries, involving the re-imagining and redefining of the Ottoman Empire and the revivification of classical ideas and imagery.[10] The Greeks preserved many accounts of dangers to individual men and masculine goals from Oriental women such as Medea, Calypso and Circe; Virgil continued this tradition in his account of Dido and Aeneas. Gibbon reports how the 'manly strength' of the ancient Romans was undermined by the importation of Oriental luxury goods, Oriental habits and Oriental religions (of which Christianity was only one). These threats from the Orient were brought together and personified in the emperor Elagabulus:

his head was covered with a lofty tiara, his numerous collars and bracelets were adorned with gems of an inestimable value. His eyebrows were tinged with black, and his cheeks painted with an artificial red and white. The grave senators confessed with a sigh, that, after having long experienced the stern tyranny of their own countrymen, Rome was at length humbled beneath the effeminate luxury of Oriental despotism. The master of the Roman world affected to copy the dress and manners of the female sex, preferred the distaff to the sceptre, and dishonoured the principal dignities of the empire by distributing them among his numerous lovers; one of whom was publicly invested with the title and authority of the emperor's, or, as he more properly styled himself, of the empress's husband.[11]

Gibbon's Elagabulus is 'dirt' personified – things out of place: a man in woman's clothing, a Syrian ruling Romans, a male emperor with a 'husband'. Striking among Gibbon's 'despots' is their shared

---

[9] Mary Shelley read *Persian Letters* in 1816. I will draw heavily upon Montesquieu's later *The Spirit of Laws*, for a 'standard' text, which there is convincing circumstantial evidence that Mary Shelley also knew well. Emily Sunstein reports that, in 1816, 'Mary and her circle were talking political philosophy and strategy, discussing monarchies and republics one evening until three in the morning with Hazlitt.' Emily W. Sunstein, *Mary Shelley: Romance and Reality* (Baltimore, 1991), p. 137. That her training was thorough is indicated by her also reading political writings by Hume, Godwin, Lady Morgan and Spinoza during the same period.

[10] For an account of this process and particularly the role played by Venice, see Lucette Valensi, *The Birth of the Despot: Venice and the Sublime Porte* (Ithaca, 1993). Valensi argues that sixteenth-century Venetians considered the Ottoman polity a state to be emulated, but inverted that image in the seventeenth century. But the earlier, positive image provided an alternative 'Orientalist' tradition for idealized Oriental potentates such as those found in the Mozart operas *Die Entführung aus dem Serail* and *Die Zauberflöte* and Inchbald's *A Mogul's Tale*.

[11] Edward Gibbon, *The Decline and Fall of the Roman Empire*, 3 vols. (New York, no date), chapter 6, pp. 126, 128.

Oriental effeminacy. Justinian is ruled by his wife Theodora; by the time of the Crusades, this effeminacy is endemic among the later emperors (the Comneni, the Angeli, the Paleologi): these men, in Gibbon's terms, seem more like women in men's bodies.

Until the eighteenth century, however, the link between moral and political corruption on the one hand and physical corruption remained accidental – until Montesquieu provided a theoretical foundation and justification for the linguistic accident of these forms of 'corruption'. Montesquieu believed there to be three essential kinds of government: monarchy, republican (subdivided into democracy and aristocracy), and despotism. Each of these 'natures' of government has a 'principle': that of democracy is virtue; of monarchy, honour. Despotisms have no law except for the caprice of their ruler; their principle is fear.

The principles of monarchies and republics are subject to 'corruption'. If this corruption proceeds far enough, rule by law is undermined and the 'nature' of the government undergoes change: democracies become anarchic or ruled by mobs, aristocracies become oligarchies and monarchies true despotisms. For Montesquieu, however, oligarchy and anarchy are equally transient, for one person (or faction) will eventually succeed in amassing all power. Of despotism, Montesquieu says 'the principle . . . is subject to a continual corruption, because it is in its very nature corrupt'.[12] Although *The Spirit of Laws* is primarily about the kinds of governments by law, the spectre of despotism haunts Montesquieu's discussion:

if through a long abuse of power, or through hurry of conquest, despotic sway should prevail to a certain degree, neither morals nor climate would be able to withstand its baleful influence: and then human nature would be exposed, for some time at least, even in this beautiful part of the world, to the insults with which she has been abused in the other three. (Book VIII, Chapter 8)

In *The Spirit of Laws*, Montesquieu makes three basic distinctions in climates: Northern, Southern, and temperate. These distinctions shape humans as well as their laws and governments. Northern peoples have 'few vices, many virtues, a great share of frankness and sincerity', but their love of independence makes it difficult for them to form lasting civilizations. In the South, however, 'the heat of the

---

[12] Montesquieu, *Spirit of Laws* (Berkeley, 1977), Book VIII, Chapter 10, p. 175. All references will be to this edition by book and chapter number.

climate may be so excessive as to deprive the body of all vigour and strength . . . ; no punishment hardly is so severe as the action of the soul, and slavery is more supportable than the force and vigour of mind necessary for human conduct' (Book xiv, Chapter 2). The problem of 'Oriental despotisms' derives then, not from their location in the 'East', but in their enervating, emasculating *Southern* climate.

Montesquieu's ideas took on new relevance for Great Britain with the great late eighteenth-century expansion in size and in economic importance of the 'Southern' Empire in both the East and West Indies. Contemporaries agreed that the effects on Great Britain itself were baleful. In 1765, the Diwani of Bengal was conferred upon the British: the East India Company became the *de facto* rulers of a rich and populous province 'as large as France' under the nominal suzerainty of the Mughal Emperor. Clive's share of the spoils after the overthrow of Siraj-ud-Daula at Plassey in 1757 had been £234,000; he later received the quit rent of territory worth £30,000 per annum.[13] On his first return to England, he bought himself a peerage and built up a 'following' of seven MPs to 'enable him to bargain for favours with successive administrations'.[14] Clive's was only the most spectacular of the success stories; the returned 'Nabob' quickly became a proverbial and literary commonplace. Samuel Foote's 1772 play, *The Nabob*, capitalizes upon popular fears of and prejudices against the returning India Merchant. The title character's name, Sir Matthew Mite, suggests the smallness of his interests, as well as his inability to adjust his India-learned behaviour to social conditions in England. The frightening impact of his return upon the morality of British life and politics is revealed through his negotiations to buy seats in Parliament from the Mayor of the 'Borough of Bribe 'em.

The activities of British males in India were often deplored. Company Servants were grossly underpaid; a writer's monthly allowance might barely cover the costs of his housing.[15] Under such conditions, young men had no choice but to engage in (often illegal) private trade or to accept bribes. The low wages paid to native

[13] K. A. Nilakanta Sastri and G. Srinivasachari, *Advanced History of India* (Bombay, 1970), p. 594.
[14] Peter J. Marshall, *Problems of Empire: Britain and India, 1757–1813* (London, 1968), p. 38.
[15] Suresh Chandra Ghosh, *The Social Condition of the British Community in Bengal, 1757–1800* (Leiden, 1970), pp. 97–99.

servants, when combined with the highly developed division of labour endemic to the caste system, meant that a well-to-do Company man might employ a multitude of servants unheard of in England. These servants were often brutally mistreated; one writer acknowledged that 'he derived much pleasure from kicking and flogging his servants for trifles'.[16] While scholars such as Sir William Jones and Charles Hamilton were praised for their immersion in and translations of ancient texts, many of their fellow colonial officials immersed themselves in other aspects of Indian life, such as employing dancing girls, smoking hookahs, and arranging circus-like spectacles of animal fights (between camels, rhinoceri, or elephants). Travellers painted a lurid picture of the Orientalization of British men during their residence in India. In an age commonly character-ized as under the spell of the 'noble savage' and the cult of Tahiti, it must have been sobering to read how quickly the touted, British, moral fibre weakened upon contact with a 'decadent' society. Company Servants became miniature despots and seemed to have no qualms about their actions towards the 'coloureds', 'niggers', or 'Blacks'. They quickly adopted not only the cruelty, but also the appetites of the despot. The pseudonymous Quiz described his shock at seeing women eat two pounds of mutton chops, while officers crammed themselves with curry, rice, beef and goat.[17] This voracity extended to the men's sexual appetites as well: Philip Francis admitted he lived with 'Black ladies without end'; even Sir John Shore, Governor-General of India and later a member of the Clapham Sect, kept a small harem.[18] Captain Thomas Williamson, calculating from twenty-years' service in Bengal, computed the maximum cost of keeping a concubine at £4 per month; Innes Munro stated it was easier to maintain 'a whole zenana of Indians than the extravagance of one English lady'.[19]

Such behaviour abroad was reprehensible enough. But the return of those who did not die of disease, of overindulgence, or in war seemed to endanger the British way of life and even the Constitution, as the threat to Parliament posed by the actions of Sir Matthew Mite, the Indian Nabob, make clear. The possibility of contamina-

[16] Ibid., p. 113.

[17] Dennis Kincaid, *British Social Life in India, 1608–1937* (London, 1938), pp. 86–87.

[18] Ghosh, *The Social Condition*, p. 113.

[19] Capt Thomas Williamson, *The East India Vade Mecum* (London, 1810), pp. 412–13; Sir Henry Yule, *Hobson-Jobson*, (London, 1886), p. 981.

tion or corruption even preceded these men's physical return to England. In 1801, William Green described how the very institution of monopoly and the importation of luxury goods by the East India Company had become wicked step-parents to England's sons: 'Commercial monopoly and Eastern opulence . . . have already *fostered* dissipation and immorality *into monsters of colossal magnitude, that every moment threatens the humbler classes of independence, with ruin.*'[20] Complaints such as these, which transform the popular icon of Britannia into a mother (the 'mother country'), and which consider both British citizens and British overseas dependencies as Britannia's children or 'sons', were voiced more or less articulately throughout the last decades of the eighteenth century. They received their most clearly stated form in an economic treatise by Henry Brougham.

Lord Brougham, who published *An Inquiry into the Colonial Policy of the European Powers* in 1803, examined the dangers of overseas colonies to the morals of the home country in great detail:

Men of property and influence have always a greater effect in modulating the habits of their fellow-citizens, then [sic] mere adventurers. The persons who repair to a colony, for the purpose of living, and acquiring an independency . . . go, however, with a design to accommodate themselves to the customs and habits of the colony; to pursue their own interest, with freedom from all restraint . . . They return men of consequence; and can choose a mode for themselves. They naturally prefer the habits which they have acquired, and which have modified their primitive manners . . . The village, or walk or fashion in which they move, becomes somewhat influenced, and the political habits which they have acquired, may still more directly affect the public affairs of the state.[21]

Knowing that the conditions in different colonies to which these European 'adventurers' resided vary greatly, and influenced by Montesquieu's theories concerning the influence of climate upon government, manners and morals, Brougham discusses both the 'national character' of the colonist, and the climate and government of the particular colony. Brougham views 'the East' as exerting a degenerative and effeminizing influence upon Europeans: 'European manners have always yielded to the more polished and luxurious

---

[20] William Green, *Plans of Economy; or the Road to Ease and Independence* (London, 1801), (my emphasis).

[21] Lord Brougham, *An Inquiry into the Colonial Policy of The European Powers* (New York, 1970), I, pp. 58–59. All references are to this edition.

manners of the Asiatics. Their forms of provincial government have been far more despotic, than either in the American colonies or in the mother country' (I, p. 81).

Brougham no longer considers Empire a unified 'body', but plural 'bodies' linked to each other by ties, like that of blood. What Montesquieu calls 'the metropolis', Brougham refers to as 'the mother country'. The 'mother country' sends out young men, metaphorical 'sons', to govern (Greek 'kratein' or 'archein') other *bodies*.[22] What happens to these young men, Brougham's 'adventurers', is overshadowed by what happens to 'the mother country' when the 'adventurers' return. Brougham sees the return of Britain's 'sons' from the East as potentially disastrous: 'In a political view, the consequences of their Asiatic habits are certainly hurtful, *at least to a free country*. Their views are ill calculated for the meridian of a government, existing for, and by the people . . .' (I, pp. 82–83, emphasis mine).

Although Brougham distinguishes between the effects on Britain's sons of residence in the East Indies and in the West Indies or the Southern United States, in terms of Montesquieu's discussion, the differences among these various climates, all of which are 'Southern', is nugatory. Brougham's rhetoric concerning the West Indies, in fact, echoes many of the charges levelled against Hastings during his lengthy, and extremely well-publicized trial. 'A colony, composed of such adventurers, is peopled by a race of men, all hastening to grow rich, and eager to acquire wealth for the gratification of avarice or voluptuousness. It is an association formed for one common end, which, in the eyes of all, justifies any means' (I, pp. 68–69).

Particularly dangerous, in Brougham's view, is 'the want of *modest* female society' (emphasis mine). For the 'sons' of the mother country at this historical moment could not yet bring 'families' with them to either the West or East Indies. The moment of transplanted English societies in the East had not yet come; and as testimony during the Hastings trial shows, there were many Heathcliffs in the East Indies as well. This inability to recreate British, family life upon foreign soils 'brutalizes the minds and manners of men, necessarily deprives

---

[22] In 1783, England had lost her major settlement colonies, the young United States – and neither Canada nor Australia had assumed the importance as settlement colonies they would soon acquire in 1802. Brougham was statistically justified in thinking of his 'adventurers' as male.

them of all the virtuous pleasures of domestic life, and frees them from those restraints, which the presence of a family always imposes on the conduct of the most profligate men' (I, p. 70).

Even more dangerous is the physical reinforcement of the class structure:

The whites form a class of superior men, proud of their palpable distinction, and viewing their slaves as creatures of a subordinate nature, made for their use or their pleasures, and bound to move by the impulse of their will. Hence arises the most disgusting contamination with which the residence of the new world stains the character of the European – a love of uncontrouled power over individuals (I, p. 72).

One cannot read Brougham's descriptions of adventurers in the West Indies without comparing them to popular images of the serail. Each colonist becomes a petty despot; each estate (plantation) structurally recapitulates an 'Oriental despotism'. Each petty despot rules in the absence of any founding law, having 'uncontrouled power' over his 'slaves'. Brougham makes it all too clear that the West Indian despot views the slaves he controls as being 'made for his use and pleasures'. This pleasurable use of slaves contaminates the West Indian colonist, and makes him physically, psychologically, and politically unfit to return to the mother country; but return he does.

Brougham's term, 'contamination', translates and paraphrases Montesquieu's 'corruption'. Brougham, like Montesquieu, leaves the sexual aspects of this 'contamination' implicit. But the 'intercourse'[23] which Brougham indicates that colonist-despots have with 'unhappy women' (I, p. 70), – precisely those 'individuals' over whom they have the most 'uncontrouled power' – heads Brougham's list of 'contaminating' influences. Colonist-despots (like Columbus's sailors, according to myth) first pick up their corruption from native women; they bring this corruption back to Europe with their ill-gotten wealth and spread both through the national 'family'.

In one sense, then, both Montesquieu and Brougham were early exponents of the 'Whiggish' view of history. Montesquieu, especially, sees the history of Western European nation states as an evolution, with high points in his own time. Yet this also perhaps unfairly simplifies his position, for Montesquieu did not believe in the

---

[23] It is not always clear whether this 'intercourse' is always sexual; any type of communication (i.e., oral communication) may lead to the European male's 'contamination'.

inevitability of 'progress', or even in a Gibbonesque 'decline'. France, and by extrapolation England, faced a choice which was really no choice: either they could continue to evolve ('change their constitutions'), participating in historical process, or they could leave history altogether (become despotisms). Europeans quite literally tried to distance themselves from this fear by coining the term 'Oriental despotism'. 'Oriental despotism' then becomes associated with the Other, the one who is not an 'Occidental' and, by implication, not even 'male'. Yet this act of displacement, the movement by which (as Said describes) the West separates itself and 'History' from despotism and a-history, entails an even deeper fear. 'Freedom' and 'civilization' had marched westward like the progress of that Enlightenment symbol of Reason, the Sun: from Greece through Rome to France and England – yet what could promise that France and England would not, as Greece and Rome, be 'benighted' in their turn by the luxury, the effeminacy, of the East?

II

The answer to this fear took the quite literal form of a 'revanche' upon the East, the areas from which Gauls, Huns, Goths, Arabs, Mongols and Turks had come. The proper response to the threat of being absorbed by 'a-history' was to eliminate the threat. Barbara Johnson sees precisely this occurring when, in *The Last Man*, Lord Raymond and the Greeks decide to expand their War of Independence:

The Western world is about to fend off definitively the threat of the East. The Greeks need only to take Constantinople for victory to be complete. But the capture of Constantinople will never happen. Where Western man expects to encounter and to master his other, he finds himself faced with the absolute Other . . . The Plague, which extends out over the entire world from the point of encounter between East and West, is thus in a sense that which replaces the victory of the West over the East.[24]

Johnson's argument provides a useful point of departure for the examination of Shelley's novel as a Romantic intervention in contemporary debates about the corrupting effects of colonialism. Shelley, like De Quincey in John Barrell's account of imperial

---

[24] Barbara Johnson, 'The Last Man', in *The Other Mary Shelley*, eds. Fisch, Mellor, Schur, p. 264.

anxieties,[25] can be seen to have symbolized in terms of bodily infection the fears of Eastern and Southern corruption developed by Gibbon and Brougham from Montesquieu. Understanding Shelley's plague as a symbol which brings political anxiety about imported corruption home to the body allows us to understand the significance of her novel's first section, which contains a long preamble to the introduction of the disease into England in which, as in Montesquieu, the tendency of government towards despotism is scrutinized.

The Last Man is a tale of two families. Lionel Verney, the eponymous hero (modelled on Mary Shelley), is the son of the intimate friend of the last, abdicated, King of England, whose son, Adrian (modelled on Percy Shelley), becomes his best friend. Shelley describes the politically tortuous two decades from the abdication of Adrian's father in 2073, in which a nation struggles to decide what the 'nature' of its government – and hence that government's 'principle' – will be. Although Adrian's father seems quite readily to dwindle from being King to being the Duke of Windsor, his wife, the former Queen, now Countess of Windsor, is by no means content with her diminished status. She is willing to sacrifice her children's happiness and even health to her attempts to restore the monarchy. The Countess had been raised in autocratic Austria, and her plan to kidnap her own daughter demonstrates that she was familiar with the tradition of European despotism however 'enlightened'. Although she 'long impelled her husband to withstand the necessity of the times', she is unable successfully to 'corrupt' her husband; she then attempts to infect her son Adrian with her corrupt principles (p. 13). Failing with Adrian, she hopes to re-establish herself through Idris's potential spouse.

The Countess is more than simply the generic foreign threat, the outside and in this case both Southern and Eastern threat to the new British Constitution. She is a thinly disguised fictionalization of another Austrian woman who was accused of using precisely the same strategies to subvert both an old and a new constitution: Marie Antoinette. Her arrogance, her lack of 'principle', her unfeelingness is a belated riposte to Burke's idealization in *Reflections on the Revolution in France*. If, like Burke's Queen of France, she is somehow 'starlike', her etherealness is nightmarish in her coldness and her aloofness

[25] John Barrell, *The Infection of Thomas De Quincey: A Psychopathology of Imperialism* (New Haven and London, 1991).

from her own children. In fact, she is very much like the Marie Antoinette of the pamphlet wars, but shorn of the erotic and pornographic overtones.[26]

Although after 2073 England no longer has a hereditary monarchy, the new form of government is not radically different. Instead of a king, there is now a 'Lord Protector', with all of the unsavoury Cromwellian overtones of that term. The Lord Protector serves for only five years, but the limits to his prerogative during that time are scarcely defined. The system combines the worst elements of monarchy and of a republic. As in a monarchy, the 'principle' of the government is largely dependent on the character and dedication of a single man. For a while Raymond is an admirable Protector, but as he becomes more deeply involved with Evadne he increasingly neglects his official duties, and there is no constitutional way to force him to perform those duties or even to remove him from his office. Resignation is Raymond's choice, it is not forced upon him.

The other constitutional innovation besides the elective, short-term 'monarchy' is the collapsing of the Lords and Commons into one deliberative body. This consolidation, in appearance democratizing, in some ways seems to increase the power of the members of the former Lords. For, although the monarchy no longer exists, titles and a certain amount of noble prerogative remain; hence Ryland's campaign to 'level' the aristocracy. Part of Lord Raymond's appeal resides in the more than vague appeal of his own title and in his close relationship to the House of Windsor. Ryland's diatribes against the aristocracy are intended to neutralize the last political pockets of resistance against demagoguery; had he succeeded, he would have undermined the rule of law and begun England's inevitable slide into despotism: 'Without any privileged classes to check its sway, despotic power is unchecked and ruthless'.[27] The 2073 Constitution institutionalizes corruption in the form of 'a bribe . . . offered to him who should voluntarily resign his pretensions'; Ryland readily accepts this bribe (p. 73).

For almost a hundred pages from the time the plague is introduced

---

[26] Recent discussions of these attacks upon Marie Antoinette can be found in Lynn Hunt, 'The Many Bodies of Marie Antoinette: Political Pornography and the Problem of the Feminine in the French Revolution' in *Eroticism and the Body Politic*, ed. Lynn Hunt (Baltimore, 1991), pp. 108–30; Sarah Maza, 'The Diamond Necklace Affair Revisited (1785–1786): The Case of the Missing Queen' ibid., pp. 63–90.

[27] Montesquieu, *Spirit of Laws*, Introduction, p. 74.

into England, Lionel Verney seems immune. For a while this is because the plague spreads slowly. But soon, the plague is everywhere, and Lionel throws himself into philanthropic work among the plague-stricken. Despite his frequent contact with the sick, dying and recently dead, Lionel remains unscathed – and moreover, somehow conscious of his continuing immunity. His repeated assurances of his knowledge of not being infected are surprising, but not as shocking as the scene of his infection, which Snyder notes is 'the sole instance of direct infection in the novel':[28]

A pernicious scent assailed my senses, producing sickening qualms, which made their way to my very heart, while I felt my leg clasped, and a groan repeated by the person that held me. I lowered my lamp, and saw a negro half clad, writhing under the agony of disease, while he held me with a convulsive grasp. With mixed horror and impatience I strove to disengage myself, and fell on the sufferer; he wound his naked festering arms round me, his face was close to mine, and his breath, death-laden, entered my vitals. (p. 245)

Although Fisch does not discuss this scene, we see here epitomized the dynamics she finds linking this novel to the discourse of the AIDS epidemic: most notably, the 'otherness' of the disease and the infection of the heterosexual white male by the African/Caribbean Other. Clearly, Lionel Verney's dark doppelgänger is no Patient Zero bent on sharing his disease (a phenomenon noted also in *Journal of the Plague Year*), but rather a projection of Verney's guilt upon the most blatantly colonial subjects of Shelley's own day. Yet this image remains ambiguous. Verney *is* the only character who survives infection, although it remains unclear whether this is due to some special, biological merit of Verney's, or whether the 'black' plague with which he is infected is less virulent.[29]

Even more noticeable is the surface heterosexism and racism of the text. Lionel Verney is immune to the dreaded disease until almost literally raped by his black Other, who 'writhes', holds Lionel 'with a convulsive grasp', winds 'naked festering arms' around Lionel and, in an almost-kiss which demonically parodies both the

[28] Robert Lance Snyder, 'Mary Shelley's *The Last Man*', *Studies in Romanticism*, 17 (1978), pp. 435–52 (p. 444).
[29] Discussion of other, particularly later, works which link race and infection can be found in Susan Meyer, *Imperialism at Home: Race and Victorian Women's Fiction* (Ithaca & London, 1996), pp. 84–95, and in Peter Stallybrass and Alison White, 'The City: The Sewer, the Gaze, and the Contaminating Touch', in *The Politics of Transgression* (Ithaca, 1986), pp. 125–48.

creation of Adam and Judas' betrayal of Jesus, sends his 'death-laden' breath into Lionel's 'vitals' (i.e., 'life-parts').

This obvious surface racism, I would like to argue, is not merely or simply racism. I do not wish to imply that Mary Shelley wasn't or somehow 'couldn't be' racist. Instead, I wish to use the insights from my overview of political economy to demonstrate that something else is also at work in this scene. Blacks, and indeed Asians (with the exception of the shadowy Turks who hold Constantinople – themselves a 'mixed' category), are otherwise absent from the novel. Although there were some blacks (both Africans and creoles born in the Caribbean or in the slave-holding states of what by then were former North American colonies) in Mary Shelley's England, relatively few were there voluntarily.[30] The majority of black men who visited or domiciled in England, including Olaudah Equiano, arrived there not from Africa but from slave-owning British colonies and former colonies. Hence, the black man's presence in the novel may by no means be politically 'innocent'. Forcibly taken from a home in Africa, he most likely has experienced the worst qualities, not of 'Oriental' but of British despotism. His skin colour is a twin indication of his 'Southernness' but more importantly of his at-best former condition of slavery.

These facts help to explain, not just Lionel's aversion to the dying man, but why it is this man and this man alone who 'succeeds' in infecting Lionel. Lionel Verney has been able to overcome or to stand away from or above the varying forms of political corruption of his England. The plague – corruption – cannot touch him because he himself is 'incorruptible': his principle, his democratic 'virtue', remains unaffected by his environment. Lionel Verney cannot, however, overcome or change history: his nation's long history of involvement with slave-trading and slavery. This national history – British despotism on an international scale – is what rises into his light from the darkness and breathes death into his face. He is infected by a man displaced and probably enslaved by British imperial power, by a black who is terrifying because, reminding Britons of the colonial guilt, his infectiousness seems poetic justice for his corruption at their hands.

I turn now to the novel's treatment of the siege of Constantinople

---

[30] Exceptions would include freemen and the children of African princes sent to England for education. For more information, see Wylie Sypher, *Guinea's Captive Kings: British Anti-Slavery Literature of the XVIII Century* (Chapel Hill, 1942).

and the characters of Lord Raymond and Evadne. Evadne undergoes transformation from princess to pauper only to re-emerge yet
again transvestized into a soldier dying in the Greek War for
Independence. As, dying, she predicts Lord Raymond's death, she
momentarily comes to embody the Plague itself which, as Paley
notes, in *The Last Man* is 'always female', despite the long tradition of
Death being personified as male.[31]

Yet Evadne also remains the personification of an Orientalized
Greece: not a virile Greece that once was, but a Greece feminized by
two millennia of domination by Macedonians, Romans, Byzantines
and Ottomans. As such, she comes to function as a latter-day Dido
who succeeds in distracting her Aeneas from his mission not simply
once, but twice (first with her design, second with her prophecy). In
the speaking silence of death she has become transgressive, transves-
tite; she loses the 'roundness of womanhood', her eyes 'sink deep',
and she needs to be muffled or 'veiled' under 'flags and heavy
accoutrements' (p. 132). She symbolizes, not the Greece of Sopho-
cles, Socrates, and Pericles, but the deadly silent yet attractive city of
Constantinople.

Here, at last, we can understand the meaning of the Greeks' and
Lord Raymond's betrayal of the War of Independence and that
war's perversion into a war of empire. The principle of virtue, the
temperate blending of co-operation and independence, is discarded
in order to pursue the vain bauble, the corrupt bubble, of empire.
Were it not for the plague, history would repeat yet again. Constantinople, this hybrid city (neither fish nor fowl, land nor sea,
Asian nor European), would emasculate its new master as it had so
many other warlike conquerors in the past: Trojans, Greeks,
Romans, Turks. The plague, endemic to the despotic Southern
climes, erupts with unprecedented malignity into temperate, lawful
Europe once this last boundary is forced. Yet this too may only be a
seeming. For Montesquieu and for his readers, the noisy, populous
seat of despotism is the appearance and silence is the grim reality.
David Wallace Carrithers sums up one of Montesquieu's *Pensées*
(1822) thus:

---

[31] Paley, '*The Last Man*', p. 120. Paley emphasizes this as a difference from *The Last Man*'s
precursors. However, the Death/Plague gender dichotomy is an important component of
another narrative about a man who is in some ways 'last': Death and Life-in-Death casting
lots for possession of the Ancient Mariner.

The despot's reach is unlimited, his touch is deadly. Void of the noisy conflict that marks a healthy polity where power is checked by power, despotisms are characterized by the silence of the cowed, by an airy tranquillity *resembling the silence of cities the enemy is about to occupy.*[32]

Lord Raymond confronts the true face of despotism, a silent but grinning skull. Instead of the fruitful and welcoming Nature-woman male Romantics fantasized on entering the capital which had come to symbolize Oriental Despotism for the West, Lord Raymond encounters the horror which Grosrichard finds at the heart of the Seraglio, the devouring Phallic Mother.[33] But when Lord Raymond, in his Satanic pride, moves past the now hellish 'fatal entrance,' the city implodes, and this unholy 'penetration' (p. 145) produces only Death.

In the grim conclusion to *The Last Man*, Mary Shelley revises Byron, combining elements of his 'Darkness' with his Orientalist fantasies. As in 'Darkness', humankind faces a natural catastrophe; Shelley's disaster (literally, a 'bad star'), however, springs from Byron's pleasure playground, Constantinople. Most tellingly, few named characters die as a direct result of the plague; Lionel's survival proves the plague not inevitably fatal. Instead, the break-down of domestic ties, symbolizing the breakdown of civil institutions, actually kills more people. It is human failings, ultimately the corruption of the human heart itself, that write 'finis' to the story of the human race.

[32] Montesquieu, *Spirit of Laws*, Introduction, p. 74, my emphasis.
[33] Alain Grosrichard, *Structure du Serail* (Paris, 1979).

Index